THE AUSTRONESIANS:
HISTORICAL AND
COMPARATIVE PERSPECTIVES

Edited by Peter Bellwood, James J. Fox and Darrell Tryon

A publication of the Department of Anthropology
as part of the Comparative Austronesian Project,
Research School of Pacific and Asian Studies
The Australian National University
Canberra ACT Australia

Canberra 1995

Published in Australia by the Department of Anthropology, as part of the Comparative Austronesian Project, Research School of Pacific and Asian Studies, The Australian National University, Canberra, 1995.

National Library of Australia
Cataloguing-in-publication data:

The Austronesians: Historical and Comparative Perspectives.

Bibliography
Includes Index
ISBN 0 7315 2132 3.

1. Anthropology/Archaeology – Islands of the Pacific. 2. Anthropology/ Archaeology – Asia, Southeastern. 3. Anthropology/Archaeology – Madagascar. 4. Austronesian languages. 5. Islands of the Pacific – History. 6. Islands of the Pacific – Social life and customs. 7. Asia, Southeastern – History. 8. Asia, Southeastern – Social life and customs. 9. Madagascar – History. 10. Madagascar – Social life and customs. I. Bellwood, Peter, 1943-   . II. Fox, James J., 1940-   . III. Tryon, Darrell, 1942-   . IV. Australian National University. Dept. of Anthropology. V. Comparative Austronesian Project.

305.89

Typesetting by Norma Chin; drawings by Theo Baumann/Jenny Sheehan
Cover design by Griffiths & Young Design/Bronwyn Dillon
Printed at ANU Printing Service, Canberra

CONTENTS

SECTION 2: TRANSFORMATIONS AND INTERACTIONS

ACKNOWLEDGEMENTS

A majority of the papers in this volume were originally presented at a Conference of the Comparative Austronesian Project. We wish to thank all those associated with that Conference, in particular Annegret Schemberg who was in charge of the organization of the Conference and that of the Comparative Austronesian Project in general.

The cover of this volume shows a single-outrigger travelling canoe from Satawal Island in the Caroline Islands of the Federated States of Micronesia. It is taken from François Edmund Pâris's *Essai sur la Construction Navale des Peuples Extra-Européens*, Plate 107. Paris: Bertrand, 1841. We are grateful to Adrian Horridge for the use of his copy of this print. The textile that forms the background for the cover comes from Kosrae Island, also in Micronesia. It is a belt of vegetable fibres consisting of knotted multi-coloured warp threads combined with supplementary weft weaving. For the reproduction of this textile, we wish to thank the National Gallery of Australia and the former curator of Asian textiles, Robyn Maxwell, who now teaches at The Australian National University. The design of the cover is by Bronwyn Dillon of Griffiths & Young Design Pty Ltd. The drawings and cartography in the volume have been done by Theo Baumann and Jenny Sheehan of the Cartography Laboratory of the Research School of Pacific and Asian Studies.

Putting together a volume of this sort with three editors and twenty contributors is by no means an easy task. All of the careful and considered copy-editing of individual contributions, the proof-reading of these papers and the preparation of the index for this volume have been done by Norma Chin to whom we wish to express our particular thanks. It would be hard to imagine a more able and more effective person with whom to work on the production of a complex collection of papers.

Peter Bellwood
James J. Fox
Darrell Tryon

April 1995

1

THE AUSTRONESIANS IN HISTORY: COMMON ORIGINS AND DIVERSE TRANSFORMATIONS

Peter Bellwood, James J. Fox and Darrell Tryon

The Austronesian languages form a single and relatively close-knit family, similar in its degree of internal diversity and time depth to other major language families such as Austroasiatic, Uto-Aztecan and Indo-European. Prior to AD 1500 the Austronesian languages belonged to the most widespread language family in the world, with a distribution extending more than half way around the globe from Madagascar to Easter Island. Today, Austronesian-speaking peoples comprise most or all of the indigenous populations of Indonesia, Malaysia, the Philippines and Madagascar. Austronesian languages are also found on Taiwan (the possible homeland of the first Austronesians), in parts of southern Vietnam and Cambodia, in the Mergui Archipelago off the coast of Burma, and on Hainan Island in southern China. Further to the east, Austronesian languages are spoken in some of the coastal areas of Papua New Guinea, in New Britain and New Ireland, and down the Melanesian chain of islands through the Solomon Islands and Vanuatu as far as New Caledonia and Fiji. From there they extend eastwards to include all of the languages of Polynesia and northwards to take in all of the languages of Micronesia.

There are estimated to be between 1000 and 1200 distinct Austronesian languages, depending on one's criteria for distinguishing languages from dialects. These languages are spoken by an estimated 270 million people whose distribution is spectacularly uneven. All but about two million Austronesian-speakers live west of a line drawn north-south at about 130° east longitude, extending from just west of the Caroline Islands to just east of the Bird's Head on the island of New Guinea. The distribution of these languages over the Austronesian-speaking area is, however, relatively more even, with something over 500 languages on either side of the 130° east longitudinal dividing line.

AUSTRONESIAN LANGUAGES AS WITNESSES FOR CULTURAL AND BIOLOGICAL ANCESTRY AT THE POPULATION LEVEL

The fact that so many people should speak related Austronesian languages is interesting, but does this linguistic fact illuminate the overall cultural and biological origins and histories of these populations in any useful way? After all, the peoples who speak these languages today are not identical in physical appearance. One would have little difficulty, for instance, in differentiating by simple visual means amongst a random mixture of Austronesian-speaking individuals of Punan (Borneo), Agta (Luzon), Fijian and Tahitian origin. Similarly, the forest-collecting Punan, the urbanized Moslem Malays of Kuala Lumpur and the atoll dwellers of Micronesia would appear to have rather little in common in the socio-economic and religious senses. Culture and physical appearance might appear to be utilized as channels of ethnic identity in many individual modern societies, yet such channels are not rigid and inflexible. Even the most cursory observation of present-day societies anywhere in the world will leave little doubt that people, often large groups of them, can intermarry with people of different biological and cultural backgrounds, change their languages, or adopt new cultures and lifestyles when conditions persuade or permit.

Yet by no means all people or societies have, by choice or obligation (excluding such extreme situations as forced population movement and slavery), undergone such fundamental transitions to any marked degree. Clearly, the vast majority of individuals in most societies, in the past perhaps much more so than in the present, have ended their lives in much the same cultural mould as they began, marrying a spouse and producing offspring very similar in physical appearance and cultural background to themselves. In some societies such relative "conservatism" would appear to have dominated through history, whereas in others there have been stronger pressures to mix with other populations and to create new biological and cultural expressions.

Austronesian societies, likewise, have varied greatly in these regards in the past. Yet for all of them there exist linguistic, biological and archaeological evidence that indicate varying degrees of common origin traceable back for a time depth of perhaps 6000 years. Austronesian societies have obviously fissioned and diversified in complex ways, and this is one of the reasons why the study of these societies of Southeast Asia and Oceania, past and present, can be so intriguing and rewarding.

Sceptics[1] might question whether any shared ancestry in the cultural and biological senses is really implied for the 270 million people who speak Austronesian languages today. This question is hard to answer in any absolute way since every Austronesian society has a different history and it would be futile and divisive to allocate degrees of inherited "Austronesian-ness". But one must surely reject any explanation for the Austronesian *languages* that would see them as spread ancestrally by borrowing or by convergence amongst static pre-existing populations. In other words, unmoving peoples, already highly diversified, did not simply "borrow" Austronesian languages from one another, even though instances of such transmission have probably occurred, especially in western Melanesia. Had all the Austronesian languages spread *only* by such means we would hardly expect to find the remarkably unbroken and enclave-free distribution pattern, relatively free of diverse substratum linguistic phenomena, which exists today in virtually all regions apart from western Melanesia and the Southeast Asian mainland.

The whole picture makes sense, and obviously so for the far-flung islands of the Pacific and Madagascar, if one accepts that the ancestral versions of the modern Austronesian languages were spread mainly by colonizing speakers. There might have been occasional exceptions to this process of spread by colonization, as we can see in the recent spreads of modern national languages such as Malay and Bahasa Indonesia. But on a whole-language-family scale with both great extent and time-depth, no other explanation apart from spread by colonization makes sense.

While the principal justification for the common Austronesian heritage is linguistic, we can also see surviving threads, despite millennia of interaction and change, in the biological and cultural arenas. For instance, the vast majority of Austronesian speakers outside Melanesia and parts of the Philippines are of "Southern Mongoloid" (or Southeast Asian) biological affiliation. Some degree of common heritage is (or was in pre-modern times) also visible in the widespread occurrence of specific cultural characteristics such as tattooing, use of outriggers on canoes, features of ethnographic and prehistoric art styles, and social characteristics such as concern with birth order of siblings and a reverence for ancestral kin group founders. Generally, however, there is little which can be characterized as *exclusively* or *uniquely* Austronesian held widely today in common across all Austronesian-speaking regions, and neither should we expect such a circumstance. We see everywhere the results of innumerable diverse transformations. The themes of this book are thus partially bipartite, focusing on shared ancestry on the one hand, and culture- and region-specific transformations on the other.

THE AUSTRONESIANS AS A PHYLOGENETIC UNIT

In order better to conceptualize aspects of shared ancestry and subsequent divergence amongst the populations within a major ethnolinguistic grouping it is appropriate to introduce here the concept of the "phylogenetic unit". This concept has been applied recently to one branch of the Austronesians, namely the Polynesians, by Kirch and Green (1987). It can also be applied carefully to the Austronesians as a whole, albeit on a much larger scale in both time and space.[2] Basically, the idea of phylogenetic relationship revolves around derivation from a common source, in cultural terms identifiable through shared patterns of language and society, in biological terms identifiable through shared configurations of the gene pool. Phylogenetic units, whether defined culturally or biologically, are subject to divergence or radiation of their internal elements through the operation of processes such as population fission with subsequent geographical separation, founder or bottleneck effects, selective adaptations to differing or changing environments, and the effects of contact with external societies.

Identifying Austronesian societies as members of an Austronesian phylogenetic unit in the broad sense does not imply that they belong, past and present, to a kind of sealed species-like entity with sharp and unbreachable boundaries. They do not, any more than do speakers of any other family of languages. We see the undeniable significance in many times and places of interaction between Austronesians and various non-Austronesian populations, not only in language but also in biology and other aspects of society. The reality of the past 5000 years of Austronesian prehistory and history reflects both "bifurcative" and "rhizotic" (or reticulate) processes of cultural change in the terminology favoured by Moore (1994).

It should be clear, therefore, that in order to approach questions of Austronesian history and common ancestry in the broad sense we need to keep separate, for heuristic purposes, biology, language and culture, even though many aspects of culture are inextricably linked to language. Languages, populations and cultures evolve, diversify and mix through different, albeit conceptually overlapping, mechanisms. When considering something on the whole Austronesian scale it would be naïve to assume that linguistic, cultural and biological entities and their boundaries must correlate precisely, or will ever have done so in any absolute way, although *relatively* high degrees of coordination and correlation, despite variations, are an essential part of the concept of a phylogenetic unit.

One of the main implications of this book is therefore that Austronesian peoples and societies are all linked by branching but not sealed lines of common ancestry spanning the past 6000 years or so. But anyone inquisitive about the nature of the human species might wish to ask why such a unit should exist. In other words, why did such a phenomenal process of colonization occur, ultimately extending over half way around the world, and what major stimuli or constraints came to bear upon its regional expressions? These are important questions which will be considered from different viewpoints spanning various time-depths in some of the chapters which follow. There may be no simple answers, but the questions are worthy of articulation and asking.

COMPARATIVE METHODS IN LINGUISTICS AND ANTHROPOLOGY

All Austronesian languages are currently considered to derive from a single parent language, probably spoken on Taiwan something over 5000 years ago. Many scholars consider that the Austronesian language family has four highest order subgroups. Three of these subgroups comprise languages confined to Taiwan. The fourth subgroup — Malayo-Polynesian — includes all of the Austronesian languages spoken outside Taiwan. In effect, therefore, it is this subgroup of Austronesian languages that constitutes the predominant focus of this volume.

The principal method used for subgrouping the Austronesian languages is the classical comparative-historical method, largely developed in the comparative study of the Indo-European languages. This method is based on the systematic comparison of regular sound correspondences between languages as a first step towards reconstructing a proto-language from which it is possible to trace the derivation of daughter languages. Once the reconstruction of a proto-language is achieved, individual languages and sets of languages can be examined to determine the innovations they reflect relative to the proto-language. It is essentially upon shared innovations (phonological, morpho-syntactic and lexical) between languages and sets of languages that subgroupings are established. Although the existence of the related Austronesian languages was already recognized in the seventeenth century, the systematic comparative research of Otto Dempwolff (1934-38) laid the foundations for much present-day linguistic research.

Comparative approaches to the study of the Austronesians in anthropology have been far more varied. Different regionally focused efforts at comparison have contributed to Austronesian studies and gradually the various separate strands of this research have begun to coalesce in a common set of comparative interests and approaches. L.H. Morgan's investigation of Hawaiian kinship and his construction of a *"punaluan"* family (1870) could be considered an early contributor to this research, as could W.H.R. Rivers' history of Melanesian society (1914). F. Eggan's research on the Philippines which, in part, led to his paper on the method of controlled comparison (1954); the work of W.H. Goodenough in Micronesia that provided a basis for his influential paper on Malayo-Polynesian social organization (1955); Sahlins' investigation of social stratification in Polynesia (1958) and I. Goldman's comparative study of status systems in ancient Polynesia (1970) all contributed to common comparative concerns.

Another important strand in this comparative mix was the work of Dutch anthropologists in Indonesia. In 1935, at a time when Dempwolff was in the midst of publishing his Austronesian research, the Leiden anthropologist, J.P.B.

de Josselin de Jong, delivered a programmatic call for the comparative study of populations of Indonesia. Inspired not by linguistic investigations but by Radcliffe-Brown's study of "The Social Organization of Australian Tribes" (1931), de Josselin de Jong's "The Malay Archipelago as a Field of Ethnological Study" (1935, 1977) set in train a program of research that has, under various guises, continued to this day.

The single most influential comparative study to draw on J.P.B de Josselin de Jong's inspiration was that of his student, F.A.E. van Wouden, whose investigation of the societies of eastern Indonesia (1935, 1968) attempted to identify certain structural features of these societies as developments from an earlier proto-form of social organization — an organization that resembled Radcliffe-Brown's model for Australia. Other Dutch anthropologists, including van Wouden himself at a later stage in his career, allowed this comparative approach to inform their ethnographic researches without committing themselves too rigidly to a single prototypic model of society. Later reformulations of this "Ethnological Field of Study" approach continued to insist on investigation of a shared "structural core" (P.E. de Josselin de Jong 1980, 1984), but also called for a linguistic focus directed to the study of a common set of shared social categories — the continuing preservation of similar metaphors for living (Fox 1980). A similar emphasis on the study of "historical metaphor" and its comparative significance was articulated and developed by Sahlins in his study of Hawaii and of the other Pacific island societies (1981, 1985). One evident inspiration for these perspectives was the work of the Indo-European comparativist, George Dumézil.

More explicitly in relation to the study of Indonesian societies, however, both Fox (1980, 1988) and Blust (1984) argued that to preserve the notion of an Ethnological Field of Study required reinterpreting it in relation to, and as part of, the comparative study of Austronesian languages. This notion was particularly critical in comparisons between Austronesian and non-Austronesian societies in areas, such as Halmahera, where contact has been continuous for periods of several millennia (Platenkamp 1984; Bellwood 1994).

The Comparative Austronesian Project under whose auspices this volume took shape was intended to draw together anthropological, archaeological and linguistic approaches for the study of the Austronesian-speaking populations and to fashion a general framework for the mutual interpretation of the complexities of the Austronesian heritage. The disciplines drawn upon to illuminate this heritage include some which focus mainly on the comparative analysis of phenomena of the present or the recent ethnographic past; these disciplines include linguistics, social anthropology, genetics and zoogeography. Cross-cutting are other disciplines which draw their data directly out of traces of humanity and human activity which survive from the remoter past. These disciplines include archaeology, palaeoanthropology and literary history.

The chapters have been organized into two sections, the first focusing on questions of origins and dispersal, the second on questions of the interactions and transformations which Austronesian peoples and societies have undergone since dispersal occurred.

ORIGINS AND DISPERSALS

The three initial chapters in the volume examine the linguistic evidence for Austronesian origins and dispersal. Tryon gives an overview of the Austronesian language family and examines the evidence for current higher level Austronesian subgrouping hypotheses and the methodology employed in comparative-historical linguistics. Pawley and Ross examine the huge Oceanic subgroup of Austronesian, of which roughly half of all Austronesian languages are members. They give an account of the culture history of the Oceanic subgroup and discuss the dispersal of the constituent languages through Melanesia and across the Pacific, looking into the question of why some Oceanic languages have changed more than other Austronesian languages. Adelaar's paper discusses the pivotal role of Borneo in terms of the original homeland and subsequent dispersal of some of the major Austronesian languages, especially Malagasy, the Malayic subgroup, the Tamanic and the Land Dayak languages.

The next three chapters deal with the archaeological record for early Austronesian dispersal. Bellwood examines questions of the ultimate homeland region for the Austronesians in southern China and Taiwan, regarding the Austronesians as a population, like many other major ethnolinguistic groups in the agricultural latitudes of the world, who began their expansion as a result of an early adoption of agriculture in a world predominantly populated by hunter-gatherers. He continues with an examination of possible reasons for the success and remarkable extent of the dispersal (reasons which clearly extended beyond a simple reliance on agriculture) and raises a number of issues about some of the early transformations which occurred as Austronesian colonists moved into new social and environmental landscapes.

The chapter by Spriggs then examines the archaeological evidence for the colonization of the Pacific Islands, focusing on the Lapita culture starting around 3500 years ago and discussing its relevance for the ancestry of the Melanesians, Micronesians and Polynesians. The Austronesians were not, of course, the first settlers of the western Pacific and they certainly did not colonize uncontested space; some of the results of the ensuing interactions are also discussed by Spriggs, as is some of the recent genetic evidence which is now becoming so important in any discussion of the origins of the actual *people* of the Austronesian world.

The early Austronesians were also advantaged in possessing an excellent sailing technology. Horridge, in his contribution to the volume, examines this Austronesian sailing technology and identifies its chief features. He concludes that early Austronesian sailing vessels consisted of a lashed-lug construction of sewn planks on a hollowed-out log base with a single outrigger and a triangular sail pushed up by a tilting pole. The nature of this sail and the way the vessel was steered made it a kind of early windsurfing craft. As Horridge makes clear, this windsurfing craft favoured sailing into the wind with a later downwind return.

In the final chapter in this section on origins and dispersal, Groves discusses the ancestors and origin regions for some of the major domestic animals of the Austronesians (water buffalo, cattle, pig and dog) and also some of the small commensal species which travelled with them. Except for Bali cattle and possibly pigs, the species discussed were all introduced into the Austronesian world from mainland Asia. Questions arise of when and how they were introduced and Groves also raises the important observation that some might ultimately have Indian homelands, a source which does not tie in well with geographical reconstructions of Austronesian prehistory prior to about 2000 years ago. The archaeological record for the species discussed, so far not a topic given much attention in the island regions of Southeast Asia, will doubtless have much to contribute to our knowledge of Austronesian dispersal in the future.

HISTORICAL INTERACTIONS AND TRANSFORMATIONS

The evidence of comparative linguistics and of archaeology for the historical origin and spread of Austronesian-speaking peoples is so overwhelming in its general conclusions that most research in other disciplines has shifted to ask more specific questions. These questions concern the transformations that occurred as a result of this spread of the Austronesians — both the internal developments within individual Austronesian cultures as well as those developments that resulted from contact among Austronesian groups and with other populations and cultures. Neither the biology, the language nor the culture of the Austronesians has remained static over the past 5000 years. It is these historical developments that the papers in the second section of this volume address.

Serjeantson and Gao, for example, in their paper argue for an evolutionary perspective that clearly recognizes the biological changes that have occurred. They focus on the evolutionary forces that have effected changes in the genetic make-up of the populations of Oceania. Whereas the Polynesians share many genetic features with Island Southeast Asians, they have also acquired genes from Melanesian populations and, importantly, have undergone further evolution, losing certain genes, in their migrations into the Pacific. The result is a genetic repertoire that is certainly different from that of the earliest Austronesians.

The Serjeantson and Gao paper also addresses a key question raised about the early Austronesians. Otto Dempwolff, who was one of the founding figures in the development of comparative Austronesian linguistics, served for a long period as a medical doctor in what was, at the time, German New Guinea. In 1904, following an earlier suggestion by another German doctor, Danneil, Dempwolff speculated that malaria may have exerted a significant selective pressure on early Austronesian populations whereas the non-Austronesian populations had, it appeared, developed a degree of immunity that gave them a selective advantage in highly malarial areas. By this argument, it was the islands with the least malaria that provided the safest pathway for the spread of the early Austronesians. Based on extensive research reported in Serjeantson *et al.* (1992), the Serjeantson and Gao paper lends support to Dempwolff's idea suggesting that the early Austronesians may indeed have arrived in Melanesia to find a malarial region inhabited by peoples comparatively well adapted to the environment and therefore it would have been prudent for them to have kept to the small islands and to have continued eastward.

The paper by Bhatia, Easteal and Kirk makes similar observations in examining the different genetic make-up of Austronesian- and non-Austronesian- (or Papuan)-speaking populations within Melanesia. Based on earlier research, Kirk has identified three patterns of linguistic and genetic differentiation based on unique allele combinations: 1) an Australoid pattern that relates to the Aboriginal populations of Australia, 2) a proto-Papuan pattern whose highest frequencies occur in the highlands of Papua New Guinea and parts of Irian Jaya, with lower frequencies along the New Guinea coast and still lower frequencies in the Solomons, Banks Islands and Polynesian Outliers, and, 3) an Austronesian pattern that is not found in Australia and rarely occurs in the Papua New Guinea Highlands. The highest frequency of this pattern is to be found in some coastal areas of north and east New Guinea, the Solomons, Banks Islands, the western Carolines and Fiji. Bhatia, Easteal and Kirk show that while language may be an indicator of genetic difference in broad geographical terms, in Melanesia it is not an adequate discriminant in specific cases.

Dutton's chapter points towards a similar conclusion. He examines the types of contact-induced change which have been observed in the Austronesian languages of Melanesia and discusses the problems posed by such change for the classification of the languages of the Oceanic subgroup of Austronesian. The complex relationships between the Austronesian- and non-Austronesian-speakers, particularly in eastern Indonesia and Melanesia where contact has had such a long history, raises fundamental questions for the study of the cultures of the region.

The past poses questions as well as providing answers. Based on the linguistic and archaeological knowledge of Austronesian expansion, the anthropological contributions to this volume consider various questions regarding the structure and distribution of contemporary Austronesian communities.

Fox looks at the diversity of Austronesian societies and the proliferation of technical terms that have been used by observers to describe these societies. In the face of these diverse descriptive appellations, he focuses on a number of common features among virtually all Austronesian societies: the concern with the tracing of local origins and the reliance on a variety of narratives for the construction of a shared past. Thus the sharing of a journey may be used to define relatedness whereas claims to precedence, often based on the order of events in particular narratives, figure prominently as means of defining social differences.

The paper considers two formal models of social differentiation among Austronesian societies, the one involving a process of "lateral expansion", the hiving-off of groups of relatively equal status to form new groups and the other involving a process of "apical demotion" among differentiated segments of society, often combined with a concomitant expulsion of high ranking segments to form new groups or opponent factions within society. Fox suggests that these two systems of differentiation rely on different structured narratives of the past to base their construction of origins and their determination of precedence. Thus, for example, in systems of lateral expansion, one encounters what Fox refers to as "spatialization of time" in origin narratives.

Sather in his paper addresses a number of questions that relate to Austronesian-speaking sea nomads and rainforest hunter-gatherers. If, as the linguistic and archaeological evidence indicates, the early Austronesians had developed, in addition to their sailing technology, the capacity to cultivate both rice and millet and, as they expanded, adopted a repertoire of other cultivated plants, such as banana and sugar cane, yams and taro, then certainly those contemporary Austronesian cultures without cultivation cannot be seen as exemplars of a prototypical Austronesian society.

Sather's examination of the case of the Sama-Bajau, who are a widespread group of nomadic fishing people, is particularly instructive. Instead of looking at Sama-Bajau sea nomads as a single distinguishable population, he considers all the Sama-speaking populations, both settled and nomadic, as a group of related peoples whose languages can be traced to a proto-form that existed in the first millennium AD. Linguistic reconstructions for proto-Sama indicate a familiarity with farming, pottery-making, weaving and even iron-forging. Although predominantly oriented to the sea, present-day Sama-speakers show a range of adaptations to land and sea. These groups include farmers as well as fishermen and traders. In fact, within this larger group, nomadic boat populations are a small minority whose way of life represents a particular historical adaptation to expanding maritime trade. Thus Sather suggests that the early Austronesians, like the early Sama populations, had a diverse economy based on both foraging and farming, hunting and horticulture which over time led to different local adaptations.

Thomas also develops a set of contrasting models to consider patterns of exchange in Oceania. One form of exchange involves the giving of like-for-like, emphasizing the quantity of goods that are exchanged, particularly the competitive exchange of food among localized regionally undifferentiated groups; the other form of exchange involves the giving of dissimilar valuables among regionally extensive and differentiated groups organized on a hierarchical basis. Thomas then illustrates the working of such models both historically and regionally in Oceania.

Differing forms of exchange, the "directionality" of exchange, the "gendering" of exchange goods, and the differential value of women in exchange have been major foci of discussion in the Austronesian literature. This is particularly true of the anthropological literature on eastern Indonesia since the time of F.A.E. van Wouden, whose dissertation made the exchange systems of the region a critical focus of his analysis. Thomas's paper is of direct comparative relevance to these continuing Austronesian research concerns.

The concluding papers in this volume examine the ways in which Austronesian societies have adapted to outside influences, particularly those of the world religions — first, Hinduism and Buddhism and then Islam and Christianity. Supomo looks at the earliest Indian contacts with Indonesian societies and the changes in religious and political organization that this brought about, particularly the dissemination of literacy that eventually led to an indigenous adaptation and transformation of Indian literary works, such as the Mahābhārata and the Rāmāyaṇa. Inscriptions in Sanskrit gave way to a number of inscriptions in Old Malay during the time of Śrīwijaya (late 7th century AD) and to a proliferation of inscriptions in Old Javanese that lasted for a period of six centuries beginning in AD 804. These early inscriptions provide some of the oldest examples of Austronesian languages preserved for examination. The Javanese inscriptions and later literary works, which Supomo refers to as "temples of language" as opposed to "temples of stone", offer glimpses of social life defined by recognizable Austronesian categories.

Supomo notes that Old Javanese inscriptions refer to local indigenous communities as *wanua* [PMP *banua*] and their inhabitants as *anak wanua*. The councils that governed these communities consisted of elders referred to as *rama* [PAn *ama* meaning 'father']. *Wanua* were grouped in territorial units referred to as *watak* and these *watak*, in turn, were headed by *rakai*, a designation which Supomo argues is derived from the term for 'elder' or 'grandfather' [PAn *aki*]. This early Javanese political system was presided over by a figure given the title *ratu* [PMP *datu*, meaning 'ancestor, chief, lord'].

The system utilizes a recognizable kinship idiom which can be related both to proto-Austronesian and to contemporary Javanese. Using the evidence from Old Javanese texts, Fox has shown that earlier Javanese kinship is entirely Austronesian in structure with little Sanskrit influence. Indeed the semantic structure of modern Javanese kinship gives evidence of a clear continuity and development from Old Javanese (Fox 1986). As Supomo points out, one must look to Bali even more than Java for many of the continuities with older Javanese traditions because the "temples of language" which he describes were transported and transplanted there after the coming of Islam. It is interesting therefore to note that local communities organized in terms of *banua* and presided over by village councils still continue to function in the upland areas of Bali today (Reuter, pers.comm. 1994).

Like Supomo, Reid also examines the continuities and changes that occurred in response to outside religious and political influences — the coming of Islam and then Christianity among the maritime populations of Southeast Asia from the fifteenth century onward. These sailing and trading populations included Malays, Javanese, Chams and Tagalogs ("Luzons") who had long-standing historical relationships with one another and with the populations of the hinterlands for whom they provided an opening to the sea. The new religions brought about rapid changes in matters of identity — dress, speech, deportment and diet — as well as more gradual but profound changes in sexual morality, in the ritual role of women, and in relationships to the sacred, including attitudes toward the spirit world and the dead.

Yengoyan's paper continues this theme in examining the diverse ways in which Christianity, promulgated through different colonial institutions and cultures, has transformed the cultures of the Philippines and the Pacific. In this transformation of local Austronesian societies, instead of fostering any one particular form of society, the combination of western colonialism and Christianity has proffered a concept of individuality, stressing the roles, rights and responsibilities of individuals in all social relationships. It is this concept that continues to exert a profound effect on Austronesian societies throughout the region.

The papers published here were all presented initially during a three-day conference entitled "The Austronesians in History: Common Origins and Diverse Transformations", held in the Coombs Lecture Theatre in the Australian

National University in November 1990. The conference was organized under the auspices of the Comparative Austronesian Project in the Research School of Pacific Studies at ANU. In accord with the aims of this project the papers were requested to be on a broad scale — comparative, interdisciplinary and historical in orientation. The results provide a survey of some of the most significant facets of the Austronesian trajectory through time and space, although as with all books of this kind there are obviously some gaps.

It is worthy of note that this volume falls into a tradition of multi-disciplinary works on the histories of the various major language families of the world. Previously, such volumes have tended to stress archaeological and linguistic information at the expense of other sources, often because they have explicitly researched the interfaces between these two disciplines (e.g. Ehret and Posnansky 1982 for Africa; Renfrew 1987, Mallory 1989, Markey and Greppin 1990 for Indo-European). It is apparent that such volumes have the potential to generate broad comparative debate. Hopefully, this volume on the Austronesians will do the same, particularly with its broadening of the disciplinary input to include anthropology, biology and documentary history. Austronesia today includes many highly significant developing nations; an understanding of its historical *raison d'être* must be seen as an important goal, both for research and for education, by and for Austronesians and non-Austronesians alike.

NOTES

1   The principal opponents of the view that Austronesian language distributions reflect human colonization are drawn not from linguistics, but from archaeology and biological anthropology. For instance, a number of Oceanic specialists in these two disciplines believe that the Austronesian-speaking populations of Polynesia and Melanesia are drawn entirely from a western Melanesian ancestry spanning the past 30,000 years (Allen and White 1989; Terrell 1981, 1986; Houghton 1991), and have never shared any significant degree of common origin with the peoples of Island Southeast Asia, except at the time of initial settlement in the Pleistocene. These opinions either ignore languages entirely, or explain the situation according to linguistic models which utilize data sets of restricted geographical and disciplinary significance. There is often a strong motivation to assert theoretical positions centred entirely on views of *in situ* diversification. For instance, according to Terrell (1981:235):

> ... resemblances between Asians and Austronesian speakers in Oceania that have been proposed are either suspect in themselves, or equally attributable to chance correspondences rather than common descent.

Such a view tends to overlook the complexity of past and present humanity in Southeast Asia, as though the narrow sea gaps immediately west of New Guinea marked an eternal barrier to all humans except, paradoxically, the first sea-borne migrants of

50,000 years ago. If the latter could move with ease from Indonesia into Australasia, why not also the navigationally better equipped Austronesians of the past 4000 years?
2   The general concept of the genetic (or phylogenetic) unit has also been applied to situations of cultural diversification in other parts of the world, e.g. Flannery and Marcus (1983) for Otomanguean-speaking populations in Mesoamerica, and Romney (1957) for Uto-Aztecans. Peoples (1993) has recently applied the concept to Micronesia. Classic anthropological applications of the idea to Polynesia have been those of Sahlins (1958) and Goldman (1970).

REFERENCES

Allen, J. and P. White
  1989   The Lapita homeland: some new data and an interpretation. *Journal of the Polynesian Society* 98:129-146.

Bellwood, P.
  1994   The archaeology of Papuan and Austronesian prehistory in the Northern Moluccas, Eastern Indonesia. Paper given at the World Archaeological Congress, New Delhi, 4-11 December.

Blust, R.A.
  1984   Indonesia as a "field of linguistic study". In P.E. de Josselin de Jong (ed.) *Unity in diversity: Indonesia as a field of anthropological study*, pp.21-37. Verhandelingen van het Koninklijk Instituut voor Taal-, Land- en Volkenkunde 103. Dordrecht: Foris Publications.

Dempwolff, Otto
  1904   Über aussterbende Völker. Die Eingeborenen der "Westlichen Inseln" in Deutsch-Neu-Guinea. *Zeitschrift für Ethnologie* 36:414.
  1934-38 Vergleichende Lautlehre des austronesischen Wortschatzes. 3 vols. Berlin: Reimer.

Eggan, Fred
  1954   Social anthropology in the method of controlled comparison. *American Anthropologist* 56:743-763.

Ehret, C. and M. Posnansky (eds)
  1982   *The archaeological and linguistic reconstruction of African history*. Berkeley: University of California Press.

Flannery, K.V. and J. Marcus (eds)
  1983   *The cloud people*. New York: Academic Press.

Fox, J.J.
  1980   Models and metaphors: comparative research in Eastern Indonesia. In J.J. Fox (ed.) *The flow of life: essays on Eastern Indonesia*, pp.327-333. Cambridge, Mass.: Harvard University Press.

1986   The ordering of generations: change and continuity in old Javanese kinship. In D.G. Marr and A.C. Milner (eds) *Southeast Asia in the 9th to 14th centuries,* pp.315-326. Singapore: Institute of Southeast Asian Studies and Canberra: Research School of Pacific Studies, The Australian National University.

1988   Review of P.E. de Josselin de Jong (ed.) *Unity in diversity: Indonesia as a field of anthropological study.* Verhandelingen van het Koninklijk Instituut voor Taal-, Land- en Volkenkunde 144(1):178-181. Dordrecht: Foris Publications.

Goldman, I.
1970   *Ancient Polynesian society.* Chicago: University of Chicago Press.

Goodenough, Ward H.
1955   A problem of Malayo-Polynesian social organization. *American Anthropologist* 57:71-83.

Houghton, P.
1991   The early human biology of the Pacific: some considerations. *Journal of the Polynesian Society* 100:167-196.

Josselin de Jong, J.P.B. de
1977   The Malay Archipelago as a field of ethnological study. In P.E. de Josselin de Jong (ed.) *Structural anthropology in the Netherlands: a reader,* pp.164-182. The Hague: Martinus Nijhoff. (Originally published in 1935 as "De Maleische Archipel als ethnologisch studieveld". Leiden: Ginsberg.)

Josselin de Jong, P.E. de
1980   The concept of the field of ethnological study. In J.J. Fox (ed.) *The flow of life: essays on Eastern Indonesia,* pp.317-326. Cambridge, Mass.: Harvard University Press.

1984   A field of anthropological study in transformation. In P.E. de Josselin de Jong (ed.) *Unity in diversity: Indonesia as a field of anthropological study,* pp.1-10. Verhandelingen van het Koninklijk Instituut voor Taal-, Land- en Volkenkunde 103. Dordrecht: Foris Publications.

Kirch, P.V. and R.C. Green
1987   History, phylogeny and evolution in Polynesia. *Current Anthropology* 28:431-456.

Mallory, J.P.
1989   *In search of the Indo-Europeans.* London: Thames and Hudson.

Markey, T.L. and J.A.C. Greppin (eds)
1990   *When worlds collide.* Ann Arbor: Karoma.

Moore, J.H.
1994   Putting anthropology back together again: the ethnogenetic critique of cladistic theory. *American Anthropologist* 96(4).

Morgan, Lewis Henry
1870   *Systems of* consanguinity *and affinity of the human family.* Smithsonian Contributions to Knowledge 218. Photomechanic reprint after the edition of 1871. Washington: Smithsonian Institution.

Peoples, J.G.
1993   Political evolution in Micronesia. *Ethnology* 32:1-18.

Platenkamp, J.D.M.
1984   The Tobelo of Eastern Halmahera in the context of the field of anthropological study. In P.E. de Josselin de Jong (ed.) *Unity in diversity: Indonesia as a field of anthropological study*, pp.167-189. Verhandelingen van het Koninklijk Instituut voor Taal-, Land- en Volkenkunde 103. Dordrecht: Foris Publications.

Radcliffe-Brown, A.R.
1931   The social organization of Australian tribes. *Oceania* 1:34-63, 206-246, 322-341, 426-456.

Renfrew, C.
1987   *Archaeology and language.* London: Jonathan Cape.

Rivers, W.H.R.
1914   *The history of Melanesian society.* Cambridge: The University Press.

Romney, A.K.
1957   The genetic model and Uto-Aztecan time perspective. *Davidson Journal of Anthropology* 3:35-41.

Sahlins, M.D.
1958   *Social stratification in Polynesia.* Seattle: University of Washington Press.
1981   *Historical metaphors and mythical realities: structure in the early history of the Sandwich Islands kingdom.* Association for the Study of Anthropology in Oceania, Special Publication No. 1. Ann Arbor: University of Michigan Press.
1985   *Islands of history.* Chicago: University of Chicago Press.

Serjeantson, S.W., P.G. Board and K.K. Bhatia
1992   Population genetics in Papua New Guinea: a perspective on human evolution. In R.D. Attenborough and M.P. Alpers (eds) *Human biology in Papua New Guinea: the small cosmos*, pp.198-233. Oxford: Clarendon Press.

Terrell, J.
1981   Linguistics and the peopling of the Pacific Islands. *Journal of the Polynesian Society* 90:225-258.
1986   *Prehistory in the Pacific Islands.* Cambridge: Cambridge University Press.

Wouden, F.A.E. van
1968   *Types of social structure in Eastern Indonesia.* The Hague: Martinus Nijhoff. Koninklijk Instituut voor Taal-, Land- en Volkenkunde, Translation Series 11. [Originally published in Dutch in 1935.]

Section 1:

Origins and Dispersals

2

PROTO-AUSTRONESIAN AND THE MAJOR AUSTRONESIAN SUBGROUPS

Darrell Tryon

The discovery of the existence of the Austronesian language family goes back to the seventeenth century, when members of the Schouten and Lemaire expedition collected a vocabulary from East Futuna (Wallis and Futuna) in the South Pacific, some of which was found later to bear a striking resemblance to Malay. However, it was not until the nineteenth century that Austronesian studies really took on a systematic flavour, particularly with the work of Dutch linguists in what is today Indonesia and that of a number of missionaries in the South Pacific. A discussion of the history of research in Austronesian linguistics is not called for here. Suffice it to say that the major advances in Austronesian studies have been made this century, beginning with the systematic comparative work of such linguists as Stresemann (1927) and Dempwolff (1934-38). Since that time there has been a great deal of systematic research carried out right throughout the vast region where Austronesian languages are spoken.

In the past twenty-five years or so there have been a number of subgrouping hypotheses advanced by scholars of Austronesian languages. Only the most recent will be considered in any detail in this overview, for the major purpose of this paper is to present current and recent Austronesian subgrouping hypotheses, to look at what may be regarded as secure and what remains the subject of ongoing research. But before undertaking this review, it is necessary to insert a couple of preliminary remarks, one on the make-up of the Austronesian language family and the other on methodological considerations, in particular the methodology of linguistic subgrouping.

THE AUSTRONESIAN FAMILY

The Austronesian language family is perhaps the world's largest, with some 1200 languages and approximately 270 million speakers, according to the most recent studies (Tryon, ed. 1994). It ranges from languages with tens of millions of speakers (Malay/Indonesian, Javanese, Tagalog) to a surprisingly large number of languages with only a handful of speakers, numbered in the hundreds. These latter are particularly prevalent in Oceania, the causes for which will be examined later in this volume by Dutton. The geographical range of the Austronesian family is displayed in Map 1. A glance at the map will show that Austronesian languages are spoken from Madagascar in the west to Easter Island in the east. They are spoken almost universally in Indonesia and the Philippines,

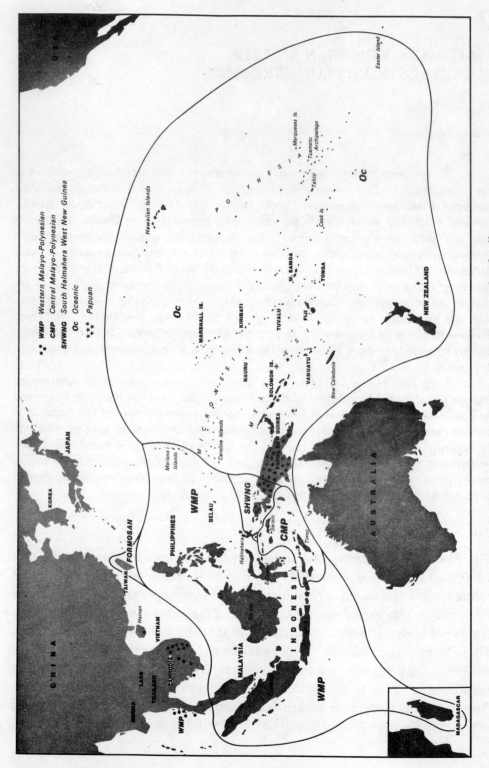

Map 1: The geographical range of the Austronesian family.

in Singapore and Malaysia, by the indigenous population of Taiwan, and by minority populations in Vietnam, Cambodia and the Mergui Archipelago off the coast of Burma (currently Myanmar). Further east, Austronesian languages occupy almost all of the islands of Oceania with the exception of the inland and most coastal areas of the great island of New Guinea (Irian Jaya and Papua New Guinea).

METHODOLOGY

The principal method that has been used to subgroup the Austronesian languages has been the traditional comparative-historical method, largely developed last century in connection with the comparative study of the Indo-European languages. Very briefly, this method systematically compares the regular sound correspondences between the languages compared as a first step towards reconstructing the proto-language from which the daughter languages have descended. Once the reconstruction of the proto-language has been achieved, then individual languages and sets of languages are examined to determine the innovations (phonological, morpho-syntactic and lexical) which they reflect relative to the proto-language. It is upon these innovations that subgrouping depends and proceeds.

Ross (1994) has made two very pertinent observations concerning the way in which these innovations are distributed across languages. He notes that innovations pattern across languages in two different ways reflecting two different developmental sequences. In the first, groups of languages share discrete bundles of innovations. Thus taking, for example languages A to Z, members of the family whose proto-language or putative ancestor language is *AZ, languages A-P may share one bundle of innovations not shared by languages Q-Z and vice versa. These languages would then fall into two distinct subgroups, AP and QZ. This is the distribution of innovations which results when languages have diversified by separation, that is when two or more communities speaking the same language become geographically separated. However, this is not the only way in which languages diversify. They also diversify without physical separation through dialect differentiation in their home territory. In this situation, instead of discrete bundles of innovations there are overlapping bundles which form a chain. Both of these distributional phenomena are observable in the Austronesian family, and will be seen to have important consequences for Austronesian subgrouping today. While the comparative method is a powerful tool, it has some limitations, especially with problems of recognizing contact-induced language change (see the chapter by Tom Dutton in this volume).

Another method used to subgroup languages is lexicostatistics, a method based on the replacement rate of the basic lexicon of a language over time. This method was employed by Dyen (1965) in his well-known lexicostatistical classification of the Austronesian family. While this method is useful as a first approximation, it is most useful with languages which are quite closely related. The major problem with this method, however, is that it is based on a premise that all languages replace vocabulary at a constant rate, which claim is demonstrably erroneous. For this reason the subgrouping hypotheses discussed in this paper are all based on comparative-historical techniques.

CURRENT SUBGROUPING HYPOTHESES

Proto-Austronesian, the ancestral language from which all other Austronesian languages descended, is considered by most scholars to have been spoken on the island of Taiwan something in the order of 5000 years ago. This ancestral language is considered to have diverged over time into four major subgroups, represented as follows:

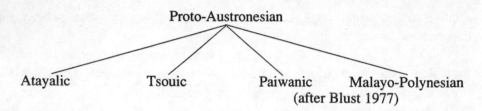

Proto-Austronesian

Atayalic   Tsouic   Paiwanic   Malayo-Polynesian
                                            (after Blust 1977)

In other words many scholars consider that three of the four highest-order subgroups of Austronesian are spoken on Taiwan and have been ever since the development of Proto-Austronesian. As discussed above, languages evolve by two different processes — gradual dialect differentiation, and separation. It is likely that the languages of the Atayalic, Tsouic and Paiwanic subgroups have arisen by gradual dialect differentiation from Proto-Austronesian, or from early descendant dialects spoken by the population which stayed behind when the languages which belong to the Malayo-Polynesian subgroup left the island. This distinction in developmental process is better signalled by the following diagram:

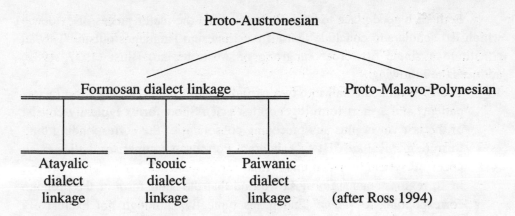

Proto-Austronesian

Formosan dialect linkage   Proto-Malayo-Polynesian

Atayalic   Tsouic   Paiwanic
dialect   dialect   dialect
linkage   linkage   linkage   (after Ross 1994)

According to this classification all of the Austronesian languages spoken outside Taiwan are descended from Proto-Malayo-Polynesian.

At this point it would be useful to consider Blust's representation of all of the major subgroups of Austronesian and then to return and consider the evidence upon which they are based, together with some alternative subgroupings currently under consideration by Austronesianists. The full Austronesian family tree devised by Blust (1978) is as follows:

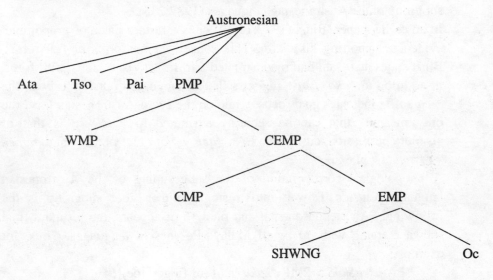

Austronesian

Ata   Tso   Pai   PMP

WMP   CEMP

CMP   EMP

SHWNG   Oc

Ata	Atayalic	CEMP	Central-Eastern Malayo-Polynesian
Tso	Tsouic	CMP	Central Malayo-Polynesian
Pai	Paiwanic	EMP	Eastern Malayo-Polynesian
PMP	Proto-Malayo-Polynesian	SHWNG	South Halmahera-West New Guinea
WMP	Western Malayo-Polynesian	Oc	Oceanic

Perhaps a good place to begin is to examine the major pieces of evidence which led scholars to conclude that all Austronesian languages outside Taiwan constitute a single first-order subgroup of Austronesian. Blust (1977, 1982) adduces the following:

1.   The PAn pronouns fall into two partially distinct sets, a long form (actor/patient) and a short form (agent/possessor). Short forms typically consist of the last vowel plus any preceding consonant of the corresponding long form (e.g. *aku: ku, '1st sg'). Internal Formosan comparison indicates an ancestral system in which this formal correspondence is regular. However, in all regions outside Formosa we find that the short form of the pronoun corresponding to *kamu '2nd pl' is typically, although not exclusively used as a singular pronoun, explained as a "politeness shift". Blust considers that symmetry and simplicity favour treating this usage as an innovation, and thus a valuable piece of subgrouping evidence. Given the unnaturalness of a plural-to-singular shift which affects the short form pronoun and not the corresponding long form, it is simplest to attribute the singular use of *-mu to one change rather than to a series of convergent innovations. Blust concludes that the change *-mu '2nd pl' > -mu '2nd sg' is therefore taken as evidence for a non-Formosan (Malayo-Polynesian) subgroup of the Austronesian languages (1982:235).

2.   In an earlier paper, Blust (1977:11-12) cites a further piece of pronominal evidence supporting his claim. This concerns long forms or full forms. Blust states that Dahl had reconstructed a form *a(N)ken '1st sg full form' in addition to *aku. Blust suggests that in languages outside Taiwan the *-en suffix indicates goal focus, while on the Proto-Austronesian level the only meaning that can be securely attributed to *a(N)ken is that of absolute possession, citing also PAn *iten v *kita '1st pl.inc.', and *amen v *kami '1st pl.exc.'.

3.   A phonological corroboration of the subgrouping of the Austronesian languages outside Taiwan into a single higher-order subgroup is the following: PAn preconsonantal and final *S disappears, the resultant final shewa merging with *a in all Malayo-Polynesian languages. Thus, for example:

   PAn *kuSkuS > PMP *kuku 'nail (of finger, toe)',
   PAn *tuqaS > PMP *tuqa 'old',
   PAn *CumeS > PMP *tuma 'clothes louse'.

4.   At the same time, another innovation which is reflected right across the Malayo-Polynesian region is the use of the PMP verbal prefixes *paŋ-, and *maŋ- to form verbs where the agent is the subject from verbs where the patient is subject (Ross 1994; Reid, pers.comm.).

5.   In addition to the above evidence, there are a number of other phonological innovations upon which the PMP subgroup is based. These include the merger of PAn *t and *ts as PMP *t. It should be noted, however, that of the languages of Taiwan both Amis and Bunun share this phonological merger. They do, however, differentiate from PMP in terms of criteria 1-4, above.

Dyen (1990) dissents from the view that all of the Austronesian languages outside Taiwan are members of a single Malayo-Polynesian subgroup. Invoking a lexical method called "homomeric lexical classification" whereby "different sets of cognates distributed over exactly the same set of languages are said to be homomerous" (1990:212), Dyen claims that "all the other classifications separate the Philippine languages from the Formosan at, or nearly at, the highest level, whereas the evidence presented here favors regarding the Philippine languages as the closest relatives of the Formosan languages, the latter being considered to form a single subgroup" (1990:224).

In his discussion of problems in Austronesian subgrouping, Ross (1994) assesses that within Taiwan there is a fair measure of agreement concerning the lower-order subgroups. Li (1980, 1981, 1985) has carried out detailed comparative work on the Atayalic subgroup, and Tsuchida (1976) has produced a substantial reconstruction of Proto-Tsouic. There is also general agreement on the core members of the Paiwanic subgroup. Beyond this there are disagreements as to subgroup affiliation, especially regarding the position of Rukai. Compare, for instance, the family trees produced in Tsuchida (1976) and Li (1985). Li (1985) proposes three major subgroups within Taiwan; a Northern group, which includes a number of languages attributed by others to Paiwanic, Tsouic, and a reduced Paiwanic group. In spite of subgrouping problems with the Austronesian languages of Taiwan, it appears clear that Proto-Austronesian diversified into a linkage of dialects and/or languages before the speakers of what later became Proto-Malayo-Polynesian (PMP) left Taiwan.

Ross (1994) has suggested that pre-PMP might have departed from the southeast coast of Taiwan, the Amis language area, since this language name appears to derive from PAn *qamis 'north'. It is possible that the Amis might have been given this name by the Malayo-Polynesian speakers to the south who might have remembered them as their relatives. Indeed, on linguistic grounds, Reid (1982) considers that an Amis-Extra Formosan node is required in the Austronesian family tree, as follows:

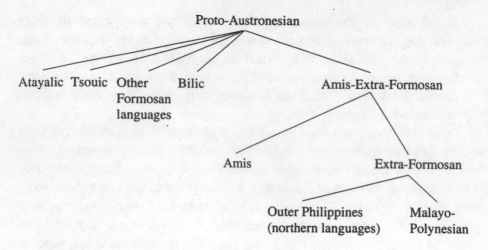

We will return to Reid's assessment of higher level Austronesian subgroups below. First, however, let us return to Blust's Malayo-Polynesian subgroup and its major constituent subgroups, thus:

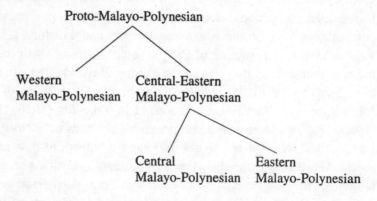

Each of the right hand nodes in the tree diagrams presented here represent the speech of a segment of the population which has migrated from a settled area, so that a new language arose by divergence as a result of separation. Together, the right hand nodes represent the main migratory path of the Austronesians from Taiwan to Oceania. It has been noted, however, that most of the left hand branches do not appear to represent a discrete proto-language, since they represent the "stay-at-homes" (Ross 1994). His further comment on the left-branching nodes is worth quoting in full:

> It looks as if the settled proto-language had already diversified into a local linkage before separation occurred. In these cases, the dialects or languages of the "stay-at-homes" have no exclusively shared ancestor. Instead they share only an ancestor at the node above, with the language of the departed migrants.

The Western Malayo-Polynesian languages include the languages of the Philippines and western Indonesia, including Chamorro, Palauan, Chamic and Malagasy. We know little about the subgrouping of the Western Malayo-Polynesian languages, and as Blust (1985) indicates, there is no clear evidence that these languages form a single subgroup of Austronesian. He is not alone in his thinking.

In fact, there is not even any real agreement as to how the Western Malayo-Polynesian languages subgroup among themselves. Ruhlen (1987), basing himself mainly on the work of Blust, assigns the members of the WMP subgroup to eleven divisions, as follows:

1. Chamorro
2. Palauan
3. Yapese
4. Northern Philippines
5. Southern Philippines
6. Meso-Philippine
7. South Mindanao
8. Sulawesi
9. Borneo
10. Sama-Bajau
11. Sundic

Ruhlen provides no justification for these subgroups, other than a geographical one. It should be noted that Chamorro, Palauan and Yapese are spoken in Micronesia to the east of the Philippines. While Chamorro and Palauan are clearly non-Oceanic, the position of Yapese is less clear.

The languages of the Philippines archipelago (including the Batan Islands between Taiwan and the Philippines) and several groups of languages spoken in the northern arm of Sulawesi have generally been believed to belong to a single Philippines subgroup regarded as having descended from Proto-Philippines (Zorc 1977, 1986). This subgrouping has been assumed rather than justified, however. Reid (1982:202) points out that the innovations which Charles (1974) lists as shared by the languages of the Philippines subgroup are based on a number of phonemic contrasts for PAn proposed by Dyen and Dempwolff which "do not stand close scrutiny, and are probably the result of unrecognized borrowing or obscured phonological processes in the history of the languages involved".

Basing himself on Reid, Ross (1994) suggests another possible scenario, as follows:

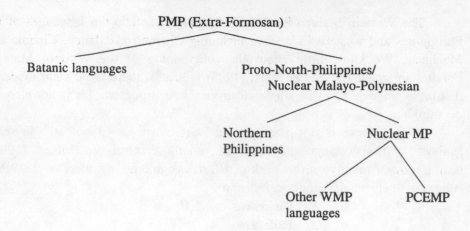

Reid (1982:212) was also unhappy about the southern Mindanao languages Blaan and Tboli (which continue to exercise his mind today, see below), quite apart from the higher order subgroups linking the languages of Taiwan and the Philippines. He found that the southern Mindanao languages reflected none of the innovations characteristic of the Malayo-Polynesian languages and may be descended from "a very early migration south of Formosa by an Austronesian-speaking people". We will return to this point in a moment, for an update on Reid's current thinking.

Zorc (1986) challenges Reid's subgrouping and defends the notion of a single Philippines grouping. His claim is based on a large number of lexical innovations shared widely by the languages of the Philippines archipelago. Commentators have remarked that it is difficult to assess Zorc's position because it is not clear that his lexical innovations are not in fact vocabulary items that have been retained from PMP but lost in extra-Philippines languages. Reid himself (1982:212) comments: "As one moves south in the Philippines ... the degree of influence of one or more of the central Philippines languages becomes more and more pervasive, so that it becomes more and more difficult to separate the strata in the languages".

Reid's thinking today has changed a little, but still centres to some extent around the problem posed by the languages of the Central Philippines, which appear to share a number of innovations with the Malayo-Javanic languages, including the formation of a set of ligatures exclusively shared by these two groups. His current position (pers.comm.) may be represented diagrammatically as follows:

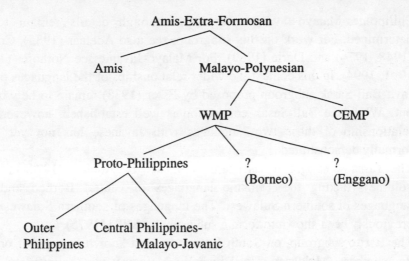

Reid is not so much concerned with the higher level subgroups in this tree diagram as the lower level attempt to resolve the problem posed by the languages of the Central Philippines and their obvious connection with the Malayo-Javanic languages, most probably through a southerly migration or series of migrations.

There are a number of other established subgroups in the Western Malayo-Polynesian area. Blust (pers.comm. to Ross) recognizes the following:

1. Moklen (on islands off the west coast of Thailand and Burma)
2. Lampung (SE Sumatra)
3. Land Dayak (Inland SW Borneo)
4. Southern Philippine/Sangir/Minahasan (Mindanao, N.Sulawesi)
5. Meso Philippine/Mongondow-Gorontalo (C.Philippines, N.Sulawesi)
6. Sama-Bajau
7. NW Sumatra/Barrier Islands (Gayo, Batak, Mentawi, Enggano)
8. NW Borneo
9. Central Sulawesi
10. Southern Sulawesi
11. Tamanic (Central Borneo)
12. Muna-Buton (off SE Sulawesi)
13. Malayo-Chamic (Acehnese, Chamic, Malayan, Sundanese)
14. Java-Bali-Sasak
15. Barito (Southern Borneo, Madagascar).

There has been further progress made with a number of these proposed lower order subgroups in recent times, as follows:
a. The Malayo-Chamic subgroup, covering substantial areas of western Indonesia (Blust 1985) is evidently closely related to Reid's Central

Philippines-Malayo-Javanic subgroup, although details remain to be determined. For work on this subgroup, see also Adelaar (1985), Cowan (1948, 1974) and Durie (1989). For Malayo-Javanic see Nothofer (1986, 1991, 1994). In this context the wider relationships of the languages of the Java-Bali-Sasak subgroup proposed by Esser (1938) remain to be worked out. While the Bali-Sasak connection is well established, however, the relationship of these two languages with Javanese has not yet been formally demonstrated.

b.   The Tamanic subgroup has been established by Adelaar (1994 and this volume), linking the Tamanic languages of central Borneo and the languages of southern Sulawesi. The languages of southern Sulawesi had previously been shown to form a subgroup by Mills (1975).

c.   The Barito subgroup, on South Borneo, is best known because of one of its members, Malagasy. Until recently Malagasy was believed to have been in Madagascar since the fourth-fifth century. Adelaar (1994) suggests that this date is at least two centuries too early.

Nothofer (1990, 1994) has made a number of fresh proposals concerning Western Malayo-Polynesian. His proposal is that much of the WMP region was once occupied by speakers of languages belonging to a group which he calls "Palaeo-Hesperonesian", and that at a later date much of this area was occupied by speakers of "Hesperonesian" languages, who became culturally dominant in western Indonesia, displacing the Palaeo-Hesperonesian languages. Some of these survive today around the periphery of the WMP region. In Nothofer's terms, the languages of northern Sulawesi and the central and southern Philippines, together with those of north-west Sumatra and the Barrier Islands, north-west Borneo and central and southern Sulawesi would be Palaeo-Hesperonesian, while the Malayo-Chamic, Java-Bali-Sasak and Barito groups are Hesperonesian. Ross (1994) notes, however, that much of the evidence which Nothofer uses is lexical and so suffers from the same difficulties as Zorc's use of such evidence in the Philippines. By the same token, however, Nothofer's hypothesis must be considered seriously.

The Central-Eastern Malayo-Polynesian subgroup of Austronesian is much more substantial. It was first proposed as Eastern Austronesian by Blust (1974), and later rebaptized Central-Eastern Malayo-Polynesian (CEMP) by the same scholar (Blust 1978). The languages which constitute the CEMP subgroup stretch from Bimanese, on the island of Sumbawa, eastward through the Lesser Sunda chain of Indonesia as far as the Aru Islands, and then north-west into the central Moluccas, inclusive of the Sula Archipelago. In addition, several still very poorly known CEMP languages appear to be scattered along the southern coast of Irian. CEMP and its lower order subgroups are as follows:

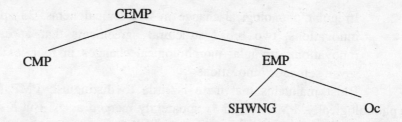

Blust (1990:2) states that "the evidence for CEMP and for some previously unrecognized subgroups within CMP is considerably stronger than the evidence for CMP itself". For, as we shall see, CMP is "united" by a number of overlapping innovations which cover many, but not all of the languages in question. This distribution of non-coincident innovations suggests to Blust that at an early stage in the Austronesian settlement of eastern Indonesia the languages now assigned to CMP formed a relatively isolated dialect chain which still shared well over 90 per cent of its basic vocabulary with languages that were not part of that chain.

In terms of culture-historical implications, after its separation from Proto-Western Malayo-Polynesian (PWMP), Proto-Central-Eastern Malayo-Polynesian (PCEMP) developed for some time in a relatively compact geographical area before splitting into Proto-Central Malayo-Polynesian (PCMP) and Proto-Eastern Malayo-Polynesian (PEMP). PEMP and its immediate descendant, Proto-Oceanic (POc) each developed in a relatively compact geographical area before splitting into descendant languages. By contrast, Proto-South Halmahera-West New Guinea (PSHWNG) and PCMP spread rapidly over a considerable distance before much dialect differentiation existed. A large number of linguistic innovations arose and spread through the CMP dialect chain in opposite directions, as they did also in SHWNG. These changes failed to reach the geographical extremes furthest from their respective centres of origin, producing differences of rule ordering in the central diffusion corridor (Blust 1978). The result is a patchy distribution of widely dispersed innovations. On the other hand, Blust maintains that some recurrent changes in the CMP languages may have been independent of contact, hence products of drift. Finally, after the differentiation of the CMP chain into distinct languages, there were limited migrations of small populations from the southern Moluccas in Indonesia to the southern coast of the Bird's Head Peninsula of New Guinea.

The evidence for the existence of a CEMP subgroup by Blust is quite substantial. It consists of the following:

1.   The reduction of consonant clusters in reflexes of reduplicated mono-syllables.

2.   Irregular phonological change in five lexical items, 33 apparent lexical innovations, two broad structural agreements that appear to involve innovations, irregular morphological changes in four lexical items and seven semantic innovations.

Blust maintains that there is little to distinguish PMP from PCEMP phonologically. PMP *c and *s apparently merged as *s. But a similar merger occurs in many WMP languages and in all Formosan languages. However, as mentioned above, there is a reduction of hetero-organic consonant clusters in the reflexes of reduplicated monosyllables. All CEMP languages have simplified medial clusters in the reflexes of PMP reduplicated monosyllables (unless the cluster consisted of a nasal followed by a stop or fricative, in which case the nasal assimilated to the place of articulation of the stop, but was not lost). Examples:

PMP *bukbuk > PCEMP *bubuk		'wood weevil'
PMP *ñamñam > PCEMP *ñañam		'tasty, delicious'
PMP *mekmek > PCEMP *memek		'crumbs'

Some WMP languages, for example Malay, have made similar simplifications — but, in Blust's opinion, the universality of this change in CEMP is best explained as the product of a single innovation in a language ancestral to the whole group.

Further evidence for the CEMP subgroup cited by Blust (1990) is as follows:

1. Irregular phonological change in five lexical items:

PMP *uliq	PCEMP *oliq	'return, go back'
PMP *i-sai	PCEMP *i-sei	'who?'
PMP *ma-qitem	PCEMP *ma-qetəm	'black'
PMP *maRi	PCEMP *mai	'come'
PMP *tudan	PCEMP *todan	'sit'

2. Apparent lexical innovations in PCEMP

1.	PMP *ka-labaw	PCEMP *kanzupay	'rat'
2.		PCEMP *liqə	'voice'
3.		PCEMP *malu	'loincloth'
4.	PMP *dilaq	PCEMP *maya	'tongue'
5.	PMP *surat	PCEMP *tusi	'scratch, draw a line, etc.'
6.	PMP *tawa	PCEMP *malip	'laugh'
7.		PCEMP *saRa	'sweep, broom'
8.		PCEMP *kandoRa	'cuscus, phalanger'
9.		PCEMP *mansar/mansər	'bandicoot'
10.		PCEMP *keRa(ŋ)	'hawksbill turtle'

11.	PMP *ñamuR	PCEMP *au	'dew'
12.		PCEMP *bai	'do, make'
13.	PMP *paen	PCEMP *bayan/payan	'bait'
14.	PMP *hazani	PCEMP *daŋi	'near'
15.		PCEMP *kese	'keep to oneself, be different'
16.	PMP *dalem	PCEMP *laman	'deep'
17.	PMP *paen	PCEMP *pani(nŋ)	'bait'
18.	PMP *muRmuR	PCEMP *pupuR	'gargle, rinse the mouth'
19.	PMP *kapal	PCEMP *təlu	'thick (of materials)'
20.		PCEMP *qumun	'earth oven'
21.	PMP *lakaw/panaw	PCEMP *ba	'go'
22.		PCEMP *balaŋ	'side, part'
23.	PMP *qa-lima	PCEMP *baRa	'hand, arm'
24.		PCEMP *lama	'spread over, cover'
25.		PCEMP *ŋaRa	'wild duck'
26.		PCEMP *papaR	'cheek'
27.		PCEMP *paRa-	'reciprocal prefix'
28.	PMP *palihi	PCEMP *tambu	'forbid'
29.	PMP *hiup	PCEMP *upi	'to blow'
30.		PCEMP *waŋka	'canoe'
31.		PCEMP *wari	'sing, song'
32.	PMP *ma-esak	PCEMP *madar	'ripe, overripe'
33.	PMP *bahu	PCEMP *mapu	'unpleasant odour'

3. Structural agreements:

Blust (1990) maintains that there are two features which are widely distributed in Eastern Indonesia and Oceania, namely:

a.   The use of proclitic subject markers on the verb.

b.   A morphologically marked distinction between alienable and inalienable possession.

However, there is a lack of established cognation in the morphemes used to express formally similar systems — thus a hypothesis of convergent development between the CMP and the Oc proclitics cannot easily be ruled out. Indeed Ross (1988:96ff.) also questions whether there is convincing evidence for an immediate common ancestor of the CMP, SHWNG and Oc subgroups.

4. Irregular morphological changes:

1.	PMP *apa	PCEMP *sapa	'what?'
2.	PMP *hepat	PCEMP *pat, *pati	'four'
3.	PMP *ma-huab	PCEMP *mawab	'yawn'
4.	PMP *ma-hiaq	PCEMP *mayaq	'shy, ashamed'

Blust (1990) concludes that the evidence for the existence of the PCEMP subgroup is fairly strong, as individual pieces of evidence are mostly mutually independent. Grimes (1990) has made an independent evaluation of the CEMP evidence and finds that Blust has a good case, even though very few of the lexical innovations which Blust lists are replacement innovations.

With respect to the Central Malayo-Polynesian subgroup (CMP), Blust and others are much less confident. These are the languages of the Lesser Sundas east of the Bima-Sumba group, and those of the southern and central Moluccas. The problems associated with this subgroup are not surprising, as we are again dealing with a "stay-at-home" rather than a migratory group. As suggested above, the most striking feature of the phonological history of the CMP languages is the extent to which similar changes are found in many but not all of the languages. This pattern of innovation suggests that PCMP underwent a short period of development apart from other contemporary Austronesian languages before it began to spread from the Moluccas to the Lesser Sundas. Many of the changes that are now widespread in these languages took place after this geographical dispersal and were the result of diffusion and in some cases drift.

The innovations which distinguish the CMP languages according to Blust (1990) are the following:

1. Loss of the prepenultimate initial vowel *hV- or *qV-. PMP trisyllables which began with a vowel or a vowel preceded by a laryngeal *h- or *q- (e.g. *qateluR 'egg') were retained as such in POc, but cognate forms in CMP languages suggest that the first syllable was lost in PCMP. However, Blust admits that forms such as Watubela /katlu/ make this claim rather doubtful.

2. Glide truncation: The monophthongization of original diphthongs through the truncation of glides, as in *-ay > -a; *-aw > -a; *-uy > -u is one of the most distinctive characteristics of the phonological history of CMP languages. This change is unattested outside eastern Indonesia. However, Blust concedes that we are forced to conclude that this was a product of independent changes in a number of languages. Truncation appears only sporadically in Leti, Kisar and Erai and is apparently unknown in Timor, Roti, Savu or Sumba.

3. Postnasal voicing: In many of the CMP languages, stops have become voiced after nasals. This is true of both consonant clusters within a morpheme and of intermorphemic clusters created by syncope. Thus, for example:

    PMP *ma-putiq > Kemak (C.Timor), Bonfia (E.Seram) buti, Buru boti, 'white'.

    As with the two previously discussed innovations, however, it appears that postnasal voicing was also a recurrent change.

4.   Irregular sound changes characterize a number of the CMP languages:
      a. PMP *pandan   PCMP *pendan   'pandanus'

      However, while examples of this irregular development are known from
      Flores to the Leti-Moa Archipelago, they are apparently not found in the
      southern and central Moluccas.
      b. PMP *baqeRu   PCMP *beqeRu   'new'

5.   Lexical Innovations:
      Blust lists the following innovations which he claims are exclusively
      shared by the languages of the Lesser Sundas and the Moluccas:

1.		PCMP *balabu	'see dimly'
2.		PCMP *balik	'mix, blend'
3.		PCMP *beta	'cut wood'
4.		PCMP *dada	'drag'
5.		PCMP *dodok	'pierce, stab'
6.		PCMP *letay	'above'
7.	PMP *kawit	PCMP *gae	'hook'
8.		PCMP *kati	'call a dog'
9.		PCMP *ketu	'pluck, break off'
10.		PCMP *lemba	'carry with a carrying pole'
11.		PCMP *lesi	'excess, overabundance'
12.		PCMP *lesu	'come out, take out'
13.		PCMP *letay	'bridge'
14.		PCMP *leu	'bend'
15.		PCMP *liRi	'sound, voice'
16.		PCMP *lolan	'cut off a piece'
17.		PCMP *lunu	'roll up'
18.	PMP *i-nu	PCMP *mpae	'where?'
19.		PCMP *peu	'bind together in a sheaf'
20.	PMP *qasu	PCMP *masu	'smoke'
21.		PCMP *silu	'lift, raise'
22.	PMP *tahiq, *zaqit	PCMP *sora	'sew'
23.		PCMP *sula	'horn'
24.		PCMP *ta	'no, not'
25.	PMP *taliŋa	PCMP *tilu	'ear'

The major problem with the lexical innovations as proposed here is that again
they are not replacement innovations.

      Blust (1990) also proposes some morphosyntactic and semantic
innovations for the CMP subgroup, but here again the problem is that they are
not shared throughout the proposed subgroup. In fact that is the very point which
Blust himself makes. Blust asks whether we should assume that the changes he

has documented are the product of completely independent innovations, that is, of drift. If so, he says, it is puzzling why the changes in question should be concentrated in the languages of the Lesser Sundas and the southern and central Moluccas.

In Blust's opinion, diffusion is the most plausible explanation for the distributions he puts forward. It is well known that diffusion can occur across major subgroup boundaries. Thus the widely shared phonological innovations among the languages of the Lesser Sundas, the southern and central Moluccas and the southern part of the Vogelkop Peninsula may simply be the products of contact among Austronesian languages that share no particularly close genetic affinity.

The Central Malayo-Polynesian subgroup of Austronesian, then, is faced with the same kinds of problems as other "stay-at-home" Austronesian groups, and its existence cannot at this stage be taken as proven any more than that of the Western Malayo-Polynesian subgroup. Nobody has really looked at the over-all relationships of the languages of Nusatenggara and Timor with the languages of Maluku. Thus we have no real idea of the first-order nodes within CMP.

The two descendants of the Eastern Malayo-Polynesian subgroup are the South Halmahera-West New Guinea (SHWNG) and Oceanic (Oc) subgroups. The SHWNG subgroup consists of all of the Austronesian languages of Halmahera and its near satellites and the various languages along the north coast of the Vogelkop Peninsula and Cenderawasih Bay, Waropen and all the Austronesian languages of Yapen Island and its satellites. The data available for many of these languages is far from adequate, making subgrouping difficult and at present uncertain. One important problem remaining to be solved concerns the boundary between CMP and SHWNG languages.

Blust (1978) set out the criteria for the SHWNG and Oc subgroups of Austronesian and need not be repeated in full here. In summary, Blust considers that the following are the most useful defining innovations for the South Halmahera-West New Guinea subgroup:

1.   Postnasal syncope (loss of a vowel between a nasal and a following stop, e.g. PMP *mata* > PSHWNG *mta* 'eye').
2.   The shift of PMP *e* > PSHWNG *o* in penultimate syllables.
3.   The replacement of PMP *anak* > PEMP *natu* 'child'.

In terms of the Oceanic subgroup (Oc), Ross (1988:30) sets out a list of ten phonological innovations which distinguish POc (Proto-Oceanic) from PAn (Proto-Austronesian). However, half of these are also reflected in the South Halmahera-West New Guinea subgroup (SHWNG) and as such are attributable to Proto-Eastern Malayo-Polynesian (PEMP), the immediate ancestor of both SHWNG and POc. There are, however, five innovations shared exclusively between PEMP and POc, as follows:

	PEMP		POc
1.	*(m)p*	*(m)b*	*(m)p, ŋp*
2	*(n)s*	*(n)z*	*(n)s*
3	*e*	*aw*	*o*
4.	*ay*	*ey*	*e*
5.	*m*		*m, ŋm*

In terms of phonological innovations between PEMP and POc, then, we are dealing with four mergers and two splits, quite substantial evidence by any standards. There is also lexical and morpho-syntactic evidence for the existence of the Oceanic subgroup presented in Pawley (1972:2-3). The development and dispersal of the Oceanic subgroup of Austronesian is discussed in the following chapter by Pawley and Ross.

CULTURAL-HISTORICAL IMPLICATIONS

The first Austronesians are believed to have originated in the South China area before moving off from the Asian mainland to settle on Taiwan somewhere about 5000-6000 years ago. There they lived relatively undisturbed for some time before one of the Taiwan-Austronesian communities, possibly from the south-east, moved south to the Philippines. Eventually they moved right through the Philippine archipelago. From there one group moved south-west, through Borneo and later Sumatra and Java, with branches penetrating the Malay Peninsula, eastern parts of Vietnam and Cambodia. A second migration from the Philippines moved south into Sulawesi. From there it is believed to have followed two major paths, one through Sulawesi and into the Seram-Ambon area and Timor, and the other towards Halmahera and Irian Jaya. From there the Austronesians are believed to have moved eastwards along the north coast of Papua New Guinea, ending up in the Bismarck Archipelago (New Britain and New Ireland), where the pre-Proto-Oceanic community is considered to have remained relatively unmolested until they were ready to move out into the Pacific.

REFERENCES

Adelaar, K.A.
   1981   Reconstruction of Proto-Batak phonology. *NUSA: Linguistic Studies in Indonesian and Languages in Indonesia* 10:1-20.
   1985   Proto-Malayic: the reconstruction of its phonology and parts of its lexicon and morphology. PhD dissertation, University of Leiden.
   1994   The classification of the Tamanic languages. In Tom Dutton and Darrell Tryon (eds) *Contact-induced change in Austronesian languages*, pp.1-41. Berlin: Mouton de Gruyter.

Blust, Robert A.
1974   Eastern Austronesian: a note. *Working Papers in Linguistics, University of Hawaii* 6(4):101-107.
1977   The Proto-Austronesian pronouns and Austronesian subgrouping. *Working Papers in Linguistics, University of Hawaii* 9(2):1-15.
1978   Eastern Malayo-Polynesian: a subgrouping argument. In S.A. Wurm and Lois Carrington (eds) *Second international conference on Austronesian linguistics proceedings*, Fascicle 1, Pacific Linguistics Series C No. 61, pp.181-234. Canberra: Department of Linguistics, Research School of Pacific Studies, The Australian National University.
1982   The linguistic value of the Wallace line. *Bijdragen tot de Taal-, Lande- en Volkenkunde* 138(2-3):231-250.
1983-84 More on the position of the languages of eastern Indonesia. *Oceanic Linguistics* 22-23:1-28.
1985   The Austronesian homeland: a linguistic perspective. *Asian Perspectives* 26(1):45-67.
1990   Central and Central-Eastern Malayo-Polynesian. Paper presented at Conference on Maluku linguistics, University of Hawaii, March 1990.

Charles, M.
1974   Problems in the reconstruction of Proto-Philippine phonology and the subgrouping of the Philippine languages. *Oceanic Linguistics* 13:457-509.

Cowan, H.J.K.
1948   Aanteekeningen betreffende de verhouding van het Atjehsch tot de Mon-Khmer-talen. *Bijdragen tot de Taal-, Lande- en Volkenkunde* 104:429-514.
1974   Evidence of long vowels in early Acehnese. *Oceanic Linguistics* 13:187-212.

Dempwolff, Otto
1934-38 *Vergleichende Lautlehre des austronesischen Wortschatzes*. 3 vols. Berlin: Reimer.

Durie, Mark
1989   Proto-Chamic and Acehnese mid vowels: towards Proto-Aceh-Chamic. *Bulletin of the School of Oriental and African Studies* 53:100-114.

Dyen, Isidore
1965   *A lexicostatistical classification of the Austronesian languages*. Bloomington: Indiana University Publications in Anthropology and Linguistics, Memoir 19; supplement to *International Journal of American Linguistics* 25.
1990   *Homomeric lexical classification*. In Philip Baldi (ed.) *Linguistic change and reconstruction methodology (Trends in Linguistics. Studies and Monographs 45)*, pp. 211-229. Berlin/New York: Mouton de Gruyter.

Esser, S.J.
1938   Talen. In *Atlas van tropisch Nederland*, 9-9b. Amsterdam: Koninklijk Nederlandsch Aardrijkskundig Genootschap.

Grimes, C.E.
    1990   Notes on Blust 1990. (Mimeo.)

Li, Paul Jen-kuei
    1980   The phonological rules of Atayal dialects. *Bulletin of the Institute of History and Philology* 51:349-405. Taipei: Academia Sinica.
    1981   Reconstruction of Proto-Atayalic phonology. *Bulletin of the Institute of History and Philology* 52:235-301. Taipei: Academia Sinica.
    1985   The position of Atayal in the Austronesian family. In Andrew Pawley and Lois Carrington (eds) *Austronesian linguistics at the 15th Pacific science congress*, pp.257-280. Pacific Linguistics Series C No. 88. Canberra: Department of Linguistics, Research School of Pacific Studies, The Australian National University.

Mills, Roger F.
    1975   Proto-South Sulawesi and Proto-Austronesian phonology. PhD dissertation, University of Michigan. Ann Arbor: University Microfilms International.

Nothofer, B.
    1986   The Barrier Island languages in the Austronesian language family. In Paul Geraghty, Lois Carrington and S.A. Wurm (eds) *FOCAL II: Papers from the fourth international conference on Austronesian linguistics*. Pacific Linguistics Series C No. 94, pp.87-109. Canberra: Department of Linguistics, Research School of Pacific Studies, The Australian National University.
    1991   Current interpretations of Western Malayo-Polynesian linguistic prehistory. *Bulletin of the Indo-Pacific Prehistory Association* 12:388-397.
    1994   The relationship between the languages of the Barrier Islands and the Sulawesi-Philippine languages. In Tom Dutton and Darrell Tryon (eds) *Contact-induced change in Austronesian languages*, pp.389-409. Berlin: Mouton de Gruyter.

Pawley, A.K.
    1972   On the internal relationships of Eastern Oceanic languages. In R.C. Green and M. Kelly (eds) *Studies in Oceanic culture history*, Vol. 3. Honolulu: Pacific Anthropological Records No.13, Bernice P. Bishop Museum.

Reid, Lawrence A.
    1982   *The demise of Proto-Philippines. Papers from the third international conference on Austronesian linguistics*, Vol. 2, pp.201-216. Pacific Linguistics Series C No. 75. Canberra: Department of Linguistics, Research School of Pacific Studies, The Australian National University.

Ross, Malcolm D.
    1988   *Proto Oceanic and the Austronesian languages of western Melanesia*. Pacific Linguistics Series C No. 98. Canberra: Department of Linguistics, Research School of Pacific Studies, The Australian National University.
    1994   Some current issues in Austronesian linguistics. In Darrell T. Tryon (ed.) *Comparative Austronesian dictionary*, pp.45-120. Berlin: Mouton de Gruyter.

Ruhlen, Merritt
  1987   *A guide to the world's languages.* Stanford, California: Stanford University Press.

Stresemann, E.
  1927   Die Lautentsprechungen in den ambonischen Sprachen. *Zeitschrift fur Eingeborenen-Sprachen,* Supplement 10, Berlin.

Tryon, Darrell T. (ed.)
  1994   *Comparative Austronesian dictionary.* Berlin: Mouton de Gruyter.

Tsuchida, S.
  1976   *Reconstruction of Proto-Tsouic phonology. Study of languages and cultures of Asia and Africa.* Monograph Series 5, Tokyo: Institute for the Study of Languages and Cultures of Asia and Africa.

Zorc, R. David
  1977   *The Bisayan dialects of the Philippines: subgrouping and reconstruction.* Pacific Linguistics Series C No. 44. Canberra: Department of Linguistics, Research School of Pacific Studies, The Australian National University.
  1986   The genetic relationships of Philippine languages. In Paul Geraghty, Lois Carrington and S.A. Wurm (eds) *FOCAL II: Papers from the fourth international conference on Austronesian linguistics,* pp.147-173. Pacific Linguistics Series C No. 94. Canberra: Department of Linguistics, Research School of Pacific Studies, The Australian National University.

3

THE PREHISTORY OF OCEANIC LANGUAGES: A CURRENT VIEW

Andrew Pawley and Malcolm Ross

The paper sketches the linguistic comparative method and reports on current results of its application to the Oceanic group of Austronesian languages. We give a brief account of the culture of Proto-Oceanic speakers as it is revealed by language, then outline our present view of Oceanic subgrouping, explaining what this implies about the location of Proto-Oceanic and the dispersion of Oceanic speakers into the Pacific. We examine patterns discernible in this dispersion, and address the question of why the languages of Melanesia have changed more than others.

INTRODUCTION

Some questions

Proto-Oceanic (POc) is the ancestor of some 450 Austronesian languages of Melanesia, Micronesia and Polynesia. Darrell Tryon has outlined in his paper for this volume the origins and position of the Oceanic subgroup within the wider Austronesian language family. Our concern here is with what historical linguistics has to say about the development of the Oceanic languages and the cultures of their speakers from Proto-Oceanic times onward.[1]

We will address the following questions:

1. How solid is the integrity of the Oceanic subgroup?
2. What was the culture of Proto-Oceanic speakers like?
3. What was the order of genetic splits among the languages of the Oceanic subgroup?
4. Where were Proto-Oceanic and later interstage languages spoken?
5. How did Proto-Oceanic and later interstage languages break up? Is a recurrent pattern discernible?
6. Why have some Oceanic languages of Melanesia changed much more than others?
7. How and why did Proto-Oceanic culture change in the daughter communities?

First, however, a few remarks on the methods of historical linguistics are in order.

The Comparative Method

The historical linguist's main tool is the Comparative Method.[2] It needs to be stressed that, in spite of its name, this method is completely different from the comparative method used in ethnological reconstruction, which is based on *typological similarities*.

The linguistic Comparative Method gains its strength from four facts associated with the sound systems of language or with the relation between sounds and meanings. Firstly, each word or morpheme in a language consists of a sequence of sounds which themselves have no meaning. Secondly, the association of meanings with sound sequences in a particular language is in almost all cases *arbitrary*. Thirdly, sound changes occur in all languages over time and, fourthly, these changes are, typically, *regular*. Regularity of sound change means that within a language community pronunciations change systematically, such that sound x becomes sound y under statable phonological conditions not just in a few words but in all words that meet those conditions. Together, these facts allow us to identify genetically related languages and to recognize genetically related morphemes or *cognates* shared by sister languages, as opposed to borrowed morphemes and accidental resemblances.

The comparative linguist takes sets of words and looks for regular sound correspondences among them. For example, among the cognate sets from widely distributed Oceanic languages in Table 1, we see a sound correspondence recurring in medial position in the words for 'paddle', 'rain' and 'name' between Manam -r-, Takia -∅-, Mangap -z-, Motu -d-, Mekeo -k-, Bali-Vitu -z-, Tolai -∅-, Nyindrou -r-, Gela -h-, Lau -t-, Bauan -ð-, and Tongan -h-. In these and later comparisons, ∅ indicates zero, i.e. loss of a sound present at an earlier stage.

Another correspondence set is reflected by initial v- in the Gela items for 'full', 'turtle', and 'paddle'. We find Manam ∅-, Takia f-, Mangap p-, Motu h-, Mekeo p-, Bali-Vitu v-, Nyindrou b-, Gela v-, Lau f-, Bauan v- and Tongan f-. Notice, however, that initial v- also occurs in the Gela items for 'woman' and 'stone', but here the Takia correspondence is p-, not f-. This is the result of phonological conditioning: Takia has f- before what was once -o-, and p- before -a-. Similarly, medial -v- in Gela *vaivine* 'woman' corresponds with Takia -∅- in *pein*, since POc *p is lost between vowels in Takia.

Where sound correspondences like those exemplified in Table 1 recur throughout the vocabularies of the languages concerned, we know that the languages are genetically related to one another. That is, we can demonstrate that the related words are formally derived in a regular manner from a common ancestral language.

Table 1:   Some Oceanic cognate sets.[a]

POc	'full' *ponuq*	'turtle' *poñu*	'paddle' *pose*	'woman' *papine*[b]	'rain' *qusan*	'stone' *patu*	'name' *qasan*[c]
Papua New Guinea north coast							
Manam	uni	...	ore	aine	ura	...	ara-
Takia	...	fon	fei	pein	ui	pat	...
Mangap	pin	pen	peze	(waine)	...	pat	za-
Papua New Guinea south coast							
Motu	honu	...	hode	hahine	...	...	lada-
Mekeo	poŋu	...	poke	papie	...	...	aka-
Bismarck Archipelago							
Bali-Vitu	vonuku	bonu	vozere	(tavine)	ɣuzaŋa	vatu	iza-
Tolai	...	pun	vo	vavina	...	vat	iaŋ
Nyindrou	...	boi	bos	...	ur	bek	ñara-
Southeast Solomon Islands							
Gela	vonu	vonu	vohe	vaivine	uha	vatu	aha-
Lau	fuŋu	fonu	fote	...	uta	fou	hata-
Central Pacific							
Standard Fijian	...	vonu	i-voðe	...	uða	vatu	yaða-
Tongan	fonu	fonu	fohe	fefine	ʔuha	...	...

Notes

[a] A blank indicates that the appropriate cognate does not occur in the linguist's data, perhaps because the cognate has been replaced by some other word, perhaps because the linguist failed to collect the cognate due to a shift in its meaning or for some other reason.

[b] From data in other languages, we know that Mangap *waine* is derived from an alternant *wapine*, Bali-Vitu *tavine* from *tapine*.

[c] Most of the words for 'name' have a hyphen on the end: this indicates that they normally occur with a suffix indicating the person and number of the possessor: 'my', 'thy', 'our', 'their', etc.

Having charted the sound correspondences among contemporary languages, one can infer the sound system of earlier stages by various established procedures, e.g. noting which languages retain distinct correspondences in sets of words that cannot be accounted for except by positing an original distinction. From data of which Table 1 gives only a tiny sample, Oceanic linguists are able to reconstruct the words[3] *ponuq* 'full', *poñu* 'turtle', *pose* 'paddle', *papine* 'woman', *qusan* 'rain', *patu* 'stone' and *qasan* 'name' for POc.

At the same time, where a word shows an apparently irregular sound correspondence, the linguist must investigate whether this is the result of an unrecognized regularity, or whether it is the result of borrowing from a language which has undergone different sound changes, or of analogical change, or perhaps simply a chance resemblance. The careful reader will notice that Nyindrou *bos* 'paddle' does not conform to the pattern displayed in other cognate sets, an indication that this item could be a borrowing from another Oceanic language rather than a direct continuation of the ancestral form. There are a number of cases in the Pacific of patterned irregularity, where a language shows two or more sets of correspondences, each reflecting the reconstructed sound system of POc. A classic case of this is Rotuman, studied by Biggs (1965), where there are three sets of correspondences: one set occurs in directly inherited words, the other two in words borrowed from Polynesian languages. Another case is Wagawaga in southeast Papua, whose vocabulary comes from two clearly different sources.

Subgrouping is usually a much harder task than establishing genetic relationship. In the Comparative Method, subgrouping is done by working out which languages share innovations relative to an earlier ancestor.[4] For example, we saw in Table 1 that Lau *fote* 'paddle' and *uta* 'rain', descended from POc **pose* and **qusan* respectively, have undergone an innovation whereby POc *-s-* has become Lau *-t-*. This innovation is one of several sound changes shared by a number of the languages of Malaita and San Cristobal (Makira) Islands in the southeast Solomons, indicating that they form a genetic subgroup, i.e. that they are probably descended from a more recent ancestor, 'Proto-Cristobal-Malaitan', in which this innovation took place.

Reconstruction and subgrouping are delicately connected: if we reconstructed POc *-t-* instead of *-s-* for this correspondence, then the Malaitan languages would not be innovators in this case, but the other languages in Table 1 would be instead. Comparative linguists use various techniques to work out the probable directions of phonetic change: some sound changes are generally known to be unidirectional (e.g. Manam *-r-* from *-s-* is an instance of a fairly common change in human language, also reflected in Latin *operis*, the genitive form of *opus* 'work'), and the reconstruction of POc **s* is also supported by non-Oceanic Austronesian languages which indicate its presence in proto-languages of higher order than POc.

Subgrouping under the Comparative Method can be applied recursively to identify subgroups within subgroups, that is, to construct what is conventionally called the "family tree" of a set of genetically related languages.

The Comparative Method produces several kinds of result in addition to subgrouping. Firstly (and we return to this in the section on kinds of subgroups) different kinds of subgroup, with different kinds of history, can be identified.

Secondly, reconstructed vocabulary, and especially reconstructed terminologies, can illuminate the culture and environment of the people who used them. And thirdly, like other scholars, linguists assume that dispersal centres are most likely to be in the areas of greatest genetic diversity. Thus, if there are two primary subgroups in a family which occupy contiguous geographical areas, the most likely dispersal centre is around the geographic seam.

One thing that comparative linguists cannot do is to provide absolute dating of the linguistic splits posited in a family tree hypothesis. Reconstructing sequences of putative splits provides only relative chronologies.[5] To give absolute dates to prehistoric linguistic events, we need to be able to relate them to archaeological events.

THE OCEANIC SUBGROUP AND PROTO-OCEANIC CULTURE

The linguistic evidence indicates that there was just a *single* early movement of Austronesian speakers into northwest Melanesia that left linguistic traces.

The need to recognize what we now call the Oceanic subgroup of Austronesian was first expressed by the Dutch linguist Hendrik Kern (1886) in a discussion of the relationships of Fijian to several Indonesian and Polynesian languages, but the foundations of modern Oceanic comparative work were not truly laid until the 1930s, when the German linguist, Otto Dempwolff, published his major work (1934, 1937, 1938) on the Austronesian family. In the second volume of this work Dempwolff reconstructed a sound system for the immediate common ancestor of the Polynesian languages and a sample of eighty-two "Melanesian" languages and found that all the languages in his sample reflect a set of sound changes to the Proto-Malayo-Polynesian ("Uraustronesisch") system he had reconstructed earlier. The quantity of these shared phonological innovations led Dempwolff to conclude that the "Melanesian" and Polynesian languages form a subgroup apart from the Austronesian languages to the west, in the Indo-Malaysian archipelago. Dempwolff labelled the interstage language ancestral to this subgroup "Urmelanesisch". Another German scholar, Wilhelm Milke, coined the more appropriate "Proto-Ozeanisch" in 1961, and since then "Proto-Oceanic" has been used. Even though some of Dempwolff's putative phonological innovations have been eliminated as a result of subsequent research, the evidence for Oceanic has on the whole been strengthened and the precision of our phonological, grammatical and lexical reconstructions has improved.[6]

The region covered by "Oceania" in this context is the Pacific east of a line drawn from north to south and dividing Chamorro (Mariana Islands) and Belau (formerly Palau) from the rest of Micronesia and crossing the north coast of Irian Jaya at 138°E longitude. This means that the seam between Oceanic and its closest Austronesian relatives is in the west of New Guinea between the Bird's Head and the Sarmi Coast. The Oceanic subgroup includes the Austronesian languages of all of Melanesia except the extreme west of New Guinea, all of Polynesia and most of Micronesia (see Map 1). Apart from languages brought by colonialism, languages of Oceania which are *not* Austronesian are found only in New Guinea and nearby archipelagoes. These are the so-called non-Austronesian or "Papuan" languages of many of the peoples of New Guinea and some island peoples as far east as Savo in the Solomon Islands (and a probable outlier area in the Reef Islands).

Reconstructed Oceanic terminologies give insight into the culture of POc speakers and of the speakers of various interstage languages.[7] It is clear that POc speakers preserved a very high proportion of Proto-Malayo-Polynesian and Proto-Eastern Malayo-Polynesian terms for a range of important cultural domains. The inference must be drawn that there was continuity in many components of the way of life of Austronesian speakers from a Proto-Malayo-Polynesian dispersal centre in Island Southeast Asia to the POc dispersal centre in northwest Melanesia, over a period of uncertain duration, perhaps 1000 years. The lexical reconstructions point to what archaeologists (e.g. Bellwood 1989) refer to as initial "founder settlement" of northwest Melanesia by Austronesian speakers.

Elaborate terminologies for seafaring and fishing and for horticulture and pottery indicate that the economy of POc speakers was based on both the sea and the land, and that some people or some local groups were specialist fishermen, farmers or potters (Pawley 1981; Pawley and Green 1984). Table 2, for example, lists reconstructed POc terms for canoe parts, seafaring and the sea (mostly from Pawley and Pawley 1994). Terms can also be reconstructed for various winds (Ross 1994d) and for numerous fish and sea creatures (Walter 1989; Pawley 1993). Table 3 shows the reconstructed forms for the growth stages of the coconut and for parts of the coconut, whilst Table 4 gives terms for food plants other than the coconut as well as some other horticultural terms (terms in both tables are from French-Wright 1983 and Ross 1993). Lichtenberk (1994) has reconstructed terms associated with food preparation (e.g. *tabiRa* 'wooden dish', *qumun* 'stone oven') and Ross (1994c) terms for pots and pottery; some of these are listed in Table 5. We can also reconstruct the names of various land animals (*boRok* 'domesticated pig', *bawe* probably 'wild pig', *kadroRa* 'cuscus', *mʷaj[oa]* 'bandicoot, marsupial rat', *kasuari* 'cassowary'). Reconstructed terminologies can also illuminate social organization, exemplified by the kinship terminology of Table 6 (based on Milke 1958; Chowning 1991): it is noteworthy that there is a gap in the system at 'father's sister' and that only two affinal terms have so far been reconstructed.

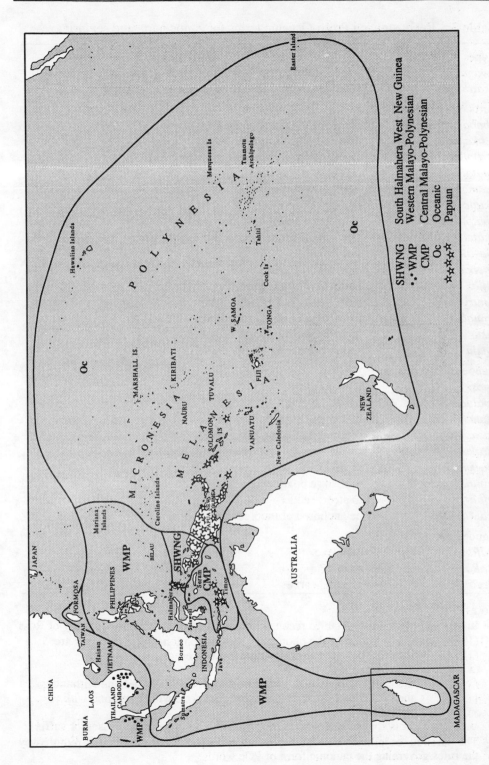

Map 1: Boundaries of the Oceanic subgroup of Austronesian languages.

Table 2:   Reconstructed Proto-Oceanic terms for canoe parts and seafaring.[a]

Types of vessel:

*waga	large sailing canoe; outrigger canoe (generic)
*katiR	small outrigger canoe (?) or canoe hull

Parts of a canoe:

*baban, *bapan	plank; canoe plank or strake
*soka(r)	thwart; collar-beam in house
*(q)oRa	strake, probably topstrake (washstrake)
*pataR	platform of any kind, inc. one erected on outrigger framework
*saman	outrigger float
*kiajo	outrigger boom
*patoto	connective sticks attaching float
*kata(q)e, kate(q)a[b]	free side of canoe, opposite the outrigger
*layaR	sail
*qeba	mat; matting sail
*jila	boom or yard of (triangular) sail
*muri-	rear, stern; back of any object
*muqa-	front, bow of boat; front of any object
*isu-	nose; projecting headboard of prow[c]
*ŋuju-	snout; projecting headboard of prow[c]

Canoe accessories:

*pose	(canoe) paddle
*paluca	to paddle
*lima(s), nima(s)	bailer
*asu	scoop or ladle out; ladle, bailer
*laŋon	rollers
*laŋon-i	place rollers under a boat
*ujan, *lujan	to load (a boat); cargo, freight
*quliŋ	to steer; rudder
*jau(q)	be anchored or moored, be stationary

Canoe making:

*kiRam	adze/axe
*taRaq	adze
*taRaq-i	to adze, carve

Notes

[a] In this and the following tables reconstructions are given in the orthography of Ross (1988), with the addition of the phoneme *p^w. Conventions in proto-forms are:

(x)	it cannot be determined whether x was present;
(x,y), xx/yy	either x or y;
[x]	the item is reconstructible in two forms, one with and one without x;
[x,y]	the item is reconstructible in two forms, one with x and one with y;
xx, yy	both x and y.
-xx	xx is always suffixed (in most cases by an inalienable possessor suffix).

[b] The parentheses indicate that the *-q- is not reflected in our data, but is required by the rules governing the canonic form of POc words.

[c] Often with ornately carved figurehead.

Table 3:   Reconstructed Proto-Oceanic forms associated with coconut culture.

The coconut and its stages of growth:

*niuR	coconut (generic); growth stage: ripe, brown but not fallen yet
*(q)abʷaji	growth stage: fruit bud
*kubo/*kubʷa	growth stage: young, green
*karu	growth stage: green, drinkable
*matuqu	growth stage: ripe, brown but not fallen yet
*maRaŋo, *goRu	growth stage: dry and ready to fall
*tabʷa	growth stage: sprouted

Parts of the coconut palm and of the coconut:

*polo	coconut water
*bʷilo, lasa	coconut shell used as liquid container or cup
*paraq	coconut embryo
*puto-	spongy centre of a sprouting coconut
*punut, *penut	coconut husk, fibres on coconut husk
*kojom[-i]	to husk a coconut
*[pa]paq[a-]	frond of a palm
*palapa(q)	palm branch
*suluq	dry coconut leaf torch
*Runut, *nuRut	sheath around base of coconut frond, used as a strainer

Table 4:   Reconstructed Proto-Oceanic terms for horticulture and food plants (other than coconuts)

Tubers and their culture:

*mʷapo(q)	taro (possibly all *Araceae*)
*talo(s)	taro, *Colocasia esculenta*
*piRaq	giant taro, elephant ear taro, *Alocasia macrorrhiza*
*bulaka	swamp taro, *Cyrtosperma chamissonis*
*kamʷa	k.o. wild taro (?)
*qupi	greater yam, *Dioscorea alata*; yam (generic)
*pʷatik	potato yam, aerial yam, *Dioscorea bulbifera*
*(s,j)uli(q)	banana or taro sucker, slip, cutting, shoot (i.e. propagation material)
*wasi(n)	taro stem (used for planting)
*bʷaŋo	new leaves or shoots, or taro tops for planting
*up(e,a)	taro seedling
*pasoq[-i]	to plant (tubers)
*kotiŋ	to cut off taro tops

Bananas:

*pudi	banana, *Musa* cultivars
*joRaga	banana, *Australimusa* group
*sakup	k.o. cooking banana: long with white flesh (presumably *Eumusa* group)

Table 4 (cont'd)

Other food plants:

*topu	sugar cane, *Saccharum officinarum*
*pijo	a kind of edible wild cane or a reed, *Saccharum spontaneum*
*[ka]timun	cucurbit (generic); cucumber, *Cucumis sativus*
*laqia	ginger, *Zingiber officinale*
*yaŋo	turmeric, *Curcuma longa*
*kuluR	breadfruit, *Artocarpus altilis*
*baReqo	breadfruit fruit (?)
*padran	pandanus (generic); coastal pandanus, *Pandanus tectorius*
*kiRe	coastal pandanus, *Pandanus tectorius*
*pakum	*Pandanus dubius*
*ima	k.o. pandanus with useful leaves
*Rabia	sago, *Metroxylon* spp., mainly *Metroxylon sagu*
*sag(u)	sago starch
*qatop	sago fronds, thatch
*talise	Java almond, Indian almond, *Terminalia catappa*
*qipi	Tahitian chestnut, Pacific chestnut, *Inocarpus fagifer*
*[ka]ŋaRi	canarium almond, *Canarium* spp.
*molis	citrus fruit or citrus-like fruit
pau(q)	mango, probably *Mangifera indica*
*wai, *waiwai	mango (generic)
*kapika	Malay apple and rose apple, *Eugenia* spp.
*ñonum	*Morinda citrifolia*
*tawan	*Pometia pinnata*
*wasa	edible greens, *Abelmoschus manihot*
*m(ʷ)asoku	wild cinnamon, *Cinnamomum* spp.
*quRis	Polynesian plum, hog plum, Tahitian apple, *Spondias cytherea*
*ñatu(q)	k.o. tree with avocado-like fruit and hard wood, *Burckella obovata*
*raqu(p)	New Guinea walnut, *Dracontomelon dao*
*buaq	areca palm, *Areca catechu*

Gardening practices:

*quma	garden
*tanoq	soil, earth
*poki	to clear ground for planting
*sara	to dig a hole
*tanum[-i]	to plant

Some prehistorians evidently find the methods of historical linguistics so arcane or the idea of such detailed lexical reconstructions so incredible, that they prefer to ignore or discount the reconstructions as irrelevant to prehistory. This attitude is no more excusable than that of a linguist who would ignore C^{14} dates for artefact assemblages because he does not understand how such dates are arrived at or who would discount the relative dating of assemblages in any archaeological site on the suspicion that worms, humans or earthquakes have disturbed the layers.

Table 5:   Reconstructed Proto-Oceanic terms associated with pots and pottery.

Types of vessel:
*kuron	cooking pot, pot (generic)
*palaŋa	frying pan
*bʷaŋa	k.o. large pot

Parts of vessel:
*tupa((n,ŋ))	lid, cover
*joŋa(n,ŋ)	plug, bung, stopper
*mʷati	herringbone pattern

Pottery manufacture:
*raRo(q)	clay
*buli	mould (clay etc.)
*tapi	paddle for beating clay into shape
*pilit	coil around, encircle; add strip of clay around top of pot

Pottery use:
*tunu	roast in the fire, fire (pot)
*nasu	cook by boiling
*napu	steam, boil
*rapu	fireplace

Table 6:   Reconstructed Proto-Oceanic kinship terms.

Consanguineal terms:
*t[i,u]bu-	grandparent, grandchild
*makubu	grandchild
*tama-	father, father's brother
*tina-	mother, mother's sister
*matuqa	mother's brother
*(qa)lawa	mother's brother, sister's child
*natu-	child, same-sex sibling's child
*tuqaka-	older same-sex sibling
*taci-	younger same-sex sibling
*mʷaqane	brother (woman speaking)
*(pa)pine	sister (man speaking)

Affinal terms:
| **qasawa-* | spouse |
| **qipaR* | spouse's opposite-sex sibling |

Note: The problem of reconstructing two terms for 'mother's brother' is discussed by Chowning (1991:65).

THE DISPERSAL AND DIVERSIFICATION OF OCEANIC LANGUAGES

Subgrouping: the sequence of genetic splits in Oceanic

Kinds of subgroups. Innovations occur in two basic patterns across languages, enabling linguists to identify subgroups. In the first pattern, all member languages of a subgroup exclusively share a common set of innovations. In the second pattern, innovations form an overlapping pattern, such that, for example, languages A, B and C reflect one bunch of innovations, languages C, D, and E another bunch, languages D, E, F, and G yet another, and languages G and H still a different bunch of innovations. A subgroup reflecting the first pattern may be termed an "innovation-defined" subgroup. One reflecting the second pattern may be called an "innovation-linked" subgroup.[8]

The two patterns allow linguists to make certain inferences about how languages have diverged.[9]

In the case of an innovation-defined subgroup, we infer that all member languages of the subgroup exclusively share a set of innovations because these innovations occurred in the language ancestral to them. That is, the subgroup has been formed because a community speaking a single language has become separated geographically and/or socially into two or more communities; after separation, changes have occurred in the speech of each of the new communities until what was one language has become two or more.

The inference that can be made about an innovation-linked subgroup is of a different order. Here, it can be inferred that the overlapping pattern of innovations reflects the fact that the languages of the subgroup once formed a network of related dialects. During this phase, innovations occurred at various places in the network, spreading from their dialect of origin into neighbouring dialects, but without affecting the whole network. Over time the dialects have diverged until they have become mutually unintelligible for practical purposes, but they continue to reflect the innovation pattern of the former network.[10]

Innovation-defined and innovation-linked subgroups are not mutually exclusive. A subgroup may be both: innovation-defined in that there are innovations shared by all members of the subgroup, and innovation-linked because there is also a pattern of overlapping innovations. In such a case, both sets of inferences apply. The subgroup is innovation-defined because its member languages are descended from a single interstage language, and innovation-linked because that interstage language diversified into a dialect network out of which the present-day languages have evolved.

With the small size and geographical isolation of political entities in Oceania, dialect networks have readily become innovation-linked subgroups of discrete languages. The result is that innovation-linked subgroups are important in Oceanic historical linguistics. But they are also problematic. The internal structure of an innovation-linked subgroup is known to us through its patterning of innovations, but, unless the subgroup is also innovation-defined, we have no direct evidence as to its origin: it may be descended from a discrete interstage language which happens not to have undergone an identifiable set of innovations, or it may simply be descended from a detached section of an earlier dialect network.

In the 1950s and 1960s, comparative linguists writing in the Austronesian field saw their primary task as genetic classification and reconstruction, and applied a simple-minded family tree model in which all language splits are assumed to be sudden and complete. But a family-tree model is often unsatisfactory for making sense of and for representing historical relationships among languages. One reason is that it forces those linguistic relationships produced by dialect differentiation (and subsequent break-up of the network) into a distorted scenario, that of the sharp separation model — and in early Oceanic, dialect differentiation and network-breaking were the rule rather than the exception. Since the early 1970s Austronesianists have given more attention to the problem of dialectal diffusion in prehistoric languages. In the Oceanic field the most incisive study of this kind is Geraghty's (1983) treatment of the relationship of the Fijian speech traditions to each other and to Polynesian. Other works that tackle dialect diffusion in particular regions include Pawley (1975) and Ross (1994b) on Central Papua; Ross (1988) on various regions of western Melanesia; Lichtenberk (1988) on Malaita; Clark (1985) and Tryon (1976) on Vanuatu; Pawley and Sayaba (1971) on Fiji; Pawley (1979) on Fiji and Rotuma; Biggs (1980), Dyen (1981) and Rensch (1987) on western Polynesia; and Jackson (1983) and Marck (1986) on Nuclear Micronesia.

The Comparative Method is not equipped to investigate certain kinds of historical change, such as structural convergence resulting from bilingualism, or from "drift" (pressures inherent in certain structural types that allegedly favour parallel changes). Recent work has begun to address these phenomena using a range of methods (e.g. Thurston 1987; Ross 1987; Ross forthcoming; and a number of the papers in Dutton and Tryon 1994).

High-order subgroups. The following high-order subgroups of Oceanic seem fairly well supported:[11]

1.   Admiralty Islands
2.   St Matthias Islands
3.   Western Oceanic
4.   Southeast Solomonic
5.   North/Central Vanuatu
6.   South Vanuatu
7.   Southern Oceanic

8.   Central Pacific
9.   Nuclear Micronesian

The regions covered by these groups are shown in Map 2. We are not seeking to claim that POc underwent a primary nine-way split, but simply that in our view persuasive arguments have yet to be presented for higher-order groupings.[12] It should be noted that Groups 3, 5 and 8 are innovation-linked subgroups: there is no innovation which all their members share relative to POc.

The **Admiralties** group is clearly established as an innovation-defined subgroup (Blust 1978b; Ross 1988:ch. 9). The **St Matthias** group is also innovation-defined, with the possibility that it is associated in some way with the Admiralties; it certainly is not a close relative of its southern neighbours, the languages of New Ireland (Ross 1988:ch. 9).

The **Western Oceanic** grouping was proposed as an innovation-linked subgroup by Ross (1988:386-389). Except in a few small relic areas the languages of the region merge POc *r and *R, share reflexes of the innovative disjunctive pronoun *idri[a] 'they' (in contrast to POc *(k)ira), and sporadically reflect other features which imply that the languages of the region are descended from a dialect network which has a history separate from that of other Oceanic groups.

The **Southeast Solomonic** group is a fairly well innovation-defined and apparently very conservative subgroup, which divides in its turn into the Guadalcanal/Gela and Malaita/Makira subgroups (Pawley 1972; Levy 1979, 1980; Tryon and Hackman 1983; Lichtenberk 1988).

North/Central Vanuatu is an innovation-linked subgroup which has been documented by Pawley (1972), Tryon (1976) and Clark (1985). Clark views the subgroup as the outcome of a dialect network which gradually differentiated out into local languages. He recognizes a major division between North and Central Vanuatu, "with the boundary running between Santo and Malekula and between Raga and the remainder of Pentecost" (1985:221).

The **South Vanuatu** group embraces the languages of the islands of Erromanga, Tanna and Aneityum, and is an innovation-defined subgroup documented by Lynch (1978).

Geraghty (1989) has proposed a **New Caledonian** group (he calls it "Southern Oceanic") which includes all the languages of New Caledonia and the Loyalty Islands. He also suggests that New Caledonian may subgroup with South Vanuatu, and implies that this grouping may form an innovation-linked subgroup with North/Central Vanuatu.[13] However, the evidence for this is limited and in our view not yet persuasive.

The **Central Pacific** grouping has been well studied (Grace 1959; Pawley 1972; Geraghty 1983, 1986, 1990). Proto-Central Pacific was evidently located

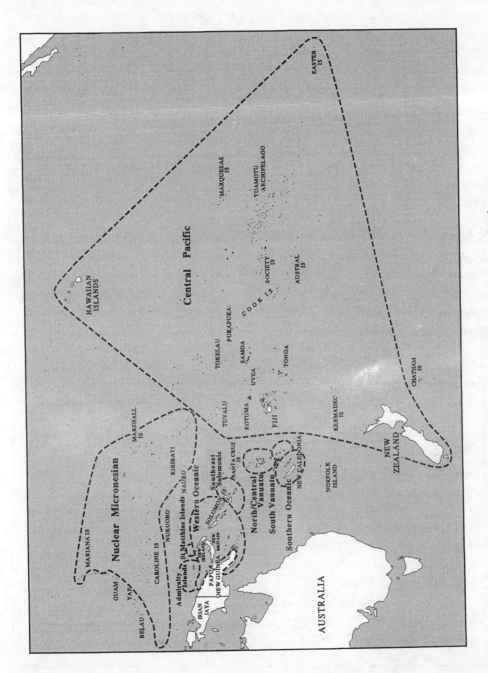

Map 2: High-order subgroups of Oceanic Austronesian languages.

in the Fijian archipelago, where it became differentiated into a dialect network with considerable variation from east to west. Speakers of an eastern dialect separated, probably by moving to Tonga and other islands in western Polynesia, where Proto-Polynesian developed (Geraghty 1983; Green 1981). Speakers of a western dialect moved to Rotuma, where a distinct language developed (Pawley 1979). Subsequently, the stay-at-home dialects in Fiji continued to interact, so that they now form an innovation-linked group, within which an eastern and a western subgroup are clearly distinguishable (Pawley and Sayaba 1971; Geraghty and Pawley 1981; Geraghty 1983). Proto-Polynesian has diversified into the languages of the Polynesian group, a very well defined subgroup of Oceanic (Pawley 1966, 1967; Biggs 1971).

Nuclear Micronesian includes all languages of Micronesia except Belau, Chamorro and probably Yapese (Bender 1971; Jackson 1983; Bender and Wang 1985).[14]

Subgroups of Western Oceanic. Ross (1988) proposes that the Western Oceanic group is made up of three subgroups or "clusters": Meso-Melanesian, Papuan Tip and North New Guinea (see Map 3).[15] The first two of these are innovation-defined subgroups, and in both cases the interstage proto-language or an early daughter interstage evidently differentiated into an extensive network. The North New Guinea grouping, however, is an innovation-linked subgroup, in that there

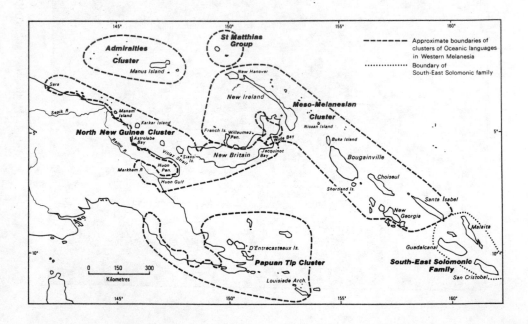

Map 3: Oceanic subgroups in western Melanesia.

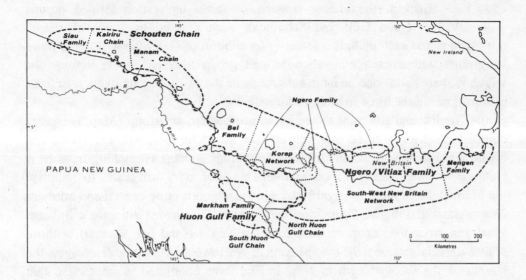

Map 4: The North New Guinea grouping and its subgroups.

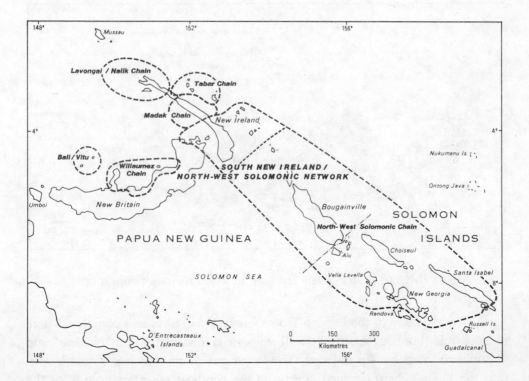

Map 5: The Meso-Melanesian grouping and its subgroups.

are no innovations shared by all languages of the cluster relative to POc (Ross 1988:120). Instead, the cluster consists of three innovation-defined groups (Ngero/Vitiaz, Huon Gulf and Schouten), each defined by a set of shared innovations and each including lower-order subgroups (see Map 4). One or more subgroups within each innovation-defined group also has some innovations which it shares with one or more subgroups of the other two innovation-defined groups, joining the three in a network relationship.[16]

The internal structure of the Meso-Melanesian subgroup (Map 5) is very complex. A primary three-way split into the Bali-Vitu language, the Willaumez chain, and the New Ireland/Northwest Solomonic linkage (stretching from New Hanover to Santa Isabel) is recognizable. The latter in its turn seems to comprise the Madak, Tabar and Lavongai/Nalik groups which occupy central and northern New Ireland and the far-flung South New Ireland/Northwest Solomonic linkage. However, since the departure from southern New Ireland (we assume) of those whose descendants became the speakers of Northwest Solomonic languages, the languages the whole length of New Ireland have continued to interact so that they form an innovation-linked group. The New Ireland communalects have thus behaved similarly to those of Fiji.

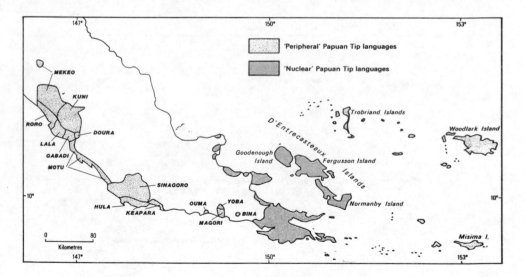

Map 6: The Papuan Tip grouping and its major subgroups.

The structure of the Papuan Tip subgroup (Map 6) is less complex. There is a possible (but not particularly well supported) initial split into "Nuclear" and "Peripheral" Papuan Tip linkages. The languages of the Nuclear network split into the Suauic chain (located mostly on the southeastern-most portion of the mainland) and the North Mainland/D'Entrecasteaux network, which forms a rough arc stretching from Normanby Island, through Fergusson and Goodenough Islands to the mainland coast at Collingwood Bay, then southeastwards along and around the coast as far as Milne Bay (Ross 1988:191, 1992).

"Melanesia". The reader will notice that nowhere do we speak of "Melanesian" languages or a "Melanesian" group. In describing the location of the Oceanic languages, one cannot avoid "Melanesia" as a geographic term. Nowadays, however, the comparative linguist referring to the genetic grouping of languages recognizes no such adjective as "Melanesian". Melanesia is occupied, as we have noted, by speakers of both Papuan and Austronesian languages, but even among Austronesian languages there is no "Melanesian" group. Instead, some languages spoken in Melanesia are more closely related to Polynesian languages than to other languages of Melanesia.

Locating the POc language community and directions of dispersal

One method for locating the probable dispersal centre (or "homeland") of a family of languages is distributional. The view that the most likely dispersal centre for a family of languages is in the area of their greatest genetic diversity was stated by Sapir (1916) some years before Vavilov applied a parallel idea to cultivated plants. More recently, its linguistic application has been substantially refined by Dyen (1956). Underlying it is the principle of parsimony, which requires that one posits the fewest and shortest moves needed to account for the geographic distribution of the subgroups. It can be seen that this method depends on subgrouping, because genetic diversity is defined in terms of subgroups.

One needs to look at both the external relationships and the internal subgrouping of the languages in question. We accept Blust's (1978a, 1983-84, 1993) conclusions that Oceanic belongs to an Eastern Malayo-Polynesian group whose other members are found around Cenderawasih Bay in northwest New Guinea and in South Halmahera, and that the closest relatives of Eastern Malayo-Polynesian also lie in Indonesia. Given this, the method requires us to conclude that Proto-Eastern Malayo-Polynesian was probably located around Cenderawasih Bay and that the separation of the Oceanic branch began with a movement of Eastern Malayo-Polynesian speakers from Cenderawasih Bay eastwards along the north coast of New Guinea.

But where did this pre-Oceanic movement end up? That is to say, what was the dispersal centre of POc itself? The internal subgrouping outlined in the section on subgrouping allows for two main possibilities, both located in northwest Melanesia. (Map 2 gives the location of high-order subgroups of Oceanic.) One possibility is that pre-Oceanic speakers moved only as far as the Sarmi Coast or Jayapura, because here we find two small and little studied Oceanic groups which may be first-order branches of Oceanic.

But if, as the limited available evidence suggests, these groups belong to Western Oceanic, then POc developed further east, in the Bismarck Archipelago, where several fairly well-established high-order subgroups meet. In the Bismarck Archipelago we find two first-order groups of Oceanic, Admiralties and Western Oceanic, and perhaps a third, St Matthias. Western Oceanic in turn divides into three large second-order groups, two of them represented in New Britain: the North New Guinea group and the Meso-Melanesian group.

Another procedure for locating linguistic dispersal centres is often called the *Wörter und Sachen* ("words and things") method, because it depends on reconstructing words for things associated with culture and physical environment. For POc, for example, it is necessary to reconstruct terms for a number of animals — cassowary, possum and bandicoot — that are found in New Guinea and at locations in the Bismarck and Solomon archipelagoes, but which are absent from southern Melanesia, Micronesia and Polynesia. These reconstructions are required not only because the cognate sets are represented in more than one primary subgroup of Oceanic but also because cognates are found in non-Oceanic Austronesian languages in eastern Indonesia (Blust 1982). It is also necessary to reconstruct words for many marine animals and other features associated with the sea. However, this line of evidence hardly allows any conclusion more specific than that POc speakers lived near the sea somewhere in eastern Indonesia, New Guinea or the Bismarck Archipelago.

Let us turn now to the break-up of POc. Primarily on the basis of distribution of subgroups, we have placed the likely dispersal centre in the Bismarck Archipelago, without favouring any particular part of this region. The distribution of first-order subgroups indicates a more or less contemporaneous movement of POc speakers in several directions over a considerable area of Melanesia. Assuming that POc was not located in the Admiralties (an assumption which needs further investigation) there was an early movement to that region, contemporaneous with the break-up of POc. The same can be said of the St Matthias group and New Britain, each of which contains a high-order subgroup of Oceanic. At about the same time there were one or more movements into the Solomons and into Remote Oceania, leading to the divergence of the Southeast Solomonic, North/Central Vanuatu, Southern Vanuatu, Southern Oceanic, Central Pacific and Nuclear Micronesian groups.

New Britain is the likely dispersal centre for the Western Oceanic group (Ross 1989). Western Oceanic is an innovation-linked subgroup, but the two innovations noted earlier are shared by the vast majority of its member languages, suggesting that it is descended from a dialect network which once occupied quite a limited area (otherwise the innovations would not have spread through almost all the network). The available evidence indicates that this area was along the north coast of New Britain, perhaps straddling the Willaumez

Peninsula, as this is the seam of two primary divisions of Western Oceanic, the Meso-Melanesian and North New Guinea groups. Furthermore, the area of greatest diversity of the Meso-Melanesian group is found in this area. Two of its three primary subgroups (Bali-Vitu and the Willaumez chain) are situated around the Willaumez Peninsula.

If the Western Oceanic homeland was on the north coast of New Britain, Western Oceanic speakers expanded in two main directions. There was progressive occupation of the New Britain coast, of New Ireland (apparently from south to north) and of the Northwest Solomonic area to form the Meso-Melanesian group.[17] The second direction of expansion was across the Vitiaz Strait to the mainland coast of New Guinea. This last movement was soon followed by a split between the North New Guinea group, occupying parts of the north coast of New Guinea and offshore islands in the Morobe, Madang and Sepik Provinces, and the Papuan Tip group, comprising the Milne Bay and Central Province languages. Within a short time the ancestral North New Guinea network split into the Schouten, Ngero/Vitiaz and Huon Gulf groups. Sequences of reconstructible innovations particularly support the south to north settlement of New Ireland and the east to west settlement of the Schouten Islands.

The weight of the subgrouping evidence, then, points to a quite rapid diaspora of Austronesian speakers across Melanesia and into the central Pacific. We have noted distributional evidence for an approximately coeval occupation by Oceanic speakers of New Britain, St Matthias, the Admiralties, the Southeast Solomons and several regions of "Remote Oceania" (the widely separated island groups and isolated islands of the Pacific beyond the Solomons chain).

Can this dispersal be accurately dated? An association between the spread of Oceanic languages and Lapita pottery and associated artefacts in the central Pacific has been argued by a number of scholars since the 1960s, but Shutler and Marck (1975) were perhaps the first to argue that the break-up of POc itself should be associated with the movements of Lapita bearers, a view that has gained increasing acceptance (Pawley and Green 1984; Spriggs 1984, 1993; Kirch 1984, 1992; Bellwood 1989; Green 1994). Lapita pottery appears in the Bismarck Archipelago around 1600 BC (Kirch and Hunt 1988; Spriggs 1989, 1990, this volume) and in several regions of Remote Oceania soon after. Archaeological dates for the first Lapita assemblages in New Caledonia, Vanuatu, Fiji, Tonga and Samoa are all between 1300 and 1000 BC. Current archaeological dates indicate that settlement of the Papuan Tip area may not have occurred until somewhat later, reaching Central Papua about 2000 years ago (Vanderwal 1973; Allen 1977a, 1977b; Bulmer 1982). At present the earliest dates which we can associate with confidence with North New Guinea speakers (on the north New Britain coast west of the Willaumez Peninsula, and on the islands and the mainland coast of the Vitiaz Strait) are only about 1500 years ago (Lilley 1988, 1990).

Rapidity of settlement bears on the conundrum of how Polynesians and Micronesians, with their Southern Mongoloid physical type, could have come out of Melanesia, where the so-called "Melanesian" physical type, marked superficially by tightly frizzy hair, dark skin and relatively large teeth, is allegedly dominant. The answer appears to be that they did not "come out of" Melanesia: some Oceanic speakers *moved through* Melanesia into the central Pacific, and they moved through rapidly enough to retain their Southern Mongoloid phenotype. Today's Austronesian speakers in Melanesia have acquired Melanesian characteristics in varying degrees by intermarriage in the intervening millennia and by gene flow after the initial dispersal of Oceanic speakers.[18] However, even in western Melanesia, pockets of Austronesian speakers' superficial Southern Mongoloid features are still found, e.g. in much of southeast Papua, and on Wuvulu and Aua. Recent work in biological anthropology (referred to in Green 1994:38) indicates that other Austronesian-speaking populations in Melanesia also exhibit genetic markers linking them with Southern Mongoloid peoples of Southeast Asia and Polynesia.

Modes of Oceanic dispersal

The fact that so many Oceanic subgroups as far east as Fiji form linkages rather than families suggests that within each major island group the main mode of settlement was a continuous expansion into neighbouring territory that resulted again and again in the formation of dialect chains and networks. Each new village maintained contact with its parent village, and only gradually did village speech communities differentiate out into separate languages. The main variation in this pattern was caused by factors which hindered contact, whether geographical (a large ocean gap or a land barrier such as a mountain range) or social (the intervention of a Papuan-speaking group). The Northwest Solomonic case is instructive. Choiseul, the New Georgia group, and Santa Ysabel are each occupied by linkages within which there are no radical breaks, yet the breaks between each network, corresponding with the intervening sea, are fairly clear. On the island of Bougainville, on the other hand, the Austronesian languages show considerable differences among themselves, a product of their separation by Papuan-speakers.

There are some, but not many, notable exceptions to this pattern. For example, within the North New Guinea group the Schouten chain is sufficiently different from its neighbours to the east, and its easternmost members are sufficiently conservative in their phonology and verbal morphology (Ross 1988:

122-132) to imply that Proto-Schouten was an early departure from the North New Guinea dialect network and became completely isolated from it.

CHANGE IN THE LEXICONS AND CULTURES OF OCEANIC SPEAKERS

In the period since the break-up of POc perhaps 3,500 years ago, many of the descendants of POc have undergone radical transformations while others have changed much less. The most conservative languages, lexically, have probably been some members of the Meso-Melanesian Cluster, especially Bali-Vitu and the Willaumez chain, all the languages located in the eastern half of the main Solomon Island chain from eastern Santa Isabel and Guadalcanal to Santa Ana, parts of central and northern Vanuatu, all the Fijian languages and some Polynesian languages (especially Tongan). Most of these languages retain reflexes of 35-45 per cent of some 250 Proto-Malayo-Polynesian basic vocabulary items reconstructed by Blust (1981, 1993). At the other extreme are languages which retain only a small percentage — in the most extreme cases, fewer than 10 per cent — of the reconstructed etyma. Most languages are somewhere between these extremes. Among Oceanic languages there is a rough — by no means exact — correlation between lexical and grammatical conservatism and a much lesser correlation between lexical and phonological conservatism. With a handful of exceptions all the lexically most innovative languages are found in the area of the New Guinea mainland and New Britain.

Linguists have for several generations been vexed by these highly innovative (sometimes called "aberrant") languages. Among the explanations that have been offered to account for their high degree of vocabulary replacement are: (i) imperfect acquisition of an Oceanic language by a non-Austronesian (Papuan) speech community, (ii) long-term bilingualism between Oceanic and Papuan neighbours, sustained by trade and intermarriage, (iii) very small size of speech communities, as the result of migration, political structures, etc., (iv) social pressures to develop a distinct language from one's neighbours, (v) taboos on using words coinciding with the names of chiefs or of the dead, (vi) changes of physical environment following migration, (vii) cultural changes generated internally, (viii) cultural changes generated by contact, and (ix) phonological change creating problematic (especially ambiguous) word forms.

By far the most controversial of these proposals, because it conflicts with the hypothesis of founder settlement, is (i), the so-called "pidginization" hypothesis, elaborated by Ray (1926) and Capell (1943). The current consensus is that few, if any, Oceanic languages show evidence of the imperfect learning and heavy substrate residue which would indicate their takeover by a community whose previous language was Papuan. To explain most cases we need to look to a combination of the other factors.

In parts of Melanesia at least as far east as the central Solomons there has been sustained interaction between Oceanic and Papuan language communities, associated with trade and intermarriage. The resultant bilingualism has in a number of cases caused a radical restructuring, especially in grammar, of Oceanic languages. Lynch (1981) argues that the subject-object-verb order and postpositions of the Papuan Tip group are attributable to Papuan influence on Proto-Papuan Tip. One Papuan Tip language, Maisin, has undergone so much Papuanization that earlier commentators could not decide whether it was Papuan or Austronesian (Ross forthcoming). Dutton (1982) has analysed the borrowing and reborrowing of vocabulary in Magori, also a Papuan Tip language. The Bel languages of the North New Guinea group show significant Papuanization in their grammatical structures (Ross 1987, forthcoming), and Lincoln (1976) describes the contrast between Papuanized Piva and un-Papuanized Banoni, two otherwise closely related languages of Bougainville. However, while such sustained language contact and bilingualism has certainly promoted linguistic change, it seems rarely to have led to the adoption of Austronesian languages by Papuan speakers which Ray and Capell argued for. Where the latter did occur, it probably wrought changes in phonology rather than grammatical structure (Ross 1994a).

It should surprise no-one that a change of physical or cultural environment led some Oceanic language communities to lose many POc words and change the meanings of others. Sometimes it is possible to work out the approximate period in the history of these languages when the terms in question were lost. For example, although New Zealand Maori no longer has terms for a great many plants and animals of the Pacific tropical environment (Biggs 1994), we can be sure that such terms were present in the immediate common ancestor of Maori, Rarotongan, Tahitian and Tuamotuan, because the latter retain Proto-Polynesian terms for many such items, and we can infer that the losses occurred only after Maori separated from these other languages. In the same way, even though in the central Pacific the megapode or brush turkey is now found only on one remote island (Niuafo'ou, between Tonga and Samoa), we know that speakers of Proto-Polynesian retained the POc (and Proto-Eastern Malayo-Polynesian) word for the megapode and that the term was lost in daughter languages only after the break-up of Proto-Polynesian. This inference can be made because the Niuafo'ou language (a Polynesian language spoken on Niuafo'ou Island between Tonga and Samoa) retains the POc term, *malau*. It is supported by the recent discovery of megapode bones in archaeological sites in Fiji. In certain Oceanic languages spoken inland on large islands in Melanesia the loss of terms for the maritime environment can be shown to be fairly recent, because the languages in question are closely related to coastal languages which retain many POc maritime-related terms.

CONCLUSIONS

It remains to sum up the implications of the linguistic evidence reviewed here for reconstructing the prehistory of the Pacific.

1. The distribution of subgroups suggests that POc developed as a distinctive speech tradition following a movement of Eastern Malayo-Polynesian speakers from the Bird's Head of New Guinea to a region further east in northwest Melanesia. It is possible that the movement was in the first instance to the Sarmi Coast and/or the Jayapura regions immediately east of the Bird's Head. However, the most probable dispersal point for all Oceanic subgroups east of Irian Jaya is in the Bismarck Archipelago, where several high-order subgroups are contiguous.

2. After a period of unified development (probably not more than a few centuries) in northwest Melanesia POc speakers spread rapidly over most of Island Melanesia and into West Polynesia and Micronesia. If we accept the connection between the fairly well-dated spread of Lapita culture and the spread of Oceanic, the initial dispersal across Island Melanesia took place in the second half of the second millennium BC. At about the same time, Oceanic speakers may have begun to settle on islands close to the New Guinea mainland around the Huon Peninsula. Settlement of the north coast of the mainland and the Huon Gulf may have been somewhat later. Following settlement of the Southeast Papuan region, speakers of a Papuan Tip language moved westwards along the south coast of Papua. This last movement can be correlated with the appearance of a pottery-bearing culture in the Central Province around 2000 years ago.

3. Partial reconstruction of various POc terminologies denoting domains and categories of social structure and material culture is possible. These reconstructions show, very clearly, that POc speakers preserved fairly completely the Proto-Malayo-Polynesian and Proto-Eastern Malayo-Polynesian terminologies for many cultural domains, e.g. the canoe complex, marine life and fishing techniques, cultivated plants, and kinship. At least five Proto-Malayo-Polynesian pottery terms[19] were retained. However, POc speakers evidently did not preserve terms for rice culture.

4. Some Oceanic communities have retained much more of the total POc lexicon than others. If we measure cultural conservatism in terms of the degree of retention of terminologies for various specific domains of technology and social structure, there is (not surprisingly) a fairly high correlation between linguistic and cultural conservatism.

NOTES

[1] We are indebted to Peter Bellwood for useful comments on the original draft of this paper. The revised version takes account of relevant developments in the field in 1991-93.

[2] The "classical" comparative method was codified by a German linguistic school, the Neogrammarians, who flourished in the last third of the nineteenth century, building on a large body of work in Indo-European comparative linguistics developed by nineteenth-century scholars.

[3] An asterisk marks reconstructed form.

[4] Another method used to subgroup languages is lexicostatistics, popularized by Morris Swadesh and others in the 1950s. Lists of words for the same set of meanings are collected from a number of languages, and for every pair of languages each pair of words is marked as either "cognate" or "non-cognate"; the percentage of the items in the list which are deemed cognate for each pair of languages is calculated. This "cognate percentage" is then taken to be a measure of the genetic relationship of the two languages. The fundamental fault of lexicostatistics is its assumption, rejected by most comparative linguists, that over long periods of time all languages replace their vocabulary at approximately the same rate. Blust (1981) is a major study of Austronesian evidence which shows great variation among languages in their replacement rates. In addition, lexicostatistics is unable to take proper account of the effects of borrowing.

[5] Glottochronology, an outgrowth of lexicostatistics, at best provides very rough indicators because of differing rates of change among languages.

[6] For references to research on Proto-Oceanic since Dempwolff (1934-38), see Blust (1978b), Ross (1988), and Pawley and Ross (1993).

[7] Examples of POc terminologies are French-Wright (1983) and Ross (1993) on horticulture and food plants; Chowning (1963) on plants; Walter (1989) on fishing; Osmond (1993) on fishing and hunting implements, Pawley (1993) on reef creatures, Clark (1994) on birds; Lichtenberk (1994) on cookery; Pawley and Pawley (1994) on canoes and canoe parts; Ross (1994c) on pottery; Ross (1994d) on meteorological terms; Milke (1938, 1958) on kinship; and the debate on the nature of leadership in POc society (Pawley 1982; Lichtenberk 1986), whilst Chowning (1991) offers a survey of POc culture. There are also works on terminologies in interstage languages. These include Geraghty (1994) on Proto-Central Pacific fish; Marck (1994) on the Proto-Nuclear Micronesian physical environment; and a variety of Proto-Polynesian terminologies in kinship and society (Pawley 1982) and other domains (Pawley and K. Green 1971; Clark 1982, 1991; Hooper 1985, 1994). POc lexical reconstructions scattered across various sources probably total close to 2000.

[8] Ross (1988:8) used the terms "family" and "linkage" (with "chain" and "network" as particular configurations of linkage) for an innovation-defined and an innovation-linked subgroup respectively. Because these terms also have other connotations for linguists, we have replaced them by the more transparent, if albeit clumsier, terms here.

[9] The two kinds of innovation pattern have been appreciated almost since the beginnings of the comparative method, and resulted in the "family tree" and "wave"

models. The latter was intended, however, to reflect the great European dialect networks of English, Dutch/German, or Western Romance, rather than language linkages like those of, say, the Milne Bay Province of Papua New Guinea.

[10] The modes of subgroup formation that result in innovation-defined and innovation-linked subgroups have been described more fully by Pawley and Green (1984) under the labels "radiation" and "network-breaking" and by Ross (1988:7-11) under "separation" and "dialect differentiation".

[11] Omitted from this grouping due to lack of evidence or the absence of studies are (i) the Oceanic languages of Irian Jaya; (ii) Yapese; (iii) the languages of Utupua and Vanikoro in the Te Motu Province of the Solomon Islands.

[12] Readers familiar with the literature on Oceanic languages may be puzzled by the absence of an "Eastern Oceanic" subgroup from our listing of high-order groups. Several attempts have been made to show the existence of such a subgroup including some or all of groups 4 to 9, but none has been convincing. It has proven difficult to establish an innovation-linked subgroup on this scale, let alone an innovation-defined one. References to various "Eastern Oceanic" hypotheses include Pawley (1972, 1977), Lynch and Tryon (1985; cf. Ross 1988:393), and Geraghty (1990).

[13] Clark (1985:219-220) has also presented innovations which link South Vanuatu to North/Central Vanuatu.

[14] Belau and Chamorro are both non-Oceanic Austronesian languages whose closest relatives are probably to be found in the Philippines. Yapese is an Austronesian language whose position in the family has yet to be clearly established.

[15] Chowning (1989) has recently questioned the integrity of the Papuan Tip group. Her arguments are discussed by Ross (1992). If they were accepted, they would result only in the exclusion from the group of the Kilivila family, i.e. three of the 54 languages attributed to the group by Ross (1988).

[16] The Jayapura and Sarmi Coast (Grace 1971) subgroups may also be part of the North New Guinea grouping, but the available data are insufficient for us to be certain.

[17] Ross (1988) has argued that if POc was located in the New Britain region, then two waves of eastward migration may have originated there: the first was ancestral to all Oceanic subgroups other than Western Oceanic, the second resulted in the Meso-Melanesian group. Under this scenario, Meso-Melanesian probably displaced first-wave languages on New Ireland and in the northwest Solomons, providing an explanation of the quite sharp differences between Meso-Melanesian languages and their neighbours in the St Matthias group to the north and the Southeast Solomonic group to the southeast. This entails the possibility that the Meso-Melanesian speakers of the second wave were more "Papuanized" than the pre-Eastern Oceanic speakers of the first wave, and were thereby better equipped to settle the Meso-Melanesian region, which was already occupied by Papuan speakers.

[18] These thoughts are not new: see Green (1963) and Wurm (1967).

[19] POc *kuron* 'pot', *palaŋa* 'frying pan', *bʷaŋa* 'k.o. large pot', *raRo(q)* 'clay' and *tapi* 'paddle for beating clay into shape'.

REFERENCES

Allen, Jim
  1977a   Fishing for wallabies: trade as a mechanism of social interaction, integration and elaboration on the Central Papuan coast. In J. Friedman and M.J. Rowlands (eds) *The evolution of social systems*, pp.419-455. London: Duckworth.
  1977b   Management of resources in prehistoric coastal Papua. In John H. Winslow (ed.) *The Melanesian environment*, pp.35-44. Canberra: Australian National University Press.

Bellwood, Peter S.
  1989   The colonization of the Pacific: some current hypotheses. In A.V.S. Hill and S.W. Serjeantson (eds) *The colonization of the Pacific: a genetic trail*, pp.11-59. Oxford: Clarendon Press.

Bender, Byron W.
  1971   Micronesian languages. In Thomas A. Sebeok (ed.) *Current trends in linguistics* 8: *Linguistics in Oceania*, pp.426-465. The Hague: Mouton.

Bender, Byron W. and Judith W. Wang
  1985   The status of Proto-Micronesian. In Andrew K. Pawley and Lois Carrington (eds) *Austronesian linguistics at the 15th Pacific science congress*, pp.53-92. Pacific Linguistics Series C No. 88. Canberra: Department of Linguistics, Research School of Pacific Studies, The Australian National University.

Biggs, Bruce G.
  1965   Direct and indirect inheritance in Rotuman. *Lingua* 14:383-415.
  1971   The languages of Polynesia. In Thomas A. Sebeok (ed.) *Current trends in linguistics* 8: *Linguistics in Oceania*, pp.466-505. The Hague: Mouton.
  1980   The position of East 'Uvean and Anutan in the Polynesian language family. *Te Reo* 22-23:115-134.
  1994   New words for a new world. In Andrew Pawley and Malcolm D. Ross (eds) *Austronesian terminologies: continuity and change*. Pacific Linguistics Series C No. 127, pp.21-29. Canberra: Department of Linguistics, Research School of Pacific and Asian Studies, The Australian National University.

Blust, Robert A.
  1978a   Eastern Malayo-Polynesian: a subgrouping argument. In S.A. Wurm and Lois Carrington (eds) *Second international conference on Austronesian linguistics: proceedings*, pp.181-234. Pacific Linguistics Series C No. 61. Canberra: Department of Linguistics, Research School of Pacific Studies, The Australian National University.
  1978b   *The Proto-Oceanic palatals*. Journal of the Polynesian Society Monograph 43. Auckland: The Polynesian Society.
  1981   Variation in retention rate among Austronesian languages. Paper presented to the Third International Conference on Austronesian Linguistics, Denpasar.

1982   The linguistic value of the Wallace line. *Bijdragen tot de Taal-, Land- en Volkenkunde* 138:231-250.

1983-84 More on the position of the languages of Eastern Indonesia. *Oceanic Linguistics* 22-23:1-28.

1993   Central and Central-Eastern Malayo-Polynesian. *Oceanic Linguistics* 32: 241-293.

Bulmer, Susan

1982   West of Bootless Inlet: archaeological evidence for prehistoric trade in the Port Moresby area and the origins of the hiri. In T.E. Dutton (ed.) *The hiri in history: further aspects of long-distance Motu trade in central Papua*, pp.117-130. Pacific Research Monograph No. 8. Canberra: The Australian National University.

Capell, Arthur

1943   *The linguistic position of South-Eastern Papua*. Sydney: Australasian Medical Publishing Company.

Chowning, Ann

1963   Proto-Melanesian plant names. In Jacques Barrau (ed.) *Plants and the migrations of Pacific peoples: a symposium,* pp.39-44. Honolulu: Bishop Museum Press.

1989   The 'Papuan Tip' languages reconsidered. In Ray Harlow and Robin Hooper (eds) *VICAL 1: Oceanic languages. Papers from the fifth international conference on Austronesian linguistics*, pp.113-140. Auckland: Linguistic Society of New Zealand.

1991   Proto Oceanic culture: the evidence from Melanesia. In Robert Blust (ed.) *Currents in Pacific linguistics: papers on Austronesian languages and ethnolinguistics in honour of George W. Grace*, pp.43-75. Pacific Linguistics Series C No. 117. Canberra: Department of Linguistics, Research School of Pacific Studies, The Australian National University.

Clark, Ross

1982   Proto-Polynesian birds. In Jukka Siikala (ed.) *Oceanic studies: essays in honour of Aarne A. Koskinen*, pp.121-143. Helsinki: Suomen Antropologinen Seura/The Finnish Anthropological Society.

1985   Languages of north and central Vanuatu: groups, chains, clusters and waves. In Andrew Pawley and Lois Carrington (eds) *Austronesian linguistics at the 15th Pacific science congress*, pp.199-236. Pacific Linguistics Series C No. 88. Canberra: Department of Linguistics, Research School of Pacific Studies, The Australian National University.

1991   *Fingota/Fangota*: shellfish and fishing in Polynesia. In Andrew Pawley (ed.) *Man and a half: essays in Pacific anthropology and ethnobiology in honour of Ralph Bulmer*, pp.78-83. Auckland: The Polynesian Society.

1994   The word is the bird: evolution, migration and extinction of Oceanic ornithonyms. In Andrew Pawley and Malcolm D. Ross (eds) *Austronesian terminologies: continuity and change*. Pacific Linguistics Series C No. 127, pp.73-86. Canberra: Department of Linguistics, Research School of Pacific and Asian Studies, The Australian National University.

Dempwolff, Otto
1934   *Vergleichende Lautlehre des Austronesischen Wortschatzes*, Band 1: *Induktiver Aufbau einer indonesischen Ursprache*. Beihefte zur Zeitschrift für Eingeborenen-Sprachen 15. Berlin: Dietrich Reimer.
1937   *Vergleichende Lautlehre des Austronesischen Wortschatzes*, Band 2: *Deduktive Anwendung des Urindonesischen auf Austronesische Einzelsprachen*. Beihefte zur Zeitschrift für Eingeborenen-Sprachen 17. Berlin: Dietrich Reimer.
1938   *Vergleichende Lautlehre des Austronesischen Wortschatzes*, Band 3: *Austronesisches Wörterverzeichnis*. Beihefte zur Zeitschrift für Eingeborenen-Sprachen 19. Berlin: Dietrich Reimer.

Dutton, T.E.
1982   Borrowing in Austronesian and non-Austronesian languages of coastal south-east mainland Papua New Guinea. In Amran Halim, Lois Carrington and S.A. Wurm (eds) *Papers from the third international conference on Austronesian linguistics* 1: *Currents in Oceanic*, pp.109-177. Pacific Linguistics Series C No. 74. Canberra: Department of Linguistics, Research School of Pacific Studies, The Australian National University.

Dutton, Tom and Darrell Tryon (eds)
1994   *Language contact and change in the Austronesian world*. Berlin: Mouton de Gruyter.

Dyen, Isidore
1956   Language distribution and migration theory. *Language* 32:611-626.
1981   The subgrouping of the Polynesian languages. In K.J. Hollyman and Andrew Pawley (eds) *Studies in Pacific languages and cultures, in honour of Bruce Biggs*, pp.83-100. Auckland: Linguistic Society of New Zealand.

French-Wright, Renwick
1983   *Proto-Oceanic horticultural practices*. M.A. thesis, Department of Anthropology, University of Auckland.

Geraghty, Paul
1983   The history of the Fijian languages. *Oceanic Linguistics* special publication No. 19. Honolulu: University of Hawaii Press.
1986   The sound system of Proto-Central-Pacific. In Paul Geraghty, Lois Carrington and S.A. Wurm (eds) *FOCAL II: papers from the fourth international conference on Austronesian linguistics*, pp.289-312. Pacific Linguistics Series C No. 94. Canberra: Department of Linguistics, Research School of Pacific Studies, The Australian National University.
1989   The reconstruction of Proto-Southern Oceanic. In Ray Harlow and Robin Hooper (eds) *VICAL 1: Oceanic languages. Papers from the fifth international conference on Austronesian linguistics*, pp.141-156. Auckland: Linguistic Society of New Zealand.
1990   Proto-Eastern Oceanic **R* and its reflexes. In J.H.C.S. Davidson (ed.) *Pacific island languages: essays in honour of G.B. Milner*, pp.51-93. London and Honolulu: School of Oriental and African Studies and University of Hawaii Press.

1994   Proto Central Pacific fish-names. In Andrew Pawley and Malcolm D. Ross
        (eds) *Austronesian terminologies: continuity and change*. Pacific
        Linguistics Series C No. 127, pp.141-169. Canberra: Department of
        Linguistics, Research School of Pacific and Asian Studies, The Australian
        National University.

Geraghty, Paul and Andrew K. Pawley
1981   The relative chronology of some innovations in the Fijian languages. In
        Jim Hollyman and Andrew Pawley (eds) *Studies in Pacific languages and
        cultures in honour of Bruce Biggs*, pp.159-178. Auckland: Linguistic
        Society of New Zealand.

Grace, George W.
1959   *The position of the Polynesian languages within the Austronesian (Malayo-
        Polynesian) language family*. Bloomington: Indiana University
        Publications in Anthropology and Linguistics, Memoir 16, supplement to
        International Journal of American Linguistics 25.
1971   Notes on the phonological history of the Austronesian languages of the
        Sarmi coast. *Oceanic Linguistics* 10:11-37.

Green, Roger C.
1963   A suggested revision of the Fijian sequence. *Journal of the Polynesian
        Society* 72:235-252.
1981   Location of the Polynesian homeland: a continuing problem. In Jim
        Hollyman and Andrew Pawley (eds) *Studies in Pacific languages and
        cultures in honour of Bruce Biggs*, pp.133-158. Auckland: Linguistic
        Society of New Zealand.
1994   Changes over time: recent advances in dating human colonisation of the
        Pacific area. In D.G. Sutton (ed.) *Origins of the first New Zealanders*,
        pp.19-51. Auckland: Auckland University Press.

Hooper, Robin
1985   Proto-Oceanic /*qi/. In Andrew K. Pawley and Lois Carrington (eds)
        Austronesian linguistics at the 15th Pacific science congress, pp.141-167.
        Pacific Linguistics Series C No. 88. Canberra: Department of Linguistics,
        Research School of Pacific Studies, The Australian National University.
1994   Proto-Polynesian fish names. In Andrew Pawley and Malcolm D. Ross
        (eds) *Austronesian terminologies: continuity and change*. Pacific
        Linguistics Series C No. 127, pp.185-229. Canberra: Department of
        Linguistics, Research School of Pacific and Asian Studies, The Australian
        National University.

Jackson, Frederick H.
1983   *The internal and external relationships of the Trukic languages of
        Micronesia*. Honolulu: University of Hawaii.

Kern, Hendrik
1886   De Fidji-taal vergeleken net hare verwanten in Indonesië en Polynesië.
        *Verhandelingen der Koninklijke Akademie van Wetenschappen, afdeeling
        Letterkunde* 16:1-242.

Kirch, Patrick V.
  1984   *The evolution of the Polynesian chiefdoms.* Cambridge: Cambridge
           University Press.
  1992   The Lapita culture of western Melanesia in the context of Austronesian
           origins and dispersals. Paper presented to the International Symposium on
           Austronesian Studies relating to Taiwan, Academia Sinica, Nankang,
           Taipei.
Kirch, Patrick V. and T.L. Hunt (eds)
  1988   Archaeology of the Lapita cultural complex: a critical review. *Thomas
           Burke Memorial Washington State Museum Monograph 5.* Seattle: Burke
           Museum.

Levy, Richard S.
  1979   The phonological history of the Bugotu-Nggelic languages and its
           implications for Eastern Oceanic. *Oceanic Linguistics* 18:1-31.
  1980   Languages of the southeast Solomon Islands and the reconstruction of
           Proto-Eastern-Oceanic. In Paz Buenaventura Naylor (ed.) *Austronesian
           studies: papers from the second eastern conference on Austronesian
           languages,* pp.213-222. Ann Arbor: University of Michigan, Center for
           South and Southeast Asian Studies.

Lichtenberk, Frantisek
  1986   Leadership in Proto Oceanic society: linguistic evidence. *Journal of the
           Polynesian Society* 95:341-356.
  1988   The Cristobal-Malaitan subgroup of Southeast Solomonic. *Oceanic
           Linguistics* 27:24-62.
  1994   The raw and the cooked: Proto-Oceanic terms for food preparation. In
           Andrew Pawley and Malcolm D. Ross (eds) *Austronesian terminologies:
           continuity and change.* Pacific Linguistics Series C No. 127, pp.267-288.
           Canberra: Department of Linguistics, Research School of Pacific and Asian
           Studies, The Australian National University.

Lilley, Ian
  1988   Prehistoric exchange across the Vitiaz Strait, Papua New Guinea. *Current
           Anthropology* 29:513-516.
  1990   Final report: Prehistoric settlement and trade in northwest New Britain,
           Papua New Guinea. Typescript. University of Western Australia.

Lincoln, Peter C.
  1976   Banoni, Piva and Papuanization. In Ger P. Reesink, Lillian Fleischmann,
           Sinikka Turpeinen and Peter C. Lincoln (eds) *Papers in New Guinea
           linguistics No. 19,* pp.77-105. Pacific Linguistics Series A No. 45.
           Canberra: Department of Linguistics, Research School of Pacific Studies,
           The Australian National University.

Lynch, John
  1978   Proto-South Hebridean and Proto-Oceanic. In S.A. Wurm and Lois
           Carrington (eds) *Second international conference on Austronesian
           linguistics: proceedings,* pp.717-779. Pacific Linguistics Series C No. 61.

Canberra: Department of Linguistics, Research School of Pacific Studies, The Australian National University.

1981   Melanesian diversity and Polynesian homogeneity: the other side of the coin. *Oceanic Linguistics* 20:95-129.

Lynch, John and D.T. Tryon

1985   Central-Eastern Oceanic: a subgrouping hypothesis. In Andrew K. Pawley and Lois Carrington (eds) *Austronesian linguistics at the 15th Pacific science congress*, pp.31-52. Pacific Linguistics Series C No. 88. Canberra: Department of Linguistics, Research School of Pacific Studies, The Australian National University.

Marck, Jeffrey C.

1986   Micronesian dialects and the overnight voyage. *Journal of the Polynesian Society* 95:253-258.

1994   Proto-Micronesian terms for the physical environment. In Andrew Pawley and Malcolm D. Ross (eds) *Austronesian terminologies: continuity and change*. Pacific Linguistics Series C No. 127, pp.301-328. Canberra: Department of Linguistics, Research School of Pacific and Asian Studies, The Australian National University.

Milke, Wilhelm

1938   Die Benennungen der Geschwister in den austronesischen Sprachen Ozeaniens. *Zeitschrift für Eingeborenen-Sprachen* 70:51-66.

1958   Zur inneren Gliederung und geschtichtlichen Stellung der ozeanisch-Austronesischen Sprachen. *Zeitschrift für Ethnologie* 83:58-62.

1961   Beiträge zur ozeanischen Linguistik. *Zeitschrift für Ethnologie* 86:162-182.

Osmond, Meredith

1993   Proto Oceanic terms for fishing and hunting implements. Paper presented to the First International Conference on Oceanic Linguistics, Vila, Vanuatu.

Pawley, Andrew K.

1966   Polynesian languages: a subgrouping based on shared innovations in morphology. *Journal of the Polynesian Society* 75:39-64.

1967   The relationships of Polynesian Outlier languages. *Journal of the Polynesian Society* 76:259-296.

1972   On the internal relationships of eastern Oceanic languages. In R.C. Green and M. Kelly (eds) *Studies in Oceanic culture history*, vol. 3, pp.1-142. Honolulu: Bernice Pauahi Bishop Museum.

1975   The relationships of the Austronesian languages of Central Papua. In T.E. Dutton (ed.) *Studies in languages of Central and South-East Papua*, pp.3-106. Pacific Linguistics Series C No. 29. Canberra: Department of Linguistics, Research School of Pacific Studies, The Australian National University.

1977   On redefining 'Eastern Oceanic'. Mimeo.

1979   New evidence on the position of Rotuman. Working Papers in Anthropology, Archaeology, Linguistics and Maori Studies 56. Department of Anthropology, University of Auckland.

1981   Melanesian diversity and Polynesian homogeneity: a unified explanation for language. In Jim Hollyman and Andrew Pawley (eds) *Studies in Pacific languages and cultures in honour of Bruce Biggs*, pp.269-309. Auckland: Linguistic Society of New Zealand.

1982   Rubbish-man commoner, big man chief? Linguistic evidence for hereditary chieftainship in Proto-Oceanic society. In Jukka Siikala (ed.) *Oceanic studies: essays in honour of Aarne A. Koskinen*, pp.33-52. *Transactions of the Finnish Anthropological Society* 11. Helsinki: Suomen Antropologinen Seura/The Finnish Anthropological Society.

1993   Proto Oceanic terms for reef and shoreline invertebrates. Paper presented to the First International Conference on Oceanic Linguistics, Vila, Vanuatu.

Pawley, Andrew and Kaye Green
1971   Lexical evidence for the Proto-Polynesian homeland. *Te Reo* 14:1-35.

Pawley, Andrew K. and Roger C. Green
1984   The Proto-Oceanic language community. *Journal of Pacific History* 19: 123-146.

Pawley, Andrew K. and Medina Pawley
1994   Early Austronesian terms for canoe parts and seafaring. In Andrew Pawley and Malcolm D. Ross (eds) *Austronesian terminologies: continuity and change*. Pacific Linguistics Series C No.127, pp.329-361. Canberra: Department of Linguistics, Research School of Pacific and Asian Studies, The Australian National University.

Pawley, Andrew K. and Malcolm D. Ross
1993   Austronesian historical linguistics and culture history. *Annual Review of Anthropology* 22:425-459.

Pawley, Andrew and Timoci Sayaba
1971   Fijian dialect divisions: Eastern and Western Fijian. *Journal of the Polynesian Society* 80:405-436.

Ray, Sidney H.
1926   *A comparative study of the Melanesian island languages*. Cambridge: Cambridge University Press.

Rensch, Karl
1987   East Uvean, Nuclear Polynesian? Reflections on the methodological adequacy of the tree model in Polynesia. In Donald C. Laycock and Werner Winter (eds) *A world of language: papers presented to Professor S.A. Wurm on his 65th birthday*, pp.565-581. Pacific Linguistics Series C No. 100. Canberra: Department of Linguistics, Research School of Pacific Studies, The Australian National University.

Ross, Malcolm D.
1987   A contact-induced morphosyntactic change in the Bel languages of Papua New Guinea. In Donald C. Laycock and Werner Winter (eds) *A world of language: papers presented to Professor S.A. Wurm on his 65th birthday*,

pp.583-601. Pacific Linguistics Series C No. 100. Canberra: Department of Linguistics, Research School of Pacific Studies, The Australian National University.

1988   *Proto Oceanic and the Austronesian languages of western Melanesia.* Pacific Linguistics Series C No. 98. Canberra: Department of Linguistics, Research School of Pacific Studies, The Australian National University.

1989   Early Oceanic linguistic prehistory: a reassessment. *Journal of Pacific History* 24:135-149.

1992   The position of Gumawana among the languages of the Papuan Tip cluster. *Language and Linguistics in Melanesia* 23:139-165.

1993   **kanaŋ ma wasa:* reconstructing food plant terms and associated terminologies in Proto Oceanic. Paper presented to the First International Conference on Oceanic Linguistics, Port Vila, Vanuatu.

1994a   Areal phonological features in north central New Ireland. In Tom Dutton and Darrell Tryon (eds) *Language contact and change in the Austronesian world*, pp.551-572. Berlin: Mouton de Gruyter.

1994b   Central Papuan culture history: some lexical evidence. In Andrew Pawley and Malcolm D. Ross (eds) *Austronesian terminologies: continuity and change*. Pacific Linguistics Series C No. 127, pp.389-479. Canberra: Department of Linguistics, Research School of Pacific and Asian Studies, The Australian National University.

1994c   Pottery terms in Proto Oceanic. Typescript. The Australian National University, Canberra.

1994d   Proto Oceanic terms for meteorological phenomena. Paper presented to the Seventh International Conference on Austronesian Linguistics, Leiden.

forth- Contact-induced change and the comparative method: cases from Papua
coming New Guinea. In Mark Durie and Malcolm D. Ross (eds) *The comparative method reviewed: irregularity and regularity in linguistic change.* New York: Oxford University Press.

Sapir, Edward
1916   Time perspective in aboriginal American culture. *Memoir* 90, *Anthropological series* 13. Ottawa: Geological Survey, Department of Mines. Reprinted in David T. Mandelbaum (ed. 1949) *Selected writings of Edward Sapir in language, culture and personality*, pp.389-462. Berkeley: University of California Press.

Shutler, Richard and Jeffrey C. Marck
1975   On the dispersal of the Austronesian horticulturalists. *Archaeology and Physical Anthropology in Oceania* 10:81-113.

Spriggs, Matthew J.T.
1984   The Lapita cultural complex. *Journal of Pacific History* 19:202-223.

1989   The dating of the Island Southeast Asian Neolithic: an attempt at chronometric hygiene and linguistic correlation. *Antiquity* 63:587-612.

1990   Dating Lapita: another view. In M. Spriggs (ed.) *Lapita design, form and composition*, pp.6-27. Canberra: Department of Prehistory, Research School of Pacific Studies, The Australian National University.

1993   Island Melanesia: the last 10,000 years. In M. Spriggs, D. Yen, W. Ambrose, R. Jones, A. Thorne and A. Andrews (eds) *Community of culture: the people and prehistory of the Pacific*, pp.187-205. Canberra: Australian National University Press.

Thurston, William R.
1987   *Processes of change in the languages of north-western New Britain.* Pacific Linguistics Series B No. 99. Canberra: Department of Linguistics, Research School of Pacific Studies, The Australian National University.

Tryon, D.T.
1976   *New Hebrides languages: an internal classification.* Pacific Linguistics Series C No. 50. Canberra: Department of Linguistics, Research School of Pacific Studies, The Australian National University.

Tryon, D.T. and B.D. Hackman
1983   *Solomon Islands languages: an internal classification.* Pacific Linguistics Series C No. 72. Canberra: Department of Linguistics, Research School of Pacific Studies, The Australian National University.

Vanderwal, R.
1973   *Prehistoric studies in central coastal Papua.* PhD dissertation, The Australian National University, Canberra.

Walter, Richard
1989   Lapita fishing strategies: a review of the archaeological and linguistic evidence. *Journal of Pacific Studies* 31:127-149.

Wurm, S.A.
1967   Linguistics and the prehistory of the south-western Pacific. *Journal of Pacific History* 2:25-38.

4

BORNEO AS A CROSS-ROADS FOR COMPARATIVE AUSTRONESIAN LINGUISTICS

K. Alexander Adelaar

The autochthonous languages of Borneo have been divided into ten separate subgroups (Hudson 1978). This paper discusses four subgroups on which the author has done research.

The Southeast Barito subgroup includes Malagasy. This language underwent considerable influence from Malay and Javanese. Malay influence appears to have lasted until after the introduction of Islam in Southeast Asia, and there are also some indications that the Arabic script was introduced to Madagascar by Indonesians (possibly Javanese). The author puts forth the hypothesis that the Malagasy, rather than having sailed to Madagascar of their own accord, may have been transported there (as subordinates) by Malays.

The Malayic subgroup includes Iban and Malay. The diversity and relative archaism of the Malayic languages spoken in West Borneo suggest that the Malayic homeland may have been in this area.

The Tamanic languages are phonologically, morphosyntactically and lexically close enough to the South Sulawesi languages to form a subgroup with them. They have some striking phonological developments in common with Buginese, with which they seem to form a separate branch within the South Sulawesi language group.

The Land Dayak languages have a few striking lexical and phonological similarities in common with Aslian languages. This suggests that Land Dayak originated as the result of a language shift from Aslian to Austronesian, or that both Land Dayak and Aslian have in common a substratum from an unknown third language.

INTRODUCTION

If one thing has become clear in the last one and a half centuries, it is that Borneo, in spite of some shallow appearances to the contrary, represents an amalgamation of ethnic groups with often very different origins. Where Hardeland in the mid-19th century (Hardeland 1858, 1859) still thought it suitable to call the language of his dictionary and grammatical sketch "Dayak", it now appears to be merely one of the Northwest Barito languages, which in turn form a branch of the West Barito grouping in the southern part of Borneo. According to Hudson (1978), the West Barito language group is but one of the ten linguistic subgroups to which the autochthonous languages of Borneo belong.

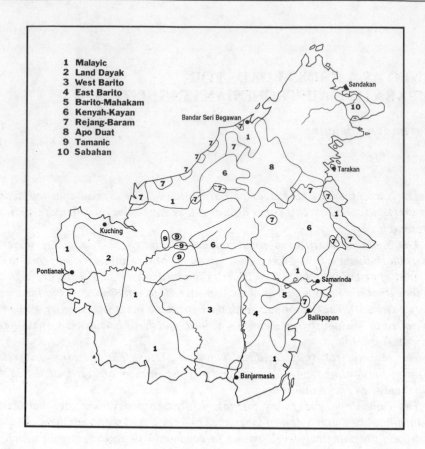

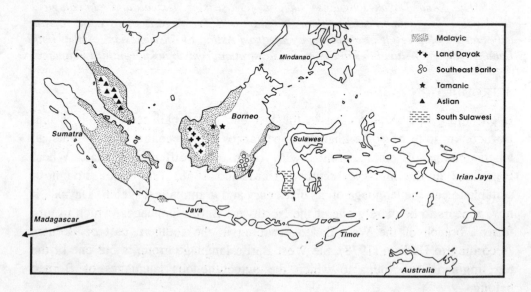

Map 1: Borneo language subgroups and their relationships to exo-Bornean subgroups.

Hudson classified the Bornean languages into seven endo-Bornean groups (Land Dayak, Rejang-Baram, Kenyah-Kayan, Apo Duat, West Barito, Barito-Mahakam and East Barito[1]) and three exo-Bornean groups (viz. Malayic Dayak, Tamanic and Sabahan[2]) (see Map 1). According to Hudson, these ten groups are at least as different from each other as they are from any other (non-Bornean) Malayo-Polynesian linguistic subgroup, and the exo-Bornean groups are each closely related to some non-Bornean languages. Malayic Dayak languages are part of the Malayic sub-family (including, among others, Malay, Minangkabau and Banjarese), Tamanic languages are most closely related to South Sulawesi languages, and Sabahan languages subgroup with the Philippine languages (Hudson 1978). Apart from the autochthonous languages, there are also several Malayic, Bajau and Chinese languages which have a long history in Borneo: they are mainly spoken in coastal areas and in towns.[3]

Although preliminary, Hudson's classification is more comprehensive and scientific than previous classifications of Bornean languages.

Through my linguistic research during the last five years I have been able to make further explorations into the history of four of Hudson's subgroups, viz. East Barito, Malayic Dayak, Tamanic and Land Dayak. I have also been doing research on the influence of Malay and other Indonesian languages on Malagasy. During four short field trips to West Kalimantan I have collected a large corpus of data on Salako (a Malayic Dayak language) and on Embaloh (a Tamanic language), and I have collected basic wordlists for a large number of Land Dayak languages.[4] These and other linguistic data allow us to make some inferences about the origin and spread of the speakers of the languages involved. The following paragraphs, which are organized according to linguistic subgroup, detail these inferences.

Many of the arguments that I present in this paper have already been treated elsewhere, and the reader is referred to the Adelaar references (1989, 1991a, 1991b, 1994 and in press) for a fuller account of these arguments and for extensive bibliographical references. In only one instance do I put forward a viewpoint that I have not discussed previously; this concerns suggested similarities between Land Dayak languages and Central Orang Asli languages.

EAST BARITO: WHO WERE THE MALAYO-POLYNESIAN MIGRANTS TO MADAGASCAR?

Dahl (1951, 1977) showed that Malagasy, the Austronesian language spoken as a number of dialects by almost all inhabitants of Madagascar, belongs to the Southeast Barito subgroup,[5] the other members of which (Maanyan, Samihim, Dusun Malang, Dusun Witu, Dusun Deyah and Paku) are spoken in the southeastern part of Borneo. Dahl observed that Malagasy has a relatively small number of Sanskrit loanwords in comparison to the large numbers in some Indonesian languages. According to him this indicated that the East Barito migrants to Madagascar must have left their homeland only just after Indian influence had begun to affect the Indonesian languages and cultures. Considering the fact that Indian linguistic influence in Indonesia can be traced to a date as far back as the fifth century AD, Dahl concluded that the migration must have taken place at this time or slightly after. He does not explicitly consider the possibility of influence from other Austronesian languages.

The first extensive studies of such influence (Adelaar 1989, 1991a and in press) show that there are many Malay loanwords in Malagasy, and that there are also a number of loanwords from Javanese. Malay and Javanese were also the vehicular languages for the Sanskrit vocabulary in Malagasy. Thus, none of the Sanskrit loanwords support the assumption of direct Indian influence on the Malagasy language. This has an important consequence for Dahl's date of the migration to Madagascar: as all Sanskrit influence in Malagasy was channelled through Malay and Javanese, we should postdate the migration to the first Malay and Javanese influence on Malagasy, rather than to the first Indian influence in Indonesia. It is as yet not possible to date the first Malay and Javanese influence on Malagasy, although it is likely that it happened at least two centuries later than the fifth century AD. The borrowed material also gives us information on the nature of the influence of Malays and Javanese on the migrating East Barito speakers, influence that must have begun some time before the migration, and that must have lasted until a considerable time afterwards.

Generally speaking, the Malay and Javanese loanwords belong to all sorts of semantic domains. But Malay loanwords are particularly well represented in the domain of maritime life and navigation, as can be seen in the following examples:

trozona 'whale' < Malay *duyuŋ* 'sea cow'

horita 'octopus' < Malay *gurita* 'id.'

fano 'turtle' < Malay *pəɲu* 'id.'

hara 'mother-of-pearl' < Malay *karah* 'patchy in colouring (of tortoise-shell)'

fanohara (dialectal) 'turtle with a particular kind of shell' < Malay *pəɲu karah* 'tortoise-shell turtle, *Chelonia imbricata*'

vontana (dialectal) 'kind of fish' < Malay *ikan buntal* 'box-fish, globe-fish or sea-porcupine'

tona 'k.o. large nocturnal snake; enormous eel' < Malay *tuna* 'name of a mud-snake or eel with yellowish body'

lamboara 'a species of fish' < Malay *ləmbuara*, Old Javanese *ləmbwara*, *ləmbora* 'a giant fish (possibly a whale)' *vidy* (dialectal) 'k.o. small fish' < Malay *ikan bilis* 'anchovy, Makassar redfish; small fish, esp. *Stolephorus* spp.'

hoala (dialectal) 'bay, inlet' < Malay *kuala* 'river mouth'

rivotra 'wind, storm' < Malay *(aŋin) ribut* 'stormwind'

tanjona 'cape, promontory' < Malay *taɲjuŋ* 'id.'

an/drefana 'West' < Malay *dəpan* '(in) front'

valaha (dialectal) 'East' < Malay *bəlakaŋ* 'back; space behind'

a/varatra 'North' < Malay *barat* 'West'

sagary 'a northeast wind' < Malay or Javanese *səgara* 'sea' (< Sanskrit)

varatraza (dialectal) 'south wind' < Malay *barat daya* 'Southwest'

tsimilotru (dialectal) 'north wind' < Malay *timur laut* 'Northeast'

harana 'coral-reef, coral-rock' < Malay *karaŋ* 'id.'

sambo 'boat, vessel' < Old Malay *sāmvaw* 'vessel' (originally from Khmer)

nosy 'island' < Javanese *nusa* (with variant forms *nusya, nuswa, nuŋsa*) 'id.'

Terms like *varatraza* and *tsimilotru* must have been borrowed from a form of Sumatran Malay, since the Malay directional terms *barat daya* and *timur laut* were originally South Sumatran developments.

Loanwords are also often found in the domain of plant names, animal names and in metallurgic terminology. Compare the following terms which are related to metallurgy:

harafesina 'rust' < Malay *karat bəsi* 'id.'

firaka 'tin, lead' < Malay *perak* 'silver'

landaizana 'anvil' < Malay *landasan* 'id.'

Higher numerals and calendrical terms are originally Malay and/or Javanese adaptations of Sanskrit terms. Sanskrit loanwords came into Malagasy via Malay or Javanese, as their shape or meaning often betray. Compare the following instances:

sisa 'remainder, rest' < Malay *sisa* 'id.' < Sanskrit *çeṣa* 'id.'

asotry (dialectal) 'Winter' < (Old) Javanese *asuji* 'September-October' < Sanskrit *açvayuja* 'id.'

tantara 'story, legend' < Malay *tantra* (obsolete), Old Javanese *tantra* 'id.' < Sanskrit *tantra-* 'chapter of a scientific book, doctrine, theory'

hetsy '100,000' < Malay *kəti*, Javanese *sa-kəti* 'id.' (both obsolete) < Sanskrit *koṭi* 'ten million'

That these terms were borrowed via Malay and Javanese is supported by the fact that, of all Sanskrit loanwords in Malagasy (at least 35 in total), there is only one word that is not also found in Malay or Javanese.[6]

A large part of the vocabulary for body-parts in Malagasy was originally Malay or Javanese:

hihy 'gums', (dialectically) 'teeth' < Malay *gigi* 'id.'

voto 'penis' < Malay *butuh* 'id.'

fify 'cheek' < Malay *pipi* 'id.'

molotra 'lip' < Malay *mulut* 'mouth'

voavitsy 'calf of leg' < Malay *buah bətis* 'id.'

sofina 'outer ear' < Malay *cupiŋ* 'lobe (usually earlobe)'

tratra 'chest' < Malay *dada* 'id.'

haranka (dialectal) 'chest' < Malay *kəraŋka* 'skeleton'

valahana 'loins' < Malay *bəlakaŋ* 'back; space behind'

lamosina, (dialectically) *lambosy* 'back' < Old Javanese *lamuŋsir* 'back; piece
   (of meat) from the back' (cf. also Minangkabau Malay *lambosiə* 'shoulder
   of a cow')

The Malagasy have a pre-colonial writing system which is an adapted
form of the Arabic script. The writing system is called *Sorabe*, which derives
from *soratra* 'writing'[7] and *be* 'big'. The name *Sorabe* and some of the
adaptations in its system indicate that the concept of writing, and possibly also
the actual writing system of the Malagasy, were introduced by Southeast Asians,
and probably Javanese. One rather idiosyncratic adaptation is also found in
Pegon, the Javanese version of the Arabic script. *Sorabe* uses Arabic *dāl* and *ta*
respectively, both with a subscript dot, for *d* and *t*: these are the same symbols as
used in Pegon for the Javanese retroflex *ḍ* and *ṭ* respectively. Javanese speakers
make a contrast between a dental series *d* and *t* and a retroflex series *ḍ* and *ṭ*, and
they perceive the alveolar consonants from other languages as retroflex
consonants. Their perception of alveolars in foreign languages as retroflexes may
have induced them to interpret Malagasy *d* and *t* as retroflexes, and to write these
retroflexes as *dal* and *ta* but with a subscript dot, as in the Pegon script. This
practice was taken over by the Malagasy, if it can be assumed that they learnt the
Arabic script from the Javanese.

If they did, this probably happened during continued contacts after the
period of migration. There is some lexical evidence that the Malagasy were still
in contact with Malays or Javanese after the latter came under the influence of
Islam. Compare the Antaimoro Malagasy *sombidy* 'to slaughter'. This term
derives from Malay *səmbəleh* or *səmbəlih* 'slaughter according to Muslim
ritual', which in turn derives from Arabic *b'ismi'llahi* [bɛsmɛlæh] 'in the Name
of God', an utterance made at slaughtering an animal according to Muslim law.

An important question now is how to interpret the linguistic data, and how
to integrate them in a theory which also takes into account archaeological,
historical and anthropological findings. The problem is that the linguistic data do
not seem to correlate with data from these other disciplines, and as a
consequence some non-linguists are reluctant to accept the linguistic evidence.

Quite apart from the fact that there is considerable regional diversity in the cultures of Madagascar themselves, many manifestations of Malagasy spiritual and material culture cannot unequivocally be linked up with the spiritual and material culture of the Dayaks of the Southeast Barito area. Some of the Malagasy are wet rice cultivators, while Dayaks are as a rule dry rice cultivators. Some Malagasy use outrigger canoes, whereas Southeast Barito Dayaks never do. The Malagasy migration to East Africa presupposes navigational skills which are found with some Indonesian peoples but which can hardly be attributed to Dayaks, who, as we know them today, are as a rule forest dwellers. Some of the Malagasy musical instruments are allegedly very similar to musical instruments found in Sulawesi, and Malagasy funeral cults are reminiscent of the Toraja funeral cults. Certain aspects of administration and statecraft of the Merina are in striking agreement with those of the Indianized Malays and Javanese, and rather unlike what has been described for the Maanyans in the Southeast Barito area. Some see a resemblance between the metallurgic practices of the Malagasy and those of the inhabitants of Nias.

The confusion caused by these data is partly due to the fact that some scholars fail to put the mass of evidence into its right perspective, which can only be done by keeping a rigorous distinction between (a) what is general Austronesian, (b) what is due to Indian influence in Southeast Asia, and (c) what is exclusively found in Madagascar and in one of the other Austronesian societies. Similarities which turn out to be general Austronesian are neither critical for a subgrouping argument nor for a cultural contact argument. In the Malagasy context (and in the context of most other regional Indonesian cultures), similarities which are the result of Indian influence only show us, in an indirect way, the extent of influence which the Indianized Malays and Javanese exerted on the Malagasy. What is relevant for a search into the Southeast Asian origins of the Malagasy people is a large concentration of similarities found in Madagascar and in one other Austronesian society in particular. Then again, these similarities are only relevant insofar as they do not turn out to be Proto-Austronesian retentions which were lost everywhere else in the Austronesian world. These similarities may point to a common inheritance or to cultural contact. Apart from (a), (b) and (c), other similarities due to chance, or due to interethnic contacts in Indonesia before the Malagasy migration, may also have to be distinguished.

But even with a rigorous distinction between (a), (b) and (c), we are still left with a number of seemingly contradictory factors. For instance, what brought some forest dwelling Dayaks to make one of the most spectacular migrations in history, and why do the Malagasy cultural data not support the linguistic evidence? These factors can be accounted for if we adopt the hypothesis that the Southeast Barito migrants did not undertake the crossing of the Indian Ocean themselves in order to colonize Madagascar, but that they were brought there as subordinates (slaves, ship crew, labourers) by Malays. Malays were seafarers, and they sailed the maritime routes all over Southeast Asia and along the Indian Ocean coast. They also took slaves from other parts of Southeast Asia with them, and it is quite likely that they took subordinates along on their trips to the Indian Ocean. Some of these subordinates may have been South Barito speakers.

If some of these subordinates were left behind in Madagascar, and if the Southeast Barito speakers among them formed a majority or a nuclear group (the first group to be left behind and to form a society), their language would have constituted the core element of what later became Malagasy. In this way their language may also have absorbed elements of languages of other subordinated Southeast Asians.[8] A certain amount of cultural mixture may have taken place through contact with subordinates from elsewhere in Indonesia, although the language of the resulting mixed community remained predominantly Southeast Barito. The members of this community would initially have lived in a state of diglossia with their leaders, who spoke Malay (and Javanese?). At some point in time, Malay was superseded by Malagasy, but its earlier prestigious position is still witnessed by the great impact it had on the Malagasy lexicon. Compare, for instance, the Malay and Javanese influence on terms for body-parts, a semantic domain which is susceptible to reflexification with prestige vocabulary. In some cases these two languages also affected the morphology of Malagasy.[9]

A development as outlined above is not unlike the history of English after the Norman invasion, where French became the language of prestige for some time and heavily affected the English lexicon, and in some cases even morphology, before it fell into disuse. In the case of English, however, this development coincided with a far-reaching simplification of the original Anglo-Saxon grammar, whereas Malagasy morphology is very conservative. It probably has the same measure of complexity as Proto-Southeast Barito had originally, a complexity which was lost in the other Southeast Barito languages.

MALAYIC DAYAK: ARGUMENTS FOR A BORNEAN HOMELAND OF MALAY

Hudson (1970) should be credited for identifying and defining the Malayic Dayak subgroup. Previous scholars were not aware of this subgroup and classified the Malayic Dayak languages either with the Malay dialects spoken by Muslims on the Borneo coast or with the Land Dayak languages. In this way they classified Iban as a Malay dialect, and Salako as a Land Dayak dialect with strong Malay influence. Kendayan Dayak was seemingly also considered as a strongly Malayicized variety of Land Dayak (cf. Cense and Uhlenbeck 1958). Hudson, however, calls Iban, Kendayan, Salako and other closely-related Dayak languages 'Malayic Dayak', and he classifies them together with Malay and other Malay-like languages[10] into the 'Malayic' linguistic group. His term 'Malayic Dayak' is meant to distinguish Malayic languages spoken by non-Muslims in Borneo from other Malayic languages. It is therefore not a linguistic term *sensu stricto*, but the term is relevant in Bornean linguistics insofar as it distinguishes autochthonous Malayic languages from Malayic languages which are the result of later migrations of (Muslim) Malays into Borneo (e.g. Banjarese, Sarawak Malay, Brunei Malay and other Malay varieties spoken by Muslims).

Hudson's classification of Iban, Salako, Kendayan and related languages into a single subgroup distinct from Land Dayak is very important, as it emphasizes the fact that these languages are relatives of Malay which have undergone a separate development, and not hybrid forms of Malay with a strong non-Malay substratum or adstratum. In other words, these languages are highly relevant for the history of Malay and for the reconstruction of Proto-Malayic. For instance, Salako and Kendayan retained the causative prefix *maka-* and the subjunctive suffix *-à?* (Kendayan *-a?*). *maka-* and *-à?l-a?* reflect Proto-Malayo Polynesian (henceforth PMP) **maka-*, a causative prefix, and PMP **-a*, a subjunctive marker respectively. Both were lost in other Malayic languages.

Examples:

Salako *rehetn* 'light' vs *maka-rehetn* 'make lighter (a punishment)'

Kendayan *lalu* 'past, further', *molot* 'mouth' vs *makalalu molot* 'keep one's promise, act according to what one has said'

Salako *mare?* 'to give' vs *mare-a?* 'in order to give, so as to give'

Salako *nabàkŋ* 'chop off' vs *nabakŋ-à?* 'in order to chop off, intending to chop off'

Compare also the following Malayic Dayak words (from Iban and Salako) which were retained from PMP, and which were usually lost in other Malayic languages:

Iban *ui*, Salako *ui?* 'rattan' < PMP **quəy* (Malay *rotan*);

Iban, Salako *asu?* 'dog' < PMP **asu* (Malay *anjiŋ*);

Iban *tama?*, Salako *tamà?* 'go inside' < PMP **tama?* (Malay *masuk*);

Salako *tau*, *talu* 'three' < PMP **təlu* (Malay, Iban *tiga*);

Iban *mua*, Salako *muhà* 'face' < PMP **muha* (Malay *muka*);

Iban, Salako *gaway* 'ceremony' < PMP **gaway* (Malay *upacara*);

Iban *sa?*, Salako *asà?* 'one' < PMP **əsa?* (Malay *suatu*);

Iban *sida?*, Salako *ne?idà?* 'they' < PMP **siDa* (Malay *məreka*);

Salako (sacral language) *uɲit*[11] 'yellow' < PMP **kuɲij* 'curcuma' (Malay, Iban *kuniŋ* 'yellow');

Iban *buuk*, Salako *bu?uk* 'hair of head' < PMP **buh(uə)k* (Malay *rambut*).

An indication of the historical relevance of Malayic Dayak is the fact that many grammatical and lexical elements retained from Proto-Malayic in the seventh century Old Malay inscriptions in South Sumatra are still found in Salako and Kendayan (the 'West Malayic Dayak' dialects), whereas other Malayic languages have lost them. This is the case with some lexical items and also with the above affixes *maka-* and (Salako) *-à?* / (Kendayan) *-a?*, which occur in Old Malay as *maka-* and *-a* (with apparently the same meanings). The passive marker in most Malayic languages is *di-*. This marker apparently did not exist in Old Malay (which used *ni-* instead), whereas in Kendayan and Salako it has not developed into a passive marker, but rather into an agent marker which is prefixed to the verb in case the agent is not expressed.

Another important aspect about Malayic Dayak languages is that until recently they kept out of the main stream of Sanskrit, Arabic, Javanese, Persian and European influences which so heavily affected the lexicons of other Malayic languages.

Hudson's classification also pays attention to the fact that the Malayic Dayak languages are indigenous, whereas other Malayic languages in Borneo were introduced from Sumatra and/or Malaysia. This is important for the search of the original Malayic homeland. Three areas have been considered as a homeland: Sumatra, the Malay peninsula and Western Borneo. Kern (1889) was in favour of a homeland in the peninsular Malay area, and he rejected the possibility of a Bornean homeland. But his arguments do not hold (Adelaar 1988). The historical and linguistic evidence suggests that the Malayic settlements in the Malay peninsula are of more recent date than those in Sumatra or in Borneo (Bellwood 1993). In view of the geographical spread (in the interior), the variety (which in some cases cannot be explained as due to contact-induced change) and the sometimes conservative character of Malayic Dayak languages, some linguists tend to favour Borneo as the homeland of the Malayic languages (cf. Blust 1988; Adelaar 1988, 1992).

TAMANIC: ON THE EXACT NATURE OF THE RELATION BETWEEN TAMANIC LANGUAGES AND SOUTH SULAWESI LANGUAGES

The dialects belonging to the Tamanic subgroup are Embaloh, Kalis and Taman. They are spoken in the Hulu Kapuas Regency of West Kalimantan near the head of the Kapuas River and its tributaries thereabouts. Until very recently, the information available on Tamanic dialects was restricted to wordlists. Much of the vocabulary in these lists agrees with Malay, but there are also some lexical items which are in striking agreement with South Sulawesi languages, and more particularly with Buginese. As a result, some scholars have classified Tamanic in the Malayic subgroup on the basis of lexicostatistics or exclusively shared lexical innovations (Blust 1981; Nothofer 1988), whereas other scholars have tended to classify it with South Sulawesi languages on the basis of rather impressionistic arguments (von Kessel 1850; Hudson 1978). During a one month field trip in the Embaloh area in January 1989 I was able to collect a sufficiently large corpus of data on this language to show on phonological, morpho-syntactic and lexical grounds that the Tamanic languages were more closely related to South Sulawesi languages than to the Malayic ones. Compare some of the shared lexical innovations between Embaloh and the South Sulawesi languages:[12]

PMP *tubuq 'body'; Proto-South Sulawesi *kale 'id.', Embaloh kale 'self; body';

PMP *qiDuŋ 'nose'; Proto-South Sulawesi *iŋi(C), Embaloh iŋar 'id.';

PMP *muqa, *(q)away, *paras, *daqəy 'face (of head)'; Proto-South Sulawesi *lindo, Embaloh lindo 'id.';

PMP *[lnø]ipən 'tooth'; Proto-South Sulawesi *isi, Embaloh isi 'id.';

PMP *liqəR 'throat, neck'; Proto-South Sulawesi *killoŋ, Embaloh kaloŋ;

N.B.:   When used verbally, Embaloh kaloŋ means 'to invoke' or 'to call', whereas many South Sulawesi languages also use the reflex of *killoŋ as the root for a verb 'to sing';

PMP *butuq, *qutiq 'penis'; Proto-South Sulawesi *laso, Embaloh laso 'id.';

PMP, Proto-South Sulawesi (no proto-form available); South Toraja ulelean, Embaloh uleʔuleʔan 'account, story';

PMP *waDa 'to be, exist'; Proto-South Sulawesi *dia(n), Embaloh dien 'id.';

PMP, Proto-South Sulawesi (no proto-form available); Makassarese, South Toraja taraue, Buginese tarauʔ, Embaloh tataraʔueʔ 'rainbow';

PMP *t(ui)DuR 'sleep'; Proto-South Sulawesi *tindo, Embaloh tindoʔ.

A close Tamanic-South Sulawesi relation automatically raises the question as to whether the South Sulawesi languages have their homeland in Borneo, or whether the Tamanic languages have their homeland in South Sulawesi. Furthermore, what is the exact relation between Tamanic and South Sulawesi languages: are both derived from a higher order proto-language, are the Tamanic languages a subgroup of the South Sulawesi ones, or are the South Sulawesi languages a subgroup of the Tamanic ones? Although the number of exclusively shared lexical innovations seems to be at least as high between Embaloh and Tae' (South Toraja) as between Embaloh and Buginese, there are some striking phonological agreements which compel me to assume a closer relation between Tamanic languages and Buginese than between Tamanic languages and other South Sulawesi languages. These phonological agreements are the reflex s for PMP *j in intervocalic position in both Tamanic and Buginese, whereas the other South Sulawesi have r, and furthermore the sporadic loss of PMP/Proto-South Sulawesi *p in a set number of Tamanic and Buginese words.

Compare:

PMP *j > Buginese and Embaloh s, South Sulawesi languages (minus Buginese) r:

PMP *pajəy 'paddy' > Proto-South Sulawesi *paze; Buginese ase, Embaloh ase (Makassarese, Mandar, South Toraja pare);

PMP *qaləjaw 'day' > Proto-South Sulawesi *ilzo; Buginese əsso, Embaloh aso (Makassarese, Mandar, South Toraja allo);

PMP *ajan 'name' > Proto-South Sulawesi *azan; Buginese asəŋ, Embaloh asan (Makassarese areŋ);

PMP *laja 'burn (a wound)'; 'be hot (spices)'; Buginese lasa 'sick', Embaloh ba-lasa 'be strong'. (Makassarese lara 'sour, bitter, e.g. a grapefruit');

PMP *siji 'to winnow' > Proto-South Sulawesi *sizi; Buginese sise? (Ide M. Said 1977: sise), Embaloh sese (South Toraja siri).

Loss of PMP/Proto-South Sulawesi *p:

PMP *pusuq 'heart' > Proto-South Sulawesi *puso 'id.'; Buginese uso 'heart-shaped blossom of the banana-tree', Embaloh uso? 'heart-shaped tip of a banana fruit-stem';

PMP *pajəy 'paddy' > Proto-South Sulawesi *paze; Buginese ase, Embaloh ase 'id.';

Proto-South Sulawesi *sa(m)po 'house' (Mills 1981:75); Buginese sao, Embaloh sao 'id.';

PMP *piliq 'choose' > Proto-South Sulawesi *pile; Buginese ile, Embaloh ile? 'id.';

PMP *punti 'banana' > PSS *punti 'id.'; Buginese utti, Embaloh unti 'id.'.

The fact that there are many shared lexical innovations in Embaloh and Tae' (South Toraja) may be the result of the fact that Tae' speakers, who only relatively recently converted to Christianity, have in many ways been less subject to changes from outside cultures than for instance the Buginese and Makassarese, their Muslim relatives.

If, as seems to be the case, Tamanic is more closely related to Buginese than to other South Sulawesi languages, it has to be included in the South Sulawesi language group in a subgroup with Buginese (or with Buginese and Campalagian, cf. Grimes and Grimes [1987] and Sirk [1989]).

It is evident that the Tamanic-Buginese link has no connection with the Buginese migrations to the coasts of East, South and West Borneo from at least the 17th century on. The Buginese kept their identity or merged with the local Malays. Their migration to Borneo is a more recent phenomenon in comparison to a Buginese-Tamanic split, which must have preceded the Islamization of South Sulawesi. It must have happened so long ago that it allowed the Tamanic speakers to adapt and assimilate to a considerable degree to their Bornean environment, and to forget their "exo-Bornean" origin.

As to the original homeland of Tamanic, as a consequence of its apparent membership of the South Sulawesi language group it is most likely that at some point in time its speakers have left South Sulawesi and have migrated to Borneo.

LAND DAYAK: SOME FEATURES THEY HAVE IN COMMON WITH ORANG ASLI LANGUAGES

According to Hudson (1978:23), it is possible that the Land Dayak languages form a subgroup with the Rejang-Baram languages, as some of the Land Dayak languages (Ribun, Pandu, Sanggau, Jongkang and Semandang) have an intervocalic *k* in their reflexes for 'two' (cf. *dukah* or *dukoh*). This corresponds to the intervocalic stop in the word for two in some of the Rejang-Baram languages (cf. *[de]gwa]*). Blust (1981) classifies Land Dayak languages in one subgroup with Malayic, Sundanese, Rejang, Tamanic (Embaloh), Acehnese and Chamic on the basis of some lexical agreements (especially in the numerals). However, Land Dayak languages are morphosyntactically rather different from Malayic (and other Austronesian) languages. If their lexicons have much in common with the Malayic languages, this might just as well be the result of borrowing, as on the whole these lexicons seem to reflect different sets of sound correspondences *vis-à-vis* PMP.

Although it is evidently far too early to make any sort of inference about the history of Land Dayak, there are some similarities between this group and some of the Orang Asli languages[13] which are striking enough to be mentioned, and which are certainly a topic for further investigation. One is the presence of a series of nasally released stops, or, as they are also called, "preploded nasals". I prefer the last term, because it does more justice to the actual phonetic change that has taken place. In Land Dayak, members of the preploded series (*-pm*, *-tn* and *-kŋ*, or, in some languages, *-bm*, *-dn*, *-gŋ*) are formed by uttering a stop without releasing the plosure, and then letting the airstream escape through the nose. In most of the Land Dayak languages, original final nasals became preploded. Compare the following examples from Sungkung, a language spoken in the West Kalimantan regencies of Sambas and Sanggau in a chain of six villages along the Sarawak border:

Proto-Land Dayak[14] *ŋarVm* 'night' > Sungkung *ŋaləpm* 'id.'
Proto-Land Dayak *madVm* 'rotten' > Sungkung *madɛpm* 'id.'
PMP *Zalan* 'road, path' > Sungkung *alatn* 'id.'
PMP *(lnø)ipən* 'tooth' > Sungkung *jipətn* 'id.'
PMP *Daqan* 'branch' > Sungkung *daʔatn* 'id.'
PMP *qiDuŋ* 'nose' > Sungkung *nukŋ* 'id.'

Proto-Land Dayak *turaŋ 'condylar bone' > Sungkung tulakŋ 'id.'

Preplosion took place in all final nasals, unless the nasal in question was historically preceded by another nasal. Compare:

PMP *[ ]ənəm 'six' > Sungkung nəm 'id.'

Proto-Land Dayak *ram[i]n 'house' > Sungkung amin 'id.'

Proto-Land Dayak *taŋan 'hand' > Sungkung taŋan 'id.'

N.B.: In the case of nukŋ 'nose' (see above), the preploded nasal is preceded by another nasal, but this nasal developed from a historical *(n)D. This *(n)D became a nasal only after preplosion had taken place.

In Orang Asli ("Aslian") linguistics, preplosion is referred to as "disintegrated nasals" (Skeat and Blagden 1906:772-773) or "predenasalisation" (Benjamin 1985:14; Diffloth 1976:230). It is observed in Central Aslian languages, including Temiar and Semai. These languages also have -jɲ, as they allow palatals in word-final position. As in Land Dayak, their preploded nasals derive historically from simple nasal consonants (Skeat and Blagden 1906:773). Some examples from Semai (taken from Diffloth 1976):

raŋɔ:jɲ 'jew's harp' (Diffloth 1976:243)

do:kŋ 'house' (cf. Old Mon ɗūŋ 'city, province'; Diffloth 1976:231)

[gmgɰ:pm] 'to winnow vertically' (Diffloth 1976:236) ʔejɲ (East Semai), ʔɛɲ (West Semai) 'I'

Skeat and Blagden (1906), Benjamin (1985) and Diffloth (1976) do not give exact phonotactic conditions for the occurrence of preploded nasals in Central Aslian, nor do their examples allow any conclusions on this matter. There are some Semai cases where preplosion seems to have been blocked by the occurrence of a preceding nasal (as in Land Dayak and Malayic Dayak languages).

Compare:

sma:ɲ 'to ask' (Diffloth 1976:231)

maɲu:ɲ 'small fruit sp.' (Diffloth 1976:243)

tuʃɛɲ '(name of a hill)' (Diffloth 1976:242)

But there are also cases where preplosion happened in spite of a preceding nasal, and, inversely, there are cases where preplosion did not take place although there is no preceding nasal:

raŋɔ:jɲ 'jew's harp' (Diffloth 1976:243)

turɔ:ɲ 'the last remaining of a series, e.g. teeth'

Again, as in Land Dayak and Malayic Dayak languages, the preceding nasal in raŋɔ:jɲ may eventually turn out to be a recent development from a stop or a nasal + stop cluster (as in Proto-Land Dayak *hi(n)duŋ 'nose' > Sungkung nukŋ, see above). But this is a speculative explanation, and the solution to this question involves a more thoroughgoing comparative historical study of Aslian languages than has been done so far.

Preploded nasals are not uncommon in other languages, but the change of final nasals to nasally released stops seems to be an areal feature which is typical for the languages of mainland Southeast Asia and some parts of Sumatra and Borneo. Preplosion also occurs in some Malay dialects spoken by Orang Asli (Benjamin 1985:14) and in some Malay dialects spoken by the Orang Darat and some of the Orang Utan in the Riau Archipelago (cf. Kähler 1960:36-37, 54-55). It must also have happened in Urak Lawoi', a Malayic language spoken off the Southwest coast of Thailand. In Urak Lawoi', -p, -t and -k must have developed from original nasals via a stage of preplosion. From Hogan's vocabulary (Hogan 1988) it appears that the phonotactic conditions for the development of Urak Lawoi' -p, -t and -k were rather similar to those applying to preplosion in Land Dayak languages. In Borneo, it is found in many Land Dayak languages, but some have not been affected by it, whereas reversely, some of the other Dayak languages did also develop the series. These other Dayak languages include West and East Barito languages in Central and South Kalimantan, and Malayic languages (such as Salako, Kendayan and varieties of Mualang) in West Kalimantan. The fact that preplosion occurs in Land Dayak languages as well as in Aslian languages is therefore not significant in itself. But it seems to correlate with some lexical similarities between these two language groups. Compare the words for 'to die' and 'to bathe' in Orang Asli languages (taken from Benjamin 1976, gloss 19 and 132):

	to die	to bathe
(Northern Aslian)		
Kensiu	kəbis	ʔənlay
Kintaq Bong	kəbis	ʔənlay
Jehai	kəbis	ʔəlay
Mendriq	kəbəs	ʔɛlay
Bateg Deq	halɔt	nay
Mintil	kəbɯs[15]	sɔuc
Bateg Nong	kəbɯs	sɔc
Che' Wong	kəbɯs	mamuh
(Central Aslian)		
Semnam	kəbəs	mamuh
Sabum	kəbəs	mamuh
Lanoh Jengjeng	kəbəs	mamuh
Lanoh Yir	kəbəs	mamuh
Temiar	kəbəs	muh
Semai I	ndat	mamuh

Semai II	*dat*	*mamuh*
Jah Hut	*kəbəs*	*maʔmūh*

(Southern Aslian)

Mah Meri	*kəbəs*	*hūm*
Semaq Beri	*kəbəs*	*mahmēh*
Semelai	*khəbəs*	*hūm*
Temoq	*kəbos*	*mahmɛh*

Almost all Orang Asli languages exhibit *kəbəs* or a related form for 'to die', and more than half of them have *mamuh* or a related form for 'to bathe'. Again, the Central Aslian languages score highest in exhibiting these forms.

Forms like *kəbəs* and *mamuh* are also generally used in Land Dayak, where the word for 'to die' is moreover related to the words for 'to kill' and 'to sleep'. (This relationship does apparently not exist in the Orang Asli languages.) Compare:

	dead	kill	sleep	bathe
(Land Dayak)				
Bekati'	*kabis*	*ŋamis*	*buus*	*mamuʔ*
Laraʔ	*kabih, [-ç]*	*ŋamíh*	*buih*	*mamū́ʔ*
Golek	*kobɨs*	*ŋkəbɨs*	*bɨis*	*mamuh*
Nonguh	*kobis*	*ŋkɔmis*	*bis*	*mamúh*
Pandu	*kɔbis*	*ŋomis*	*biis*	*maneʔ*
Ribun I	*kobis*	*ŋkobis*	*biʰis*	*mandeyʔ*
Ribun II	*kɔbis*	*ŋkɔmis*	*biis*	*mandeyʔ*
Jangkang	*kɔbɪʔ*	*kɔmɪʔ*	*biʔ*	*manɪʔ*
Lintang	*k(oɔ)bis*	*ŋkɔmis*	*biis*	*manɪʔ*
Aye-aye	*kubəs*	*ŋkuməs*	*bɨs*	*manī́ʔ*
Sungkung	*kabəs*	*nnabəs*	*bəʔəs*	*mamuh*
Sekayam	*kɔbis*	*ŋkɔmis*	*bis*	*mắmúh*

N.B. The forms *maneʔ, mandeyʔ, manɪʔ* and *manī́ʔ* are adaptations of Malay *mandi* or Malayic Dayak *man(d)iʔ*.

The fact that the Aslian languages share preplosion and a similar form for the word for 'to die' with (Land) Dayak languages was already pointed out (or hinted upon) by Skeat and Blagden (1906:773 and 435-438).

Generally speaking, similarities as the ones under discussion here may be due to (1) genetic relationship, (2) chance or (3) contact, whether in the form of cultural borrowing or a substratum. A genetic relationship will not account for the similarities, as all other evidence leaves little doubt about the classification of Land Dayak languages as Austronesian, and about the classification of Orang Asli languages as Austro-Asiatic. It would be possible to maintain that the lexical similarities are due to chance, but this seems to be a less suitable explanation for preplosion, the spread of which should be described in terms of an areal feature. If there was contact, this must have been a very long time ago, as there is, as far as I know, no evidence for it in historical times. The nature of the similarities, two rather basic vocabulary items and a phonological areal feature, suggest intimate borrowing. Allowing for the fact that our present knowledge is too scanty to draw any definite conclusion, I tend towards explaining these similarities as the result of language shift. It may have been the case that original Aslian speakers in Borneo shifted from their original language to Land Dayak, whereby few words of the original language, such as the words for 'to die' and 'to bathe' were maintained and resisted replacement by the well-attested Proto-Austronesian roots *anDuy 'to bathe' and *maCey 'to die'. It is also possible that once there was a third (unknown and now extinct) language spoken in Borneo and on the Malay Peninsula, and that its speakers in Borneo shifted to Land Dayak, while its speakers on the Malay Peninsula shifted to Aslian. Although forms like kəbis and mamuh are quite common in Aslian, at this stage it is not clear whether they are inherited and can be attributed to Proto-Aslian. It therefore remains possible that they are innovative in both Aslian and Land Dayak.

Preplosion is found in many languages that do not belong to the same linguistic subgroup or even the same language family. Both Land Dayak and Aslian have members that have never been affected by it. Preplosion is therefore younger than the splits that led to the emergence of different Austronesian linguistic subgroups such as Malayic Dayak and Land Dayak. It is clearly not diagnostic for language classification in Southeast Asia.

POST SCRIPTUM

1) Since the final edition of this paper in 1991, Dr Bernard Sellato brought to my attention that the Land Dayak word kəbis 'to die' and its variant forms has cognates in many of the languages spoken by Punan people in Borneo.

2) Also after the final edition of this paper, O.C. Dahl published a book on the Indonesian origins of the Malagasy people (Dahl 1991).

NOTES

1   East Barito includes Malagasy.
2   Hudson himself and earlier authors used "Idahan", but this term is confusing as it turns out also to be the name of a community in Sabah using a language which does not belong to Hudson's "Idahan" subgroup. Prentice therefore proposes "Sabahan" as a less

ambivalent term (Prentice, pers.comm.; see Wurm and Hattori 1981-3, note 14 on the back of map 41).

[3]   The Malayic languages include the Sambas, Sarawak, Brunei and Kutei dialects of Malay, and Banjarese; the Chinese languages include Hakka, Chaozhou and Hokkien (Wurm and Hattori 1981-3:map 47). There is also a Mandarin-speaking community from Shandong Province in Sabah (D.J. Prentice, pers.comm.). I am not sure if any of the descendants of Buginese immigrants in Borneo have maintained their original language. It is remarkable that none of the bibliographical sources mention the fact that the Chinese of Pontianak and surroundings are for a large part Chaozhou.

[4]   The first three field trips took place in the years 1986-89 and were funded by NWO, the Netherlands Organisation for Scientific Research. A fourth field trip (in 1990) was funded by the Research School of Pacific Studies, The Australian National University, Canberra.

[5]   A branch of the East Barito group.

[6]   Viz. Merina Malagasy *sakarivo*, Sakalava Malagasy *sakaviro* 'ginger' < Sanskrit *çṛŋgavera* 'id.' See Adelaar (1989 and in press) for the number of 35 Sanskrit loanwords, which is higher than the number (30) counted by Dahl (1951:97).

[7]   A Malay or Javanese loanword, cf. Malay *surat* 'thing written; letter; epistle'; Javanese *surat* 'stripe (of colour); beam (of light); letter'.

[8]   But this remains to be studied (and is far less obvious than the fact that Malagasy has a Southeast Barito core and underwent Malay and Javanese influence).

[9]   Compare the *ra-* prefix in kinship terms, which must be borrowed from Javanese, and some instances of prefixation of *tafa-* (expressing non-controlledness) and *ba-* (to stative verbs) which point to influence from Malay and/or Banjarese.

[10]   Such as, e.g., Minangkabau and Banjarese.

[11]   With unexplained loss of *k.

[12]   Proto-South Sulawesi etyma are taken from Mills (1975 and 1981).

[13]   These are Austro-Asiatic (i.e. non-Austronesian) languages spoken in West Malaysia.

[14]   Proto-Land Dayak has not yet been reconstructed, and the etyma that I label here as such are very tentative reconstructions made on an overall impression from corresponding forms in different Land Dayak languages in my field notes and in other sources.

[15]   I.e. a high-back unrounded vowel.

REFERENCES

Adelaar, K.A.
    1988   More on Proto-Malayic. In Mohd. Thani Ahmad and Zaini Mohammed
            Zain (eds) *Rekonstruksi dan cabang-cabang Bahasa Melayu induk*, pp.59-
            77. Siri monograf sejarah bahasa Melayu. Kuala Lumpur: Dewan Bahasa
            dan Pustaka.
    1989   Malay influence on Malagasy: linguistic and culture-historical inferences.
            Oceanic Linguistics 28(1):1-46.

1991a   New ideas on the early history of Malagasy. In H. Steinhauer (ed.) *Papers in Austronesian linguistics No.1*, pp.1-22. Pacific Linguistics Series A No. 81. Canberra: Department of Linguistics, Research School of Pacific Studies, The Australian National University.

1991b   A phonological sketch of Salako. In Ray Harlow (ed.) *VICAL 2 Papers from the fifth international conference on Austronesian linguistics*, pp.1-19. Auckland: The Linguistic Society of New Zealand.

1992   *Proto-Malayic: a reconstruction of its phonology and part of its morphology and lexicon*. (Revised version of 1985 PhD thesis.) Pacific Linguistics Series C No. 119. Canberra: Department of Linguistics, Research School of Pacific Studies, The Australian National University.

1994   The classification of Tamanic languages (West Kalimantan). In Tom Dutton and Darrell Tryon (eds) *Language contact and change in the Austronesian world*, pp.1-41. Trends in Linguistics. Studies and Monographs. Berlin: Mouton de Gruyter.

in press   The nature of Malay and Javanese linguistic borrowing in Malagasy. (Paper presented at the 2nd Tamadun Melayu conference held in Kuala Lumpur in August 1989.)

Bellwood, Peter
1993   Cultural and biological differentiation in peninsular Malaysia: the last 10,000 years. *Asian Perspectives* 32:37-60.

Benjamin, Geoffrey
1976   Austroasiatic subgroupings and prehistory in the Malay peninsula. In Philip N. Jenner, Laurence C. Thompson and Stanley Starosta (eds) *Austroasiatic studies Part I*, pp.37-128. Honolulu: University of Hawaii Press.

1985   On pronouncing and writing Orang Asli languages: a guide for the perplexed. In *Orang Asli Studies Newsletter* No.4. Hanover (USA): Dartmouth College, Department of Anthropology; pp.4-16.

Blust, R.A.
1981   The reconstruction of Proto-Malayo-Javanic: an appreciation. *Bijdragen tot de Taal-, Land- en Volkenkunde* 137(4):456-469.

1988   The Austronesian homeland: a linguistic perspective. *Asian Perspectives* 26:45-67.

Cense, A.A. and E.M. Uhlenbeck
1958   *Critical survey of studies on the languages of Borneo*. Bibliographical series II of the Royal Institute of Languages and Cultures. The Hague: Nijhoff.

Dahl, Otto Christian
1951   *Malgache et Maanyan. Une comparaison linguistique*. Avhandlinger utgitt av Instituttet 3. Oslo: Egede Instituttet.

1977   La subdivision de la famille Barito et la place du Malgache. *Acta Orientalia* (Copenhagen) 38:77-134.

1991   *Migration from Kalimantan to Madagascar*. Oslo: The Institute of Comparative Research in Human Culture, Norwegian University Press.

Diffloth, Gérard
    1976   Minor-syllable vocalism in Senoic languages. In Philip N. Jenner,
            Laurence C. Thompson and Stanley Starosta (eds) *Austroasiatic studies
            Part I*, pp.229-247. Honolulu: University of Hawaii Press.

Grimes, Charles E. and Barbara D. Grimes
    1987   *Languages of South Sulawesi*. Pacific Linguistics Series D No. 78.
            Canberra: Department of Linguistics, Research School of Pacific Studies,
            The Australian National University.

Hardeland, August
    1858   *Versuch einer Grammatik der Dajackschen Sprache*. Amsterdam: Muller.
    1859   *Dajacksch-Deutsches Wörterbuch*. Amsterdam: Muller.

Hogan, David W. (in collaboration with Stephen W. Pattemore)
    1988   *Urak Lawoi': basic structure and dictionary*. Pacific Linguistics Series C
            No. 109. Canberra: Department of Linguistics, Research School of Pacific
            Studies, The Australian National University.

Hudson, Alfred B.
    1970   A note on Selako: Malayic Dayak and Land Dayak languages in West
            Borneo. *Sarawak Museum Journal* 18:301-318.
    1978   Linguistic relations among Bornean peoples with special reference to
            Sarawak: an interim report. In *Sarawak. Linguistics and development
            problems*, No.3, pp.1-45. Williamsburg, VA: Studies in Third World
            Societies.

Kähler, Hans
    1960   *Ethnographische und linguistische Studien über die Orang darat, Orang
            akit, Orang laut und Orang utan im Riau-Archipel und auf den Inseln an
            der Ostküste von Sumatra*. Veröffentlichungen des Seminars für
            Indonesische und Südseesprachen der Universität Hamburg Band 2. Berlin:
            Dietrich Reimer.

Kern, H.
    1889   Taalkundige gegevens ter bepaling van het stamland der Maleisch-
            Polynesische volkeren. *Verslagen en mededeelingen der Koninklijke
            Akademie van Wetenschappen, Afdeeling Letterkunde* (3rd Series) 6:270-
            287 (also published in *H. Kern Verspreide Geschriften* 6:105-121).

Mills, Roger F.
    1975   *Proto-South-Sulawesi and Proto-Austronesian phonology* (2 volumes).
            PhD dissertation, University of Michigan, Ann Arbor (University
            Microfilms International 1978).
    1981   Additional addenda. In R.A. Blust (ed.) *Historical linguistics in Indonesia
            Part I. NUSA: Linguistic Studies in Indonesian and Languages in
            Indonesia* Volume 10. Jakarta: NUSA, Universitas Atma Jaya.

Nothofer, Bernd
    1988   A discussion of two Austronesian subgroups: Proto-Malay and Proto-
            Malayic. In Mohd. Thani Ahmad and Zaini Mohammed Zain (eds)

Rekonstruksi dan cabang-cabang Bahasa Melayu induk, pp.34-58. Siri monograf sejarah bahasa Melayu. Kuala Lumpur: Dewan Bahasa dan Pustaka.

Said, Ide M.
1977   *Kamus bahasa Bugis–Indonesia.* Jakarta: Pusat Pembinaan dan Pengebangan Bahasa.

Sirk, Ülo
1989   On the evidential basis for the South Sulawesi language group. In James N. Sneddon (ed.) *Studies in Sulawesi languages Part I*, pp.55-82. *NUSA: Linguistic Studies in Indonesian and Languages in Indonesia* Volume 31. Jakarta: NUSA, Universitas Atma Jaya.

Skeat, Walter William and Charles Otto Blagden
1906   *Pagan races of the Malay peninsula* (Vol. II). London: Macmillan.

von Kessel, O.
1850   Statistieke aanteekeningen omtrent het stroomgebied der rivier Kapuas, Wester-afdeeling van Borneo. *Indisch Archief (Tijdschrift voor de Indien*, Batavia) I.2:165-204.

Wurm, S.A. and Shirô Hattori
1981-3 *Linguistic atlas of the Pacific area.* Pacific Linguistics Series C Nos. 66-67. Canberra: Department of Linguistics, Research School of Pacific Studies, The Australian National University.

5

AUSTRONESIAN PREHISTORY IN SOUTHEAST ASIA: HOMELAND, EXPANSION AND TRANSFORMATION

Peter Bellwood

Austronesian origins are here presented as an example of a frequent phenomenon in world prehistory, whereby populations who develop agriculture in regions of primary agricultural origins are provided with essential economic advantages over surrounding hunter-gatherers. These advantages allow them to undertake the colonization of very large regions, and the records of such colonizations are visible in the archaeological and linguistic records. The pattern of Austronesian expansion, possible reasons for it, and some major factors influencing subsequent differentiation of Austronesian cultures are all discussed, commencing from about 4000 BC in southern China and Taiwan.

QUESTIONS OF ULTIMATE HOMELAND

This paper will commence by focusing on the question of where the immediate ancestor of Proto-Austronesian was located, and when. Proto-Austronesian is the hypothesized linguistic entity, perhaps a single language or perhaps a dialect network (see Pawley and Ross, this volume), ancestral to all subsequent and existing Austronesian languages. But like all languages it also had an ancestor, prior to the budding of the Austronesian (henceforth An) family as a linguistic taxon with its own unique history.

An observation relevant for this question, one particularly intriguing in terms of its relevance for world prehistory, is that the general homeland regions of many of the major language families which have had long histories of association with agriculture seem to be geographically correlative with regions of *primary* (i.e. indigenously-generated) agricultural origins (Bellwood 1990b, 1991, in press b). In the Old World such language families include Indo-European, Elamo-Dravidian, Afro-Asiatic, Niger-Kordofanian, Nilo-Saharan, Sino-Tibetan, Austroasiatic, Thai-Kadai (or Daic of Ruhlen 1987) and Austronesian. The first two of these families, and possibly Afro-Asiatic, have arguable homelands in or closely adjacent to southwest Asia, the second two in northern sub-Saharan Africa, and the last three (with Sino-Tibetan being uncertain) in central and southern China. These three geographical regions are known from archaeological data to have witnessed major local developments of plant and animal domestication, in each case well before any such developments

96

in intervening regions of the Old World (MacNeish 1992). Because of these widespread correlations between early centres of agriculture and major language family homelands (Renfrew 1992), one may posit a process whereby demographically-expanding agricultural populations moved outwards from primary agricultural homeland regions, perhaps slowly but certainly inexorably occupying lands previously occupied by foragers (as suggested for Europe by Ammerman and Cavalli-Sforza 1984; Renfrew 1987).

If one examines the geographical distributions of these major language families and the geography of diversity between and within them, one sees that areas of agricultural origin reveal *both* a larger-than-average number of different language families *and* high levels of internal language family diversity, as revealed by the close proximity of subgroups which have long histories of separation. This is true for the three areas listed, and also for the early agricultural homeland regions of central Mexico, the northern Andes of Peru and Ecuador, and New Guinea. Directly relevant for this paper, the Austronesian, Thai-Kadai, Hmong-Mien and Austroasiatic language families seem to have arisen by a process of dispersal out of subtropical southern China and northern Mainland Southeast Asia, a zone lying between the Yangzi and northern Thailand/Indochina,[1] where the cultivation of rice and other crops developed widely between about 6000 and 3000 BC. Some of the Papuan language families of New Guinea are also associated with an early and primary centre of agriculture, although in this case the result seems to have been population maintenance and increase *in situ* rather than actual dispersal into new territories.

The Neolithic "revolutions" of China evidently occurred in two culturally-connected regions. The first, in the basin of the Yellow River, led to the domestication of foxtail and broomcorn millet by 6000 BC. The second, in the middle and lower Yangzi basin, led to the domestication of rice by about the same time (Yan 1991). However, although Chinese archaeologists tend to regard the Yellow and Yangzi basins as supporting unrelated Neolithic cultures, we perhaps need now to regard central and eastern China as one single centre for the early development of Asian monsoon agriculture.

Both rice and foxtail millet have been found in Chinese early Neolithic sites in storage pits and habitation layers, in quantities sufficiently large to suggest that they rapidly attained a major dietary importance.[2] There is little doubt that they would have fuelled an increase in population numbers which was perhaps quite rapid, given the archaeological appearance of the oldest Neolithic cultures across huge areas of China by about 5000 BC (Chang 1986). One result of this would have been an outward expansion of those populations involved into areas which hitherto had been inhabited entirely by foragers.

By 5000 BC, settlements of rice cultivators were in existence down the eastern coastline of China to as far south as Guangdong, and by perhaps 4000

BC in northern Vietnam and Thailand. In their archaeological remains are found assemblages of artefacts which leave no doubt about the overwhelming impact of the new lifestyle. For instance, the 7000-year-old village of pile dwellings at Hemudu, near the southern shore of Hangzhou Bay in Zhejiang Province, has yielded pottery, stone adzes, wooden and bone agricultural tools, evidence for carpentry and boatbuilding, paddles, spindle whorls for weaving, matting, rope, and large quantities of harvested rice. In addition, the site produced the bones of domesticated pigs, dogs, chickens and possibly domesticated cattle and water buffalo. Such a large village settlement and such a range of tools suggest a fundamental and drastic shift from the presumed mobile foraging lifestyle of the East Asian Late Palaeolithic. The inhabitants of Hemudu and other contemporary Chinese agricultural settlements lived during an episode of cultural evolution which was ultimately to have repercussions over the whole of temperate and tropical eastern Asia and the Pacific. One of these repercussions, albeit one which developed its first momentum a thousand kilometres or more south of Hemudu, was the ultimately-phenomenal expansion of the speakers of Austronesian languages.

THE PATTERN OF AUSTRONESIAN EXPANSION

It is necessary to return again to the linguistic evidence in order to plot the geographical axes of expansion of early An-speaking peoples. Beginning with the Pre-Austronesian level, a number of claims have been made for ancient genetic relationships between An and other Asian mainland language families (see footnote 1). Perhaps the best-known of these claims is the Austro-Tai hypothesis of Paul Benedict (1975; Reid 1984-5), which postulates that the Tai-Kadai and Austronesian language families once shared a common ancestral language or chain of languages spoken on the southern Chinese mainland. Benedict has suggested a number of important vocabulary reconstructions for this ancestral language, including terms for field, wet field (for rice or taro), garden, rice, sugarcane, cattle, water buffalo, axe, and canoe. The overlap between this list and that presented above for Hemudu and other coastal southern Chinese Neolithic sites needs little emphasis. One has to consider very seriously the possibility that the initial expansions of Austronesian and Tai-Kadai languages (and probably also Austroasiatic) began among Neolithic rice-cultivating communities in China south of the Yangzi. The archaeological record agrees very well and provides a date range for initial developments between 5000 and 4000 BC.

Moving beyond Austro-Tai into Austronesian proper, the reconstruction of linguistic prehistory which is most widely used today is that postulated by Robert Blust (1984-5). This is based on a "family tree" of subgroups and a hierarchy of proto-languages extending from Proto-Austronesian (PAn) forwards in time. Reduced to its essentials, Blust's reconstruction favours a geographical expansion beginning in Taiwan (the location of the oldest Austronesian languages, including PAn), then encompassing the Philippines, Borneo and Sulawesi, and finally bifurcating, one branch moving west to Java, Sumatra and Malaya, the other moving east into Oceania (see Darrell Tryon's more detailed summary in this volume).

A wealth of linguistic detail can be added to this framework, but here I will restrict myself to some implications of broad historical and cultural significance. During the linguistic stage before the break-up of PAn it would appear that some colonists with an agricultural economy moved across the Formosa Strait from the Chinese mainland to Taiwan (Bellwood 1984-5, 1992). Here developed the Initial Austronesian language(s), and after a few centuries some speakers of one of these languages made the first moves into Luzon and the Philippines. This movement led to the division of Austronesian into its two major subgroups, Formosan and Malayo-Polynesian (or Extra-Formosan). The reconstructed PAn vocabulary, which relates generally to this early Taiwan-Luzon phase, indicates an economy well suited to marginal tropical latitudes with cultivation of rice, millet, sugarcane, domestication of dogs and pigs, and the use of some kind of watercraft.

As a result of further colonizing movements through the Philippines into Borneo, Sulawesi and the Moluccas, the Malayo-Polynesian (MP) subgroup eventually separated into its several lower-order Western and Central-Eastern branches. The break-up of Central-Eastern MP probably occurred initially in the Moluccas, and Eastern MP contains all the Austronesian languages of the Pacific Islands apart from some in western Micronesia. The vocabulary of Proto-Malayo-Polynesian (PMP), a linguistic entity which might have been located somewhere in the Philippines, is of great interest because it contains a number of tropical economic indicators which were absent in the earlier and more northerly PAn stage. These include, according to Blust (1984-5), *Colocasia* taro, breadfruit, banana, yam, sago and coconut. Their presences may reflect a shift away from rice, a plant initially adapted to sub-tropical latitudes, towards a greater dependence on tubers and fruits in equatorial latitudes (Bellwood 1980a, 1985). The PMP vocabulary also has terms for pottery, sailing canoes and several components of substantial timber houses (Zorc 1994).

It may now be asked how the archaeological record relates to this reconstruction of the directions and cultural components of Austronesian expansion. Specific archaeological cultures cannot logically be equated with specific ancestral languages in prehistoric time. However, the appearance of certain technological and economic components of PAn and PMP can be searched for profitably in the archaeological record of the area now occupied by

Austronesian speakers. As already indicated, it is a reasonable inference that both PAn and PMP represent agricultural societies who, amongst other things, grew rice, made pots, lived in well-made timber houses and kept domesticated pigs. As it happens, direct material evidence for all these items survives in the archaeological records of the islands of Southeast Asia, and all of them make an initial appearance in widespread excavated sites between about 4000 and 1500 BC. Furthermore, their appearances (especially pottery) show a time trend — earliest in the northerly regions of China, Taiwan and Luzon, and progressively later as one moves southwards into equatorial Indonesia and western Oceania (Spriggs 1989). Given this seeming correlation between the linguistic and archaeological records (Bellwood 1985), we may hypothesize a direct association with the dispersal of the Austronesian language speakers, rather than dispersal of these cultural items by diffusion alone.

The Neolithic archaeological records in Taiwan began around 3000-4000 BC with archaeological assemblages of southern Chinese type, presumably carried initially by small groups of agricultural settlers across the Formosa Strait from Fujian (Tsang 1992). Characteristic artefacts of the oldest sites include cord-marked pottery, polished stone adzes and slate spear points. Other items such as slate-reaping knives and baked clay spindle whorls (for spinning thread for weaving) perhaps arrived a little later. By 3000 BC in Taiwan there is evidence for rice and, from pollen records, for inland forest clearance for agriculture.

Between 2500 and 1500 BC related archaeological assemblages with plain or red-slipped pottery, rather than the older Taiwan cord-marked type, appeared in coastal and favourable inland regions of the Philippines, Sulawesi, northern Borneo, Halmahera, and (with domestic pigs) to as far southeast as Timor. No sites of this period have yet been reported from the large islands of western Indonesia, but research on pollen history in the highlands of western Java and Sumatra suggests that some fairly intensive forest clearance for agriculture was underway there by at least 2000 BC, and probably earlier (Flenley 1988). In the equatorial latitudes of Indonesia there may also have been a shift away from rice cultivation towards a much greater dependence on the tropical fruit and tuber crops listed above for the PMP vocabulary. No cereals were ever introduced into the Pacific Islands, with the exception of rice to the Marianas.

By 1500 BC, therefore, agricultural colonists had spread from Taiwan to the western borders of Melanesia. The continuing expansion through Melanesia into western Polynesia, represented by the Lapita culture, seems to have been even more rapid than preceding movements, perhaps because food producing (as opposed to purely foraging) Papuan-speaking populations were already occupying some coastal regions of the large islands of New Guinea, the Bismarcks and the Solomons. Finely decorated Lapita pottery has been found in coastal or offshore island sites from the Admiralties in the west to Samoa in the east, a distance of about 5000 kilometres (see following chapter). This Lapita expansion occurred between 1600 and 1000 BC and to north and east of the Solomons it involved, for the first sustained period in Austronesian prehistory, the settlement of previously uninhabited islands. Between 1000 BC and AD 1000 the settlement of these uninhabited regions continued onwards (Irwin 1992), ultimately to incorporate all the islands of Polynesia and Micronesia and, on the other side of the world, Madagascar (Map 1).

WHY DID THE EXPANSION OCCUR?

The main points of the linguistic and archaeological records as they relate to early Austronesian dispersal, and possible reasons for it, can now be summarized. Austronesian-speaking agricultural colonists underwent a fairly continuous expansion (albeit divided into periods of relative stasis punctuated by rapid movement), over a period of about 4000 years, from the agricultural heartland region of southern China through many thousands of kilometres of coastline and across increasingly wide sea gaps eastwards into the Pacific. This expansion, which seems to have ignored island interiors in its early stages, met with stiff cultural resistance only in regions with prior histories of agriculture, these being restricted to mainland Southeast Asia and western Melanesia, the latter area being one where archaeology has indicated the existence of a prior and independent development of agriculture (Golson 1985; Golson and Gardner 1990).

The rate at which the early Austronesian colonization occurred must surely be one of the most rapid on record from the prehistoric agricultural world, although admittedly much of it was across sea rather than into large and absorbent land masses. It was probably not caused simply by an over-reliance on land-hungry shifting cultivation, an explanation which I have favoured in the past (Bellwood 1980b), but by a number of different stimuli. These include, not necessarily in order of significance:

(1)   continuous population growth based on an agricultural food supply, allowing a continuous generation-by-generation "budding-off" of new families into new terrain (cf. Ammerman and Cavalli-Sforza 1984 for a European model);

(2)   the inherent transportability and reproducibility of the agricultural economy to support colonizing propagules, especially on resource-poor small islands;

(3)   the presence of a deep and absorbent "frontier zone" available for colonization adjacent to the area of early Austronesian agricultural development, occupied purely by foraging populations (i.e. Taiwan and

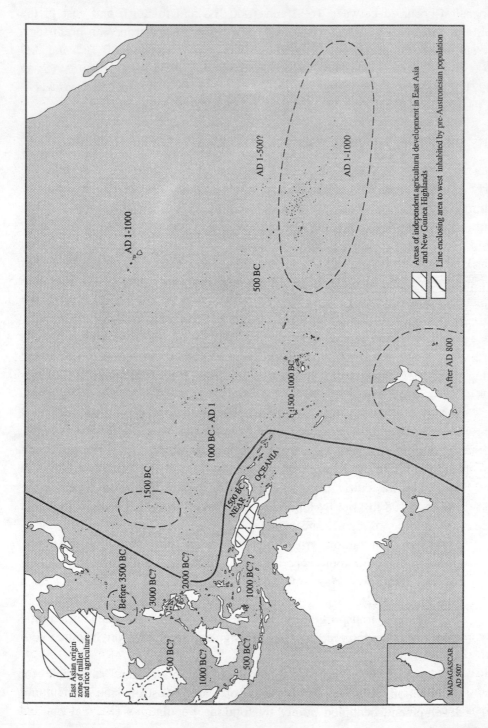

Map 1. Approximate dates for initial Austronesian colonization.

the Philippines in the early days of expansion), most of whom would presumably have shown little interest in adopting a systematic agricultural economy for themselves (Bellwood 1990b, 1991);

(4)   a developing tradition of sailing-canoe construction and navigation (see Adrian Horridge in this volume);

(5)   a predilection for rapid coastal movement and exploration, probably to find the most favourable environments for cultivation and sheltered inshore fishing, and thus promoting a colonization pattern of wide-ranging settlement followed, often only centuries later, by territorial infilling;

(6)   a culturally-sanctioned desire to found new settlements in order to become a revered or even deified founder ancestor in the genealogies of future generations (presumably this evolved hand-in-hand with the colonization process itself — see Bellwood, in press a);

(7)   a desire to find new sources of raw materials for "prestige goods" exchange networks (Friedman 1981; Hayden 1983; Kirch 1988).

Not all of these stimuli were present before the process of Austronesian expansion began; those listed at (4) and (6) in particular surely evolved in part as a result of the process itself, as might (7) if it was of major significance as an agency of colonization (which I doubt; Bellwood in press a). However, it is my suspicion that the tap-root of the expansion process, a *sine qua non*, was the possession of a systematic agricultural economy capable of supporting continuous population growth.

The sceptic here may ask why, if agriculturally-induced population growth was so important, all early agricultural peoples did not simply expand in this way. I would reply that perhaps the majority of them did, and this becomes highly significant if one takes the view that early agriculture was an uncommon development in a primary form (i.e. as a result purely of local evolution from an indigenous foraging cultural base), restricted to only a very few specific environmental and floral/faunal regions of central Africa, southwestern Asia, China, New Guinea, Mesoamerica, the northern Andes and the Mississippi basin. As I have already noted, it is perhaps these early expansions, flourishing in a lightly populated, healthy and resource-rich world,[3] which laid the bases for the distributions of many of the major language families of the Old World today.

TRANSFORMATIONS

The early Austronesians began their ethnolinguistic career as subtropical coastal and riverine peoples with a Neolithic economy based on cereal and tuber cultivation and a set of domesticated animals. Their ethnographic descendants in island Southeast Asia managed to create for themselves a much wider range of subsistence economies, including rainforest foraging and collection-for-trade; sea nomadism (see Sather, this volume); varied forms of both irrigated and rainfed rice cultivation; shifting cultivation of cereals, fruits and tubers; and even palm exploitation (Fox 1977). Underlying causes for specific transformations can only be hypothesized, but such hypotheses will not proceed very far unless it is recognized that the early An colonists and their descendants must have been influenced by two kinds of landscape, the environmental *and* the human.

In terms of environmental factors, the Austronesian expansion would never have begun at all had its early participants been unable to cross the gaps of about 120 km between China and Taiwan, and between Taiwan and the Batan Islands. Zorc (1994) has recently pointed out how difficult it is to reconstruct terms for boats and navigation for Proto-Austronesian (as opposed to Proto-Malayo-Polynesian) and he suggests that much An seafaring terminology might have been lost in Taiwan owing to the heavy overlay of Chinese settlement in coastal regions. If so, the Proto-Austronesian vocabulary would once have contained more seafaring terms than it does now. Therefore, the obvious place to seek archaeological evidence for innovations in boat construction and navigation[4] may be amongst the hundreds of small islands which flank the coasts of Zhejiang and Fujian Provinces. To my knowledge these islands have produced few archaeological remains, apart from the fifth millennium BC pottery assemblage from the Fuguodun shellmound on Quemoy (Chang 1977; see also Chang 1992 for a recent update). However, if the Austronesians ever required a maritime "nursery", it might have been here.

A second environmental factor which affected the results of An expansion would have been the gradual shift from a seasonal sub-tropical climate into an ever-wet equatorial one as colonists moved southwards from Taiwan and the Philippines towards the Equator. Eventually, of course, the settlement of Java and southeastern Indonesia placed Austronesians back into a zone of markedly seasonal climate. But in the equatorial islands proper — Sumatra, Borneo, central Sulawesi, Halmahera — the prevailing climatic conditions probably promoted an economic reliance on tubers and fruits rather than the major cereals, rice and millet. I have argued this before in several publications (e.g. Bellwood 1980a, 1985) and see no reason to change my views, which do offer a convenient explanation as to why cereals should have been absent in Oceanic economies beyond western Micronesia; the northern New Guinea passageway into Oceania is completely equatorial.

Concerning the pre-existing *human* landscape of what is now western Austronesia an interesting and varied pattern can be reconstructed. Most of Island Southeast Asia was probably inhabited by foragers in pre-Austronesian times, and in the rainforests of Sundaland there probably would have been only very sparse settlement, mostly focused in coastal regions, many of which are now of course beneath sea level as a result of the postglacial ice melt (Bellwood

1990a). Denser populations doubtless existed in the more seasonal environments of Java, the Lesser Sundas and the central and northern Philippines, as witnessed in the Philippines by the existence of Agta foragers of a Melanesian-related physical type (albeit now An-speaking; Reid 1990) to the present. Indeed, in order to settle the Wallacean islands (Philippines, Sulawesi, Lesser Sundas, Moluccas), as also Australia and New Guinea, the original Pleistocene colonists must have had some degree of seafaring capacity, even if rudimentary, by at least 40,000 years ago. Did the Austronesians learn a number of seafaring skills from them, together with perhaps the uses of a number of equatorial crop plants such as breadfruit and coconut, which first appear in An linguistic history in the PMP vocabulary? I have already referred to Zorc's observation that rather little seafaring terminology is reconstructible for Proto-Austronesian. While it would be unwise to deny Proto-Austronesians the knowledge at least of canoes, it is worth remembering that much of the early expansion of the Austronesian-speaking peoples was through Wallacea, especially the Philippines and Sulawesi with their manifold satellite islands. It is amongst the more watery topography of Late Pleistocene Wallacea, rather than land-bridged Sundaland, that one might expect pre-Austronesian maritime traditions to have flourished and to have been transmitted to later arrivals (Irwin 1992).

Outside the islands of Southeast Asia the early Austronesians met with far stronger cultural resistance, both to the west and east. A different world again of course awaited colonists in the Pacific Islands beyond the Solomons — empty and inviting, with no attested pre-Austronesian populations at all (see following chapter).

The archaeological record now makes it clear that Neolithic populations occupied the whole region of Mainland Southeast Asia, including Peninsular Malaysia, by at least 2000 BC (Higham 1989; Bellwood 1993). The relevant archaeological affinities of all these cultures lie within the mainland region itself rather than across to the islands; perhaps it can be hypothesized that the majority of the agricultural populations of Thailand, Indochina and Peninsular Malaysia at this time spoke languages related most closely to the modern Austroasiatic family. In southern Vietnam the ancestors of the Austronesian Chamic-speaking peoples probably had to intrude into a landscape already peopled quite densely by such pre-existing cultivators. The Austronesian expansion into Peninsular Malaysia surely occurred long after the expansion of Austroasiatic cultivators (early speakers of Aslian languages) southwards from Thailand during the third millennium BC. Indeed, Austroasiatic-speaking cultivators might originally have colonized onwards quite rapidly into parts of Sumatra and western Borneo if one takes a broad view of the pollen evidence[5] and some linguistic substratum hints (see Adelaar, this volume). The pre-existence of such agricultural populations in at least Malaya and Vietnam can explain why the mainland of Southeast Asia was only a region of small-scale prehistoric settlement by Austronesians, just as, under rather different cultural circumstances, was New Guinea.

As on the mainland of Southeast Asia, so in New Guinea and western Melanesia the Austronesian colonists also met a major level of resistance — biological, cultural and linguistic. The existence of primary agricultural development in New Guinea is no longer in doubt, even if it is unclear where it was focused (highlands or coasts?) and exactly how the participating economies functioned (Golson and Gardner 1990). Cultivation of plants, especially taro, is likely, but many coastal populations might have lifted their population densities to outsider-resistant levels by other forms of tree exploitation (sago and *Canarium*) or exchange of foodstuffs. Many of these peoples, like their Wallacean cousins, also knew how to cross sea, as witnessed by the Late Pleistocene discovery and distribution of New Britain obsidian (Allen *et al.* 1989). However, their seafaring skills were perhaps more limited than those of the later Austronesian settlers who, at about 1000 BC, were able to colonize far into western Polynesia and to trade Talasea obsidian from New Britain across a distance of 6500 kilometres from northern Borneo in the west to Fiji in the east (Bellwood 1989). This probably makes Talasea obsidian the furthest-distributed commodity of the whole Neolithic world.

SOME FINAL GENERALIZATIONS

Perhaps I may finally sketch, in brief, some of the major transformations which I believe prehistoric Austronesian societies underwent in Island Southeast Asia between about 4000 BC and AD 1.

(1)   4000-3500 BC; Initial Austronesian expansion to Taiwan; settled cereal and tuber agriculture, limited seafaring.

(2)   3000 BC; Proto-Austronesian expansion to the northern Philippines; improvement of seafaring technology, stylistic shift from cord-marked to plain or red-slipped pottery.

(3)   Late third and second millennia BC; Proto-Malayo-Polynesian dispersal from the southern Philippines to Borneo, Sulawesi and the Moluccas; equatorial enhancement of fruit and tuber production *vis-à-vis* cereals, except in more southerly and climatically-seasonal islands such as Java where rice has presumably always maintained its pre-eminence. One development of great interest which might have occurred about this time might have been the beginnings of forager adaptations to the rainforests of Borneo and Sumatra (see Sather, this volume).

(4)   Second/first millennia BC? Beginnings of mobile maritime (proto-sea nomad?) adaptations around the Sulu and Sulawesi Seas (cf. Bellwood 1989 for a maritime economy with long-distance exchange at Bukit

Tengkorak, Sabah, around 1000 BC), and possibly elsewhere. These, in turn, might have laid some of the seafaring groundwork for:

(5) Middle and late second millennium BC; Lapita colonization of Remote Oceania to as far as Tonga and Samoa. Seafaring skills were here developed further amidst an ever-expanding vista of uninhabited islands, but with few opportunities to settle on large western Melanesian islands (especially New Guinea) already inhabited by Papuan-speaking peoples.

(6) Second/first millennia BC? Austronesian settlement in Vietnam and Malaya, in both regions in competition with pre-existing agriculturalists.

(7) 500 BC and after. Introduction of bronze and iron metallurgy into Island Southeast Asia. Dong Son drums were also traded from Vietnam into the Sunda islands, extending from Sumatra to the southern Moluccas.

Perhaps the metallurgical introductions listed last above were no more than side effects of something much greater; the incorporation of parts of Island Southeast Asia into a network of Old World trade stretching from the Mediterranean to eastern Indonesia. Indian pottery of c.200 BC to AD 200 has now been unearthed in Java and Bali (Ardika and Bellwood 1991), and at the same time the archaeological record reveals a hitherto-unprecedented level of similarity in local pottery design and manufacture across a huge region which includes coastal regions of the Sunda islands, Borneo, Sulawesi and the Philippines. It is possible that a great deal of linguistic assimilation of prior diversity occurred from this time onwards, for instance by the Malayic languages (especially Old Malay itself), Javanese and perhaps other languages or subgroups (cf. Blust 1991 for the possibility of some kind of linguistic levelling in the Philippines). By AD 500 the Western Austronesian area was perhaps a zone of continuously-flourishing inter-island travel and trade, with the odd proviso that Taiwan, where so many crucial developments had once occurred, was now divorced into an almost total isolation from the rest of Island Southeast Asia (Meacham 1984-5). Such are the enigmas of history.

NOTES

[1] While no comparative linguists appear to have addressed themselves specifically to an elucidation of this point, it does seem to me to be inherently likely if one accepts the opinions of, *inter alia*, Benedict (1975, 1976), Ballard (1981), Bayard (1975), Diffloth (1979) and Norman and Mei (1976). At a conference on Asia Mainland/Austronesian Connections, held at the University of Hawaii in May 1993, differing opinions were presented linking Austronesian genetically with Thai-Kadai, Austroasiatic and Sino-Tibetan. Although such opinions provoke much lively linguistic debate, owing to the unavoidable ambiguity of any claimed evidence at such great time depth, my own

suspicion is that the ancestors of all these four language families might have been geographically contiguous early in the centuries of agricultural development in China, and that they should therefore share some degree of remote genetic relationship, or at least connections through early borrowing.

[2]   For instance, Yan Wenming (1993) has suggested that the site of Cishan in Hebei (c.6000 BC) contained sufficient pit storage space for 100 tonnes of foxtail millet, and that Hemudu in Zhejiang (c.5000 BC) contained waterlogged rice remains equivalent to a yield of 120 tonnes of fresh grain.

[3]   Agricultural production and resultant demographic crowding might have lowered human health standards in the long run. But the *first* agriculturalists to develop systematic food production should have enjoyed high levels of health and fertility, such that local groups might have increased their numbers at similarly rapid rates to agricultural colonists in recent centuries in Australia and the USA. I have never been convinced that European so-called "colonial" experiences were totally unique to the past two centuries.

[4]   Such evidence would be unlikely to extend to actual boats or canoe parts, except under waterlogged conditions. However, evidence of frequent mainland-island contact could be gleaned from data on pottery and stone tool transport and on fishing methods (bones of offshore fish, for instance, might suggest the use of canoes). See Tsang (1992) for evidence of early contacts between Fujian, the P'eng-hu (Pescadores) Islands and Taiwan.

[5]   Flenley (1988) posits some degree of pre-4000 BP forest clearance in the Sumatran Highlands.

REFERENCES

Allen, J., C. Gosden and J.P. White
   1989   Human Pleistocene adaptations in the tropical island Pacific. *Antiquity* 63:548-560.

Ammerman, A.J. and L.L. Cavalli-Sforza
   1984   *The neolithic transition and the genetics of populations in Europe.* Princeton: Princeton University Press.

Ardika, I.W. and P. Bellwood
   1991   Sembiran: the beginnings of Indian contact with Bali. *Antiquity* 65:221-232.

Ballard, W.L
   1981   Aspects of the linguistic history of south China. *Asian Perspectives* 24(2):163-186.

Bayard, D.
   1975   North China, South China, Southeast Asia, or simply "Far East". *Journal of the Hong Kong Archaeological Society* 6:71-79.

Bellwood, P.S.

1980a Plants, climate and people: the early horticultural prehistory of Austronesia. In J.J. Fox (ed.) *Indonesia, the making of a culture*, pp.57-74. Canberra: Research School of Pacific Studies, The Australian National University.

1980b The peopling of the Pacific. *Scientific American* 243(5):74-85.

1984-5 A hypothesis for Austronesian origins. *Asian Perspectives* 26(1):107-117.

1985 *Prehistory of the Indo-Malaysian Archipelago*. Sydney: Academic Press.

1989 Archaeological investigations at Bukit Tengkorak and Segarong, southeastern Sabah. *Bulletin of the Indo-Pacific Prehistory Association* 9:122-162.

1990a From late Pleistocene to early Holocene in Sundaland. In C. Gamble and O. Soffer (eds) *The world at 18,000 BP*, Vol. 2, *Low latitudes*, pp.255-263. London: Unwin Hyman.

1990b Foraging towards farming. *Review of Archaeology* 11(2):14-34.

1991 The Austronesian dispersal and the origins of languages. *Scientific American* 265(1):88-93.

1992 Southeast Asia before history. Chapter 1 in N. Tarling (ed.) *The Cambridge history of Southeast Asia*. Cambridge: Cambridge University Press.

1993 Cultural and biological differentiation in Peninsular Malaysia: the last 10,000 years. *Asian Perspectives* 32:37-60.

in press a Hierarchy, founder ideology and the Austronesian expansion. In J.J. Fox and C. Sather (eds) *Origin, ancestry and alliance*. Canberra: Department of Anthropology and Comparative Austronesian Project, Research School of Pacific and Asian Studies, The Australian National University.

in press b Prehistoric cultural explanations for widespread language families. In P. McConvell and N. Evans (eds) *Understanding ancient Australia: perspectives in archaeology and linguistics*. Oxford: Melbourne University Press.

Benedict, P.K.

1975 *Austro-Thai language and culture*. New Haven: Human Relations Area Files Press.

1976 Austro-Thai and Austro-Asiatic. In P.L. Jenner *et al.* (eds) *Austroasiatic Studies*, pp.1-36. Honolulu: University of Hawaii Press.

Blust, R.A.

1984-5 The Austronesian homeland: a linguistic perspective. *Asian Perspectives* 26(1):45-68.

1991 The greater Philippines hypothesis. *Oceanic Linguistics* 30(2):73-129.

Chang, K.C.

1977 A new prehistoric ceramic style in the southeastern coastal area of China. *Asian Perspectives* 20:179-182.

1986 *The archaeology of ancient China* (4th edition). New Haven: Yale University Press.

1992 Taiwan Strait archaeology and Protoaustronesian. Paper presented to International symposium on Austronesian studies relating to Taiwan, Academia Sinica, Taipei, December 1992.

Diffloth, G.
    1979   Aslian languages and Southeast Asian prehistory. *Federation Museums Journal* 24:3-18.

Flenley, J.R.
    1988   Palynological evidence for land use changes in South-East Asia. *Journal of Biogeography* 15:185-197.

Fox, J.J.
    1977   *Harvest of the palm.* Cambridge, Mass.: Harvard University Press.

Friedman, J.
    1981   Notes on structure and history in Oceania. *Folk* 23:275-295.

Golson, J.
    1985   Agricultural origins in Southeast Asia: a view from the east. In V.N. Misra and P. Bellwood (eds) *Recent advances in Indo-Pacific prehistory*, pp.307-314. New Delhi: Oxford and IBH.

Golson. J. and D.S. Gardner
    1990   Agriculture and sociopolitical organization in New Guinea Highlands prehistory. *Annual Review of Anthropology* 19:395-417.

Hayden, B.
    1983   Social characteristics of early Austronesian colonizers. *Bulletin of the Indo-Pacific Prehistory Association* 4:123-134.

Higham, C.
    1989   *The archaeology of mainland Southeast Asia.* Cambridge: Cambridge University Press.

Irwin, G.
    1992   *The prehistoric exploration and colonization of the Pacific.* Cambridge: Cambridge University Press.

Kirch, P.V.
    1988   Long-distance exchange and island colonization: the Lapita case. *Norwegian Archaeological Review* 21:103-117.

MacNeish, R.
    1992   *The origins of agriculture and settled life.* Norman: University of Oklahoma Press.

Meacham, W.
    1984-5 On the improbability of Austronesian origins in South China. *Asian Perspectives* 26(1):89-106.

Norman, J. and T-L. Mei
    1976   The Austroasiatics in ancient south China: some lexical evidence. *Monumenta Serica* 32:274-301.

Renfrew, C.
    1987   *Archaeology and language.* London: Jonathan Cape.
    1992   Archaeology, genetics and linguistic diversity. *Man* 27:445-478.

Reid, L.R.
   1984-5   Benedict's Austro-Tai hypothesis: an evaluation. *Asian Perspectives* 26(1):19-34.
   1990   The search for original Negrito: Negrito languages as creolized Austronesian. Paper given at 14th IPPA Congress, Yogyakarta, August 1990.

Ruhlen, M.
   1987   *A guide to the world's languages*. Volume 1: *Classification*. California: Stanford University Press.

Spriggs, M.
   1989   The dating of the island Southeast Asian Neolithic. *Antiquity* 63:587-612.

Tsang Cheng-hwa
   1992   *Archaeology of the P'eng-hu Islands*. Taipei: Institute of History and Philology, Academia Sinica, Special Publication 95.

Yan Wenming
   1991   China's earliest rice agriculture remains. *Bulletin of the Indo-Pacific Prehistory Association* 10:118-126.
   1993   The origins of agriculture and animal husbandry in China. In C.M. Aikens and Song Nai Rhee (eds) *Pacific Northeast Asia in prehistory*, pp.113-123. Pullman: Washington State University Press.

Zorc, R.D.P.
   1994   Austronesian culture history through reconstructed vocabulary (an overview). In A. Pawley and M. Ross (eds) *Austronesian terminologies: continuity and change*, pp.541-594. Pacific Linguistics Series C No. 127. Canberra: Department of Linguistics, Research School of Pacific and Asian Studies, The Australian National University.

6

THE LAPITA CULTURE AND AUSTRONESIAN PREHISTORY IN OCEANIA

Matthew Spriggs

The Lapita culture (1600 BC to 500 BC/AD 1) represents the archaeological record of the first substantial Austronesian colonization into Melanesia and Polynesia. The situation prior to Lapita in western Melanesia (near Oceania) is discussed, together with the archaeology of the Lapita culture itself and questions of correlations with early Oceanic languages and colonizing people. Some observations relevant for an understanding of Austronesian migration are also presented.

INTRODUCTION

The most widespread cultural horizon in Oceania is the Lapita culture, defined initially on the basis of its highly distinctive decorated pottery (see Green 1990 for a "potted" history of Lapita studies). Its geographic spread is from Manus (Admiralties) and the Vitiaz Straits (between New Guinea and New Britain) in the west to Tonga and Samoa in the east (Map 1). On New Guinea itself sherds from a single pot only have been found at Aitape on the north coast of West Sepik Province (Papua New Guinea). The Lapita culture dates from about 1600 BC to between 500 BC and the time of Christ in different areas, by which time it had lost its more general but distinctive features (see Spriggs 1990a for a discussion of Lapita distribution and chronology).

When the widespread distribution of Lapita was first recognized in the late 1960s and 1970s, it was linked with the spread of Austronesian (An) languages in the region and on occasion interpreted as representing the migration of speakers of these languages from Island Southeast Asia, through Melanesia and out into the Pacific (Bellwood 1978:255; Pawley and Green 1973; Shutler and Marck 1975). In the 1980s, perhaps inevitably, reaction set in against this simple equation, at least as far as Island Melanesia was concerned. The equation for Fiji and Western Polynesia remains generally uncontroversial. The ANU Lapita Homeland Project was formulated in 1983-84 specifically to examine the possibility of local development of the Lapita culture in the Bismarck Archipelago to the immediate east of New Guinea from indigenous roots (Allen 1984). Perhaps equally inevitably the mass of information on the prehistory of Island Melanesia gained from this project and a number of related projects which

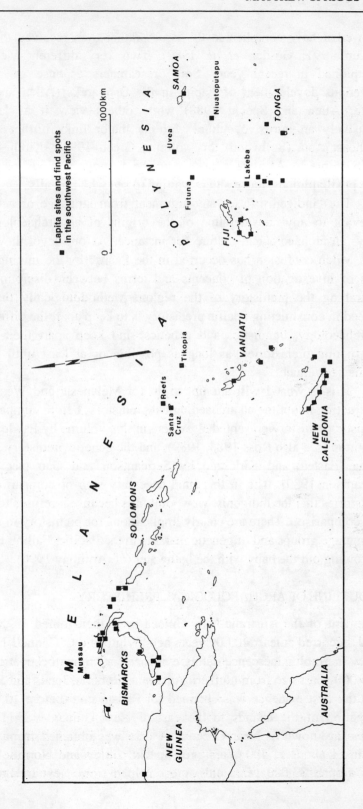

Map 1: Lapita sites and find spots in the southwest Pacific.

followed it have complicated the issues rather than resolved them (Allen and Gosden 1991; Gosden *et al.* 1989). Two very different views have been championed in recent years. Some researchers espouse an almost entirely indigenous development of Lapita in the Bismarcks (Allen and White 1989; White, Allen and Specht 1988) while others view it as largely but not exclusively an intrusive culture with its major links further west to Island Southeast Asia (Bellwood, this volume; Green 1991a; Kirch 1988a; Spriggs 1991b, in press). As always there is a tribe of more cautious, or perhaps simply more pusillanimous, fence sitters waiting to see who prevails.

The "indigenists" see any argument from language or genetics as being irrelevant to any consideration of the origins of an archaeologically defined entity, an archaeological culture for instance. At one level they are of course right. Much confusion has occurred in the Pacific by the mixing at too early a stage of investigation of concepts and terms between disciplines involved in researching the prehistory of the region. Methodologically the best way to proceed in constructing Pacific prehistory is to keep apart the different data bases of archaeology, linguistics and genetics, and keep apart their arguments for constructing prehistories, as long as possible or at least until the excitement becomes too much.

This is what I will attempt to do for Melanesia and Western Polynesia, constructing in outline an archaeological prehistory, before comparing it with the linguistic prehistory presented elsewhere in this volume by Pawley and Ross and by Dutton (see also Ross 1988, 1989), and the genetic prehistory summarized by Bhatia, Easteal and Kirk and by Serjeantson and Gao (see also Hill and Serjeantson 1989). It is in this final necessary step of comparing the different prehistories that the indigenist viewpoint fails because it refuses to engage in any such comparison. There are clearly implications for prehistory in the distribution of language groups and of genetic markers in the Pacific. Failing to address them is throwing out the baby with the bathwater (cf. Anthony 1990).

AN OUTLINE OF ARCHAEOLOGICAL PREHISTORY

Settlement of the Australia-New Guinea area, then joined as the continent of Sahul, occurred at least 40,000 years ago (White and O'Connell 1982), and there is now thermoluminescence dating evidence for human occupation on the order of 55,000 years ago from northern Australia (Roberts, Jones and Smith 1990). In 1980 the first evidence was obtained for Pleistocene (before 10,000 years ago) occupation of the islands to the east of New Guinea, within the region in Melanesia known as Near Oceania. A date was obtained from a site on New Britain of about 11,400 years ago (Specht, Lilley and Normu 1981). In 1986 dates around 33,000 years old were obtained from New Ireland (Allen *et al.*

1988; Allen, Gosden and White 1989), and in 1988 came evidence from Buka at the northern end of the Solomons chain for occupation by 29,000 years ago (Wickler and Spriggs 1988). Finally, in 1990 Pleistocene occupation was confirmed for Manus in the Admiralty Islands by research conducted by Wal Ambrose, Spriggs and Clayton Fredericksen.

Initial occupation of New Guinea and the rest of Near Oceania (the Bismarck and Solomon archipelagoes) was by hunting and gathering populations, but possibly by 7000 BC and more certainly by about 4000 BC an indigenous development of agriculture occurred in the New Guinea Highlands, and almost certainly in the lowlands of the island as well. The evidence is from ditching of swamps in the Highlands, significant forest clearance revealed in pollen records (Golson 1977, 1989) and plant macrofossils of several important New Guinea domesticated nut and tree species at the Dongan site in the Sepik-Ramu Basin at 4700 BC (Swadling, Araho and Ivuyo 1991). Equivalent evidence has not been found in the Bismarcks and Solomons, apart from the exploitation of *Canarium* nut trees apparently introduced from the mainland of New Guinea (Yen 1985:320, 1990:262, 268) before the end of the Pleistocene. It is thus possible that an agricultural focus existed in New Guinea, with the adjacent islands pursuing more of a hunting and gathering economy in the immediately pre-Lapita period. This contentious issue is discussed in more detail elsewhere (Spriggs 1993).

Until recently the evidence for an indigenous development of agriculture in New Guinea seemed to sit, at least to me, rather uneasily with introduced pig remains in the New Guinea Highlands at 4000 BC and more uncertainly at 8000 BC. The pig is not indigenous to Melanesia and would have had to have been brought in from Island Southeast Asia (see Groves, this volume). Recent direct dating by accelerator mass spectrometry of pig remains claimed to be from early contexts now raises the possibility that pigs have only been in the Highlands for a much shorter period (David Harris, pers.comm.), although new claims of pig in a 4000 BC context have recently been made for the north coast of New Guinea (Gorecki, Mabin and Campbell 1991:120).

South and east of the main Solomons chain, however, in the area known as Remote Oceania (see Bellwood Map 1, this volume), there is no clear evidence of human settlement earlier than the Lapita culture, dating in Vanuatu and New Caledonia to about 1200 BC. For this part of Melanesia and for Western Polynesia, Lapita appears to be the founding culture (see Green 1991b and Spriggs 1989b for discussion).

As mentioned at the beginning of this paper, Lapita was initially defined on the basis of its highly distinctive pottery, decorated by dentate (toothed-stamp) impression. With the possible exception of the Sepik-Ramu pottery (Swadling, Araho and Ivuyo 1991), it is the earliest pottery tradition in

Melanesia. Lapita-like decoration is not found in earlier pottery assemblages in Island Southeast Asia (it does occur there slightly later — Spriggs 1989a:607), but the range of vessel forms and the use of red-slip decoration are shared between the two regions.

There are now three sub-styles of Lapita recognized (Anson 1983, 1986), which have geographical and chronological significance (Spriggs 1990b).

1. Far Western, or as I would prefer "Early Western", Lapita is limited to the Bismarck Archipelago and dates from about 1600 to 1200 BC or slightly later. This sub-style has produced the most complex vessel forms and the most elaborate decorative motifs, often executed using extremely fine dentate stamps.

2. Western Lapita is found after 1200 BC in the Bismarcks and represents the earliest Lapita pottery in the Solomons, Vanuatu and New Caledonia. It consists of less elaborate decoration, fewer vessel forms and generally the use of coarser stamps. This sub-style lasts until about the time of Christ in some areas while in others dentate-stamping as a decorative technique had ceased by 500 BC. An example is given in Figure 1.

3. Eastern Lapita is found in Fiji and Western Polynesia starting around 1000 BC. The motifs are simpler still and there are fewer vessel forms. A coarse dentate-stamping is often used. In Tonga the sub-style may have continued in use until about 2000 years ago, whereas in Samoa it appears to have ceased much earlier by about 800 BC. This sub-style is related most closely to the Western style Lapita assemblage of Malo in northern Vanuatu.

The tendency in Lapita pottery is for simplification through time, and as the style spread from west to east. In all areas of its distribution vessel forms and decoration became less elaborate over time. Finally the vessels either become entirely plain or are decorated with incised and/or applied relief designs. These latter decorative techniques are present but rare in earlier Lapita assemblages.

But Lapita is not just pots. There is a whole "package" of material culture items and other distinctive features which like the pottery are not found in earlier cultural assemblages. The existence of this distinctive assemblage is often underplayed by those who argue that Lapita developed in Melanesia with minimal external input. Evidence that Lapita does represent some kind of break with preceding assemblages in Melanesia is evident from the following observations:

1. South and east of the main Solomons Lapita is the founding culture, representing the first human occupation of Remote Oceania.

2. Everywhere Lapita is found it marks the first appearance in Island Melanesia of the three Oceanic domesticates — the pig, dog and chicken,

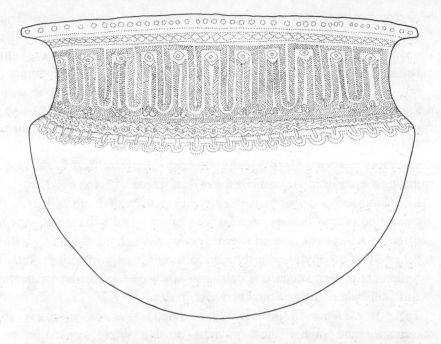

Figure 1:   A dentate-stamped pottery vessel from Malo Island, Vanuatu. The bottom figure is a simplified version of the dentate-stamped composition shown above.

all derived from Island Southeast Asia, as well as the commensal Polynesian rat (*Rattus exulans*), again of Asian origin.

3.   There is a distinctive Lapita stone adze kit, in part an innovation of the Lapita culture and in part derived from Island Southeast Asian adze forms (Green 1991a).

4.   There are distinctive Lapita shell ornament types (Kirch 1988b), some of which also occur in Neolithic Island Southeast Asian assemblages.

5.   A major extension in the range of distribution of Talasea (New Britain) and Lou Island (Admiralties) obsidian occurs with Lapita. Lou Island obsidian is not found outside the Admiralties Group in pre-Lapita times. But it is found in Lapita sites throughout the Bismarcks, Solomons and into Vanuatu. Talasea obsidian was distributed pre-Lapita to the west on the New Guinea mainland as far as the Sepik-Ramu Basin,[1] and to the south and east in New Ireland and on Nissan, an island between New Ireland and the Northern Solomons (Spriggs 1991a). In Lapita times its distribution encompassed Sabah in Borneo (Bellwood and Koon 1989) to the west and Fiji in the east (Best 1987), a spread of some 6500 km.

6.   Lapita possesses a distinctive settlement pattern of large villages, often consisting of stilt houses over lagoons or on small offshore islands, and certainly always within a kilometre or two of the shore. Lapita sites do not generally re-occupy previously used locations except in rockshelters. The settlement pattern suggests a defensive posture or avoidance of mainland situations where malaria might have been rife.

7.   There is evidence in the vicinity of Lapita sites for extensive forest clearance and higher than previous erosion rates, suggestive of an agricultural basis to the economy (Gosden et al. 1989:573).

8.   Lapita also represents the movement out into the Pacific of a wide range of domesticated plants, of either Southeast Asian or New Guinea origin. Macrofossils of these plants are found in many Lapita sites, but in Island Melanesia have not so far been found in earlier archaeological contexts (Gosden et al. 1989:573-574).

The question of the origin of the Lapita crop complex remains unresolved. Island Southeast Asian Neolithic cultures were at least initially rice-using and yet rice was not transferred across to Melanesia. Yen (1982, 1985, 1990) has challenged the earlier assumption that the crop complex carried into the Pacific by the Lapita culture was also of Asian or Southeast Asian origin. The wild progenitors of many of these crops can now be seen as of New Guinea origin, in line with the evidence mentioned previously for an early centre of plant domestication in this area.

Three questions are raised by this. How far in the islands to the west of mainland New Guinea did the process of pre-Lapita domestication extend? Secondly, how much further had the domesticates themselves spread in pre-Lapita times? Thirdly, could some of the plants in question have been domesticated independently in areas of Southeast Asia and in New Guinea? As the area immediately west of New Guinea, and indeed the western half of New Guinea itself, are still little explored archaeologically, no answers to these questions can yet be formulated. To the extent that the Lapita crop complex may have been picked up from the New Guinea region rather than Island Southeast

Asia, there is a wide area in which any crop transfer could have occurred — from eastern Indonesia and along the north coast of New Guinea to the Bismarcks. The lack of evidence so far for many of these plants in pre-Lapita contexts in the Bismarcks gives no reason to suggest primacy for that area in any such transfer. It may have occurred earlier and far to the west.

What does Lapita culture represent in the various areas where it occurs? In Remote Oceania including Polynesia it represents initial colonization by human groups, equipped with a fully agricultural economy. In Near Oceania (the Bismarcks and Solomons) it represents the first appearance of domestic animals, a range of new artefact forms including pottery, a shift in settlement patterns, dramatic changes in obsidian exchange networks and the first clear evidence for an agricultural base to the economy.

Because of a dearth of immediately pre-Lapita sites, it is hard to assess continuities in Lapita from pre-Lapita cultures in Near Oceania. Where these do occur some continuities are apparent. *Canarium* nut exploitation remains an important part of the economy. There is continuity too in some artefact types: *Tridacna* (clam) shell adzes, *Trochus* shell armrings, simple shell beads and probably simple one-piece shell fishhooks (Spriggs 1991b). The discontinuities, however, seem more substantial, given the many new artefact types in the Lapita inventory listed previously. In the Talasea area of New Britain comparison is hampered by preservation conditions such that organic materials (including shell) are not preserved. Pre-Lapita and Lapita period obsidian technologies there, however, are extremely different with an earlier elaborate blade industry not continuing into Lapita levels (Torrence, Specht and Fullagar 1990). Apart from the Talasea area, there are few obviously pre-Lapita open sites and many of the previously inhabited rockshelters went out of use between about 6000/4000 BC and the Lapita or immediately post-Lapita period.

On the island of New Guinea itself, Lapita does not represent anything apart from the fragments of a single pot, seemingly of a late Lapita style. There is a comparable but somewhat later phenomenon, however, in the archaeologic- ally instantaneous spread of the Papuan red-slipped pottery style found west to east along the south coast of Papua at about AD 200 (Irwin 1980, 1991). The spread is again associated with a distinctive settlement pattern, long-distance movement of obsidian (this time from Fergusson Island sources in Milne Bay Province, PNG) and other items of material culture ultimately derivable from the Lapita culture of the Bismarcks. This pottery tradition is the earliest along the south coast of the island of New Guinea. Slightly later again after AD 500 pottery appears along the north coast and on islands offshore from Madang Province, related again to the Bismarcks assemblages (Lilley 1988). As already mentioned the status and age of the Sepik-Ramu pottery styles are not yet clear, but they are certainly not in the Lapita style.

I would argue that the dates for pottery in Island Melanesia in relation to Southeast Asia, the rapid spread of Lapita culture, the nature of the new material culture items, the Southeast Asian links for the domestic animals and the pottery vessel forms and red slip, and the distinctive settlement pattern argue for Lapita culture representing a migration into the Bismarcks from areas to the west in Island Southeast Asia. Lapita culture, though intrusive, did not exist isolated from the already existing cultures of the area and there is some carry-over in material culture items and continuing exploitation of the major obsidian sources. There appears to have been a pause of some 400 or so years in the Bismarcks, ample time for significant interaction with local populations, before the culture spread through the Solomons and out into Remote Oceania at about 1200-1000 BC.

When the Lapita design system disappears in Island Melanesia and Fiji between about 500 BC and AD 1, different pottery styles derivable from the non-dentate-stamped "domestic ware" of Lapita appear from Manus to Fiji. Vanuatu obsidian and pottery types appear in Fiji at this time (Best 1984, 1987), evidence of renewed contacts to the west. The changes in pottery style might represent further population movements or alternatively continuity of groups who remained in interaction over the previous range of Lapita in Melanesia as I have argued previously (Spriggs 1984; see also below).

The archaeology of Micronesia is much less understood (see Craib 1983 for summary). The Mariana Islands appear to have been first settled at about 1200-1000 BC (Bonhomme and Craib 1987) and there are some very specific parallels with Island Southeast Asian pottery of the same general period. The rest of Micronesia has so far only produced sequences for the last 2000 years. Plain and rim-notched pottery from Eastern Micronesia could plausibly be derived from late Lapita assemblages (Athens 1980).

COMPARISON WITH LINGUISTIC PREHISTORY: A LAPITA LANGUAGE?

The details of current thinking on linguistic prehistory in Oceania are presented elsewhere in this volume, where detailed references should be sought. If we compare the two prehistories there is indeed a striking fit, although diversity in interpretations among linguists should be acknowledged. Ross (1988, 1989) situates the Proto-Oceanic homeland in the general area of the Willaumez Peninsula (Talasea area), on the north coast of New Britain (cf. Grace 1961:364), which was as we have seen an important centre for the distribution of obsidian in Lapita times. The distribution of the Oceanic An languages and the distribution of Lapita and its successor cultures are also coincident. Ross sees an early movement of An languages to Manus, the other centre for obsidian distribution in the Lapita period, and another movement out through the Solomons into

Vanuatu and New Caledonia, and ultimately to Fiji and Polynesia. This spread of a branch of Oceanic into and beyond the Solomons is matched by the distribution of the Western and Eastern Lapita sub-styles. The Central Pacific languages (Fijian, Rotuman and Polynesian) have their closest relatives in northern Vanuatu and the Eastern Lapita sub-style, which covers the same area, has its closest relation to the pottery from Malo in northern Vanuatu (Anson 1983, 1986).

In Polynesia the break-up of Proto-Polynesian into the Tongic and Nuclear Polynesian linguistic groups matches exactly the division between Tonga and Samoa in material culture during the Lapita period. Almost immediately after initial settlement at about 1000 BC dentate-stamped pottery was replaced by plainware in Samoa, while in Tonga use of some dentate stamping continued until almost the time of Christ (Kirch, Hunt and Tyler 1989; Poulsen 1987). When evidence for settlement further out into the Pacific occurs at about 200 BC or later in the Marquesas it is associated with plainware generally similar to that from Western Polynesia and Fiji (Kirch 1986). All Eastern Polynesian languages are derived from the Nuclear rather than the Tongic branch of Polynesian (see Clark 1979 for a succinct discussion of Polynesian languages).

The clear correlation of the distribution of Lapita with the distribution of Oceanic An languages suggests that Proto-Oceanic split up by about 1200 BC with the movement of Lapita culture beyond the Bismarcks. Linguistic change after that may have been extremely rapid. Proto-Central Pacific must have developed its few distinctive features around 1000 BC and Proto-Polynesian could have developed soon afterwards, possibly already starting to diverge into what became the Tongic and Nuclear Polynesian groups soon after 800 BC.

The languages of the Marianas and Belau (formerly Palau) and possibly Yap in Western Micronesia are An but not Oceanic, being of Western Malayo-Polynesian type (see Tryon, this volume). The other Micronesian languages are assigned to a subgroup of Oceanic termed Nuclear Micronesian. Although various subgrouping arguments have been put forward to link Nuclear Micronesian with other subgroups within Oceanic, there is no general agreement as to their immediate external relationships (Jackson 1986). Archaeology does not yet suggest a more specific point of dispersal in Island Melanesia. The generally plain or notched-lip pottery found in Micronesian contexts back to about 2000 years ago can be matched in a wide area of Island Melanesia from Manus to Vanuatu at the same time period.

The situation in the Bismarcks and the north-western Solomons has been complicated according to Ross (1988) by the subsequent spread of the Western Oceanic languages of the Meso-Melanesian cluster from New Britain, which may have in part replaced An languages of probable Southeast Solomonic type in Bougainville and presumably also in New Ireland. It is tempting to link this hypothesized language spread to the replacement of recognizably Lapita pottery by the incised and applied relief styles which are found from the Bismarcks to Fiji. While the linguistic influence is argued by Ross to have stopped at the southern end of Santa Ysabel in the Western Solomons, at the so-called Tryon-Hackman line, the suggested archaeological signature of this process continued further south, ultimately to Fiji. If there was a secondary movement of population from the Bismarcks to the south and east, it was a movement from the same general area as the original Lapita spread and so may not have been represented by a distinctive material culture apart from a new pottery style. It should be noted that Ross' idea of a two-stage spread of An languages in the New Ireland-Solomons area has yet to convince other linguists working in the region (Andrew Pawley, pers.comm.).

The two other branches of Western Oceanic An, the Papuan Tip Cluster and the North New Guinea Cluster (Ross 1988), also have close parallels with the distribution of archaeological phenomena. The distribution of the Papuan red-slipped ware and its attendant material culture almost exactly matches the distribution of the Papuan Tip Cluster languages. The pottery making centre of Mailu along the South Papuan coast is now Non-Austronesian (NAn) speaking, but this is obviously a recent switch (Dutton 1982). Genetically the Mailu population is grouped with other South Coast Papuan An-speaking populations (Kirk 1989:100-101). Although much less studied, the spread of pottery use along the North New Guinea coast, and indeed up the Markham Valley as well, corresponds to the distribution of the North New Guinea Cluster An languages. The association between archaeological and linguistic distributions suggests that the movement of Papuan Tip Cluster speakers to the west along the Papuan coast took place rapidly about 1800 years ago and the time depth for the spread out from the Bismarcks area of North New Guinea Cluster languages is almost certainly within the last 2500 years.

One feature of many of the Western Oceanic languages is that they have undergone linguistic change as a result of contact with Non-Austronesian (NAn) languages, initially in the New Britain area, and subsequently as they spread to New Guinea and probably along already-trodden An paths in the Bismarcks and northern Solomons. These languages would have been the first An languages to be spoken in at least the eastern half of the island of New Guinea, which prior to 500 BC was entirely NAn-speaking. Although the associated incised and applied relief pottery styles have their origins in Lapita, they are presumably also heavily informed by the NAn cultural traditions of neighbouring groups. In this sense we can see the intrusive Austronesian Lapita tradition becoming progressively "Melanesianized" by contact-induced change and innovation to produce the range of local cultural styles found in the area in the recent past.

The movement of An speakers to mainland New Guinea in the last 2500 years may have marked the introduction of the pig, so important in the ethnographically recorded cultures particularly of the Highlands. It is noteworthy that the pig is a case where archaeological and linguistic prehistories did not at first appear to match. It has been known for some time that the word for pig is an An loan word in many New Guinea NAn languages (Blust 1976). How was this fact to be squared with evidence for pig in New Guinea at 6000 or even 10,000 years ago? The advances in archaeological dating techniques mentioned earlier now suggest that the pig may be late in New Guinea, late enough to have been brought in by An speakers.

A LAPITA PEOPLE? THE EVIDENCE FROM GENETICS

As with the linguistic evidence, genetic studies are treated elsewhere in this volume. For many of the more recently discovered genetic systems, sample coverage is spotty compared to that in archaeology and linguistics. For example, there has not been a great deal of work in the Bismarcks, an area critical for comparison with the archaeological and linguistic pictures. Many of the genetic data were collected for purposes of applied medical rather than historical research and this should also be remembered. That said, the genetic prehistory established so far does seem consonant with the prehistories derived from the other two disciplines.

If we start with Polynesia and work backwards, the pattern is clearer. Initial settlement of Polynesia by the Lapita culture and lack of evidence for any but Polynesian sub-group languages there would suggest Polynesians, a genetically homogeneous group, are direct descendants of the bearers of Lapita culture. An ultimate origin in Island Southeast Asia for the "Pre-Polynesians" now seems certain, with some evidence of genetic admixture with populations in northern Island Melanesia, as summarized by Serjeantson and Hill:

> The lack of particular coastal New Guinea [genetic] markers in Polynesians, such as the high-frequency $-\alpha^{4.2}$ thalassaemia deletion, the albumin NG variant, the HLA-B13.Cw4 haplotype, and the B allele of the ABO blood group, all argue that the pre-Polynesians moved rapidly through this part of Melanesia. However, the presence of a substantial frequency of the Melanesian α-globin haplotypes IIIa and IVa in all Polynesians indicates that at some point there was significant interbreeding with Melanesians. The presence of the $-\alpha^{3.7}$III but not the $-\alpha^{4.2}$ α thalassaemia deletion indicates that this contact was probably mainly in northern island Melanesia rather than in New Guinea (1989:287-288).

Not all bearers of the Lapita culture moved to Polynesia of course. The genes of the "stay at homes" can be found in coastal and island Melanesian groups who are genetically the descendants both of the pre-Lapita populations in the area and of the intrusive Southeast Asian populations who also gave rise to the Polynesians. The latest evidence indicates that Fijians have undergone admixture with Island Melanesians since first settlement by Lapita groups, thus reinstating an earlier and partly discredited view of Fijian culture history (Serjeantson and Hill 1989:288-289). The original Fijian population would have been more Polynesian in appearance. This might also have been true of the initial settlers of Vanuatu and New Caledonia. The new genetic evidence is also against any direct link between Polynesians and Micronesians. Micronesian populations are diverse but in general are a distinct Island Southeast Asian population with genetic input from Melanesia in varying degrees (Serjeantson and Hill 1989:290-291). Polynesian populations cannot be derived from Micronesia, as Howells (1973) once believed.

Thus there may have been a moment in the Bismarcks when there was a single people using Lapita pottery, genetically, linguistically and culturally distinct from their neighbours. But this unity and distinctiveness would have been shortlived. Lapita-using populations which spread to Polynesia and those in Island Melanesia subsequently had divergent genetic and linguistic histories. The end of Lapita culture in these two areas also meant very different things. In Island Melanesia rapid transformations in material and other aspects of culture occurred, previous An languages in parts of the Bismarcks and Northern Solomons were replaced by languages of Western Oceanic An-type, and there was perhaps another phase of migration through Island Melanesia of Bismarcks area populations which further swamped the "pre-Polynesian" genotypes. In Polynesia seemingly more gradual changes occurred to produce the cultures of the area recorded in the recent past, their An languages conservative and their art forms still clearly recognizable as Lapita-derived.[2] Their homogeneous physical type compared to the more differentiated populations of Island Melanesia bears witness to these developments having occurred in comparative isolation.

THE STRUCTURE OF AUSTRONESIAN MIGRATION IN OCEANIA

Anthony (1990) has urged that prehistoric migrations be considered as structural processes, the study of which can be approached through general principles derived from recent studies of migration in demography and geography. It may be worth examining some of these postulated principles in the light of the Lapita evidence.[3] Anthony notes that a common feature of long-distance migration is leapfrogging, great distances being crossed and large areas bypassed, "through the agency of advance 'scouts' who collect information on social conditions and resource potentials and relay it back to the potential migrants" (1990:902). He suggests that archaeologically this should be recognizable by an earlier small-scale penetration prior to the large-scale migration, and notes significantly that the archaeological signature of leapfrogging, "should resemble 'islands' of settlement in desirable or attractive locations, separated by significant expanses of unsettled, less desirable territory" (1990:903).

This of course is precisely the Lapita settlement pattern. "Scouts" too may explain anomalous Lapita assemblages such as the somewhat ephemeral rock-shelter occupation on Nissan, at the northern end of the Solomons, of the Halika phase, contemporary with the earliest Lapita further to the north and west and stratigraphically below a classic Lapita assemblage at one of the excavated sites (Spriggs 1991a). Lapita rockshelter occupations on Lakeba in Eastern Fiji, interpreted by Best (1984) as representing a "strandlooper" phase of Lapita before the establishment of a fully agricultural economy, would also fit the pattern.

Another feature of long-distance migration discussed by Anthony is its resemblance to a stream, the migrants proceeding along well-defined routes towards specific destinations, and often originating from a highly restricted point of origin. The archaeological signature would be distribution of regionally defined artefact types from a circumscribed home region to a specified destination. The pattern of obsidian distribution in the western Pacific could certainly be interpreted in this framework (cf. Green's (1987:246) discussion of maintaining "ties" with the homeland by continuing to import obsidian from Bismarcks sources when a local alternative was available). Anthony further notes that migration streams often continue to flow in a given direction despite circumstances quite changed from those that prompted the initial movement:

> Kinship linkages, dependence, and the reduction of obstacles may attract a secondary flow that is quite different in goal orientation and composition from the initial migrant group. Such a chronological shift in group composition and organization might well have archaeological effects (1990:904).

The changes which occur at the end of Lapita may form an example of such a secondary stream. Migration streams, Anthony notes, favour the creation of "apex-families" which might establish more permanent status differentiation as communities mature. The suggested hierarchical nature of Lapita society (see Kirch 1988b for discussion) could well have been related to such processes.

A third feature of migration is return migration, a counterstream returning back to the migrants' place of origin, particularly when opportunities are similar at the origin and destination points. Some examples of long-distance "trade" might represent goods carried by return migrants. In this regard it is worth remembering the Talasea obsidian in Sabah and the similarities in pottery decoration to Lapita of assemblages in various parts of Island Southeast Asia which date a few hundred years later than the earliest Lapita in Island Melanesia (see above).

A fourth feature is migration frequency, migrants tending to belong to groups who have a tradition of migration. Within particularly the younger age groups of a population, migration increases the probability that further migration will occur. Anthony (1990:905) suggests that this self-propagating tendency can partially explain flurries of migratory activity that characterize some portions of the archaeological record. The rapidity of spread of Lapita from the Bismarcks to Samoa in only a few hundred years would seem to be a classic example of this pattern.

Anthony mentions as a final pattern, that of migration demography, often skewed towards males in the initial stages of more recently documented migrations. Some of the "bottlenecks" detected by mitochondrial DNA studies, for instance in the settlement of Eastern Polynesia, might usefully be examined with this in mind. Further modelling of Lapita-period population dynamics along the lines started by McArthur, Saunders and Tweedie (1976) and Black (1978) are clearly needed.

CONCLUSIONS

Peter Bellwood (this volume) has already discussed possible reasons for the expansion of An speakers into the Pacific, although as Anthony (1990:898) points out, the causes of migrations are often extremely complex and in many prehistoric cases proximate causes can no longer be clearly identified. The migrants' initial success in establishing settlements in the Bismarcks and Solomons may well have been due to the demographic muscle imparted by a full-on agricultural economy moving into a basically hunter-gatherer area. The existence of an already in-place agricultural economy on the mainland of New Guinea may well explain why An settlement there appears to have been delayed for over a thousand years after the Bismarcks were settled (Bellwood 1984). It would be wrong, however, to see the new colonists immediately blanketing the Bismarcks and Solomons. Initial numbers would have been low, settlements were marginal to the larger islands and even before the push through to Polynesia some limited recruitment from local NAn-speaking populations must have taken place to explain certain genetic markers found in Polynesian populations.

The diffusion of agriculture across the An-NAn linguistic boundary must have occurred at some time, as all Bismarcks and Solomons populations are agricultural today whatever language they speak. Over time there must also have been a tendency for whole groups to switch from NAn to An languages in areas such as Manus and New Ireland. On Bougainville the majority of the population never adopted An languages, which mimic the mainland New Guinea pattern in occurring peripherally around the coast (Spriggs 1992). The archaeological study of the An and agricultural "frontier" in the region has barely begun but will produce a much more complex prehistory than we can outline with our present state of knowledge.

Although this and other papers in this volume have inevitably given an Austronesian-centred view of the region, all present Austronesian groups, whether in Melanesia or Polynesia, also share a heritage derived from a Non-Austronesian Melanesian origin, whether it be in the food crops they cultivate, aspects of their material culture and art, certain genetic markers, or in aspects of the structure and lexicon of their languages. This should not be forgotten because (with apologies to Rupert Brooke) there is a corner of an Austronesian field that is forever Non-Austronesian.

ACKNOWLEDGEMENTS AND DEDICATION

I would like to thank Andrew Pawley for particularly trenchant criticisms of an earlier draft of this paper and Nancy Sharp for more restrained comments. It has also been honed by comments on oral presentations of an earlier version by audiences at the Universities of Copenhagen, Lund, Sheffield, Oxford and Cambridge, as well as those at the Austronesians in History Conference at the Australian National University. This paper is dedicated to my wife Ruth Vatoa Saovana of the Wa-Do (Tinputz) language area, part of the Meso-Melanesian Cluster of Western Oceanic Austronesian languages, descendant too of those Bougainville non-Austronesian speakers who got there first.

NOTES

[1] The evidence for this is the finding of two tanged obsidian blades at Mangum Village, East Sepik Province which have been sourced to Talasea (Swadling *et al.* 1988:20). In the Talasea area this blade industry is only found in pre-Lapita contexts (Torrence, Specht and Fullagar 1990). Another tanged obsidian artefact, presumably of similar age and source, was found between the Sepik and mountains south of Wewak, East Sepik Province (Swadling *et al.* 1988:19-20).

[2] The derivation of Polynesian art from Lapita is discussed by Green (1979).

[3] Some previous examinations of the prehistory of settlement in the Pacific and the cultural and linguistic diversity of the area have had recourse to geographic and particularly biogeographic principles (see for instance Pawley 1981 and Terrell 1986). Pawley's paper makes useful suggestions of processes which may have led to linguistic diversification in Pacific Island groups. His broader attempt at a "unified" explanation for Polynesian homogeneity and Melanesian diversity in language relies too much on a postulated much greater time depth for Lapita and Austronesian settlement in Melanesia (Pawley 1981:273-275) which is not sustainable on current archaeological evidence. His hypothesis has also been challenged on linguistic grounds (Lynch 1981). Terrell (1986) uses biogeographical principles which seem to me to be far too general

in comparison with the detailed processes of specifically human migration discussed in Anthony's (1990) paper.

REFERENCES

Allen, J.
  1984   In search of the Lapita homeland. *Journal of Pacific History* 19:186-201.

Allen, J. and C. Gosden (eds)
  1991   *Report of the Lapita homeland project*. Occasional Papers in Prehistory No. 20. Canberra: Department of Prehistory, Research School of Pacific Studies, The Australian National University.

Allen, J., C. Gosden, R. Jones and J.P. White
  1988   Pleistocene dates for human occupation of New Ireland, northern Melanesia. *Nature* 331:707-709.

Allen, J., C. Gosden and J.P. White
  1989   Human Pleistocene adaptations in the tropical island Pacific: recent evidence from New Ireland, a greater Australian outlier. *Antiquity* 63:548-561.

Allen, J. and J.P. White
  1989   The Lapita homeland: some new data and an interpretation. *Journal of the Polynesian Society* 98(2):129-146.

Anson, D.
  1983   Lapita pottery of the Bismarck Archipelago and its affinities. PhD thesis, University of Sydney.
  1986   Lapita pottery of the Bismarck Archipelago and its affinities. *Archaeology in Oceania* 21:157-165.

Anthony, D.W.
  1990   Migration in archaeology: the baby and the bathwater. *American Anthropologist* 92:895-914.

Athens, J.S.
  1980   Pottery from Nan Madol, Ponape, Eastern Caroline Islands. *Journal of the Polynesian Society* 89:95-99.

Bellwood, P.S.
  1978   *Man's conquest of the Pacific*. London: Collins.
  1984   The great Pacific migration. In *Yearbook of science and the future for 1984*, pp.80-93. Encyclopaedia Britannica.

Bellwood, P. and P. Koon
  1989   'Lapita colonists leave boats unburned!' The question of Lapita links with Island Southeast Asia. *Antiquity* 63:613-622.

Best, S.
  1984   Lakeba: the prehistory of a Fijian Island. PhD thesis, University of
          Auckland. Ann Arbor: University Microfilms.
  1987   Long distance obsidian travel and possible implications for the settlement
          of Fiji. *Archaeology in Oceania* 22:31-32.

Black, S.
  1978   Polynesian Outliers: a study in the survival of small populations. In I.
          Hodder (ed.) *Simulation studies in archaeology*, pp.63-76. Cambridge:
          Cambridge University Press.

Blust, R.A.
  1976   Austronesian culture history: some linguistic inferences and their relations
          to the archaeological record. *World Archaeology* 8:19-43.

Bonhomme, T. and J. Craib
  1987   Radiocarbon dates from Unai Bapot, Saipan: implications for the
          prehistory of the Mariana Islands. *Journal of the Polynesian Society* 96:95-
          106.

Clark, R.
  1979   Language. In J.D. Jennings (ed.) *The prehistory of Polynesia*, pp.249-270.
          Cambridge, Mass.: Harvard University Press.

Craib, J.
  1983   Micronesian prehistory: an archaeological overview. *Science* 219:922-927.

Dutton, T.
  1982   Borrowing in Austronesian and Non-Austronesian languages of coastal
          South-East Mainland Papua New Guinea. In A. Halim, L. Carrington and
          S.A. Wurm (eds) *Papers from the third international conference on
          Austronesian linguistics*, vol.1: *Currents in Oceanic*, pp.109-177. Pacific
          Linguistics Series C No. 74. Canberra: Department of Linguistics,
          Research School of Pacific Studies, The Australian National University.

Golson, J.
  1977   No room at the top: agricultural intensification in the New Guinea
          Highlands. In J. Allen, J. Golson and R. Jones (eds) *Sunda and Sahul:
          Prehistoric studies in Southeast Asia, Melanesia and Australia*, pp.601-
          638. London: Academic Press.
  1989   The origins and development of New Guinea agriculture. In D.R. Harris
          and G.C. Hillman (eds) *Foraging and farming: the evolution of plant
          exploitation*, pp.678-687. London: Unwin Hyman.

Gorecki, P., M. Mabin and J. Campbell
  1991   Archaeology and geomorphology of the Vanimo coast, Papua New Guinea.
          Archaeology in Oceania 26(3):119-122.

Gosden, C., J. Allen, W. Ambrose, D. Anson, J. Golson,
R. Green, P. Kirch, I. Lilley, J. Specht and M. Spriggs
  1989   Lapita sites of the Bismarck Archipelago. *Antiquity* 63:561-586.

Grace, G.
1961   Austronesian linguistics and culture history. *American Anthropologist* 53:359-368.

Green, R.C.
1979   Early Lapita art from Polynesia and Island Melanesia: continuities in ceramic, barkcloth and tattoo decorations. In S.M. Mead (ed.) *Exploring the visual art of Oceania*, pp.13-31. Honolulu: University of Hawaii Press.
1987   Obsidian results from the Lapita sites of the Reef/Santa Cruz Islands. In W. Ambrose and J. Mummery (eds) *Archaeometry: further Australasian studies*, pp.239-249. Canberra: Department of Prehistory, Research School of Pacific Studies, The Australian National University.
1990   Lapita design analysis. The Mead system and its use: a potted history. In M. Spriggs (ed.) *Lapita design, form and composition: Proceedings of the Lapita design workshop*, Canberra, December 1988, pp.33-52. Occasional Papers in Prehistory No.19. Canberra: Department of Prehistory, Research School of Pacific Studies, The Australian National University.
1991a   The Lapita cultural complex: current evidence and proposed models. *Bulletin of the Indo-Pacific Prehistory Association* 11:295-305.
1991b   Near and remote Oceania: disestablishing 'Melanesia' in culture history. In A.K. Pawley (ed.) *Man and a half: Essays in Pacific anthropology and ethnobiology in Honour of Ralph Bulmer*, pp.491-502. Auckland: The Polynesian Society.

Hill, A.V.S. and S.W. Serjeantson (eds)
1989   *The colonization of the Pacific: a genetic trail*. Oxford: Clarendon Press.

Howells, W.
1973   *The Pacific Islanders*. London: Weidenfeld and Nicolson.

Irwin, G.J.
1980   The prehistory of Oceania: colonization and cultural change. In A. Sherratt (ed.) *The Cambridge encyclopedia of archaeology*, pp.324-332. Cambridge: Cambridge University Press.
1991   Themes in the prehistory of Coastal Papua and the Massim. In A.K. Pawley (ed.) *Man and a half: essays in Pacific anthropology and ethnobiology in Honour of Ralph Bulmer*, pp.503-510. Auckland: The Polynesian Society.

Jackson, F.H.
1986   On determining the external relationships of the Micronesian languages. In P. Geraghty, L. Carrington and S.A. Wurm (eds) *FOCAL II: Papers from the fourth international conference on Austronesian linguistics*, pp.201-238. Pacific Linguistics Series C No. 94. Canberra: Department of Linguistics, Research School of Pacific Studies, The Australian National University.

Kirch, P.V.
1986   Rethinking East Polynesian prehistory. *Journal of the Polynesian Society* 95(1):9-40.

1988a   The Talepakemalai Lapita site and Oceanic prehistory. *National Geographic Research* 4:328-342.

1988b   Long-distance exchange and island colonization: the Lapita case. *Norwegian Archaeological Review* 21(2):103-117.

Kirch, P.V., T.L. Hunt and J. Tyler
1989   A radiocarbon sequence from the Toaga Site, Ofu Island, American Samoa. *Radiocarbon* 31(1):7-13.

Kirk, R.L.
1989   Population genetic studies in the Pacific: red cell antigen, serum protein, and enzyme systems. In A.V.S. Hill and S.W. Serjeantson (eds) *The colonization of the Pacific: a genetic trail*, pp.60-119. Oxford: Clarendon Press.

Lilley, I.
1988   Prehistoric exchange across the Vitiaz Strait, Papua New Guinea. *Current Anthropology* 29(3):513-516.

Lynch, J.
1981   Melanesian diversity and Polynesian homogeneity: the other side of the coin. *Oceanic Linguistics* 20(2):95-129.

McArthur, N., I.W. Saunders and R.L. Tweedie
1976   Small population isolates: a micro-simulation study. *Journal of the Polynesian Society* 85(3):307-326.

Pawley, A.
1981   Melanesian diversity and Polynesian homogeneity: a unified explanation for language. In J. Hollyman and A. Pawley (eds) *Studies in Pacific languages and cultures in Honour of Bruce Biggs*, pp.269-309. Auckland: Linguistic Society of New Zealand.

Pawley, A. and R. Green
1973   Dating the dispersal of the Oceanic languages. *Oceanic Linguistics* 12:1-67.

Poulsen, J.
1987   *Early Tongan prehistory*, 2 vols. *Terra Australis* No.12. Canberra: Department of Prehistory, Research School of Pacific Studies, The Australian National University.

Roberts, R.G., R. Jones and M.A. Smith
1990   Thermoluminescence dating of a 50,000 year old human occupation site in northern Australia. *Nature* 345:153-156.

Ross, M.
1988   *Proto-Oceanic and the Austronesian languages of Western Melanesia*. Pacific Linguistics Series C No. 98. Canberra: Department of Linguistics, Research School of Pacific Studies, The Australian National University.

1989   Early Oceanic linguistic prehistory. *Journal of Pacific History* 24:135-149.

Serjeantson, S.W. and A.V.S. Hill
   1989   The colonization of the Pacific: the genetic evidence. In A.V.S. Hill and
           S.W. Serjeantson (eds) *The colonization of the Pacific: a genetic trail*,
           pp.286-294. Oxford: Clarendon Press.

Shutler, R. and J.C. Marck
   1975   On the dispersal of the Austronesian horticulturalists. *Archaeology and
           Physical Anthropology in Oceania* 10:81-113.

Specht, J., I. Lilley and J. Normu
   1981   Radiocarbon dates from West New Britain, Papua New Guinea. *Australian
           Archaeology* 12:13-15.

Spriggs, M.
   1984   The Lapita cultural complex: origins, distribution, contemporaries and
           successors. *Journal of Pacific History* 19(3-4):202-223.
   1989a   The dating of the Island Southeast Asian Neolithic: an attempt at
           chronometric hygiene and linguistic correlation. *Antiquity* 63:587-613.
   1990a   Dating Lapita: another view. In M. Spriggs (ed.) *Lapita design, form and
           composition: Proceedings of the Lapita design workshop*, Canberra,
           December 1988, pp.6-27. Occasional Papers in Prehistory No. 19.
           Canberra: Department of Prehistory, Research School of Pacific Studies,
           The Australian National University.

Spriggs, M. (ed.)
   1989b   The Solomon Islands as bridge and barrier in the settlement of the Pacific.
           In W.S. Ayres (ed.) *Southeast Asia and Pacific archaeology*. Pullman:
           Washington State University Press.
   1990b   *Lapita design, form and composition: Proceedings of the Lapita design
           workshop*, Canberra, December 1988. Occasional Papers in Prehistory No.
           19, Canberra: Department of Prehistory, Research School of Pacific
           Studies, The Australian National University.
   1991a   Nissan: the island in the middle. In J. Allen and C. Gosden (eds) *Report of
           the Lapita homeland project*, pp.222-243. Occasional Papers in Prehistory
           No. 20. Canberra: Department of Prehistory, Research School of Pacific
           Studies, The Australian National University.
   1991b   Lapita origins, distribution, contemporaries and successors revisited.
           Bulletin of the Indo-Pacific Prehistory Association 11:306-312.
   1992   Archaeological and linguistic prehistory in the North Solomons. In T.
           Dutton, M. Ross and D. Tryon (eds) *The language game: Papers in
           memory of Donald C. Laycock*. Pacific Linguistics Series C No. 110,
           pp.417-426. Canberra: Department of Linguistics, Research School of
           Pacific Studies, The Australian National University.
   1993   Island Melanesia, the last 10,000 years. In M. Spriggs *et al.* (eds) *A
           community of cultures*, pp.187-205. Occasional Papers in Prehistory No.
           21. Canberra: Department of Prehistory, Research School of Pacific
           Studies, The Australian National University.

Swadling, P., N. Araho and B. Ivuyo
  1991   Settlements associated with the inland Sepik-Ramu sea. *Bulletin of the Indo-Pacific Prehistory Association* 11:92-112.

Swadling, P., B.H. Schäublin, P. Gorecki and F. Tiesler
  1988   *The Sepik-Ramu: an introduction.* Port Moresby: National Museum.

Terrell, J.
  1986   *Prehistory in the Pacific Islands.* Cambridge: Cambridge University Press.

Torrence, R., J. Specht and R. Fullagar
  1990   Pompeiis in the Pacific. *Australian Natural History* 23(6):456-463.

White, J.P., J. Allen and J. Specht
  1988   Peopling the Pacific: the Lapita homeland project. *Australian Natural History* 22(9):410-416.

White, J.P. and J.F. O'Connell
  1982   *A prehistory of Australia, New Guinea and Sahul.* Sydney: Academic Press.

Wickler, S. and M. Spriggs
  1988   Pleistocene human occupation of the Solomon Islands, Melanesia. *Antiquity* 62:703-706.

Yen, D.E.
  1982   The history of cultivated plants. In R.J. May and H. Nelson (eds) *Melanesia: beyond diversity*, Vol. 1, pp.281-295. Canberra: Research School of Pacific Studies, The Australian National University.
  1985   Wild plants and domestication in Pacific Islands. In V.N. Misra and P.S. Bellwood (eds) *Recent advances in Indo-Pacific prehistory*, pp.315-326. Delhi: Oxford University Press and IBH.
  1990   Environment, agriculture and the colonisation of the Pacific. In D.E. Yen and J.M.J. Mummery (eds) *Pacific production systems*, pp.258-277. Occasional Papers in Prehistory No. 18. Canberra: Department of Prehistory, Research School of Pacific Studies, The Australian National University.

7

THE AUSTRONESIAN CONQUEST OF THE SEA — UPWIND

Adrian Horridge

This chapter discusses the history of canoe construction and rig design in the Pacific region — pre-Austronesian, Austronesian, and Southeast Asian early historical. Sailing conditions in the Pacific are described, together with sailing techniques and zones of traditionally-remembered interisland contact. Austronesian exploration is considered to have favoured sailing into the wind, with a downwind return.

INTRODUCTION

The built-up dug-out or planked canoe with an outrigger and sail has been the principal technology for survival and colonization for the sea-going peoples who spread over Island Southeast Asia and far over the Pacific for at least the past few thousand years. We deduce this from the present and presumed past distributions and structures of the canoes. With the ability to carry fire, family, dogs, chickens, tuberous roots, growing shoots and seeds by sea, the Austronesians eventually occupied the Pacific Islands, travelling into Melanesia about 3500 years ago and onwards into Polynesia. I propose to deal with two questions, whether it was in fact a problem for the early Austronesian colonists to travel against the prevailing winds and currents, and how much we can infer about their vessels.

THE SOUTHEAST ASIAN ARCHIPELAGO, AN EASY FIRST STEP

The relatively shallow waters of the continental Sunda Shelf of Southeast Asia end at a line drawn through the Straits of Lombok, northwards through the Straits of Makassar, between the island of Palawan and the remainder of the Philippines, then south of Taiwan. To the east of this line are deep water channels that have always isolated the islands of Sulawesi, the Philippines, Timor and other islands of the Moluccas. Further east we come to the shallow Sahul Shelf between New Guinea and the north coast of Australia, once a land bridge for marsupials and also for humans. Whereas land mammals and freshwater fishes were restricted by these narrow seas, humans spread from the Sunda to the Sahul Shelf at least 50,000 years ago when sea-levels were lower than now and sea-crossings were perhaps shorter as a result of the build-up of glacial ice sheets. Even so, people must have crossed at least 70 km of open sea in order to reach Sahul. We may infer that they used bamboo rafts because these are an easily constructed form of transport and they could be made with the crude stone tools then available. There is no problem about movement over these relatively enclosed seas because the winds and currents reverse every season with the monsoons.

MOVEMENTS INTO THE PACIFIC

From 5000 years ago, Island Southeast Asia was progressively colonized by people who spoke languages in the Austronesian family. These people spread southwards through the Philippines and Moluccas and eastwards into the Pacific. They made pottery and fine elbow-hafted and polished adzes. They kept pigs, dogs and chickens, but their chief characteristic was a mastery of the sea and a predisposition to spread from island to island with maritime cultures. By at least 2000 BC, according to comparative reconstructions, their technology must have included the making of pottery, bark cloth, dug-out canoes, mat sails, ropes, fishing gear and anchors. What little evidence we have, based upon the widespread construction methods of Neolithic boats, suggests that they already had a boatbuilding technology based upon lashings, protruding pierced lugs, and a hollowed base for the hull with added planks. At this stage, however, they must have adopted their own unique triangular sail and the outrigger construction. Along the margins of the large Melanesian islands they were not able to replace the local populations as they eventually did in Indonesia. Passing through Melanesia they left a distinctive incised pottery, called Lapita ware (Spriggs 1984, and this volume; Allen and White 1989). From Melanesian coastlands, about 3000 years ago, they colonized onwards to Tonga and Samoa and continued to develop their maritime cultures. By about 2500 years ago they were ready to make even longer sea voyages, with more substantial cargoes, possibly because they had by that time perfected the *double canoe*. They carried the large and varied cargoes essential for colonization, including dog, chicken, bamboo, banana, sugar cane, taro, yams, plant medicines and poisons, many fruits and tree seeds.

Travelling eastwards against the prevailing winds and currents, the Polynesians reached the Marquesas by about 200 BC. By about AD 500 they had colonized Hawaii and Easter Island, New Zealand by AD 1200, and eventually almost all of the habitable islands of the central and eastern Pacific. The golden age of occupation of new island groups was recorded in the folk memories and myths that were later written down by the earliest missionaries. Moreover, different schools of navigators in recent times kept open communication by sea within their own island groups by knowing the positions of many islands and the take-off points and shortest sea routes from one group of islands to another (Lewis 1972).

The curious fact is that, although the Austronesians carried out of Asia many cultural features of possible origin in central and southern China, such as making bark cloth, tattooing, certain decorative patterns, pottery making, adze styles, domestic pig, dog and chicken, house and granary designs and many useful plants, there is no trace of Chinese boat technology in Austronesian boats, or vice-versa. Similarly, there is little trace of the Pacific boats among the relatives of the Austronesians in Mainland Southeast Asia. This supports the idea that those details of the boat designs that are characteristic of the Austronesians were adopted in the islands at or after the time that they left Mainland Asia. After all, the combination of outrigger and Oceanic triangular sail is not suitable for lakes or rivers. The peculiarities of the single-outrigger canoes of Melanesia, Micronesia and Polynesia very likely had their origin in pre-Austronesian times in what are now Indonesia and the Philippines.

BOAT CONSTRUCTION BEFORE THE AUSTRONESIANS

Nothing contradicts the view that excellent sailing rafts and sewn boats existed in the Indo-Malaysian Archipelago long before the Austronesian ancestors are thought to have moved out of Taiwan. The earliest edge-ground axe-like stone tools that could have made a crude dug-out canoe date from more than 20,000 years ago in Australia and 30,000 years ago in Japan. Humans were obliged to cross the sea to reach Australia, perhaps at first on bamboo rafts and later in dug-out canoes. Bamboo rafts are traditional over much of Indonesia and Melanesia as far as Fiji. Other lightweight timbers for rafts, such as *Erythrina* which is still used for outrigger floats, are available on the shoreline. Most of the boatbuilding timbers are also extremely widespread and must have been spread by humans, for only some species have seeds that are viable after floating in sea-water. Also, boat technology and agriculture are interconnected because the production of domestic hybrids depends on transporting parent stocks which would otherwise not be brought together.

RELATIONS WITH THE INDIAN OCEAN

Most likely the earliest trade routes of the Indian Ocean developed about 5000 years ago between the Indus Valley and the Persian Gulf, possibly contemporary with initial Austronesian expansion in Southeast Asia. However, Indian Ocean boatbuilding seems to have contributed nothing to Austronesian designs until effectively historical times. Whether the original Austronesian and Indian Ocean hull was a dug-out log extended upwards by a plank or two, or whether it was built entirely of planks, the seams must have been sewn. It is astonishing how widespread were sewn planks, over Europe, Asia and Oceania, and how long they persisted into modern times, with interesting variants. We can assume that this common heritage extended to Southeast Asia and that the Austronesians also acquired it. In early Egypt, boatbuilders evolved another technique to hold planks edge-to-edge by using flat tenons embedded in slots in the edges of the planks and then locked in with transverse wooden pins. In Mesopotamia and the Indus Valley they used dowels or treenails within carved hardwood planks which were placed edge-to-edge and then sewn. These additional techniques must have been very ancient but they are linked to the use of bronze tools.

The fixed mast, dowelling techniques,[1] the quarter rudder and the trapezoid sail appear to have spread eastwards into Indonesia from the Indian Ocean during the past 2000 years, since the initiation of trade through the Straits of Malacca. Before the arrival of western explorers these details spread no further than the early trade routes to the Philippines and New Guinea.

Theories that Austronesian rigs were derived from those of the Indian Ocean, or even from Egypt, are mistaken because the Austronesians had left Mainland Asia long before contacts spread eastwards. On the contrary, the westward spread of the Austronesian triangular sail into the Indian Ocean about 200 BC provides us with the probable origin of the Arab triangular lateen sail that spread into Egypt and even into the Mediterranean by late classical times, say AD 200. A thousand years later the Portuguese adopted the lateen on the mizzen masts of their caravels, enabling them to manoeuvre closer to the wind and reach the Pacific.

Although influences from the Indian Ocean were too late to influence the Pacific Austronesians, Sanskrit words and possibly some rigging techniques could have started to spread east of Peninsular Malaysia by 200 BC. Trade routes were also open between Vietnam and eastern Indonesia about 200 BC, as shown by the distribution of the Dong Son bronze drums along the natural sea route dictated by the monsoons in the South China and Java Seas. Recent excavations at Sembiran in Bali have also revealed evidence of drum casting and deposits of South Asian rouletted ware pottery, most likely dated before AD 200 (Ardika and Bellwood 1991). Annual trade between China and India through the Malacca Straits had opened by about 200 BC. Perhaps by that time Austronesian sailors were regularly carrying cloves and cinnamon to India and Sri Lanka, and perhaps even as far as the coast of Africa in boats with outriggers. Certainly they have left numerous traces in canoe design, rigs, outriggers and fishing techniques, and a mention in Greek literature (Christie 1957).

About 1300 years ago or less (Adelaar, this volume), Austronesian-speaking people from Indonesia reached Madagascar and some of the small islands off the east coast of Africa, at that time all apparently uninhabited. Although they later mixed with African Bantu people they preserved their languages and canoe styles. Whether they navigated in both directions in short stages along the coasts of Africa and South Asia, or directly across the Indian Ocean, is unknown, but both routes are probable. Not all the islands of the Indian Ocean were colonized; for example, the Mascarene group (remember how the dodo survived in seclusion there) and the Seychelles were not inhabited when occupied by the French in the seventeenth century, although they were known to explorers and pirates before that. The incomplete coverage suggests that the Malay wanderers did not regularly cross the central Indian Ocean, where we find none of the folklore of navigation and voyaging that was abundant until recently among Pacific Islanders.

THE AUSTRONESIAN CONTRIBUTION

Rafts, skin boats, dug-out canoes and particularly sewn boats were all clearly so widespread over Asia when archaeological and historical records began that they must predate the Austronesians. We might try to list the features of characteristic recent Austronesian boats and decide which ones can be considered as uniquely Austronesian.

The basis of all Austronesian boats, beyond the simple dug-out and the raft, is the lashed-lug construction technique, in which projecting perforated lugs are left in the dug-out base of the hull and on the additional planks which are sewn on to its sides (Figure 1). Thwarts and flexible ribs are lashed down to these lugs, so further compressing the planks added to the hull. The same lashing technique holds down the transverse booms for the outrigger and may well have originated for that purpose. The ends are each closed by a stem and stern piece carved from a fork which runs a little way along the sides of the hull. Early Austronesian boats did not necessarily have outriggers; excellent fishing boats and especially war-canoes with a single hull persist ethnographically in Botel Tobago and as the *mon* of the Solomons. This lashed-lug technique spread into the Pacific, sometimes with stitches through holes in the planks or through projections from the planks, and sometimes strengthened by bindings between projections on the inside of the planks. The seams could be packed with absorbent fibre that expanded when wet, sometimes the plank edges were polished to a perfect fit by rubbing them together, and sometimes the seams were overlaid by padded laths under the stitches. Until the curved metal chisel or other tools became available for drilling straight dowel holes, the joints were sewn and sealed with resin. This technique is widespread from Hawaii to Madagascar and throughout Micronesia, Polynesia and Indonesia. It was modified in only two ways; (a) by modernization; (b) by a different, probably very ancient, tradition of long thin canoes without outriggers in which men often stand to propel the boat

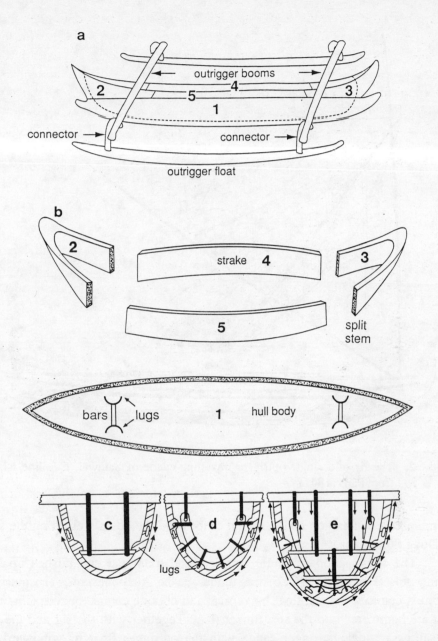

Figure 1. Basic construction of the Austronesian lashed-lug built-up outrigger canoe:
(a) The 5-part canoe; (b) exploded view of the upper hull; (c) (d) and (e) sections of hulls of increasing complexity.
(c) Downward compression; (d) arch compression; (e) combined downward and flexible rib construction. The details and variations on these themes were different for different island groups.
(The drawings are based on modern Indonesian canoes — the use of dowels is not a prehistoric feature, as indicated in the text.)

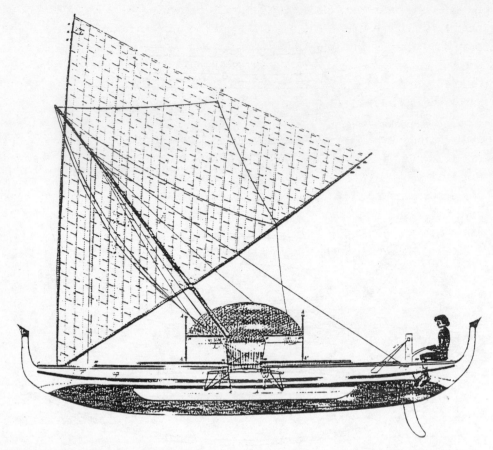

Figure 2.   The rig of a single-outrigger travelling canoe of Satawal, Caroline Islands, from Pâris (1841).

along, e.g. Asian dragon boats, Asmat canoes and the boats incised on the sides of Dong Son drums.

The combination of single outrigger and triangular sail pushed up by a tilting pole (Horridge 1986:86) was unique to the Austronesians. The outrigger boom is connected to the float by vertical and oblique connector rods (Figure 1) that are hammered into the soft timber float. Together with the rig and the way of sailing a single-outrigger canoe with the outrigger float to windward, we observe that the Austronesians had a sailing machine with a combination of features that, once perfected, would always have to be built and sailed in the same way. The two-boom triangular sail (see Figure 2) is also unique to the Austronesians in its Austronesian form. This sail pivots on its point, can be tilted fore and aft to steer the boat (as on a windsurfer), is spread transversely across the boat to go downwind, and when the sheet is pulled in and towards the stern the boat is almost self-steering fairly close to the wind. There was therefore no need to invent the fixed rudder, and the sail can be pushed up with a movable prop so there was no need to invent the pulley or the fixed mast with fixed shrouds and stays. In fact, the rig does not allow shrouds and is therefore totally different in principle from the rigs with fixed mast that might have spread eastwards much later from the Indian Ocean.

When we ask why the outrigger canoe plus tilting sail technology was evolved, there are so many interacting factors that the only quick answer seems to be that there was no other solution to all the simultaneous challenges that had to be met. This answer itself is sufficient to explain the remarkably conservative copying of the successful designs for generation after generation. Some of the numerous technical factors which make the technology appropriate are as follows:

1. Available natural materials are wood, which is good in compression, and plaited fibres such as rotan or palm fibre sennit which are good in tension.
2. Cellulose-based materials are essentially weak for construction and therefore loads must be distributed, avoiding stress concentrations. This consideration governed the whole design.
3. Cellulose-based materials rot and the whole boat has to be dismantled for replacement of parts and sometimes for drying out when temporarily not in use.
4. At sea the main engineering problem is to avoid fatigue fractures caused by the working of the waves and wind, especially if the outrigger is in the water. The solution was to use fibrous materials and to make the structure flexible, more like a basket chair than a rigid four-legged table.
5. As with an eggshell, the double curvature of the hull gives an unexpected bonus in strength and stiffness.
6. Without a pulley (which they did not have) the size of the sail is limited by its weight when wet and by the strength of the pole that pushes it up. To maximize the compression strength of the pole, it was free to pivot on its end so that lateral forces were all transferred to the stay in tension and there were no bending forces on the pole.
7. Planks swell in width when wet and the lashing fibre shrinks, so the lashed-lug construction tightened up at sea; compressing the planks together.

The basic principles of sewn and lashed-lug construction are remarkably homogeneous across the whole Austronesian range, except for subsequent influences that have spread eastwards from the Indian Ocean and as a result of the introduction of metal tools and pulleys into Indonesia and the Philippines in historic times. A significant detail is that traditional Pacific canoes had sewn seams with the internal lugs often taking the form of a raised ridge along the whole seam. In the Southeast Asian Archipelago sewing was replaced over the past 2000 years by edge-to-edge planking with internal dowels. Another detail is that Pacific traditional canoes have several short straight sticks hammered into the outrigger float to connect it to the outrigger boom. In contrast, in Indonesia several later designs of connector were adapted to the use of giant bamboo for the floats. In the Southeast Asian Archipelago, except for Madura, the triangular rig gave way to the trapezoid sail on a fixed mast and this meant also the adoption of the fixed quarter rudder. The limit of spread of these technological changes corresponds well to the limit of spread of metal tools and other goods by traders from Asia. The conclusion is that there was little opportunity or reason for technological change in the Pacific after the basic design was taken east of Indonesia.

There are also social factors. Like a house or fish-trap, a boat is a shared structure from which many gain an advantage. In Austronesian communities, typically, every maritime village has its own boat design and they say that the details of construction have been handed down from their ancestors. The apprentices learn the exact way to build every detail and the conservative attitude is reinforced by memorized chants that must be repeated without error, and by universal belief that any deviation from tradition would cause a disaster at sea. Because the use of them is dangerous, boats are particularly conservative structures and all cultures adhere to their own proven designs. Rigs are more easily copied than hull structures (Horridge 1986). When changes in design are introduced they are not admitted. In consequence, boatbuilding techniques may survive unchanged for 1000 years or may be quickly modified in a single generation, as happens when designs are transferred from elsewhere. There is a negative side to this valuable conservation of the best available designs: inventions that are not immediately needed do not get invented, witness the pulley, the fixed rudder, the keel, the jib sail, the fixed mast or the multiple mast in the Pacific.

SAILING CONDITIONS IN THE PACIFIC

Many early accounts describe canoes more than 15 m long carrying 30 to 50 people and a few larger ones carrying more than 100 people. Other reports mention the high speeds of lightly loaded canoes, about 10 knots with the wind on the beam. There are also many mentions of voyages of more than 800 km, and flotillas of many canoes. One of the critical details was the sealed hull, others the warm water, the availability of rain and the use of dried provisions for long journeys. Pâris (1841) mentions that breadfruit was fermented to make it sugary and then baked into hard cakes which kept indefinitely at sea. In the tropical Pacific, the flying fish leap into the boat at night, especially if an oil-nut can be lit to make a light, as modern voyagers describe. If we survey the whole of Polynesia, Micronesia and Melanesia, there are only a few areas that would have been out of reach of exploration with such boats as we know of, equipped as we know they could have been. Recently there have been successful re-enactments of several of the voyages described in myths (Finney 1985; Irwin 1989). The difficult laps were on either side of Easter Island and to islands around New Zealand, and yet people successfully reached even the Chatham Islands in prehistoric times.

Making use of periods of mixed winds (Finney 1985), a month's journey of exploration eastwards between 20°N and 20°S in the Pacific Ocean would easily cover about 1000 km. To be on the safe side a drift back downwind might take two months. Carbohydrate for three months for eight people would weigh about 300 kg, which is not an unreasonable load for a 12 m single-outrigger canoe. Double canoes would carry a tonne with ease, but because of the larger investment in construction labour they were more suitable for carrying family, plants, animals and cargo to places already discovered.

Voyaging was always seasonal, even when not forced by the winds, because the stars are seasonal. Charts of the tropical Pacific prepared for the days of sail show the trade winds blowing fairly strongly but not consistently all the year from the north-east to the north of the equator and from the south-east to the south of the equator. However, from October to June over the whole area of Melanesia and Polynesia to the south of the equator, from New Guinea to the Tuamotus, the winds blow from the north-east about as frequently as they do from the south-east. With normal trade winds the prevailing surface currents average 15 to 25 km per day (Figure 3) and can assist sailing downwind, but are not very significant for a boat that covers 50-150 km per day. As far east as about Tonga, westerly winds accompany the cyclones in December to March. In Micronesia the winds are more consistently from the east or north-east and cyclones are less predictable. In Cook's account of Tahiti, Tupaia said that his people knew very well how to make use of the westerly winds (Lewis 1972: 297). In Polynesia, westerlies are more likely in December and January. Bearing all this in mind, the obvious time to set out eastwards into the unknown would have been the beginning of December, starting with a westerly wind, and always with the expectation of an easy return home.

Voyages by outrigger canoe would ultimately have been limited by the sea-water surface temperature. Apart from New Zealand, the Austronesian colonization was all within the isotherm of 21°C (70°F) in the warmest season. The Austronesian agricultural crops were mostly limited to this zone, and in New Zealand different storage methods and crops, such as hardy varieties of sweet potato, were used at the limits imposed by cold. The whole culture —

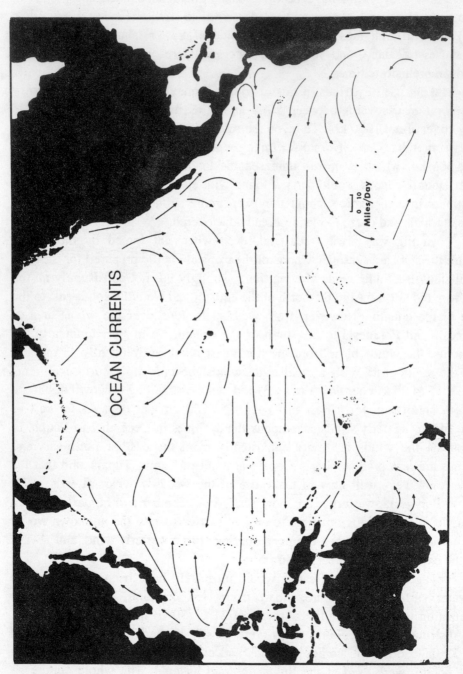

Figure 3.   Drift currents in the Pacific with the length of each arrow indicating velocity in nautical miles per day. (1 km approx. = 0.625 nautical mile). Seasonal differences (given by Lewis 1972:102) are small.

plants, housing, dress, boat design and aquatic lifestyle — was adapted to the warm terrestrial climate.

Boat size was not a problem, as large canoes of 25 m long could carry 30 or 50 people plus cargo. Speed was not a problem either as the small single outrigger canoes (the flying proas of Micronesia) could do up to 20 knots but were limited to a few weeks sailing. The problem was that such speeds would quickly smash up a large canoe in a heavy sea because the construction materials could not stand the repeated stresses. The upper limit was set by the scale effect acting on the limits of the materials, as for wooden aircraft, windmills and all similar structures. The best compromise seems to have been the travelling canoe of medium size, large enough for one or two families.

THE SEAWAYS WERE OPEN, ONCE EXPLORED

For the end of the 18th century, when the major Western explorations and descriptions had been completed but the local traditions were not destroyed, we have firm accounts from most parts of the Pacific. When these are brought together they reveal an open seaway in a series of separate stages from Indonesia and the Philippines to the extreme east of Polynesia, and north/south to Hawaii and New Zealand. Lewis (1972) pointed out that almost all the Pacific islands can be reached by sea crossings of no more than 500 km, and his analysis of navigation methods shows that planned passages could be much longer. Information about inter-island movement and trade has been summarized from old accounts for each area by Haddon and Hornell (1936-38), along with sizes of boats, performance and numbers of people carried. Many of the same data, and new material, are given by Lewis (1972).

Let us start with the Palau (Belau) Islands, a group 100 km across, only about six days sailing by local canoe from Mindanao in the Philippines. The long-distance *kaep* canoes for travel within the group were single-outriggers up to 10 m long. Stone money was carried regularly from Palau to Yap, and there is a tradition that *trepang* was taken to Chinese merchants in the Philippines. There were Micronesian colonies on Tobi and Sonsorol, almost in the Moluccas, and traditions of voyages southwards to the coast of New Guinea and of raiding parties coming the other way. All the island groups of Micronesia had regular trade, visits or wars within the main groups, with many traditions of war parties venturing further afield. From Palau there was a continuous route for trade and war through the Carolines past Puluwat, then from Kosrae to Jaluit in the Marshall Islands, then to Tarawa in Kiribati (Gilbert Islands), each stage with a slightly different type of double-ended long-distance single-outrigger canoe (Haddon and Hornell 1936-38, I:439, quoting Hambruch). The Marshall Islanders raided other islands from Kosrae in the west to the Ellice Islands

(Tuvalu) in the south (Haddon and Hornell 1936-38, I:439). There was no longer a tradition of exploration, but instead there were extremely well-organized schools of navigators who learned the inter-island routes and the seasons for travel. The large single-outrigger canoes sail more safely into the wind than downwind, but go fastest and most steadily with the wind on the beam. In the Carolines the *popo* canoes ran regular passenger routes (mainly north and south) over a total range of 3000 km and every year parties of them visited the Marianas (Haddon and Hornell 1936-38, I:438, from an account of the Freycinet voyage). It is an interesting detail that in Micronesia the navigation classes for learning star tracks were conducted on the beaches facing *east* to mark the rise of the stars (Haddon and Hornell 1936-38, I:439).

Another route to the south lay along the island chain past New Ireland and the Solomons to the Santa Cruz islands, to Fiji and on to Tonga. The boats here were more solid single outriggers. From Tonga the route continued into Polynesia to Samoa, thence to Tahiti, from where there were routes in all directions, eastwards to the Tuamotus and thence to the Marquesas, northwards to Hawaii, south to the Cook Islands. From Tonga and Samoa there were traditions of raiding parties to the Santa Cruz islands, carrying Polynesian populations to the Polynesian Outliers such as Tikopia. There is a tradition that many generations ago there were voyages between Tahiti and Hawaii, and between Rarotonga and the Marquesas. Tangi'ia-nui was a great voyager who claimed to be familiar with island groups from Fiji to Easter Island and who ended his life in Rarotonga. Tupaia, the Raiatean high priest friend of Cook, knew of many islands in the Australs, Societies, Cooks, Tuamotus, and westwards as far as Fiji. According to some Maori traditions, Kupe from Tahiti discovered New Zealand about the 10th century. Toi and Whatonga followed 8-10 generations later and then Nuku sailed there via Rarotonga with four canoes. For a while, mainly in the early nineteenth century, until they disappeared, these canoe journeys persisted within the island groups in the central and eastern Pacific, and a few survived into the twentieth century (Lewis 1972).

The voyages we learn about in Polynesian traditional myths were different from those of Micronesia, being less frequent, over longer distances, and related to the original exploration rather than to regular routes. The Polynesian long-distance vessel was the double canoe in which a voyage would be more likely to carry plants, seeds, women and animals, so requiring more time and expense to prepare. The only surviving and regular long-distance inter-island trade that we know of from eighteenth and early nineteenth century accounts of Polynesia occurred in the Societies and Tuamotus in eastern Polynesia and in the Fiji-Tonga-Samoa triangle in western Polynesia.

THOR HEYERDAHL, GOING WESTWARD

The maps of currents (Figure 3) and winds of the Pacific Ocean show the trade winds that blow from east to west over the area of warm water encompassing most of the Pacific Islands, and steady currents of 8 to 35 km per day that flow in the same direction. Driftwood, rafts and square-rigged ships have been moved on these currents, witness the Kon-Tiki balsa raft (Heyerdahl 1978:185). In 1913, the *Dagonar*, a derelict sailing ship, took only 170 days to go 8000 km from Peru to the Tuamotus in this current (Hornell 1945). Heyerdahl's basic premise was that early boats *followed* winds and currents, but he thought only of rafts and reed boats. Rafts and reed boats were known world-wide in Neolithic times so people could have drifted eventually to many unlikely places, and perhaps from Peru to Polynesia. Easter Island was known to the Incas and archaeological remains there strongly suggest that some aspects of South American culture and plants spread there, and perhaps into other parts of eastern Polynesia as well (Heyerdahl 1978). Probably the Asiatic chicken was taken to Ecuador via Polynesia, and the South American sweet potato, some cotton, gourds, and other plants travelled westwards by balsa raft into Polynesia. The arguments have raged for years but the evidence for transport in both directions before AD 1500 gets firmer every decade. Drifting downwind on an inefficient boat, however, is an inefficient way to colonize new islands because there is no return (Irwin 1992).

Just drifting in the Kuro Siwo current from Japan to the northwest coast of America takes 3-4 months, and many Japanese fishermen have survived this journey over the past few centuries (Hornell 1945). There are Japanese words in the coastal dialects of the northwest American Indians and ancient planked boats of Austronesian type on the islands off the coast of California. The current continues southwards along the Californian coast almost to the equator. One of the most controversial archaeological records is the discovery of the Valdivia complex on the coast of Ecuador, with pottery dated about 3200 BC resembling that in northeast Asia at that time (Estrada and Meggers 1961). In my view, this Pacific crossing was possible as a way of no return, and therefore unattractive, but some plants, the chicken (Langdon 1989) and craftsmen skills may have travelled this way. As a branch on this line, the current turns westward well out to sea off the coast of Oregon and regularly brought pine logs from the northwest American coast to Hawaii where they were stored and used for building large canoes. Possibly people also went that way occasionally, long before the Austronesians moved into Polynesia.

Rafts were known in the Marianas, Yap, Fiji and Melanesia when Western explorers arrived. There was a persistent tradition of sea-going sailing rafts in Tonga, there were transport rafts in Mangareva, and in New Zealand there were reed boats 18 m long made of bulrushes and flax. Bamboo rafts were commonly used in Japan, Taiwan and Indonesia, some with steering by fore and aft centre boards as in South America. Rafts were Neolithic if not older and perhaps humans are today all members of one species because gene-pools were continually mixed by raft crews.

EXPLORATION WAS UPWIND

Sufficient has been said to demonstrate that in the Pacific, *once the way was known*, there were sufficient travellers. Maybe a voyage was not repeated for a century or so, but so long as the route by wave patterns and stars was remembered by the traditions in the schools of navigators, the way was open. It was fear of people, not fear of the sea, that kept the canoes near home.

Let us now consider the exploration of the unknown with the available boats. For much of the year, the winds anywhere in the Pacific came from the direction of unknown islands, so that flotsam would float ashore *proving that more land lay to windward*. The earliest Austronesian colonists in the Pacific were in the situation of the Vikings on the coast of Norway, the Portuguese and later the English and the Dutch, faced by the prevailing south-west winds of the Atlantic. The situation creates a continual stimulus for sailors. In periods when the winds are reversed you can sail out to sea if you are confident that you will be blown back near home, or past home to islands downwind from home. Irwin (1989, 1992) deals with the questions of accessibility and winds in great detail, and stresses that the known art of latitude sailing fits well into a pattern of progressive exploration eastwards with a carefully remembered return at each stage. The only condition is that you have seaworthy boats that sail reasonably well to windward, or even poorly to windward if time is not pressing. You can spend time, maybe centuries, improving your boats and ability to survive at sea. Even in the early exploration phase, colonists must have had fast watertight boats to carry food, plant shoots and seeds.

When we look at the large Micronesian single-outrigger canoes of historical times (see cover photograph), we notice the triangular sail, the outrigger construction, the double-ended arrangement for tacking, the deep well and sealed hulls for safety at sea, and the high speed when travelling light on the best point of sailing. Anson (1740-4), quoted by Haddon and Hornell (1936-38, I:415), noted that the single outriggers of the Marianas were "designed to sail as close as possible to the wind", and "by the flatness of their lee side they lie much closer to the wind than any other vessel known, and have the advantage of being able to go faster than the wind, like the sails of a windmill." He gave the speed as 20 knots for a hull of 12 metres. Lewis (1972:269) gives the average performance of a single outrigger as 75°-80° off the trade wind. Pâris (1841) described how the single outriggers of the Carolines sailed best when close to the wind and that otherwise they had difficulty in staying on course, even with the wind on the quarter. Pâris also reported that the double canoe of Tonga (the *kalia*) sailed badly with the wind behind, and the Tongan single outrigger (the *hamatafua*) was difficult to handle with the wind at the side or behind but easy when sailing as close to the wind as possible. Basically the triangular sail pivoted on a universal joint and behaved like that of a windsurfer, self-steering when balanced on the wind, but the hull sailed closer to the wind than a windsurfer because it gripped the water. The modern windsurfer gives some idea of the performance of a triangular sail on a flat hull; a canoe with the lee side flattened must have been an improvement on a windsurfer, if the materials could withstand the stresses.

Downwind from an undiscovered island there is a scent of land and an interference pattern of the wind-created waves converging behind the island, besides flotsam on the surface, as numerous sailors have described. Therefore Nature assists by providing clues of land on the approach side of the island exactly where they are needed. In contrast, remember how Heyerdahl's Kon-Tiki raft (with a square sail) ended its journey by crashing helplessly on the windward side of a reef. That is not the way to explore or colonize. Sensible seamen approach land upwind and lay-off until they find a calm landing, as you could certainly do in an outrigger canoe with a tilting triangular sail. Those hypothetical younger sons of chiefs, looking for new land, had to sail eastwards because that is the direction their boats would naturally take them on the least foolhardy explorations with expectation of safe return. Let me add that, apart from the early explorers, who saw Pacific craft first-hand, it has been the small-boat sailors, notably Lewis (1972), Finney (1985) and Irwin (1989, 1992), who have the correct interpretation of Pacific sailing and colonization.

CONCLUSION

The problem of how the Pacific was colonized against prevailing winds and currents is solved if we accept that the earliest path-finders had boats of similar design to the fast, long-distance single-outrigger with a tilting triangular sail, because these boats sail best a little upwind or with the wind on the beam. They must have had these outrigger canoes, otherwise they could never have made exploration probes and then colonized, and exploration is an easier proposition than subsequent colonization. For several reasons, the natural way to go is eastwards with the aid of occasional westerly winds.

NOTES

[1] Dowelling was used for carpentry joins as early as 5000 BC in China (Chang 1986:211, for the Neolithic site of Hemudu), but there is no evidence that the technique was used in boatbuilding.

REFERENCES

Allen, J. and J.P. White
  1989   The Lapita homeland: some new data and an interpretation. *Journal of the Polynesian Society* 98:129-146.

Ardika, I.W. and P. Bellwood
  1991   Sembiran: the beginnings of Indian contact with Bali. *Antiquity* 65:221-232.

Chang, K.C.
  1986   *The archaeology of ancient China.* 4th edn. New Haven: Yale University Press.

Christie, A.
  1957   An obscure passage from the Periplus. *Bulletin of the School of Oriental & African Studies* 19:345-353.

Estrada, E. and B.J. Meggers
  1961   A complex of traits of probable trans-Pacific origin on the coast of Ecuador. *American Anthropologist* 63:913-939.

Finney, B.R.
  1985   Anomalous westerlies, El Niño and the colonization of Polynesia. *American Anthropologist* 87:9-26.

Haddon, A.C. and J. Hornell
  1936-38 *Canoes of Oceania.* 3 volumes. Honolulu, Hawaii: Bishop Museum Press, Special Publication Nos. 27, 28 and 29.

Heyerdahl, T.
  1978   *Early man and the ocean.* London: Allen and Unwin.

Hornell, J.
  1945   Was there pre-Columbian contact between the peoples of Oceania and South America? *Journal of the Polynesian Society* 54:167-191.

Horridge, G.A.
  1986   The evolution of Pacific canoe rigs. *Journal of Pacific History* 21:83-99.

Irwin, G.
  1989   Against, across and down the wind: a case for the systematic exploration of the remote Pacific Islands. *Journal of the Polynesian Society* 98:167-206.

1992   *The prehistoric exploration and colonization of the Pacific*. Cambridge: Cambridge University Press.

Langdon, R.
1989   When the blue-egg chickens come home to roost. *Journal of Pacific History* 24:164-192.

Lewis, D.H.
1972   *We, the navigators*. Canberra: Australian National University Press.

Pâris, François Edmund
1841   *Essai sur la construction navale des peuples extra-européens*. Paris: Bertrand.

Spriggs, M.
1984   The Lapita cultural complex: origins, contemporaries and successors. *Journal of Pacific History* 19:202-223.

8

DOMESTICATED AND COMMENSAL MAMMALS OF AUSTRONESIA AND THEIR HISTORIES

Colin P. Groves

A discussion is here presented of the origins and histories of the main domestic and commensal mammals of the Austronesian world. Some, such as the water buffalo, the dog and a number of rodent species, were introduced from Mainland Asian sources. Others, such as Bali cattle and the Celebes pig, were domesticated locally in Indonesia.

INTRODUCTION

A variety of animal species have travelled with Austronesians on their migrations through Southeast Asia, and some have gone further into the Pacific. In this paper I will discuss the ecology of some of these species, trying to understand their geographical distributions and the natures of their associations with Austronesian-speaking people. I will try also to identify the regions of their aboriginal wild distributions. In this way we can possibly make some statements about prehistoric Austronesian culture, subsistence and migration history.

PARTNER IN THE PADI FIELDS: THE WATER-BUFFALO

Water-buffalo are so closely associated with wet rice cultivation that it is difficult to see how an efficient wet rice (*sawah*) economy could function without them. Their broad splaying hooves spread their weight out in swampy ground and they plod through the soft ricefields without sinking in as cattle would, hauling ploughs behind them and at the same time puddling the soil. If they need to spend long hours soaking in ponds or streams, that is a small price to pay for their services.

Asian buffaloes (*Bubalus arnee*), of which the water-buffalo is the domestic form, are restricted to floodplain and deltaic regions. Genuinely wild representatives still occur in Assam, especially along the Brahmaputra River; in the Mahanadi Delta extending inland to Bastar district; and on the borders of Nepal (Map 1). Until the turn of the century they also lived in the Sunderbans of Bengal, and the Mughal Emperors hunted them in the Indus Valley. Wild-living buffaloes in Sri Lanka, on the upper Chindwin, in the Chao Phraya Valley of Thailand and (until at least the 1920s) in the Irrawaddy Delta of Burma are also

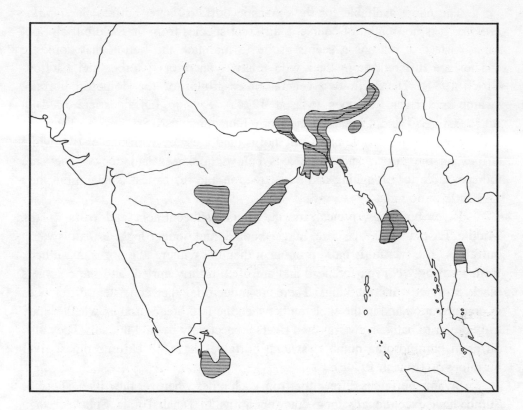

Map 1.   The distribution, within the past century, of wild Asian buffalo (*Bubalus arnee*). The distributional areas marked represent Sri Lanka, the Bastar region, Mahanadi Delta, southeast Nepal, Sunderbans, Brahmaputra Valley, upper Chindwin, Irrawaddy Delta, and Chao Phraya Valley. Evidence also suggests that wild buffalo existed in southern China within the last millennium.

probably truly wild, although it remains possible that they may be feral. Those of Vietnam, Cambodia, Lampung, the Miri River in Sarawak and the Baluran National Park in Java are almost certainly feral; a wild buffalo was present in Java up to the early Holocene (remains occur in the Sampung Cave) but has since become locally extinct.

Names available for subspecies of the wild Asian buffalo, if they should prove distinguishable, are:

> *Bubalus arnee arnee* — Bengal
> *Bubalus arnee fulvus* — Upper Assam
> *Bubalus arnee septentrionalis* — Sunderbans
> *Bubalus arnee migona* — Yala, Sri Lanka

Other populations which may be distinct are so far unnamed.

The name available for the domestic buffalo (water-buffalo) is *Bubalus bubalis*. It is not really, of course, a different species from the wild buffalo, but for a variety of reasons it seems useful to maintain the fiction that domestic species are different from their wild relatives/ancestors (Corbet and Clutton-Brock 1984). There are two general breed-groups of the domestic buffalo: swamp and river buffaloes (Mason 1974a). Swamp buffaloes are bred in Southeast Asia and China, northeastern India and also Sri Lanka. They are heavily built, with simple crescentic horns, and are grey with one or two white stripes on the throat, and white legs below the knees and hocks. They are indispensable for ploughing and other traction and their meat is eaten, but they give little or no milk.

River buffaloes, typical for the Indian subcontinent and parts of the Middle East and Europe, are longer-bodied and longer-legged than swamp buffaloes. The sacrum is more prominent than the withers, the horns curve back from a strongly convex forehead and are often tightly curled, and the colour is black, without white markings. There are numerous other consistent differences in conformation and in the skeleton between the two breed-groups; whether they truly prefer to bathe in swamps and rivers respectively I could not say. They also differ in chromosome number: swamp buffaloes have 48 chromosomes, river buffaloes 50 (Mason 1974b).

Swamp buffaloes differ little from each other wherever they live. Those of Sumba have exceptionally long, outswept horns. In Tanah Toraja, Sulawesi, they are very large and often piebald. In Thailand, Yunnan and South Sulawesi there are high frequencies of albinism. However, there are no true breeds. On the other hand, river buffaloes have given rise to a number of highly specialized breeds such as the Murrah, which is an excellent milker, and they have been exported to Egypt, Brazil and the West Indies. They are also replacing swamp buffaloes in parts of Thailand, Malaysia and the Philippines. The replacement by river buffaloes of the more primitive swamp type seems to have been going on for a long time; we not only have the oddity of the swamp type surviving in a peripheral region such as Sri Lanka, but the Toda buffaloes of the Nilgiri Hills are of swamp type, separated from the swamp buffaloes of Southeast Asia by most of the Indian subcontinent where only river buffaloes are used. Prehistoric depictions of domestic buffaloes with the characteristic crescentic horns of the swamp form are known from Mohenjo-Daro and from Ur, dating from the mid-third to early second millennia BC.

The wild Indian buffalo resembles an enormous version of the domestic swamp buffalo and is surely its direct ancestor, although its chromosomes are unknown. Mean skull lengths for different wild populations are as follows (in millimetres, followed by sample size in brackets):

	Male	Combined	Female
Assam	603 (13)		585 (12)
Bastar, Orissa	574 (2)		555 (3)
Thailand	556 (5)		545 (8)
Nepal		557 (4)	
Sri Lanka		539 (6)	

In comparison, domestic buffaloes have skull lengths around 450-500 mm, the river breeds tending to be smaller than most swamp buffaloes.

In order to get some idea of which wild population most resembled the domestic ones in skull form, and so forms the most suitable candidate for their ancestor (always assuming that river and swamp types do have a common domestic ancestor), I have undertaken a discriminant analysis on craniometric variables. The variables used were greatest skull length, biorbital breadth, postorbital breadth, occipital breadth (greatest), occipital breadth (constriction), breadth of horn base, nasal breadth posterior, nasal breadth anterior, nasal length, and basal skull length. It should be explained that not all measurements were available for every skull.

The results are shown in Figure 1. The first discriminant function (horizontal) accounts for 67.5 per cent of the total variance and is in part at least dependent on size, but also contrasts wide nasal tip with narrow nasal base and emphasizes relatively slender horn bases. The second function, which accounts for 14.6 per cent of total variance, contrasts a broad occipital constriction and broad nasals with a narrow postorbital constriction and short nasals. No other function accounted for more than 8 per cent of the total variance.

In Figure 1, means and one-standard-deviation circles have been plotted for all geographic samples, and individual specimens from other regions have been plotted separately. Assam, Nepal and Thailand are well separated from Bihar and the domestic samples, with individual specimens from central India (Bastar) and Sri Lanka falling between. The fact that the Bihar/Orissa sample (centring on the Mahanadi delta) is the only wild one whose dispersion widely overlaps that of the domestic samples suggests that, if skull form is any guide, this is the best bet for a wild ancestor. Did this important component of the wet-rice complex come from that region of India? This would be surprising, given that this is well outside the Austronesian area and that the oldest putative domestic buffaloes come from Neolithic sites in southern China, although northeastern India is within the Austroasiatic (Munda-speaking) area. In what follows, we will see whether there is any analogy for such a distribution and inferred place of origin.

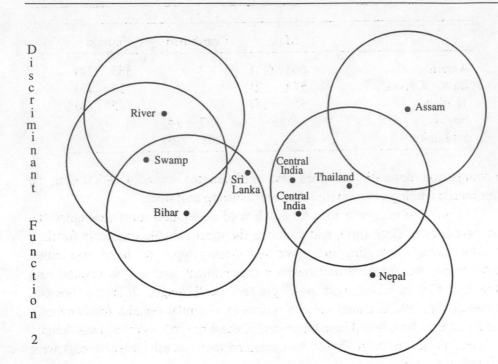

Figure 1.   Discriminant analysis of cranial measurements in Asian buffaloes. The circles represent one-standard-deviation limits of samples from Assam, Thailand, Nepal and Bihar/Orissa (wild) and swamp and river samples (domestic).

TABLE-SHARERS: RODENTS OF THE RICEFIELDS

Groves (1984a) has surveyed a number of murid rodents that appear to have been introduced into Island Southeast Asia and are closely tied to wet rice landscapes. These animals are "commensal", meaning "sharing the same table", that is they live among humans and in their cultural landscape. *Mus caroli, Mus cervicolor* (Map 2) and *Rattus argentiventer* are widely distributed in Mainland Southeast Asia north of the Malay Peninsula; their distributions are spotty in the archipelago and invariably restricted to wet rice growing areas. If the pests travelled initially with the *padi* then a Burma/Thailand/Vietnam centre for the rice complex is suggested; if they came afterwards then a general importance for this area in later rice trading is indicated.

One species whose distribution does extend into the Mahanadi delta region, and so might have travelled with the water-buffalo from India, is the lesser bandicoot-rat, *Bandicota bengalensis*, a noted ricefield pest in Indonesia (Map 3). It is especially significant that, in Thailand, Indochina and most of

Map 2. Distribution of *Mus cervicolor*. Solid dots represent approximate locations recorded. From Groves (1984b).

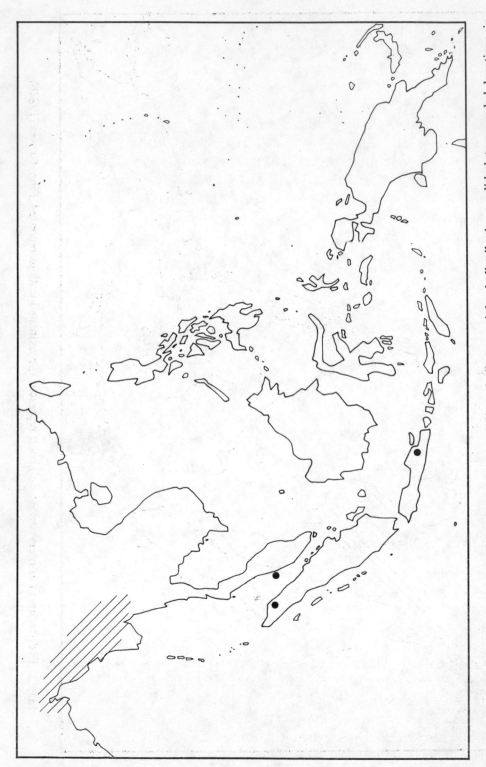

Map 3.   Distribution of *Bandicota bengalensis*. Diagonal lines indicate mainland distribution; solid dots recorded locations in Sundaland. From Groves (1984b).

Burma, it is replaced by an ecologically equivalent species, *B. savilei*, which did not get introduced into the archipelago.

Two somewhat unexpected ricefield pests in Indonesia are *Mus dunni*, a small mouse indigenous to northwestern India, and *Rattus nitidus*, indigenous to Nepal. Surely no explanation to do with early rice expansion will suffice in these cases.

Finally, among the agricultural pests must be mentioned the Pacific rat, *Rattus exulans*, which is wild in both Mainland and Island Southeast Asia. Smaller than the worldwide commensal rats *R. rattus* (black rat, roof rat) and *R. norvegicus* (brown rat, ship rat, Norway rat), this was the only species occurring on the Pacific islands, where it was commonly eaten, in pre-European contact times. Unfortunately its very versatility precludes us from associating it with any particular subsistence mode.

LOCAL CONTRIBUTIONS: *SAPI* AND *BABI*

Cattle

Despite their inferiority to buffaloes in a wet rice context, cattle can be similarly employed for ploughing, and Indonesia has even supplied a home-grown variety. This is the *sapi Bali* (Bali cow), a small type with white legs and white rump. Adult males are black with thick horns joined across the forehead by a cornified zone, and females, much smaller, are brown with simpler horns. Bali cattle are descended not from the same stock as other cattle, but from the *banteng* (*Bos javanicus*), a wild species still living in Southeast Asia. *Banteng* come in three subspecies:

> *Bos javanicus javanicus* — Java
>
> *Bos javanicus lowi* — Borneo
>
> *Bos javanicus birmanicus* — mainland, north of the Malay Peninsula (it is one of the unexplained oddities of zoogeography that there are no *banteng* in Sumatra or Malaya south of Kedah).

Only the Java subspecies fulfils the criteria for an ancestor of Bali cattle; the other two are unlike them in characteristic ways. So the origin of Bali cattle must have been in Java (unless wild *banteng* at one time occurred in Bali as well: there is no evidence on this point).

Bali cattle are bred throughout Bali, but also in other areas of Indonesia such as Riau and Lampung in Sumatra, southeastern Borneo, east Java, south and southeast Sulawesi, and Timor (Rollinson 1984). In general, they are found wherever the introduced Indian humped cattle (*zebu*) are not found. We assume that, being inferior to these in size and so presumably in traction and beef yield, they have been widely replaced by them, though in some places (especially Bali itself) Bali cattle are protected by religious sentiment. Meijer (1962) mentions a depiction of a humped ox before a plough on the Borobudur, so the replacement had already begun by the ninth century AD. On the other hand, he records that Bali cattle were still being exported from Java in the 14th century.

Pigs

So to the pigs (Groves 1981, 1984a). An Indonesian species, *Sus celebensis*, indigenous to Sulawesi, still occurs today as a domesticate on Roti and Timor. It occurs wild on Timor, Flores, Halmahera and, unexpectedly, Simuleue (west of Sumatra). Such a bizarre distribution strongly suggests past human introduction — presumably in domestic form. On Halmahera, pigs of unknown species are present at c.3500 BP (P. Bellwood, pers.comm.). Pigs descended from the species *Sus scrofa*, the widespread Eurasian wild pig, are today the domestic stock in most non-Muslim areas, but interspecies hybrids are the basis of the New Guinea pigs.

Even within *S. scrofa* there are informative divisions. Domestic and feral pigs of this species in Indonesia have the skull characters of *S. scrofa vittatus*, the wild pig of the region. Similar characteristics mark the pigs of the Andaman Islands, Flores, Admiralty Islands and Espiritu Santo (Vanuatu) as being of western Indonesian origin. On Tinian and Saipan, however, domestic and/or feral pigs occurred with the skull characteristics of wild Chinese (including Taiwanese) pigs. I am grateful to Robert Langdon for discussing these with me; they might be of rather recent origin, evidence for historic trade rather than ancient population movements. All these distributions are mapped in Map 4 (note that other species — *Sus barbatus*, *S. verrucosus* and the Philippine species — are not involved in domestication problems and are not mapped).

SNAPPERS-UP OF UNCONSIDERED TRIFLES:
DOGS AND, WHO KNOWS, DINGOES TOO?

Gollan (1985) found similarities between prehistoric dogs of the Indus Valley and the Australian dingo. Surely, one thought, not a direct connection jumping over Southeast Asia? Corbett (1985), however, was able to demonstrate that dingo-like dogs are widespread in Southeast Asia and studied the skulls of a series from Thailand, where apart from being pariah-like scavengers they are sold for food. The recency of the dingo's appearance in Australia makes sense if it was derived from an Austronesian pariah/table dog.

At the same time, there are both tame and feral dogs in the region which are not of dingo type: chiefly the New Guinea "singing dog" and the Tengger dog of eastern Java. It is tempting to see in these a relict of pre-Austronesian stocks, although there is no archaeological evidence either way.

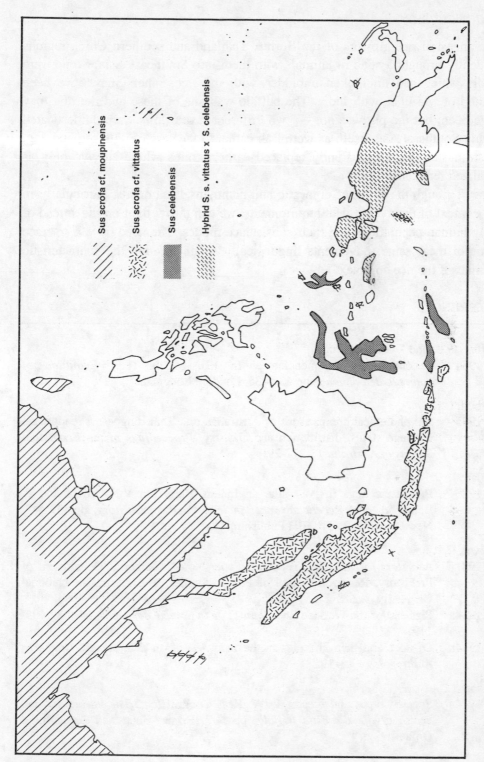

Map 4. Distribution of wild *Sus scrofa*, *Sus celebensis* and hybrids in Southeast Asia. From Groves (1984b).

Sus scrofa cf. moupinensis

Sus scrofa cf. vittatus

Sus celebensis

Hybrid S. s. vittatus x S. celebensis

IN CONCLUSION

The ancestral rice-growers of the Burma, Thailand and southern China regions evidently brought a suite of animals with them into Southeast Asia. Some were locals which had hitchhiked unbidden with the rice; others may have been grafted on via links with India. The buffalo was one of these and the dog may have been, but the pig was not — two different taxa of *Sus* were domesticated within Southeast Asia itself, as were Bali cattle. In the case of both pig and dog, Austronesian strains apparently replaced earlier strains which survive only as localized remnants.

Through the study of domestic and commensal mammals, particularly in the context of their ecological requirements, we can throw light on the spread of early human populations and their subsistence modes. The need now is to trace some of these same movements linguistically, again through the characteristic animals of the rice complex.

REFERENCES

Corbet, G.B. and J. Clutton-Brock
    1984   Taxonomy and nomenclature. In I.L. Mason (ed.) *Evolution of domesticated animals*, pp 434-438. London: Longman.

Corbett, L.K.
    1985   Morphological comparisons of Australian and Thai dingoes: a reappraisal of dingo status, distribution and ancestry. *Proceedings of the Ecological Society of Australia* 13:277-291.

Gollan, K.
    1985   Prehistoric dogs in Australia: an Indian origin? In V.N. Misra and P. Bellwood (eds) *Recent advances in Indo-Pacific prehistory*, pp.439-443. New Delhi: Oxford & IBH Publishing Co.

Groves, C.P.
    1981   *Ancestors for the pigs*. Technical Paper No. 3. Canberra: Department of Prehistory, Research School of Pacific Studies, The Australian National University.
    1984a   Pigs east of the Wallace line. *Journal de la Société des Océanistes* 39:105-119.
    1984b   Of mice and men and pigs in the Indo-Australian archipelago. *Canberra Anthropology* 7:1-19.

Mason, I.L.
    1974a   Species, types and breeds. In W. Ross Cockrill (ed.) *The husbandry and health of the domestic buffalo*, pp.1-47. Rome: Food and Agricultural Organization.

1974b   Genetics. In W. Ross Cockrill (ed.) *The husbandry and health of the buffalo*, pp.57-81. Rome: Food and Agricultural Organization.

Meijer, W.Ch.P.
    1962   *Das Balirind*. Wittenberg Lutherstadt: Ziemsen Verlag (Die Neue Brehm-Bücherei).

Rollinson, D.H.L.
    1984   Bali cattle. In I.L. Mason (ed.) *Evolution of domesticated animals*, pp.28-34. London: Longman.

SECTION 2:

TRANSFORMATIONS AND INTERACTIONS

9

HOMO SAPIENS IS AN EVOLVING SPECIES: ORIGINS OF THE AUSTRONESIANS

S.W. Serjeantson and X. Gao

This paper commences with a survey of genetic markers thought to give protection from malaria, in connection with the issue of differentiation between An and NAn populations in Oceania. The closely-linked, highly polymorphic human leukocyte antigen (HLA) class II genes, HLA-DR and -DQ, are then examined for evidence of in situ *evolution in some Austronesian-speaking populations of Oceania. The authors define the evolutionary forces of founder effect, genetic drift, mutation, migration and selection and look for evidence that these evolutionary forces shaped the genetic profiles seen in contemporary populations of Austronesian speakers. Genetic data confirm an ultimate East Asian origin for Polynesians but also indicate some degree of past gene flow from island Melanesian populations.*

INTRODUCTION

Homo sapiens is an evolving species. We make this point because the archaeological debate relating to the development of Lapita pottery in Melanesia has focused on whether it represents an intrusive culture (Spriggs, this volume) or an indigenous development (Allen and White 1989). This debate has been carried over to the question of whether the pre-Polynesians were a colonizing group from Island Southeast Asia, or a group that evolved within Melanesia. The genetic record shows that contemporary Polynesians do indeed share many genetic features with Island Southeast Asians, but they have also undergone further and probably rapid evolution in the past two or three millennia. That is, in the same way that red-slip decoration of early pottery and vessel forms was shared between Island Southeast Asia and Melanesia (Bellwood, this volume), with a local evolution of Lapita decoration in Melanesia (Spriggs, this volume), contemporary Polynesians have ancestral ties with other Mongoloid populations but also have unique genetic features suggesting further evolution.

In the case of Polynesians, much of the evolution appears to have taken place east of Melanesia, in contrast to Lapita decoration, with the population continuously losing genes on the voyage through the Pacific; not many Polynesian genes have been acquired from Melanesians. This was pointed out 30 years ago by the late Roy Simmons of the Commonwealth Serum Laboratories in Melbourne who noted that Eastern Polynesians lacked the B antigen of the

ABO blood group system (Simmons 1962). Those early Austronesians who remained in Fiji and New Caledonia have evolved also, of course, in the sense that the original genetic repertoire has been overlain by Melanesian genetic elements. Western Melanesians in coastal areas have also evolved through genetic admixture with early Austronesian settlers (Serjeantson *et al.* 1983).

The debate on the origin of the Polynesians has polarized viewpoints, so that the concept of continuing evolution may have been trivialized inadvertently. This has led to criticisms that the geneticists have been studying the wrong populations. That is, if only geneticists would look at the right contemporary populations the missing links would be found. We doubt this. While agreeing there is a frustrating dearth of genetic information for Island Southeast Asia and for the Lapita homeland area in the Bismarck Archipelago, there is substantial evidence that the evolutionary forces of selection, mutation and genetic drift have resulted in the unique genetic profile seen in contemporary Polynesians. Further, the populations from whom the pre-Polynesians derived were also subject to evolutionary forces, as well as to inward migration by other groups. The missing link may not exist and we may need to accept that if, for example, the nine base-pair deletion in mitochondrial DNA (mtDNA) that is almost universally present in Polynesians (Hertzberg *et al.* 1989) is found also in 18 per cent of East Asians (Stoneking and Wilson 1989), then that is as good a link as we are likely to get. There is simply not going to be an as-yet-undetected population, somewhere in Island Southeast Asia, where everyone tests positive for the mtDNA deletion and negative for blood group B!

THE IMPACT OF MALARIA ON HUMAN GENETICS

The linguistic dichotomy of populations in Melanesia into Austronesian and non-Austronesian-speaking peoples has tempted some scholars to over-simplify the genetic characteristics of these populations as malaria-resistant and malaria-susceptible, on the basis of gamma-globulin genetics (Clark and Kelly 1993). Kelly (1992) argues that if malaria in Melanesia did indeed have an antiquity greater than about 3600 BP, the malarious coastal lowlands would have been open for settlement by Austronesian-speaking immigrants because the non-Austronesian-speakers did not have the genetic capability to live permanently in malarious environments.

The data do not support this scenario. First, it is not clear how malaria could have been sustained without some minimal human population density in the low-lying regions. Second, continuous occupation of a malarious region induces some immunity to malaria among the inhabitants. The sporadic forays of non-Austronesian-speakers into the lowlands, as envisaged by Kelly, are much more likely to be deleterious than continuous occupation. This is evidenced by the finding that in New Guinea, hyperreactive malarious splenomegaly is confined to the Watut people, resident at an altitude of about 1000 m where malarial transmission is intermittent.

The third factor to be taken into consideration is the genetic profile of the contemporary population of coastal lowland Melanesia. There are several genetic markers, widespread in non-Austronesian-speaking lowlanders, which are thought to provide some protection against malaria. A description of these genes together with their population distribution is given by Serjeantson *et al.* (1992) and includes the thalassaemias, glucose-6-phosphate dehydrogenase deficiency, hereditary ovalocytosis and the Gerbich negative blood group. The population distributions of these genes provide some insights into genetic prehistory in Melanesia.

For instance, the gene causing hereditary ovalocytosis, a slight distortion of the red blood cell shape, has a frequency of about 10 per cent throughout lowland Papua New Guinea. The distortion in the red cell membrane arises from a 27 base pair deletion in the DNA encoding Band 3 protein, first shown in a Southeast Asian donor and confirmed as the same gene as that in some Melanesians. The Band 3 defect distorts a number of receptors on the red cell surface and may inhibit malarial invasion. Further evidence that hereditary ovalocytosis provides some protection from high density, lethal parasitemias is provided by epidemiological data and by the apparent absence from the population of people homozygous for the mutant Band 3 gene. That is, despite the apparent lethality of the mutant Band 3 gene when it is inherited from both parents (i.e. a double dose), a high population gene frequency is maintained, presumably through a selective advantage in malarious areas for those with a single dose.

Was this gene introduced to lowland coastal Melanesia, together with malaria, by early Austronesian speakers? The gene's antecedents lie in the Aboriginal populations of Southeast Asia, but it is otherwise rare in contemporary populations of this region. It is found in appreciable frequencies in the Orang Asli populations of Malaysia, has been reported in the Austronesian-speaking Land Dayaks and Iban of Borneo, is prevalent in the hinterland of north and south New Guinea, is absent from New Guinea Highlanders, and is rare in populations east of the New Guinea mainland. This gene thus indicates the likely arrival in Melanesia of a non-Austronesian-speaking wave of immigrants before the early Austronesian-speakers.

The non-Austronesian-speaking Melanesians in malarious areas of New Guinea have other characteristic genetic mutations, such as the Gerbich-negative blood group that is a consequence of a large deletion in the glycophorin C gene. This mutation may have arisen in one of the populations of the Torricelli Mountains, where it is particularly prevalent, as the gene has a more limited distribution than hereditary ovalocytosis in New Guinea and is not found in the Gulf and Western Provinces. We have detected, using DNA analyses, the glycophorin C gene deletion in low frequency in Micronesia but not in Polynesia.

Among other genetic markers thought to be related to malaria, the most frequent in non-Austronesian-speaking peoples in lowland New Guinea is a 3.7 kb deletion in the alpha-globin gene, a mutation that has occurred on an unmistakably Melanesian-area chromosome as attested by the flanking DNA markers. This marker was carried into Polynesia, where it has sporadic occurrence, although it has attained appreciable frequency in New Zealand Maoris, presumably through genetic drift.

GENETIC MARKERS FOR AUSTRONESIANS AND NON-AUSTRONESIANS?

As already noted, the hypothesis that gamma-globulin (Gm) allotypes are associated with differential resistance or susceptibility to malaria is unsupported by any evidence. Is there then a clear dichotomy between non-Austronesian and Austronesian-speaking peoples in lowland New Guinea with Gm and other genetic markers? The answer, as given in detail by Serjeantson *et al.* (1983), is that there is not. For Gm, as for other genetic markers, geographic distance is a much stronger determinant of genetic affinity than is language, and this is true also for Markham Valley populations where Gm allotypes were originally proposed as sensitive indicators of Austronesian ancestry.

The human leukocyte antigen (HLA) profiles for populations in Melanesia support the notion that there is genetic diversity within non-Austronesian-speaking peoples that must have predated the overlaying of Austronesian elements in some coastal and island non-Austronesian-speaking peoples. A simple test is whether lowland coastal non-Austronesian-speaking people represent a hybrid pool of New Guinea Highlander and Polynesian genes, or whether they have their own separate genetic profile. The HLA-DR system shows that hybridity is not the case. For instance, DRB1*1408 has a frequency of 18 per cent in New Guinea Highlanders but is absent from lowland non-Austronesian-speakers. The latter have some unusual genes, DRB1*1104 and 1602, that are found neither in Highlanders nor Polynesians. The Polynesian gene pool, characterized by high frequencies of DRB1*1201 and 0901 can be drawn from the east Asian but not the Melanesian gene pool.

In a perspective on evolution and population genetics in Papua New Guinea, Serjeantson *et al.* (1992) showed that populations cluster into four main groups on the basis of ABO blood group and other genetic markers. These are: 1. Austronesian-speaking Melanesians from the New Guinea Islands and Papuan south coast, 2. An and NAn-speaking populations from Madang and Sepik

Provinces, 3. speakers of the New Guinea Highlands NAn languages, and 4. non-Austronesian-speakers from New Britain and Papua. The diversity of colonizers in Melanesia is confirmed by the study of mitochondrial DNA, which has shown that at least 18 surviving maternal lineages colonized Papua New Guinea, all deriving from Southeast Asia.

Austronesian settlements have rarely penetrated the hyperendemic malarial hinterland of New Guinea, but rather, are found on offshore islands and in coastal regions. It seems that early Austronesians may have arrived in Melanesia to find a malarious region inhabited by peoples comparatively well adapted to the environment. For many early Austronesians, it may have been prudent to continue east. It is no coincidence that the majority of Lapita sites are found on small islands.

In the remainder of this paper, we examine the closely-linked, highly polymorphic human leukocyte antigen (HLA) class II genes, HLA-DR and -DQ, for evidence of *in situ* evolution in some Austronesian-speaking populations of Oceania. We define the evolutionary forces of founder effect, genetic drift, mutation, migration and selection and look for evidence that these evolutionary forces shaped the genetic profiles seen in contemporary populations of Austronesian speakers.

The analyses are based on new data generated by using the polymerase chain reaction (PCR) technique to amplify the HLA-DRB1, DRB3, DRB5, DQA1 and DQB1 genes, followed by hybridization with sequence-specific oligonucleotides (SSOs). The PCR-based HLA typing protocol is rapid and sensitive, and looks directly at the gene of interest rather than at flanking regions of DNA as is often the case in restriction fragment length polymorphism (RFLP) analysis. Using the PCR approach, it has been possible to examine many more individuals in many more populations than was possible with traditional serological techniques or RFLP analysis. We have examined more than 2,600 chromosomes from Asia, Oceania and Australia and have identified 82 DR,DQ haplotypes (there are additional haplotypes in Caucasoids); this compares with less than ten DR haplotypes identified in early serological studies (Serjeantson *et al.* 1982) and with 32 DR,DQ haplotypes detected in RFLP studies (Kohonen-Corish *et al.* 1988). That is, subtle variation in HLA class II alleles, sometimes a single DNA base change, was not detected in less-sensitive serological and RFLP analyses. In the following, we examine these data for evidence of the impact of evolutionary forces.

EVOLUTIONARY FORCES: DEFINITIONS

The forces of evolution include founder effects, genetic drift, mutation, migration and selection.

Founder effects. Founder effects arise when the subgroup colonizing previously uninhabited territory is not fully representative, in a genetic sense, of the parental population from which the subgroup derived. Since fission of groups is more likely to occur along family lines than at random (Neel 1968), founder effects may be expected in any colonizing group. The intensity of the founder effect is directly related to the size of the colonizing group — the smaller the number of colonizers, the greater the chance that genes from the parental group will be under- or over-represented, or lost altogether.

Genetic drift. Genetic drift occurs when the distribution of genes in a given generation differs from the distribution in the previous generation. This can occur by chance. For instance, all offspring in a given mating may be female, by chance, so that the paternal Y chromosome is lost to that and future generations, by chance. If all offspring in a given mating are male, the maternal mitochondrial DNA lineage will terminate. The impact of genetic drift is directly related to population size — the smaller the population, the greater the fluctuations in gene frequencies from one generation to the next and the greater the chance that rare or infrequent genes will be lost from the gene pool. The effects of genetic drift can be brought on by catastrophes such as drought, cyclones, epidemics and boating accidents that can dramatically reduce population size, causing in genetic terminology a "bottleneck". If the numbers of males and females in a population are unequal, then the effective population size is closer to the smaller number.

It should be noted that chance can also determine the particular individuals selected for study, so that they may not faithfully represent the larger population from which they are drawn. The smaller the sample size, the greater the chance of sampling effects. Analysis of contemporary populations cannot discriminate readily between founder effects and genetic drift. Bottlenecks may have been more important than founder effects in a population where mtDNA is less diverse than nuclear DNA (Birky *et al.* 1989).

Mutation. When cells replicate, DNA also replicates and is not always a faithful copy of the original; the error is called a mutation. If the mutation occurs in the germ-line it may be passed to the next generation. Mutations may be a single DNA base substitution, a deletion, a gene duplication and so on. Some mutations, present initially as a single copy in the population, will be lost in genetic drift, but other new mutations will become established in the population, especially if the new mutation has a selective advantage. A point mutation in a functional gene is silent if it occurs in a redundant nucleotide (explained below); otherwise, it results in an amino acid change in a molecule and is then possibly subject to selection.

Selection. Selection operates when a particular gene has a survival advantage, through differential fertility or in survival to reproductive age. Post-reproductive survival differentials are not selected because genes have already been passed to the next generation. Amino acids are encoded by a sequence of three nucleotides called a codon, but the third nucleotide (and sometimes the second) is often redundant. For example, the codons CCA, CCC, CCG and CCT all encode the amino acid residue proline, so that the nucleotide in the third position is redundant. For a given gene, comparison of the rate of nucleotide substitutions in the first and third nucleotides of the codon can indicate whether there is positive selection for variability, negative selection for variability, or whether variability is no greater than expected by chance. The extreme polymorphism at the HLA loci has been attributed to selection for diversity *per se*, due to frequency-dependent selection for high genetic diversity where individuals with a rare allele have some selective advantage, or due to over-dominant selection where individuals carrying different alleles at a single locus (i.e. heterozygotes) have a selective advantage. Frequency-dependent and over-dominant selection can save rare or new alleles from extinction.

THE HLA DATA

HLA-DR and -DQ antigens. The HLA-DR and -DQ human leukocyte class II antigens are encoded by alleles at the closely-linked loci DRA1, DRB1, DQA1 and DQB1. The DRA1 locus is not polymorphic, but the WHO nomenclature committee (Bodmer *et al.* 1991) recognizes 47 alleles at DRB1, eight at DQA1 and 15 at DQB1. Chromosomes carrying DR2 alleles at the DRB1 locus have a second functional locus, DRB5, while some other chromosomes have an alternative second functional locus, DRB3. Not all DR and DQ alleles are found in all populations.

The DR and DQ loci are so closely linked on chromosome six that there are no confirmed reports of a recombination between DRB1 and DQB1, although the occasional recombinational event must have occurred in human evolutionary history to give rise to observed distributions of DR,DQ haplotypes in contemporary populations. For instance, the DR2 allele DRB1*1502 is invariably linked with DRB5*0102 in Caucasoids. However, a unique haplotype DRB1*1502, DRB5*0101 occurs commonly in Australian Aborigines, Papua New Guinea Highlanders, and in coastal and island Melanesians. This haplotype occurs sporadically in Javanese and Polynesians but not in northern or southern Chinese (Gao and Serjeantson 1991a). This is only one example of how DR,DQ haplotypes can be powerful indicators of population affinities. Further, the number of DR,DQ haplotypes in a given population tends to reflect historic events. A small number of haplotypes indicates founder effects and bottle-necks in population size, and genetic isolation, while a large number of haplotypes can be indicative of historic mixing of populations.

Evidence from HLA studies for founder effects and genetic drift. In a study of DR2-related DR,DQ haplotypes in Asia, Oceania and Australia we identified 15 DRB1, DRB5, DQA1, DQB1 haplotypes (Gao and Serjeantson 1991a). The most diversity was seen in southern Chinese, with nine distinct DR2-related haplotypes, reflecting a great ancestral mixing of populations. The least diversity was seen in Polynesians, with sporadic occurrence of only two DR2-related haplotypes. A similar distribution of haplotype diversity was seen with respect to DR4-related haplotypes (Gao and Serjeantson 1991b). A total of 12 DR,DQ combinations was observed in Asia, Oceania and Australia. Ten of these haplotypes were seen in Chinese, but only two were represented in Papua New Guinean Highlanders and a different two in Micronesians. DR4-related

Table 1.   The most common HLA-DR,DQ haplotype in each of 19 populations of Asia-Oceania.

Population	Number tested[a]	Most common haplotype[b]				Frequency (per cent)
		DRB1	DRB	DQA1	DQB1	
Kimberley	149	AB4	DRB3*0101	0501	0402	20.7
East Cape York	148	0803	-	0103	0601	29.1
West Cape York	112	0803	-	0103	0601	24.0
PNG Highlands	114	1501	DRB5*0101	0102	0602	29.8
Madang	130	1101	DRB3*0202	0501	0301	45.4
New Britain	120	1101	DRB3*0202	0501	0301	36.7
New Caledonia	130	1101	DRB3*0202	0501	0301	26.2
Fiji	114	1101	DRB3*0202	0501	0301	33.3
Western Samoa	102	1201	DRB3*0101	0501	0301	18.6
Niue	140	1201	DRB3*0101	0501	0301	30.0
Rarotonga	156	1101[c]	DRB3*0202	0501	0301	20.5
Nauru	134	1202	DRB3*0301	0601	0301	28.4
Kiribati	124	1202	DRB3*0301	0601	0301	37.9
Java	154	1202	DRB3*0301	0601	0301	46.1
Hong Kong	78	0901	DRB4	0301	0303	14.0
Singapore	92	0901	DRB4	0301	0303	18.5
Xinjiang	184	07	DRB4	0201	0201	18.5
Xian	160	0901	DRB4	0301	0303	14.8
Beijing	182	0901	DRB4	0301	0303	14.4

[a]   No. of haplotypes.

[b]   Haplotype refers to the joint occurrence of the given alleles at the closely-linked DRB1, DRB3 (or DRB4 or DRB5), DQA1 and DQB1 loci.

[c]   DRB1*1201 had a frequency of 14.7 per cent.

haplotypes were not detected in Javanese. While some haplotypes are lost in genetic drift, others can become well-established.

Table 1 gives the most common DRB1, DRB3 (or DRB4 or DRB5), DQA1 and DQB1 haplotypes found in traditional populations of Asia, Oceania and Australia and their frequencies. In Asia, we have studied Javanese, the Chinese minority population of Xinjiang, northern Chinese from Beijing and Xian, and southern Chinese from Hong Kong and Singapore. Micronesians were from Nauru and Kiribati while Melanesians were from coastal Papua New Guinea (Madang and New Britain), New Caledonia, Fiji and the New Guinea Highlands (Goroka). Polynesians were from Western Samoa, Rarotonga and Niue. Aborigines were from the Kimberley region and from eastern and western Cape York communities.

The most frequent haplotype in Kimberley Aborigines was not seen in any of the other study populations, including Cape York. The most common Cape York haplotype was also found in the Kimberley region Aborigines (18.9 per cent) and in Papua New Guinean Highlanders (7.0 per cent). The DRB1*1201 haplotype that predominated in western Polynesians was not seen in other populations, while the DRB1*1202 haplotype in Micronesians and Javanese was otherwise detected only in southern Chinese. Populations less affected by genetic drift, such as those of mainland China, have a more diverse genetic repertoire at HLA-DR so that the frequency of common haplotypes (14-19 per cent) is lower than in Java and Oceania (19-46 per cent). In northern China there were 34 DR,DQ haplotypes but only ten in Nauru, for example.

Evidence from HLA Studies for Mutation

A new DRB1 allele, a variant of DRw14 called DRB1*1408, has been found in Polynesians (Gao *et al.* 1992a); this allele equates with 'DRw6P' described in earlier RFLP studies. Among Austronesian speakers tested to date this allele is essentially confined to Polynesians in whom it occurs with moderate frequency (5-7 per cent), but it is absent from Madang, New Britain and Fiji. Four instances of the novel allele have been seen in Melanesians from New Caledonia, but this could represent recent admixture with Polynesians from the Wallis Islands. Closer dissection of the novel Polynesian-specific variant at the DNA level shows that it represents a single nucleotide substitution in an allele still found in contemporary Polynesians, so is almost certainly an example of recent mutation. In Kimberley region Aborigines, three novel HLA-DRB1 mutations, not seen elsewhere, account for about 50 per cent of the HLA-DRB1 allele frequency (Gao *et al.* 1992b).

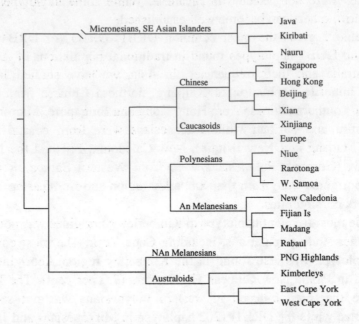

Figure 1.   Phylogenetic analysis of the distributions of HLA-DR,DQ haplotypes in 20 populations. In Asia-Oceania there were 82 haplotypes; additional haplotypes found in Caucasoids were pooled to generate a 20×83 matrix for genetic distance calculations.

Evidence from HLA Studies for Selection

The mutation giving rise to DRB1*1408 in Polynesians is of functional significance in that it results in an amino acid change at position 57 in the DR beta molecule. The PCR-based protocol is capable of detecting silent mutations in hypervariable regions of the DRB1 gene, and no novel silent mutations have been found in Polynesians. This suggests that the new functional mutation may have survived and flourished due to some selective advantage. Other evidence in favour of this hypothesis is that the same mutation has occurred in Australian Aborigines on a different DRB3 haplotype, suggesting independent mutations and convergent selection. The role of natural selection in shaping HLA-DR profiles is subject to debate (Hughes and Nei 1989), but it is possible that rare HLA types have been advantaged in epidemics.

Evidence from HLA Studies for Migration Effects

Phylogenetic analyses of HLA-DR,-DQ haplotype distributions in the populations listed in Table 1 and in Caucasoids (Fernandez-Viña *et al.* 1991) are

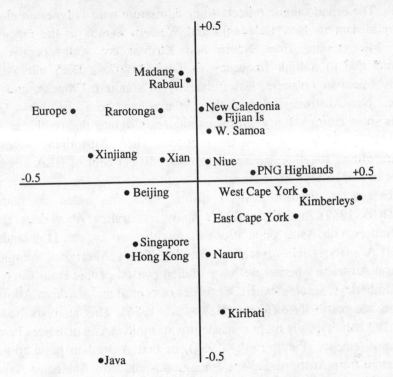

Figure 2. Eigenvector representation of genetic distances between 20 populations based on HLA-DR,DQ haplotype frequency distributions.

given in Figures 1 and 2, based on Nei's distance statistic (Nei 1973). Figure 1 shows the extraordinary power of this small segment of the human genome, clustering populations in a manner partially expected from linguistic, anthropological and archaeological evidence (Bellwood 1989). The complete separation of Javanese and Polynesians, who show virtually no overlap in HLA-DR,DQ haplotypes (Gao and Serjeantson 1991a), is unexpected on linguistic grounds. The eigenvector (Figure 2) makes better use of the genetic data, representing genetic distance in two dimensions. Java is well-isolated from the other populations due to a near absence of DR4- and DRw6-related haplotypes; these haplotypes are well-represented in the other populations and account for the majority of HLA-DR types seen in Polynesia. The northern and southern Chinese populations cluster to the left of the eigenvector, while Xinjiang, a minority group with known Caucasoid ancestry, is positioned midway between Caucasoid and northern Chinese populations. The Polynesian groups have a position intermediate between northern China and coastal Melanesia. In the phylogenetic analysis, Melanesians from the north Papua New Guinea coast (Madang) cannot be discriminated from the Tolai of New Britain and these groups have a DR,DQ profile similar to that in Melanesians from New

Caledonia. The Fijian sample reflects some admixture with Polynesian elements and is equidistant to New Caledonia and Western Samoa in the eigenvector diagram. Micronesians from Nauru and Kiribati are well-separated from Polynesians due to a high frequency of DRB1*1202, a DR5 allele that is commonly found in Javanese, less frequently in southern Chinese, and rarely elsewhere. Non-Austronesian-speaking Melanesians from the New Guinea Highlands show closer affinity with Australian Aborigines than with any of the Austronesian-speaking Melanesian groups. The Australian Aboriginal populations cluster together, even though about 50 per cent of HLA-DR alleles are unique to Kimberleys Aborigines.

This genetic distance analysis differs from that based on non-HLA markers (Kirk 1989) in that, in Kirk's study, Australian Aborigines showed closer affinities with Asian populations than with New Guinea Highlanders in the non-HLA analysis. However, we note that Kirk's Aboriginal sample was from central Australia whereas we have studied coastal people from Cape York and the Kimberleys; serological HLA profiles of central and northern Aboriginal populations are markedly different (Hay *et al.* 1986). This analysis based on HLA-DR,DQ haplotypes is more consistent with multivariate distances based on cranial measurements (Pietrusewsky 1984), in that Australian populations are well-separated from Austronesian-speaking groups and from Southeast Asia, and in that Java clusters with Southeast Asia rather than with Polynesia. The affinity between Fiji and Polynesia seen in the HLA-DR,DQ analyses was not seen by Pietrusewsky (1984) but was evident in the anthropometric analysis of Howells (1970).

COMPARATIVE OBSERVATIONS FROM OTHER GENETIC SYSTEMS

Thus the combined forces of founder effect, genetic drift, migration and mutation have undoubtedly shaped the genetic profiles seen in contemporary Austronesian speakers. This conclusion based on HLA data is supported by studies of the distributions of the nine base-pair (bp) mitochondrial DNA deletion and of the 3.7 kb deletion in the α globin genes. The nine bp mitochondrial DNA deletion is another example of the role of chance in determining genetic profiles; since mtDNA is maternally-inherited, the number of copies in a colonizing group is equivalent to the number of females in that group. Thus we see the gradual loss of the wild-type or common non-deleted mtDNA as the early Austronesian-speakers moved through the Pacific. The deleted form has a frequency of 16 per cent in the Moluccas, 10-40 per cent in coastal Melanesia, 77 per cent in Tonga, 87 per cent in the Cook Islands, but reaches near fixation (frequency of 100 per cent) in Samoans and the New Zealand Maori (Hertzberg *et al.* 1989).

The common form of mtDNA was not the only genetic material lost to the pre-Polynesians as they moved eastwards through the Pacific. There are other examples of clines in gene frequencies from west to east, with final and irretrievable loss of the allele. At the HLA-B locus, for instance, HLA-B27 is not represented in eastern Polynesia, although this is a common antigen in island Melanesia (11 per cent in New Caledonia) and occurs in Mauke Island (6 per cent) (Serjeantson 1989). Similarly, HLA-B13 is found in western but not eastern Polynesia.

Another example of chance effects is the 3.7 kb deletion in the α globin genes ($\alpha^{-3.7}$), which has a frequency of 15 per cent in Maoris. This deletion is clearly carried on a chromosome of Melanesian origin, because there are particular features in the DNA flanking the deletion (restriction enzyme sites) that are otherwise seen only in Melanesians. This has given rise to claims of substantial Melanesian genetic input into the contemporary Polynesian genome (Hill et al. 1989). However, the gene can be seen to increase in a cline from western to eastern Polynesia, increasing from 1 per cent in Tongans to 12 per cent in Cook Islanders to 15 per cent in Maoris (Hill et al. 1989). Thus the $\alpha^{-3.7}$ marker does not provide evidence that Polynesians evolved out of Melanesia; rather, it suggests that pre-Polynesians recruited at least one Melanesian into the mating pool.

It is clear that the recent PCR-based technological revolution in molecular genetics (Scharf et al. 1986), permitting rapid screening for the newly-sequenced alleles, will result in an explosion in knowledge of the genetic profiles of contemporary populations. PCR amplification of DNA from aged material has attracted much attention, but application of the PCR technique in reconstruction of genetic prehistory by analysis of contemporary populations is potentially very informative indeed.

How can the scholar of Austronesian prehistory best make use of the emerging PCR-based data? First, there will be an important role for the prehistorian who is prepared to examine the genetic tabulations and reinterpret them in language understood by his colleagues, wresting the data from the geneticists who with great abandon muddle geographic, anthropological and linguistic terms and muddle the reader (Houghton 1991)! Second, for the data to be relevant to archaeology they will need to be interpreted with due attention to the main thrust of this paper — that Homo sapiens is an evolving species. We conclude, from this small sample of the human genome, that founder effects, bottlenecks and mutations have resulted in a unique genetic profile in contemporary Polynesians, so that their origins are forever blurred. The Polynesian genetic repertoire at HLA-DR,DQ can largely be drawn from the East Asian gene pool, but has been irrevocably altered by evolutionary forces to generate the unique genetic repertoire that is distinctively Polynesian.

ACKNOWLEDGEMENTS

We thank many colleagues who have assisted us in the collection of, or who have collected, blood specimens: Michael Alpers, Kuldeep Bhatia, Max Blake, Gary Dowse, Brian Hawkins, Hilary King, R.L. Kirk, George Le Gonidec, Ken Mickleson, Ruby Newlands, Ray Pace, Salam Safro, Yiping Sun, Kiki Thoma, Ron Trent, A. Veale and Paul Zimmet.

REFERENCES

Allen, J. and White, P.J.
  1989   The Lapita homeland: some data and an interpretation. *Journal of the Polynesian Society* 98:129-146.

Bellwood, P.
  1989   The colonization of the Pacific: some current hypotheses. In: A.V.S. Hill and S.W. Serjeantson (eds) *The colonization of the Pacific: a genetic trail*, pp.1-59. Oxford: Clarendon Press.

Birky, C.W., P. Fuerst and T. Maruyama
  1989   Organelle gene diversity under migration, mutation and drift: equilibrium expectations, approach to equilibrium, effects of heteroplasmic cells, DNA comparison to nuclear genes. *Genetics* 121:613-627.

Bodmer, J.G., S.G.E. Marsh, E. Albert *et al.*
  1991   Nomenclature for factors of the HLA system, 1990. *Tissue Antigens* 37:97-104.

Clark, J.T. and K.M. Kelly
  1993   Human genetics, paleoenvironments, and malaria: relationships and implications for the settlement of Oceania. *American Anthropologist* 95(3): 612-630.

Fernandez-Viña, M., X. Gao, M.E.M. Moraes and P. Stastny
  1991   Alleles at four HLA class II loci and their associations determined by oligonucleotide hybridization in five different ethnic groups. *Immunogenetics* 34:299-312.

Gao, X. and S.W. Serjeantson
  1991a   Heterogeneity in HLA-DR2-related DR,DQ haplotypes in eight populations of Asia-Oceania. *Immunogenetics* 34:401-408.
  1991b   Diversity in HLA-DR4-related DR,DQ haplotypes in Australia, Oceania and China. *Human Immunology* 32:269-276.

Gao, X., P. Zimmet and S.W. Serjeantson
  1992a   HLA class II sequence polymorphisms in Pacific islanders. I. HLA-DR,DQ genes in Polynesians, Micronesians and Javanese. *Human Immunology* 34:151-161.

Gao, X., A. Veale and S.W. Serjeantson
    1992b   HLA class II diversity in Australian Aborigines: unusual HLA-DRB1 alleles. *Immunogenetics* 36:333-337.

Hay, J., G. Bennett, A. Sheldon and P. Hetzel
    1986   Aboriginal Australians. In M. Aizawa *et al.* (eds) *HLA in Asia-Oceania 1986*, pp.295-297. Sapporo: Hokkaido University Press.

Hertzberg, M., K.N.P. Mickleson, S.W. Serjeantson, J.F. Prior and R.J. Trent
    1989   An Asian-specific 9-bp deletion of mitochondrial DNA is frequently found in Polynesians. *American Journal of Human Genetics* 44:504-510.

Hill, A.V.S., D.F. O'Shaughnessy and J.B. Clegg
    1989   Haemoglobin and globin gene variants in the Pacific. In A.V.S. Hill and S.W. Serjeantson (eds) *The colonization of the Pacific: a genetic trail*, pp.246-285. Oxford: Clarendon Press.

Houghton, P.
    1991   The early human biology of the Pacific: some considerations. *Journal of the Polynesian Society* 100:167-196.

Howells, W.W.
    1970   Anthropometric grouping analysis of Pacific peoples. *Archaeology and Physical Anthropology in Oceania* 5:192-217.

Hughes, A.L. and M. Nei
    1989   Nucleotide substitution at major histocompatibility complex class II loci: Evidence for overdominant selection. *Proceedings of the National Academy of Science U.S.A.* 86:958-962.

Kelly, K.M.
    1992   On the genetic basis of hyperreactive malarious splenomegaly and the selection of G3m alleles. *American Journal of Physical Anthropology Suppl.* 14:98.

Kirk, R.L.
    1989   Population genetic studies in the Pacific: red cell antigen, serum protein, and enzyme systems. In A.V.S. Hill and S.W. Serjeantson (eds) *The colonization of the Pacific: a genetic trail*, pp.60-119. Oxford: Clarendon Press.

Kohonen-Corish, M.R.J., H. Dunckley and S.W. Serjeantson
    1988   HLA-DR and -DQ genotyping in seven populations of Asia-Oceania and Australia. *Tissue Antigens* 32:32-40.

Neel, J.
    1968   The demography of two tribes of primitive relatively unaccultivated American Indians. *Proceedings of the National Academy of Science U.S.A.* 59:680-689.

Nei, M.
    1973   The theory and estimation of genetic distance. In N.E. Norton (ed.) *Genetic structure of populations*, pp.45-51. Honolulu: University of Hawaii Press.

Pietrusewsky, M.
   1984   Metric and non-metric cranial variation in Australian Aboriginal populations compared with populations from the Pacific and Asia. *Occasional Papers in Human Biology*, No. 3. Canberra: Australian Institute of Aboriginal Studies.

Scharf, S.J., G.T. Horn and H.A. Erlich
   1986   Direct cloning and sequence analysis of enzymatically amplified genomic sequences. *Science* 233:1076-1078.

Serjeantson, S.W.
   1989   HLA genes and antigens. In A.V.S. Hill and S.W. Serjeantson (eds) *The colonization of the Pacific: a genetic trail*, pp.120-173. Oxford: Clarendon Press.

Serjeantson, S.W., P.G. Board and K.K. Bhatia
   1992   Population genetics in Papua New Guinea: a perspective on human evolution. In R.D. Attenborough and M.P. Alpers (eds) *Human biology in Papua New Guinea: the small cosmos*, pp.198-233. Oxford: Clarendon Press.

Serjeantson, S.W., R.L. Kirk and P.B. Booth
   1983   Linguistics and genetic differentiation in the Pacific. *Journal of Human Evolution* 12:77-92.

Serjeantson, S.W., D.P. Ryan, P. Zimmet, R. Taylor,
R. Cross, M. Charpin and G. Le Gonidec
   1982   HLA antigens in four Pacific populations with non-insulin-dependent diabetes mellitus. *Annals of Human Biology* 9:69-84.

Simmons, R.T.
   1962   Blood groups and genes in Polynesians and comparisons with other Pacific peoples. *Oceania* 32:198-210.

Stoneking, M. and A.C. Wilson
   1989   Mitochondrial DNA. In A.V.S. Hill and S.W. Serjeantson (eds) *The colonization of the Pacific: a genetic trail*, pp.215-245. Oxford: Clarendon Press.

10

A STUDY OF GENETIC DISTANCE AND THE AUSTRONESIAN/NON-AUSTRONESIAN DICHOTOMY

Kuldeep Bhatia, Simon Easteal and Robert L. Kirk

Data on genetic distance and unique allele distributions are presented for a number of Austronesian and non-Austronesian (Papuan) linguistic populations in the western Pacific. These data confirm separate origins for both of these major populations, but also suggest the existence of much subsequent gene flow between them. Genetic links between Australia and New Guinea are probably very remote in time.

INTRODUCTION

In 1965, Giles, Ogan and Steinberg claimed a clear-cut discrimination based on tests for the Gm system between Austronesian (An) and non-Austronesian (NAn) speakers in the Markham River Valley of Papua New Guinea. Because of a failure later to find a similar discrimination between An and NAn speakers on Bougainville, there has been critical and sometimes heated debate on (a) the usefulness of genetics for studying An and NAn origins, and (b) the validity of the model which suggests that An and NAn-speakers have different biological origins.

These competing views have been highlighted from differing perspectives by John Terrell in his *Prehistory of the Pacific Islands* (1986), Jonathan Friedlaender in his concluding chapter of *The Solomon Islands Project* (1987), and by Sue Serjeantson and Adrian Hill in *The colonization of the Pacific* (1989). The last conclude (Serjeantson and Hill 1989:287):

> ... the extreme view taken by Terrell (1986) and White *et al.* (1988), that Polynesians evolved within Melanesia from a population resident there for at least 30,000 years, is untenable in the light of the genetic evidence.

In the present volume Serjeantson and Gao provide further evidence for this position, based on information derived from analysis of HLA genes. The present discussion complements the HLA analysis by reviewing evidence collected over the past 20 years for a large number of blood-genetic traits and subjecting the data to newer multivariate analytical techniques.

THE NATURE OF THE EVIDENCE

We are not concerned here with discrimination using anthroposcopic or anthropometric characters. In passing, however, it should be noted that such studies, particularly those for teeth and fingerprints, can be very informative. Our own surveys have been restricted to traits detectable in samples of blood under simple genetic control by loci on many different chromosomes. The enzyme and other protein systems used, and their distributions in Pacific populations, have been reviewed recently by Kirk (1989), and in more detail for Papua New Guinea by Kirk (1992).

The data can be analysed in two ways. Some genetic differences are unique to certain populations and their patterns of distribution suggest common ancestry. In addition, variations in frequency of genetic factors can be subjected to multivariate analysis to give "genetic" distances between populations. These distances can be used to construct evolutionary trees by a number of methods including cluster and maximum likelihood analysis, or by principal component analysis, to obtain the distribution patterns of populations.

Unique Allele Distributions

Kirk (1992), reviewing previous studies of the distribution of unique alleles in the western Pacific, recognized three patterns relevant to understanding the relationships between linguistic and genetic differentiation. The first of these patterns, the "Australoid", is associated with the transferrin allele Tf*D1 and the GC*1A1 allele of the vitamin D-binding protein system. The second, or "Proto-Papuan", is characterized by alleles such as PGM1*3, PGM2*9, PGM2*10, PGK*4 and MDH*3. None of these alleles is found in Australia, suggesting that they were brought to, or originated in, New Guinea after the separation of New Guinea and Australia at the end of the Pleistocene, 8-10,000 years ago. These "Proto-Papuan" alleles all have relatively high frequencies in the Papua New Guinea Highlands and in parts of Irian Jaya, with lower frequencies in New Guinea coastal areas and even lower frequencies in the Solomons, Banks Islands and Polynesian Outliers.

The third pattern is "Austronesian". Alleles in this group are not found in Australia and rarely in the Papua New Guinea Highlands. They have their highest frequencies in the Solomons, Polynesian Outliers, Banks Islands, some coastal areas in the north and east of Papua New Guinea, the western Carolines and Fiji. These alleles include PGM1*7, PGK*2, probably HB*Tongariki, Albumin*NG, GPT*3 and GPT*6.

Genetic Distance Studies

Previous studies, reviewed by Kirk (1986, 1989, 1992), have shown discrimination between Waskia (NAn) and Takia (An) on Karkar Island. However, for 17 other populations in the north coastal regions of Papua New Guinea the An speakers are not clearly differentiated from NAn speakers. In these cases more detailed analysis shows that geographic location is more important than linguistic division (Serjeantson *et al.* 1983).

Nevertheless, consideration of populations over a wider geographic area, including many from the Highlands of Papua New Guinea and others from coastal areas and other parts of the western Pacific, show that language is an important discriminant, with the exception of the Mailu in southeast Papua. The exceptional position of the Mailu is due probably to the incorporation of An genetic components from neighbouring populations into a group which continues to speak a NAn language (see Kirk 1992 for further details).

In a detailed comparison of genetic distances between An-speaking Indonesian and other western Pacific populations, Sofro (1982) has shown that the Indonesian populations, including Ternatens and Galelarese from Halmahera whose languages are NAn, cluster with the An-speaking populations of New Guinea and elsewhere in the Pacific but are distinctive from the NAn-speaking populations both in Papua New Guinea and Irian Jaya.

To examine further the question of linguistic and genetic relationships in the Pacific area we have used more recently developed statistical procedures to re-analyse some of our previous data, and have included some populations for which new genetic marker information is now available. Multi-locus allele frequency data were used to estimate the phylogeny of two population groups, using a partial maximum-likelihood method (Felsenstein 1981).

This method has been shown by Kim and Burgman (1988) to be more accurate than the more commonly used unweighted pair-group arithmetic average clustering (UPGAA) method of estimating phylogeny from allele frequency data, particularly when a relatively small number of loci are analysed and where rates of evolution may vary among populations. The maximum-likelihood approach results in an estimate of the evolutionary history of a group of populations in the form of a maximum-likelihood network (or tree) connecting them. The reliability of the estimate can be tested by comparing the "likelihood" of the maximum-likelihood network with that of other networks connecting the same populations through different patterns of branching.

The first group of populations analysed consisted of the same 17 populations referred to above, investigated by Serjeantson *et al.* (1983) and located in the Bogia District and Gogol Valley in northern coastal Papua New Guinea, and on the adjacent Manam, Karkar and Siassi Islands. These populations include both An and NAn speakers. The second group consists of An and NAn speakers from various localities on New Guinea and from throughout Indonesia, Island Melanesia, Micronesia and Polynesia (Map 1).

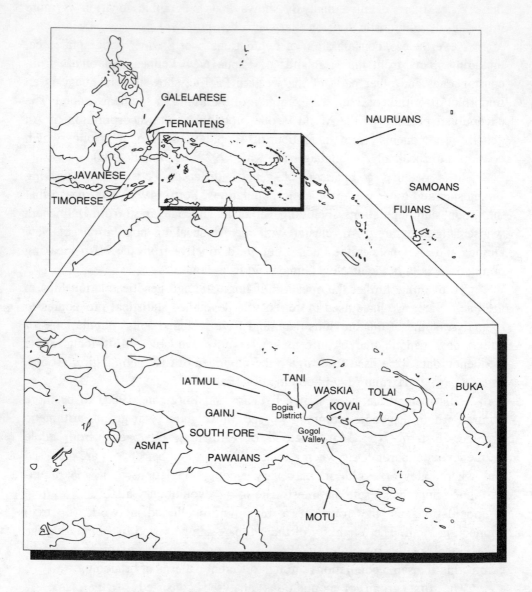

Map 1.   Localities of sampled populations. The linguistic groups sampled from the Bogia District are Saiki, Pila, Tani, Pay, Monumbo, Mikarew, and Manam; those sampled from the Gogol Valley are Munit, Sehan, Ham, Amaimon, and Bemal.

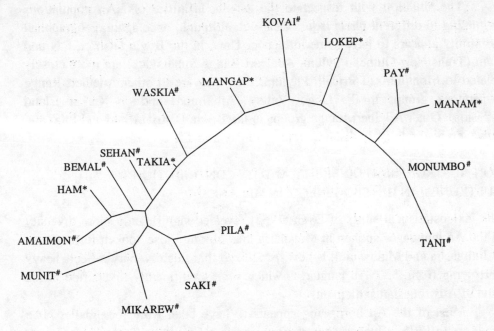

* Austronesians; # non-Austronesians

Figure 1. Maximum likelihood network connecting Austronesian and non-Austronesian-speaking populations from the Bogia District and Gogol Valley on the north coast of Papua New Guinea and from adjacent islands. Branch lengths are drawn in proportion to genetic distance.

AUSTRONESIAN AND NON-AUSTRONESIAN POPULATIONS ON THE NORTH COAST OF PAPUA NEW GUINEA

Our maximum-likelihood analysis of the data of Serjeantson *et al.* (1983) (Figure 1) confirms their conclusions that no clear genetic distinction exists between the An and NAn speakers residing along the north coast of Papua New Guinea, and that population affinities are based more on geographical proximity than on linguistic similarity. There are some differences between the branching patterns of our network and their dendrogram, but it remains the case that, for the most part, populations that are geographically close to each other are relatively similar genetically, irrespective of their linguistic affiliations. Thus, for example, the An Ham are more closely related to other NAn groups in the Gogol Valley than they are to the other An populations. Similarly, the An Manam resemble their NAn neighbours in the Bogia District more than they do other An populations. Two groups on Karkar Island (An Takia and NAn Waskia) are also close to each other in the network, as are the three groups from the Siassi Islands (An Mangap and Lokep and NAn Kovai).

The situation with respect to the genetic affinities of NAn populations belonging to different phyla is less clear-cut, although, once again, geographical proximity appears to have some influence. Thus, in the Bogia District, Pay and Tani (Trans New Guinea Phylum, Adelbert Range Superstock) are more closely related to Monumbo (Torricelli Phylum) than they are to other Adelbert Range Superstock groups in the Gogol Valley (Amaimon) and on Karkar Island (Waskia). Other Adelbert Range groups in the Bogia District (Saki and Pila) are, however, also relatively distantly related to Pay and Tani.

NON-AUSTRONESIAN DIVERSITY AND ITS CONTRIBUTION TO AUSTRONESIAN HETEROGENEITY IN MELANESIA

The lexicostatistical study of Dyen (1965) revealed significantly more diversity in the An languages spoken in Melanesia than among those spoken further west in Indonesia and Malaysia. It is now recognized that this diversity reflects heavy borrowing from the NAn languages which were significantly diversified at the time of Austronesian settlement.

Most of the An borrowing appears to have been from the smaller NAn phyla, with little influence from the two major NAn phyla, Trans New Guinea and Sepik-Ramu. The geographical distributions of these two phyla only overlap with the Austronesian speakers on mainland New Guinea, and that also marginally. Besides, the speakers of languages belonging to these phyla have only recently expanded into their present areas of distribution. The Highlands migration of the Trans New Guinea Phylum languages is considered to have begun around 5,000 to 2,000 years ago. The occupation, west to east, of the coastal areas of Sepik and Madang provinces by Sepik-Ramu speakers, who are essentially a riverine people, is much more recent a phenomenon. Investigation of the An/NAn dichotomy in Melanesia therefore must take into consideration this diversity of NAn languages and the extent to which it has influenced the An substratum.

To evaluate the relationships among An and NAn speakers on a wider scale we selected for analysis representatives of three different NAn phyla, namely, the North Halmahera Stock of West Papuan Phylum (Ternatens and Galelarese), the Iatmul of the Sepik-Ramu Phylum, and speakers of languages in the Trans New Guinea Phylum. In view of the extensive diversification of Trans New Guinea Phylum languages, we selected one population each from five different regions of New Guinea: the north coast (Pila), the northern Highlands-fringe (Gainj), the Highlands proper (South Fore), the southern Highlands-fringe (Pawaia) and the south coast (Asmat). In addition, two populations were added from the islands off the coast of New Guinea (Waskia and Kovai). We also included widely distributed An speakers (Figure 1).

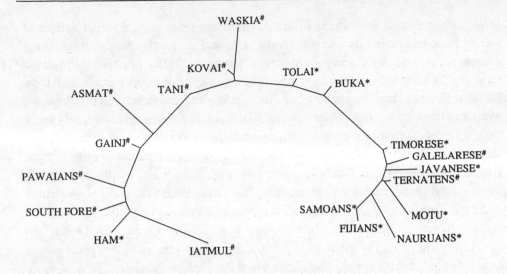

* Austronesians; # non-Austronesians

Figure 2. Maximum likelihood network connecting representative Austronesian and non-Austronesian-speaking populations from Indonesia, Melanesia, Micronesia and Polynesia. Branch lengths are drawn in proportion to genetic distance.

The linguistic diversity among NAn speakers is reflected by their genetic diversity (Figure 2). Differences in the branching order between Figures 1 and 2 for those populations represented in both are due to slight differences in the data used in the two analyses.

The Ternatens and Galelarese from Indonesia (both belong to the West Papuan Phylum) are closely related to the majority of An speakers. They are quite distinct from the other NAn groups, which are themselves loosely clustered with no hierarchical structure to their relationships. It appears that the Trans New Guinea Phylum speakers failed to homogenize the genetic diversity underlying the linguistic substructure already in place at the time of their arrival.

Among the An populations, Ham clusters well within the NAn populations indicating that they have acquired an Austronesian language from outside. With the exception of Tolai and Buka (see below), the remaining An populations are relatively tightly clustered. This indicates close genetic affinities, despite the populations being widely distributed geographically. The pattern is consistent with these populations having spread rapidly and recently to occupy their present location.

It is now accepted that the Bismarck Archipelago was home to the progenitors of Lapita cultures, although an opposing view suggests that these cultures arrived fully formed into the region. Supporters of both these views, however, agree that the islands of the Archipelago were central to the spread of Lapita people further east into the Pacific. Unfortunately, the genetic data on the contemporary Bismarck populations are scanty and the above argument is unlikely to be resolved without some information from New Ireland and New Britain. Genetic data on populations surrounding the Bismarck Archipelago are available, and it may be argued that the Bismarck populations are unlikely to be very different from these neighbouring populations. We argue, on the one hand, that the populations settled on both sides of St George's Channel, between New Britain and New Ireland, would more likely to have been influenced by the Lapita movement than those surrounding the Vitiaz Strait, between New Britain and New Guinea, if the colonizers of Polynesia originated in Southeast Asia and largely bypassed Melanesia. On the other hand, if the Lapita populations *did* develop entirely in the Bismarck Archipelago then one might expect greater genetic homogeneity among populations in the region of the Bismarck Sea.

To test these two opposing hypotheses we have included in the analyses populations bordering St George's Channel and the Vitiaz Strait. The Tolai occupy the western end of St George's Channel, whereas the Buka are located further east. For the Vitiaz Strait we have selected two NAn-speaking populations, the Kovai from Umboi Island and Waskia from Karkar Island.

The analysis reveals that the four Papua New Guinean island populations do not join either the group composed of Polynesians, Micronesians and Indonesians, or the remaining NAn populations (Figure 2) occupying an intermediate position in the network between the two. Waskia and Kovai share a common branch in Figure 2. Tolai and Buka branch quite separately and distinctly, but are closer to the remaining An populations. There is thus no homogeneity among the populations surrounding the Bismarck Sea and greater affinity between the main group of An populations and those adjacent to St George's Channel consistent with the hypothesis of a movement of Lapita culture through the region.

LINGUISTIC LINKS BETWEEN SEPIK-RAMU AND EARLIER AUSTRALIAN LANGUAGES

The diversity of NAn languages raises the issue of their possible links with the languages which are now found in Australia. Wurm (1983) has suggested that linguistic traces of an early Australian (or Australoid) population, mixed with later arriving NAn speakers, can be seen in the languages of the Sepik-Ramu Phylum. According to him, Laycock (1973) has pointed out the general resemblance between the phonology of the languages of Ndu Family in the Middle Sepik Stock of the Sepik-Ramu Phylum and the general phonological features of the Australian languages. In addition, the occurrences in the Sepik-

Ramu region of Australian cultural elements such as spearthrowers, bullroarers, flat surface and bark painting, and the resemblances of slit-gong melodies to didgeridoo melodies, are all considered to indicate possession of common cultural traits. The connection between the speakers of Sepik-Ramu Phylum languages and Aboriginal Australians has been explained by a southward migration route passing through the Purari River area, possibly because there are similarities between the Sepik art styles and those of the Purari (Spieser 1937), where bullroarers are also found (Williams 1936).

However, further analysis of our data provides no indication of a connection between the Sepik-Ramu populations and Aboriginal Australians via the Purari River area. First, there is no close affinity between the Iatmul (Sepik-Ramu) and the Pawaians (Purari River) (Figure 2). Second, we repeated the analysis of the populations shown in Figure 2 with the inclusion of a population from central Australia (Waljbiri). The resulting network (not illustrated here) shows the Waljbiri are very distantly related to all other populations. The branch leading to the Waljbiri is nearly eight times as long as the next longest terminal branch on the network (leading to Iatmul), and the position at which it connects to the rest of the network could not reliably be determined. It would seem that if there are any genetic affinities underlying the cultural and linguistic similarities between Sepik-Ramu and Australian Aboriginal populations, as discussed by Wurm (1983), these are extremely remote.

CONCLUSIONS

Our extensive data support the model that An speakers had a different biological origin from the NAn speakers in the western Pacific. However, the differences are not clear-cut in all cases and suggest that in many populations other factors, including intermarriage to various extents, have occurred to blur the edges of the linguistic boundaries.

REFERENCES

Dyen, I.
   1965   A lexicostatistical classification of the Austronesian languages. *International Journal of American Linguistics*, Memoir 19.

Felsenstein, J.
   1981   Evolutionary trees from gene frequencies and quantitative characters: finding maximum likelihood estimates. *Evolution* 35:1229-1242.

Friedlaender, J. (ed.)
   1987   *The Solomon Islands Project*. Oxford: Oxford University Press.

Giles E., E. Ogan and A.G. Steinberg
1965   The gamma globulin factors (Gm and Inv) in New Guinea: anthropological significance. *Science* 150:1158-1160.

Kim, J. and M.A. Burgman
1988   Accuracy of phylogenetic-estimation methods under unequal evolutionary rates. *Evolution* 42:596-602.

Kirk R.L.
1986   Human genetic diversity in south-east Asia and the western Pacific. In D.F. Roberts and G.F. de Stefano (eds) *Genetic diversity and its maintenance in tropical populations*, pp.111-134. Cambridge: Cambridge University Press.
1989   Population genetic studies in the Pacific: red cell antigen, serum protein and enzyme systems. In A.V.S. Hill and S.W. Serjeantson (eds) *The colonization of the Pacific: a genetic trail*, pp.60-119. Oxford: Clarendon Press.
1992   Population origins in Papua New Guinea. In R.D. Attenborough and M.P. Alpers (eds) *Human biology in Papua New Guinea: the small cosmos*, pp.172-197. Oxford: Clarendon Press.

Laycock, D.C.
1973   *Sepik languages — checklist and preliminary classification.* Pacific Linguistics Series B No. 25. Canberra: Department of Linguistics, Research School of Pacific Studies, The Australian National University.

Terrell, J.
1986   *Prehistory in the Pacific Islands*. Cambridge: Cambridge University Press.

Serjeantson, S.W. and A.V.S. Hill
1989   The colonization of the Pacific: the genetic evidence. In A.V.S. Hill and S.W. Serjeantson (eds) *The colonization of the Pacific: a genetic trail*, pp.286-294. Oxford: Clarendon Press.

Serjeantson, S.W., R.L. Kirk and P.B. Booth
1983   Linguistic and genetic differentiation in New Guinea. *Journal of Human Evolution* 12:77-92.

Sofro, A.S.M.
1982   Population genetic studies in Indonesia. PhD thesis, The Australian National University, Canberra.

Spieser, F.
1937   Eine initiationszeromonie in Kambrango am Sepik, Neuguinea. *Ethnologischer Anzeiger* 4:153-157.

White, J.P., J. Allen and J. Specht
1988   Peopling the Pacific: the Lapita Homeland Project. *Australian Natural History* 22:410-416.

Williams, F.E.
1936   *Bullroarers in the Papuan Gulf* (Territory of Papua, Anthropological Report 12). Port Moresby: Government Printer.

Wurm, S.A.
    1983   Linguistic prehistory in the New Guinea area. *Journal of Human Evolution* 12:25-35.

11

LANGUAGE CONTACT AND CHANGE IN MELANESIA

Tom Dutton

*This paper surveys the kinds of contact-induced language change that have so far been observed in the languages of Melanesia, linguistically one of the most diverse areas of the world, if not **the** most diverse. It then draws on this survey to draw attention to the problems that these pose for the classification and reconstruction of the history of Melanesian languages. In some ways Melanesia is typical of the rest of the Austronesian world, but in other ways it is not.*

INTRODUCTION

The topic of language contact and change in Melanesia is a vast one, and one that I cannot possibly do justice to in detail in the space available here. My aim will therefore be merely to give an overview of the types of contact-induced change that have so far been observed in that part of the Pacific that is popularly known as Melanesia (Map 1), with a view to drawing attention to certain problems that these pose for the classification and reconstruction of the history of Melanesian languages. In some ways Melanesia is typical of the rest of the Austronesian world but in other ways it is not.

Let us begin with the, now somewhat well worn, observation that Melanesia is one of the most diverse linguistic areas in the world, if not the most diverse. Here, scattered across New Guinea, the Solomon Islands, Vanuatu, New Caledonia, the Loyalty Islands and Fiji are to be found over one thousand languages,[1] or approximately one-quarter of those spoken in the world today.[2]

Languages in this area are usually classified into two major types: Austronesian (An) and Non-Austronesian or Papuan (NAn), the latter being a general cover term for all those languages that are not An in origin without necessarily implying genetic relationship. For the most part speakers of An languages occupy the smaller islands and coastal areas of the larger islands. These languages are most closely related genetically to the languages of Polynesia and Micronesia and form with them the Oceanic (Oc) subgroup of An languages (see Pawley and Ross, this volume). Approximately 400 of the Oceanic languages are spoken in Melanesia. They belong to different first order subgroups of Oc although not everyone agrees on just what these subgroups are.

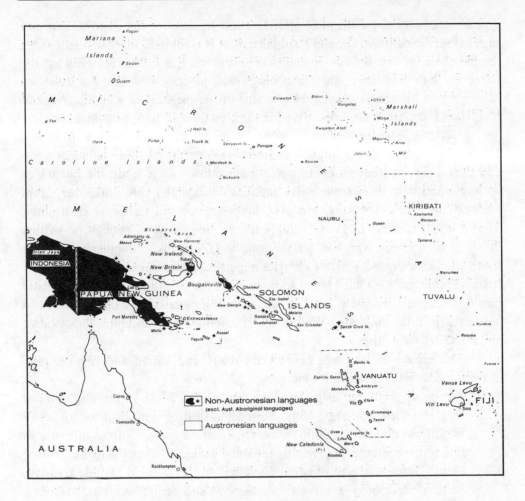

Map 1: The distribution of language types in Melanesia.

Thirteen of them are Polynesian in origin and are known as the Polynesian Outliers.[3]

NAn languages, on the other hand, are genetically unrelated to An languages.[4] They vary widely amongst themselves and do not belong to one large family like the An languages do, although some 75 per cent or so of them are thought to be distantly related to one another and to form a super-family called the Trans-New Guinea Phylum. Even so, no such relationship has yet been firmly demonstrated and the best that linguists are prepared to accept is that there are many families (about 60) which look as if they could group together in a large number of stocks and phyla. Speakers of these languages occupy the area not occupied by speakers of An languages, which for the most part is the interior of some of the larger western Melanesian islands. They are especially concentrated on the mainland of New Guinea. Because of the distributions and internal relationships of An and NAn languages it is thought that NAn languages are the older and that the An languages are intrusive. It is further believed (on the basis of both linguistic and archaeological evidence) that the Austronesian settlement of Melanesia was by descendants of the speakers of a single ancestral language, Proto-Oceanic, who arrived in the area three to four millennia ago.

Given a situation where so many languages are concentrated in such a small area it comes as no surprise to find that speakers of these languages are, and have been, in frequent contact with each other.[5] As a result the languages undergo, and have undergone, what linguists colloquially call "influence" from each other. Strictly speaking, however, languages do not influence each other. They cannot, because languages only exist as entities when spoken or written down. It is speakers who transfer the aspects of one on to another when they make choices about what to say or write in particular circumstances. But for this to happen the speakers must know some or all of the other language. In linguistic terms there must be some level of bi- or multilingualism in communities in contact before the languages used in those communities can come into contact and influence each other.

The effects of language contact are many and varied and can be quite dramatic. The main possibilities include:

a)   one group giving up its language in favour of another. In linguistic circles this is called language shift. Language shifting is sensitive to social conditions and, although it is not yet a settled issue, cultural pressure in one form or another is generally regarded as the important shift-motivating factor. Some of the most common factors in this context include prestige, cultural superiority, militaristic dominance and demographic superiority.[6] If the dominant group is large it is likely that the shifting group will eventually learn the target language. However, if the relationship changes (as for example, if the dominant group is reduced in size for some reason or loses power) or if the shifting group is able to survive as a homogeneous or close-knit subgroup within the target language community (as happens with some ethnic minorities in Australia), the shifting group's form of the language may become established as the norm. In this case the norm will show the effects of borrowing, often called language shift interference or substratum influence — the subordinate speakers have influenced the language in the direction of their original language.

b)   two or more languages existing side by side without any interference. This can only happen in very special circumstances, when, for example, neither group utters a word of the other's language even though the two groups may come together for certain purposes (such as trading), or when speakers of one language learn to understand the other but never use it.

Speakers in this latter situation are said to be passively bilingual (that is understand a language but not speak it) or to be dual lingual (as, for example, when two people speak different languages and converse by doing so, each being passively bilingual in the other's language).

c)   borrowing of elements of one language into another. This is the most common type of influence one language has on another and may involve all aspects of a language, from sounds to grammar and vocabulary. Theoretically any feature of a language may be borrowed, although this has only recently been acknowledged. For a long time it was assumed, for example, that grammatical elements would only be borrowed between dialects (or variants of a language) or very similarly structured languages. Nevertheless, in practice we find that given the right social conditions any aspect of a language can be borrowed. For this to happen, however, special social circumstances have to be operating. In general, social factors are the most important determinants for borrowing, although linguistic factors such as the similarity of the structure of the two languages (or what linguists call typological distance between them) are not unimportant.[7] Although there is a range of terms used by linguists to talk about borrowing there are three well-known if somewhat old fashioned terms which cover most cases. These are what Bloomfield (1933:444-495), the so-called Father of American Linguistics, called "dialect borrowing", "cultural borrowing" and "intimate borrowing", although in Melanesia it is often difficult to distinguish between the results of partial language shift, heavy cultural borrowing and intimate borrowing.

i) Dialect borrowing. As the name suggests this is the kind of borrowing that occurs between dialects or varieties of a language. It is also applied to that between typologically very similar languages. In this kind of borrowing changes introduced are generally very minute and result mainly from groups of speakers favouring one way of saying something over another, rather than from the adoption of wholly new forms of vocabulary or grammar. Dialect borrowing is perhaps the most difficult problem that linguists have to deal with in trying to classify languages and in reconstructing their histories, because it often goes undetected.[8]

ii) Cultural borrowing. This is the term used to describe the kind of borrowing that occurs when two or more groups of people come into contact and learn words for things they do not have and are interested in obtaining from each other. This kind of borrowing implies casual contact and is most likely to occur where there are cultural differences. It is ordinarily mutual (as the rather crude definition above suggests), but it does not have to be. It is one-sided only to the extent that one group has more to give than the other. Because it is associated with casual contact the borrowing usually only involves vocabulary. This kind of borrowing is also usually very easy to identify because it is restricted to certain kinds of items and is usually phonologically irregular in some way. Finally the borrowing process does not affect the borrowing language's sound system. Consider, for example, how little the pronunciation of British citizens in India was affected by the adoption of many words of Indian origin.

iii) Intimate borrowing. This type of borrowing occurs when a group of speakers attempts to learn the language of its contacts. As a result it implies some degree of second language learning, some kind of bilingualism (or multilingualism) although it does not necessarily imply language shift.[9] That may be an unintended result, however. Thus, as will be pointed out later, where language differences serve group identity (or emblematic) functions, as in Melanesia, a group of speakers may come to regard another language as part of its "pool of linguistic resources" (Grace 1981:264) for various social purposes. That is, speakers keep their mother tongue for group identity purposes but become so familiar with the second language that they may transfer the features of that language to their mother tongue. As a result the structure and vocabulary of their mother tongue may be influenced by that of the second language. The learning of the second (or third or however many) language normally takes place as a result of some "felt need" or perceived social advantage on the part of the learners. Borrowing or linguistic influence in this case implies close or intense contact. Often the first indication that intimate borrowing has taken place is that the language proves difficult to classify or that the original status of the language as An or NAn is not immediately clear. In Melanesia a number of such difficult-to-classify languages have been called "mixed languages" (Capell 1976), although the term is a controversial one and not accepted by everyone.

d)   the development of a third language not identical to either. This is the case again when special social conditions prevail, such as, for example, when communities come into contact to trade[10] or when one group of people is imprisoned by or forced to work for another (as happened in the Pacific last century for example). In these situations there is a need to communicate before there is time to learn one or the other of the languages spoken by the contacting groups or when there are other barriers to doing so. Such languages are usually restricted in vocabulary and simplified in structure compared with the languages in contact. They are specific purpose languages and are not spoken natively. They are called pidgin languages.[11]

LANGUAGE CONTACT AND CHANGE IN MELANESIA

Language Shift and Obsolescence

Although we do not have records to show how often this occurred in the past — Melanesian societies kept no written records and were apparently not sufficiently concerned about the demise of languages to keep oral traditions about them for any significant length of time — there were sufficient numbers of cases of languages in the last stages of obsolescence at the time of European contact for us to presume that it was a reasonably regularly occurring event prehistorically. It would appear that the conditions favouring language shift in Melanesia are similar to those noted elsewhere — the absorption of remnants of larger groups seeking refuge from intertribal warfare and natural disasters (such as droughts, floods and epidemics) or small numbers of people pursuing perceived economic or cultural advantages. In any case, both An and NAn languages were involved (Dutton and Mühlhäusler 1991).

No Influence

It is hard to find cases in this category because the potentially instructive ones either have not been fully described or do not live up to expectations on further investigation. For example, even though we have reported cases of dual lingualism involving An and NAn language speakers, in the best described one the An languages involved, Banoni and Piva, do show low levels of cultural borrowing from neighbouring Papuan languages (Lincoln 1976:97-99).

BORROWING

Dialect Borrowing

By its very nature this kind of borrowing is difficult to identify. It usually shows up, however, in detailed comparative work as inconsistent sound correspondences and/or as dialect chaining. Thus, for example, in Papuan Tip (PT) languages in the Milne Bay Province of Papua New Guinea some reflexes of PPT *b, *d and *g occur voiced instead of being voiceless as expected (Ross 1988:198-202). These voiced reflexes are evidently the result of dialect borrowing from neighbouring languages.

Chaining occurs when a string of communities share sets of features with each other in an overlapping fashion so that community A shares some features with community B, which in turn shares some features with community C, and so on. The phenomenon was first described by Wurm and Laycock (1961-62) in discussing problems of classification in Papua New Guinea. Its existence introduces a certain arbitrariness in the definition of "language" and "dialect" in

Melanesia and explains why linguists differ about the number of languages actually spoken therein. In his detailed study of the An languages of western Melanesia, Ross (1988:8) distinguishes between "chains" and "networks", the former being used for "communalects that are typically spread along a coastline, each related most closely to its neighbour on either side", and the latter for "communalects scattered over a land area or an archipelago, typically having neighbours on more than two sides and often sharing different innovations with several of these".

Dialect borrowing therefore poses problems for the traditional family tree model of language diversification. To cope with it linguists are forced to adopt models that allow for diversification through contact-induced change, as Ross (1988) did in his exemplary study.

Cultural Borrowing

This is the most common kind of borrowing noted in Melanesia — at least it is the one most easily identified and most often reported. It is particularly common in NAn languages in contact with An ones and in Melanesian An languages in contact with Polynesian Outlier ones. In both these cases it is particular cultural items that seaboard or incoming Austronesians have that other resident communities seek and hence borrow vocabulary for. Thus, for example, the NAn Koita around Port Moresby have borrowed sailing and sea terminology (including terms for marine life) from their Austronesian neighbours, the Motu (Dutton 1994). The An languages near Polynesian Outlier languages have done very much the same thing, borrowing not only Polynesian terms for the sea and sailing but also words associated with kava drinking and artefacts made from coconut fronds (Clark 1994). This picture is repeated many times in the literature and is part of the folk wisdom of Oceanic linguists.[12] By definition this kind of borrowing is one sided or at most unequal, although it is not always quite as straightforward as this suggests. Indeed it is very sensitive to socio-cultural realities and may be bound up with intimate borrowing as well. Thus, for example, Clark (1986) describes how the Polynesian Outlier languages of Emae and Mele-Fila in Vanuatu have borrowed intimately from neighbouring An languages which in turn only show effects of cultural borrowing.[13] The reasons for this are apparently demographic — the Polynesians were (and still are) much fewer in number than their Melanesian neighbours and in seeking wives and in trading they would have had to, as Clark says,

> deal with Melanesian speakers more often than not, whereas Melanesian speakers, on average, would have had only a minority of Polynesian contacts. Melanesian wives, in particular, marrying into Polynesian villages, bearing and rearing children, speaking a Melanesian-influenced second-language variety,

would have accomplished both the physical and the linguistic assimilation of the immigrants (Clark 1986:341).

Such cases show that, even though the principles of cultural borrowing are clear, it is not possible to predict the effects in particular cases without knowing the social conditions operating. Consequently it is often not possible to distinguish between the effects of heavy cultural borrowing and intimate borrowing.

Intimate Borrowing

It has long been known that, structurally, the An languages of the Papua New Guinea area fall into two main types, those with a basic SOV (subject – object – verb) word order and those with a basic SVO word order.[14] Practically all of the mainland An languages and those of south-eastern Papua and its associated offshore islands are of the first type while those of the second type are found mainly in New Britain and New Ireland. As well, the basic word order SOV coincides with that of most NAn languages. It has therefore been suggested that the structural difference between these two groups of An languages is to be attributed to contact with NAn languages some time in the past. Although it has not been possible to identify any particular NAn language or group of such languages to support this claim it seems highly likely that this difference was the result of intimate borrowing.

Apart from this case and a number of other well known cases of language "mixing" described briefly below (which derive from intimate borrowing between An and NAn languages),[15] relatively few cases of this kind of borrowing have appeared in the literature until recently. One such case is Labu, an An language spoken near Lae, Papua New Guinea. This is a small language of 1700 speakers that is surrounded by speakers of two other An languages, Bukawa and Kela. For many years the genetic position of Labu *vis-à-vis* related languages in the same area has been ambiguous. Holzknecht (1994) shows, however, that Labu is a member of the Markham Family that has been heavily influenced by Bukawa and possibly also Kela (both closely related to one another and members of the North Huon Gulf Chain) in phonology, grammar and vocabulary. Although she does not say as much this case appears to be one of intimate borrowing between An languages. This is not only evident from the fact that all aspects of the structure have been influenced but also from the fact that the Labu have been socially in "more or less intense" contact with the Bukawa. Indeed, some of the early Labu "spent some time within Bukawa-speaking communities in a client (Labu)-patron (Bukawa) relationship" as refugees (Holzknecht 1994:371), and some children grew up bilingual in Labu and Bukawa. This is not regarded as a case of dialect borrowing, however, because, even though the languages are An, they are not sufficiently closely related or typologically similar to fit the definition given above.

More elaborate cases are those described briefly by Clark (1994), who discusses a complex situation obtaining amongst the Polynesian Outlier languages. He notes that none of the Polynesian languages is "pure" in the sense of having undergone no influence but the influence is scaled — it is greatest on those languages geographically closest to non-Polynesian languages and least in the most remote or isolated communities. Two languages, Mele-Fila and Emae, show unmistakable signs of intimate borrowing from non-Polynesian languages nearby. Two others, Rennellese and Fagauvea, show signs of cultural and intimate borrowing at work together. In other cases it is not clear if the evidence is indicative of intimate borrowing or the influence is a secondary effect of cultural borrowing on a large scale. The picture is further complicated by the fact that (i) at least in one case, Anuta, multiple settlements have occurred from Polynesia on the one island, (ii) in other cases there has been contact with neighbouring Polynesian communities that have a common settlement history. On the other hand, none of the non-Polynesian languages has undergone anything like the borrowing seen in the more affected cases of Polynesian languages. In general they have only borrowed culturally relevant vocabulary of a kind already noted above. The explanation for the observed borrowing pattern is demographic — the Polynesian communities are all small even by Melanesian standards.

So-called "Mixed" Languages

These are special cases of intimate borrowing where the languages have undergone so much influence from some other language or languages that there has been considerable debate about their original status. They include Magori, Maisin and the Reef-Santa Cruz languages, and in a slightly different category, Lusi.

Magori is an An language of the southeast coast of Papua New Guinea. At the time of European contact it was only spoken in two small villages in the Bailebo River valley almost opposite Mailu Island where the principal village of the NAn Mailu (or Magi) is situated. When first recorded it was thought that Magori was part of the Mailu language, if apparently somewhat aberrant. Subsequent investigation showed, however, that it was originally an An language from which the Mailu had initially borrowed. Later, it appears that something happened to put the Magori in a position where at first contact they were living in fear of the Mailu and were learning their language. In the process they were borrowing back words that the Mailu had originally borrowed from them in a different form (Dutton 1982). This borrowing has been very heavy but so far it does not seem to have affected the grammar and phonology very much. However, Magori and remnants of three other closely related An languages, Ouma, Yoba and Bina, have become more alike as a result of mutual loaning and borrowing with other neighbouring An languages. Lexically, they now appear to be co-ordinate between eastern and western groups of An languages along the south coast of Papua (Dutton 1976, 1982).

Maisin is spoken in two areas corresponding to two dialect divisions in the Northern Province of Papua New Guinea — one in the coastal area of Collingwood Bay and one in several villages in the swamps between the mouths of the Musa and Bariji Rivers in Dyke Ackland Bay (Dutton 1971). For many years this language had been an enigma, some scholars classifying it as originally An and others as originally NAn. In 1977, however, Lynch showed fairly conclusively that although it had a vocabulary of mixed origins its grammar was basically An. It is now clear that it originally belonged to the Are-Tauopota Chain of Papuan Tip languages (Ross 1988). Its present "mixed" status arises from the fact that it was evidently in close contact with some (as yet unidentified) NAn language or languages in which the speakers were bilingual and as a result has been heavily influenced by it or them.

The Reefs-Santa Cruz languages spoken in the islands of the same name in the eastern Solomon Islands are similar to Maisin in that investigators have disagreed about their original status. Wurm (1978), for example, argued that they were originally NAn and Lincoln (1978) argued that they were An. This controversy has not been satisfactorily resolved to date.

Lusi is an An language spoken in the West New Britain Province of Papua New Guinea. According to Thurston (1982), Lusi is a creole language (that is, a pidgin language that has become the native language of a group of speakers) which has developed from a pidginized An language through contact with the NAn language Anêm (Thurston 1982:71). Thurston's use of the word "pidginized" is aimed at emphasizing the rapid nature of change that was involved in this transformation and the changes the language has undergone.[16] It was an exaggerated position adopted to draw attention to the normally accepted view that language change is gradual. In reality it is no different from related languages in the area. While it has undergone changes not undergone by others, most probably as a result of contact with Anêm, it is not so different for it to be put in a special category.

PIDGINS

So far, seven of these have been reported involving An languages in Melanesia, only five of which have been documented in any way.[17] Of these two had to do with the *hiri* trade in central Papua involving An and geographically distant NAn language speakers (Dutton 1985). Another two developed with trade between the An Mekeo and neighbouring NAn language speakers in central Papua (Jones 1985). In a slightly different but related category was a kind of "foreigner talk" used by the An Motu of the Port Moresby area to communicate with visiting foreigners. An administrative language called Police Motu which developed in Papua after European contact is thought to have developed out of this special variety of Motu (Dutton 1985).

This number of reported pidgin languages is surprisingly small, given the linguistic diversity of Melanesia and the number of trading networks in which there was contact between An and NAn languages, as well as between An and An languages including Polynesian Outlier languages. Amongst the more important reasons for this are possibly the following:

a)   that where trading was between neighbouring groups, bi- or multi-lingualism took care of the problem of communication;

b)   that pidgin languages have not been considered worthy of any attention by linguists until recently and have therefore gone unreported in the past.

It is to be particularly noted that there are no examples of pidgins arising out of An-An contact.[18]

IMPLICATIONS FOR CLASSIFICATION AND HISTORICAL RECONSTRUCTION

If there is one point that stands out above all others in this survey it is that there has been much more contact between the different types of languages in Melanesia than most scholars have been prepared to acknowledge in the past. As a result, we must be prepared to accept that the linguistic and archaeological prehistories of the area are that much more complicated than hitherto suspected or acknowledged.

Scholars interested in the classification and origin of An languages have long known about and been fascinated by the diversity aspect of Melanesian languages. While those languages share what Grace called "a characteristic uniformity" (or "tendency to sameness") in some respects, they also display a "remarkable diversity" in others (Grace 1968:67). However, those same scholars have often argued at cross purposes about the underlying reasons for this because they have generally failed to recognize that there is not just one kind of diversity, but several.

The first kind of diversity to be recognized is that which is referred to in the opening paragraph to this paper, notably, the sheer number of languages concentrated in a small area. Actually it is not merely the absolute number that is the interesting and significant thing, but, as Pawley (1981) points out, the number of languages per island group. Thus, when compared with Polynesia, for example, Melanesia has many languages per island group while Polynesia usually has only one. Why is this so? Pawley's answer was that Melanesian diversity was not "brought about by mechanisms of a radically different kind from those which operated in Polynesia" (Pawley 1981:273). Rather, the sequence of diversification was much the same in both areas, the only difference being that "the cycle of linguistic diversification" had more time to apply in Melanesia than in Polynesia (Pawley 1981:298). While he saw various socio-economic and political factors as important in this speciation process, Pawley did not see contact with NAn communities as a "necessary ingredient in the recipe for Melanesian linguistic diversity" (Pawley 1981:274-275). He did acknowledge, however, that the presence of such populations may have hastened the process. As he himself noted on a later occasion (Pawley 1990), this type of diversity is not much of a puzzle. It can be accounted for by the sorts of mechanisms outlined in his paper.

Two other kinds of diversity are more interesting. They have to do with variation between An languages in Melanesia. In the first kind the focus is on the way some languages differ markedly from other An languages and reconstructed proto-languages in their sound systems and grammars. The second type has to do with the distribution of cognates across languages, some languages having relatively few. Those that are most divergent in these senses are often referred to as "aberrant" or "problematic" (Grace 1990), and those that have changed least as "conservative" or "exemplary". Between these two are degrees of aberrancy so that languages can be ranged on a scale (although no one has actually tried to do this) from least to most aberrant (Grace 1990). The Markham River languages in Papua New Guinea, New Caledonian languages and those of south Tanna in Vanuatu in particular have reputations of being the most aberrant. Indeed, although An languages in Melanesia are classified as An, that is, as descendants of Proto-Oceanic, they vary so widely in structure and vocabulary that linguists are still debating how they should be classified internally (see Pawley and Ross, this volume).

Scholars have long puzzled over the reasons for these two kinds of diversity and have sought to explain them in varying ways. The first to do so was S.H. Ray (1926), who suggested that the present forms of An languages in Melanesia resulted when incoming An speakers from Indonesia settled in Melanesia and came into contact with resident NAn populations. Later, Capell (who was actually a student of Ray's) carried this idea forward in various publications, giving rise to what is known as the "pidginization hypothesis". Both Ray and Capell pointed to the small proportion of vocabulary in Melanesian An languages that could be related to Indonesian vocabulary.[19] Capell (1943) further claimed that a study of this vocabulary shows that the languages of southeast Papua, for example, derived their particular features from having been in contact with a number of "regional" NAn languages, certain features of which could be reconstructed from that same vocabulary.

For a long time this pidginization hypothesis was rejected by later linguists as based on false assumptions and bad methodology.[20] Grace (1962), in summing up the controversy, challenged supporters of it to find a Melanesian language in which the non-An elements could be attributed to a specific NAn language. Thurston (1982) took up this challenge and provides evidence from Lusi in West New Britain that he says is "capable of resolving the argument in favour of Capell and Ray" (Thurston 1982:2). His examination of both lexical and grammatical evidence leads him to conclude, as already pointed out, that Lusi is a creole language which has developed from a pidginized An language through contact with the NAn language Anêm. Thurston is so convinced by what he finds in Lusi and other languages of the same area that he believes that pidginization (in his sense) was the major factor in the diversification of Mn languages (1987, 1994).

Meanwhile, Lynch (1981) also took up the challenge implicit in Pawley's 1981 paper referred to above and argued that the many-languages-per-island-group type of diversity as found in Melanesia was not solely a reflection of different time depths and particular socio-economic and political conditions. He felt that contact between An and NAn languages was also an important factor. In support of his claim he appealed to the specific mixed-language-type case studies of Magori, Maisin, Lusi and Reefs-Santa Cruz that have been mentioned above.

Since then Grace, responding to more recent detailed work by a number of younger scholars including those already mentioned, has acknowledged that there is much that is left unexplained by the traditional views of language diversification and change based on the family tree model. He has called for a reassessment of "all the facts" (1985:3).

Part of the problem in the past has been, of course, that scholars have attempted to provide a unified "solution" to what has often been called "the Melanesian problem" (Grace 1968), without distinguishing between the different types of diversity described above and without attempting to find separate "solutions" for each kind. What such scholars failed to acknowledge was that there are many factors besides time depth and language contact that have been involved in producing the kinds of diversity found in Melanesia today. Attitudes to language, and what Don Laycock used to call "conscious human monkeying with language", are two such factors. Laycock describes how in one dialect of Buin, a NAn language of south Bougainville, gender distinctions in grammar are the exact reverse of those in other dialects — what is male in other dialects is female in this dialect (1982:35). Melanesians thus appear to foster linguistic diversity purposefully because they see linguistic differences as important badges of group identity. It is, as it were, a Melanesian choice to promote diversity (Laycock 1982:34).

One thing is certain, and that is that diversity must be functional in some way; otherwise, as Grace points out, it is maintained at too great a social cost — why learn to be different when being the same would be less taxing? Nor can diversity be explained solely by migration, as that would require too many independent moves (Grace 1975; Thurston 1987:94ff.). At the same time, Melanesian societies have placed a high value on multilingualism. The public display of knowledge of other languages has long been noted as an important means of gaining prestige in Melanesia (Salisbury 1962; Sankoff 1977).

Another factor that needs to be taken into account in attempting to explain linguistic diversity in Melanesia is word tabooing. This is the social action of forbidding the use of a word that is associated in some way with a member of the community who has just died. It is a common feature of many Melanesian societies and leads to "unnatural" replacement of vocabulary (Simons 1982; Holzknecht 1988).

FUTURE RESEARCH NEEDS

Notwithstanding the marked improvement in knowledge of particular Melanesian languages and groups of languages in recent years, there are still many questions that have to be answered before we can say that the field of language contact and change has been adequately covered. Just how far we still have to go can perhaps be most simply illustrated by pointing out that, whereas the results of An-NAn contact figure prominently in the discussion above, those of An-An contact do so only to a much lesser degree. This can be shown by a table such as the following that displays the types of contact studies that have figured in the discussion above. In this '#' indicates that no case has been adequately described to date and '+' means one or more cases have been reported:

Type (resulting from):	An-An contact	An-NAn contact
a) obsolescence	#	+
b) dual lingualism	#	+
c) borrowing		
dialect borrowing	+	#
cultural borrowing	+	+
intimate borrowing	+	+
"mixed" language	#	+
d) pidgin language	#	+

Although crude, this table is nevertheless quite instructive because it clearly shows that the types of reported cases are skewed in favour of An-NAn contact. Thus, while An-NAn contact has produced all possible results, An-An contact seems to result only in different types of borrowing. To what can this skewing be attributed? Does it merely represent poor socio-linguistic investigation and reporting, or are there other explanations? To answer these sorts of questions we need more in-depth studies of particular cases focused not only on traditional descriptive and comparative historical questions, but also on such aspects as the following that Grace (1975, 1985, 1990) has drawn attention to:

- societal attitudes to language correctness and accelerated language change;
- the way sound changes are introduced and spread;
- social isolation and its effect on rate of change;
- inter- versus intra-community diversity;
- the definition of "the language of a community".

In other words we need much more detailed information than we have had hitherto. With many new scholars entering the field, better trained than in the past, there is every prospect of achieving the desired goals.

NOTES

[1] The word "language" is here used in the sense that when two people speak their respective mother tongues they do not understand each other (unless one has learnt the other's language). That is, it is not the same as "dialect" or varieties of a language like British English and Australian English. These two terms are confusing because until early this century the word "dialect" was often used to mean what we refer to as "language" today.

[2] The claim is based on the following figures.

Location	Area (in km^2)	Number of languages*	Estimated population*
Irian Jaya	400,000 (approx)	700-750[†]	3,000,000
Papua New Guinea	476,500		3,000,000
Solomon Islands	29,000	120	200,000
Vanuatu	14,763	200	100,000
New Caledonia	19,103	27	135,000
Fiji	18,200	2	600,000
Total	957,566	1049-1099	7,035,000

* Based on figures in Wurm and Hattori (1981).
† The variation here reflects differences of opinion on how "language" should be defined.

[3] These include Nukuria off New Ireland in Papua New Guinea, Nukumanu, Luangiua, Sikaiana, Pileni, Taumako, Tikopia, Anuta, and Rennell-Bellona in the Solomon Islands, Takuu, Mae (or Emae), Futuna-Aniwa in Vanuatu and Fagauvea in the Loyalty Islands off New Caledonia — see Wurm and Hattori (1981).

[4]   See Wurm (1982) and Foley (1986) for further details on NAn languages of Oceania.

[5]   This is not a necessary result, however. As will be pointed out later some scholars have emphasized the isolation of Melanesians in attempting to explain the diversity of languages found in this part of the world.

[6]   This is a large topic and readers are referred to Dorian (ed.) (1989) and references therein for further details.

[7]   There is an extensive and growing literature on contact linguistics. See Thomason and Kaufman (ed.) (1988), for example, and references therein for further reading.

[8]   This is quite an involved topic and the best I can do is direct readers to Trudgill (1986), for example, for further reading.

[9]   See Guy (1990) for a survey of the relationship between social conditions of change and their linguistic outcomes and Ross (1991) for a refinement on Guy's treatment.

[10] Trading does not always produce new languages. Instances of "silent" trading between different linguistic groups have been reported in Papua New Guinea for example (e.g. Harding 1967:64). In these trading sessions goods were exchanged but no language was spoken.

[11] There is again a vast and ever growing literature on pidgins and pidginization and the reader is directed to Holm (1988), Mühlhäusler (1986), and Valdman (ed.) (1977) and references therein for further details. Pidgin languages are said to become creolized (or to become creole languages) when they are spoken natively by a population although linguists do not yet agree about what the distinguishing features of creoles are.

[12] For some other examples see Geraghty (1994), Lynch (1994), Bugenhagen (1994), Tryon (1994) and Ross (1994).

[13] Clark (1986:341) notes that it may also be the case that the Pn languages borrowed culturally as well but that such borrowings may have been swamped by intimate borrowing.

[14] See for example Capell (1962, 1971).

[15] These include Lusi (Thurston 1982, 1987, 1994) (although Thurston prefers to use the term pidginization to describe this case), Magori (Dutton 1976), Maisin (Lynch 1977; Ross 1984) and Reefs-Santa Cruz (Lincoln 1978; Wurm 1978).

[16] Thurston's use of the word "pidginization" is not the normal one. For example, the resulting or affected language does not cease to be someone's native language.

[17] The two which have not been documented are one reported by Jones (1985) and one reported by Harding (1967:6, 203). The former was a Mekeo-based pidgin similar to two others reported in the same place. However, as it had fallen into desuetude at the time of recording nothing more is known about it. The second pidgin is said to have been a pidgin form of the Siassi language. At one time Hees' so-called "Tolai-Nakanai" trade language was also thought to be a pidgin (Dutton 1978:352, fn. 12). However, closer examination shows that it was most probably not a pidgin but was basically Minigir with a little Meramera/Nakanai mixed in (Dutton and Ross 1992).

[18] This is in contrast to a number that have been reported arising out of NAn-NAn contact (Foley 1986:30-31).

[19] See Grace (1985, 1990) for defining features of Ray's and Capell's ideas.

[20] Isolation has often been proposed as an explanation for diversity but this is so opposed to the sort of evidence discussed here that it cannot be maintained even as a

part explanation. People will cross the apparently most inhibiting terrain to be in contact with others. Also, as Laycock (1982:2) points out, the largest languages are in the most isolated (from our point of view) areas (e.g. the Highlands of Papua New Guinea), whereas the most diverse are in areas of easy terrain where extensive contacts abound. People have been trading, marrying and fighting with each other for aeons.

REFERENCES

Bloomfield, Leonard
   1933   *Language*. London: Allen & Unwin.

Bugenhagen, Robert
   1994   Language change on Umboi Island. In Tom Dutton and Darrell Tryon (eds) *Language contact and change in the Austronesian world*, pp.43-108. Berlin: Mouton de Gruyter.

Capell, Arthur
   1943   *The linguistic position of south-eastern Papua*. Sydney: Australasian Medical Publishing Co.
   1962   Oceanic linguistics today. *Current Anthropology* 3:371-428.
   1971   The Austronesian languages of Australian New Guinea. *Current Trends in Linguistics* 8:240-340.
   1976   Austronesian and Papuan 'mixed' languages: general remarks. In S.A. Wurm (ed.) *New Guinea area languages and language study*, vol. 2: *Austronesian languages*, pp.527-579. Pacific Linguistics Series C No. 40. Canberra: Department of Linguistics, Research School of Pacific Studies, The Australian National University.

Clark, Ross
   1986   Linguistic convergence in central Vanuatu. In P.A. Geraghty, Lois Carrington and S.A. Wurm (eds) *FOCAL II: Papers from the fourth international conference on Austronesian linguistics*, pp.333-342. Pacific Linguistics Series C No. 94. Canberra: Department of Linguistics, Research School of Pacific Studies, The Australian National University.
   1994   The Polynesian Outliers as a locus of language contact. In Tom Dutton and Darrell Tryon (eds) *Language contact and change in the Austronesian world*, pp.109-139. Berlin: Mouton de Gruyter.

Dorian, Nancy (ed.)
   1989   *Investigating obsolescence: studies in language contraction and death*. Cambridge: Cambridge University Press.

Dutton, T.E.
   1971   *Languages of South-East Papua: a preliminary survey*, pp.1-46. Pacific Linguistics Series A No. 28. Canberra: Department of Linguistics, Research School of Pacific Studies, The Australian National University.

1976   Magori and similar languages of South-East Papua. In S.A. Wurm (ed.) *New Guinea area languages and language study*, vol. 2: *Austronesian languages*, pp.581-631. Pacific Linguistics Series C No. 40. Canberra: Department of Linguistics, Research School of Pacific Studies, The Australian National University.

1978   Language and trade in central and southeast Papua. *Mankind* 11(3):341-353.

1982   Borrowing in Austronesian and non-Austronesian languages of coastal south-east mainland Papua New Guinea. In Amran Halim, Lois Carrington and S.A. Wurm (eds) *Papers from the third international conference on Austronesian linguistics*, Vol 3: *Accent on variety*, pp.109-177. Pacific Linguistics Series C No. 76. Canberra: Department of Linguistics, Research School of Pacific Studies, The Australian National University.

1985   *Police Motu: iena sivarai (its story)*. Port Moresby: The University of Papua New Guinea Press.

1994   Motu-Koiarian contact in Papua New Guinea. In Tom Dutton and Darrell Tryon (eds) *Language contact and change in the Austronesian world*, pp.181-232. Berlin: Mouton de Gruyter.

Dutton, T.E. and Malcolm Ross
1992   A note on Hees' 'Tolai-Nakanai' trade language. *Language and Linguistics in Melanesia* 23(2):198-204.

Dutton, Tom and Darrell Tryon (eds)
1994   *Language contact and change in the Austronesian world*. Berlin: Mouton de Gruyter.

Dutton, Tom and Peter Mühlhäusler
1991   Are our languages dying? *Occasional papers in language and literature*, 1(1):50-72. Port Moresby: The University of Papua New Guinea.

Foley, William A.
1986   *The Papuan languages of New Guinea*. Cambridge: Cambridge University Press.

Geraghty, P.A.
1994   Linguistic evidence for the Tongan Empire. In Tom Dutton and Darrell Tryon (eds) *Language contact and change in the Austronesian world*, pp.233-249. Berlin: Mouton de Gruyter.

Geraghty, P.A., Lois Carrington and S.A. Wurm (eds)
1986   *FOCAL II: Papers from the fourth international conference on Austronesian linguistics*. Pacific Linguistics Series C No. 94. Canberra: Department of Linguistics, Research School of Pacific Studies, The Australian National University.

Grace, George W.
1962   Comment. *Current Anthropology* 3:408-410.
1968   Classification of the languages of the Pacific. In A.P. Vayda (ed.) *Peoples and cultures of the Pacific*, pp.63-81. New York: Natural History Press.

1975   Linguistic diversity in the Pacific: on the sources of diversity. *Working Papers in Linguistics, University of Hawaii* 7(3):1-7.

1981   Indirect inheritance and the aberrant Melanesian languages. In [K.J.] Jim Hollyman and Andrew Pawley (eds) *Studies in Pacific languages & cultures, in honour of Bruce Biggs*, pp.255-268. Auckland: Linguistic Society of New Zealand.

1985   Oceanic subgrouping: retrospect and prospect. In Andrew Pawley and Lois Carrington (eds) *Austronesian linguistics at the 15th Pacific Science Congress*, pp.1-18. Pacific Linguistics Series C No. 88. Canberra: Department of Linguistics, Research School of Pacific Studies, The Australian National University.

1990   The 'aberrant' (vs. 'exemplary') Melanesian languages. In Philip Baldi (ed.) *Linguistic change and reconstruction methodology* [Trends in Linguistics. Studies and Monographs 45], pp.155-173. Berlin/New York: Mouton de Gruyter.

Guy, Gregory R.
1990   The sociolinguistic types of language change. *Diachronica* 7(1):47-67.

Halim, Amran, Lois Carrington and S.A. Wurm (eds)
1982   *Papers from the third international conference on Austronesian linguistics*, Vol 3: *Accent on variety*. Pacific Linguistics Series C No. 76. Canberra: Department of Linguistics, Research School of Pacific Studies, The Australian National University.

Harding, T.G.
1967   *Voyagers of the Vitiaz Strait: a study of a New Guinea trade system.* Seattle and London: University of Washington Press.

Holm, John
1988   *Pidgins and creoles*, 2 vols. Cambridge: Cambridge University Press.

Hollyman, [K.J.] Jim and Andrew Pawley (eds)
1981   *Studies in Pacific languages & cultures, in honour of Bruce Biggs.* Auckland: Linguistic Society of New Zealand.

Holzknecht, Susanne
1988   Word taboo and its implications for language change in the Markham family of languages, Papua New Guinea. *Language and Linguistics in Melanesia* 18(1):43-69.

1994   The mechanisms of language change in Labu. In Tom Dutton and Darrell Tryon (eds) *Language contact and change in the Austronesian world*, pp.351-376. Berlin: Mouton de Gruyter.

Jones, Alan
1985   Two Mekeo pidgins. Unpublished MS. Research School of Pacific Studies, The Australian National University.

Laycock, D.C.
1982   Linguistic diversity in Melanesia: a tentative explanation. In Rainer Carle, Martina Henschke, Peter W. Pink, Christel Rost and Karen Stadtlender

(eds) *GAVA': studies in Austronesian languages and cultures, dedicated to Hans Kähler*, pp.31-37. Berlin: Dietrich Reimer.

Lincoln, Peter C.
1976   *Banoni, Piva and Papuanization*, pp.77-105. Pacific Linguistics Series A No. 45. Canberra: Department of Linguistics, Research School of Pacific Studies, The Australian National University.
1978   Reef-Santa Cruz as Austronesian. In S.A. Wurm and Lois Carrington (eds) *Second international conference on Austronesian linguistics: proceedings*, pp.929-967. Pacific Linguistics Series C No. 61. Canberra: Department of Linguistics, Research School of Pacific Studies, The Australian National University.

Lynch, John
1977   Notes on Maisin — an Austronesian language of the northern province of Papua New Guinea. Unpublished MS. Port Moresby: University of Papua New Guinea.
1981   Melanesian diversity and Polynesian homogeneity: the other side of the coin. *Oceanic Linguistics* 20:95-129.
1994   Melanesian sailors in a Polynesian sea: maritime vocabulary in Southern Vanuatu. In A. Pawley and M. Ross (eds) *Austronesian terminologies: continuity and change*, pp.289-300. Pacific Linguistics Series C No. 127. Canberra: Department of Linguistics, Research School of Pacific and Asian Studies, The Australian National University.

Mühlhäusler, Peter
1986   *Pidgin and creole linguistics*. Oxford: Blackwell.

Pawley, Andrew K.
1981   Melanesian diversity and Polynesian homogeneity: a unified explanation for language. In K.J. Hollyman and A. Pawley (eds), *Studies in Pacific languages & cultures, in honour of Bruce Biggs*, pp.269-309. Auckland: Linguistic Society of New Zealand.
1990   A simple linguist's view of Pacific prehistory. Unpublished seminar paper, Research School of Pacific Studies, The Australian National University.

Pawley, Andrew and Lois Carrington (eds)
1985   *Austronesian linguistics at the 15th Pacific Science Congress*. Pacific Linguistics Series C No. 88. Canberra: Department of Linguistics, Research School of Pacific Studies, The Australian National University.

Ray, Sidney H.
1926   *A comparative study of the Melanesian Island languages*. Cambridge: Cambridge University Press.

Ross, Malcolm D.
1984   *Maisin: a preliminary sketch*, pp.1-82. Pacific Linguistics Series A No. 69. Canberra: Department of Linguistics, Research School of Pacific Studies, The Australian National University.

1988   *Proto-Oceanic and the Austronesian languages of western Melanesia.* Pacific Linguistics Series C No. 98. Canberra: Department of Linguistics, Research School of Pacific Studies, The Australian National University.

1991   Refining Guy's sociolinguistic types of language change. *Diachronica* 8:119-129.

1994   Central Papuan terms for the maritime environment. In A. Pawley and M. Ross (eds) *Austronesian terminologies: continuity and change*, pp.389-479. Pacific Linguistics Series C No. 127. Canberra: Department of Linguistics, Research School of Pacific and Asian Studies, The Australian National University.

Salisbury, R.F.
1962   Notes on bilingualism and linguistic change in New Guinea. *Anthropological Linguistics* 4(7):1-13.

Sankoff, Gillian
1977   Multilingualism in Papua New Guinea. In S.A. Wurm (ed.) *New Guinea area languages and languages study*, Vol. 3: *Language, culture, society and the modern world*, pp.265-307. Pacific Linguistics Series C No. 40. Canberra: Department of Linguistics, Research School of Pacific Studies, The Australian National University.

Simons, Gary
1982   Word taboo and comparative Austronesian linguistics. In Amran Halim, Lois Carrington and S.A. Wurm (eds) *Papers from the third international conference on Austronesian linguistics*, Vol. 1: *Currents in Oceanic*, pp.157-226. Pacific Linguistics Series C No. 74. Canberra: Department of Linguistics, Research School of Pacific Studies, The Australian National University.

Thomason, Sarah Grey and Terrence Kaufman
1988   *Language contact, creolization, and genetic linguistics.* Berkeley: University of California Press.

Thurston, William R.
1982   *A comparative study of Anêm and Lusi.* Pacific Linguistics Series B No. 83. Canberra: Department of Linguistics, Research School of Pacific Studies, The Australian National University.

1987   *Processes of change in the languages of north-western New Britain.* Pacific Linguistics Series B No. 99. Canberra: Department of Linguistics, Research School of Pacific Studies, The Australian National University.

1994   Renovation and innovation in the languages of north-western New Britain. In Tom Dutton and Darrell Tryon (eds) *Language contact and change in the Austronesian world*, pp.573-609. Berlin: Mouton de Gruyter.

Trudgill, Peter
1986   *Dialects in contact.* Oxford: Blackwell.

Tryon, Darrell
1994   Language contact and contact-induced language change in the Eastern Outer Islands, Solomon Islands. In Tom Dutton and Darrell Tryon (eds)

Language contact and change in the Austronesian world, pp.611-648. Berlin: Mouton de Gruyter.

Valdman, Albert (ed.)
1977   *Pidgin and creole linguistics*. Bloomington: Indiana University Press.

Wurm, S.A.
1978   Reefs-Santa Cruz: Austronesian, but ...? In S.A. Wurm and Lois Carrington (eds) *Second international conference on Austronesian linguistics: proceedings*, pp.969-1010. Pacific Linguistics Series C No. 61. Canberra: Department of Linguistics, Research School of Pacific Studies, The Australian National University.
1982   *Papuan languages of Oceania*. Tübingen: Gunter Narr.

Wurm, S.A. and Lois Carrington (eds)
1978   *Second international conference on Austronesian linguistics: proceedings*. Pacific Linguistics Series C No. 61. Canberra: Department of Linguistics, Research School of Pacific Studies, The Australian National University.

Wurm, S.A. and Shirô Hattori
1981   *Language atlas of the Pacific area*. Pacific Linguistics Series C No. 66. Canberra: Department of Linguistics, Research School of Pacific Studies, The Australian National University.

Wurm, S.A. (ed.)
1976   *New Guinea area languages and language study*, vol. 2: *Austronesian languages*. Pacific Linguistics Series C No. 40. Canberra: Department of Linguistics, Research School of Pacific Studies, The Australian National University.
1977   *New Guinea area languages and language study*, vol. 3: *Language, culture, society and the modern world*. Pacific Linguistics Series C No. 40. Canberra: Department of Linguistics, Research School of Pacific Studies, The Australian National University.

Wurm, S.A. and D.C. Laycock
1961-62 The question of language and dialect in New Guinea. *Oceania* 32:128-143.

12

AUSTRONESIAN SOCIETIES AND THEIR TRANSFORMATIONS

James J. Fox

This paper examines the common Austronesian reliance on similar idioms and metaphors to define ideas of origins and on the use of narratives for the construction of a shared past. Thus common origin — not just "descent" — becomes a prime marker of identity. Among Austronesians, the sharing of a journey may be part of this reckoning of social ancestry. Within this cultural framework, the paper considers two formal systems of differentiation: the one, a system of lateral expansion; the other, a system of apical demotion with concomitant predatory expulsion. Each system relies on a differently structured narrative of the past on which to base its construction of origins.

INTRODUCTION

Austronesian societies offer a spectacle of diversity. There are at least eight hundred contemporary Austronesian societies, each of which can be considered to possess a distinct, if not distinctive, social organization; and, if one were to add to this number those Austronesian societies on whose early social formations we possess reasonable historical information, this diversity is further increased.

Such social diversity ranges from that of simple hunter-horticulturalists such as the Buid of Mindoro, the Ilongot of Luzon, the Penan of Borneo, the Sakkudei of the Mentawai islands, or the Huaulu of Ceram to the elaborate command states of the Merina of Madagascar, the Javanese of the Majapahit and Mataram periods, or the complex island kingdoms of Tonga, Tahiti, and Hawaii; from migratory sea populations such as the Sama-Bajau, or the trading societies of the Moluccas and of the Massim with their inter-island networks of ritualized exchange valuables to the predatory seafaring societies of the Malays, Bugis, Makassarese and Tausug.

A diversity of island environments has called forth adaptations that have also spawned great social variety: coastal sago palm exploiters such as the Waropen; elusive jungle nomads like the Kubu of Sumatra; tiny fishing populations on atolls in the Pacific; riverine peoples such as the Dayak, Kenyah or Kayan of Borneo; the maize-cultivating mountain populations like the Atoni Meto of Timor, for whom a view of the sea was once considered distressing; dryland palm tappers such as the Rotinese and Savunese in eastern Indonesia; cattle herding peoples such as the Bara of south central Madagascar; yam, taro,

214

and sweet-potato gardeners of the Melanesian islands, some of whom, like those on Goodenough Island or the Trobriands, flaunt their harvests in feasting for recognition; expansive swidden-rice cultivators like the Iban of Borneo; or settled rice farmers like the Ifugao of Luzon with centuries of collective investment in elaborate terraces.

Religion has also contributed to this diversity. Islam has influenced the societies of western Austronesia as has Hinduism and Buddhism; and Christianity has had its influence through the whole of the Austronesian world from Madagascar to Hawaii and from the Philippines to Timor. There are also scattered Austronesian populations who have taken on no world religion — or, have even formally rejected such possibilities. Such populations are often identified, by the nineteenth century categorical designation, as "animists". These Austronesians share with most other Austronesian peoples, though perhaps in more explicit fashion, a general belief in life and in the interrelationship of different forms of life. In the Austronesian world, the mosque, the temple, the church, or simply a tree set among a pile of rocks is part of the diversity of social life.

Confronted with this spectacle of diversity, the question is whether there exists among these many societies social features that may be identifiable as characteristically Austronesian. Certainly in answer to this question, anthropologists investigating societies in different regions of the Austronesian world have fashioned a formidable array of technical designations. We have cognatic and non-cognatic societies; lineal and nonlineal, patrilineal, matrilineal, bilineal, quasi-unilineal, ambilineal, and double unilineal societies; societies with kindreds, with ramages, with bilateral descent groups, with optative descent groups, with status lineages, with circulating connubium, generalized exchange, symmetric and asymmetric marriage. Sorting one's way through the formal technicalities of all of this apparatus is almost as daunting as investigating the original diversity of societies which this apparatus was intended to illuminate.

A singular difficulty with the current sociological apparatus available for the study of Austronesian societies is that it has been shaped within specific regions. Reflecting the particularities of these regions, the terminology of one area does not travel well — and certainly not as well as the Austronesians themselves — from one region to another. Instead of encompassing the full sweep of Austronesian diversity, our present terminology is partisan to particular variants of the whole. Another less apparent difficulty is that this sociological apparatus makes implicit assumptions about the nature of social life which the Austronesians themselves do not seem to share. Austronesian ideas about persons, about the union of persons, about social derivation and identity, about sociability itself, such ideas are not — or, were not — those of nineteenth century Europe from which our sociological traditions derive.

In the study of Austronesian societies and their transformations, it is best to reexamine our own premises and to focus on a few basic features of a general nature. At the same time, it is essential to attend closely to the concepts of the Austronesians themselves expressed in idioms and metaphors of a common linguistic and cultural heritage. In the process, it is inevitable that we abandon some of our previous preoccupations[1] and with them jettison the conceptual encumbrances that have limited a comparative understanding of the Austronesians.

This effort may give us a fresh start on a new voyage of investigation. My purpose in this paper therefore will be to examine a few key ideas that recur throughout the Austronesian-speaking world and to consider their implications in the transformation of Austronesian societies. In this paper, I will look first at the concept of "origin" among the Austronesians and then, from this vantage point, at specific formal structures of social differentiation. I will illustrate my discussion by selective citations of particular well-known Austronesian ethnographies. My intention is not to create a composite picture of Austronesian society but just the opposite — to identify differences that derive from shared similarities.

THE CONCEPT OF ORIGIN

Our own ideas of origin — either the Judeao-Christian-Muslim or the evolutionary view of human derivation — ill prepare us to appreciate Austronesian ideas of origin or to take seriously the implications of these ideas. Our ideas look to a unitary, if not unified, conception of origin whereas the Austronesians tolerate — or, rather relish — the notion of multiple origins. Often this multiplicity derives from an initial unity that is shattered — the destruction of a cosmic tree, the internal rupture of a universal egg, or the separation of a primary couple — but once this unity is shattered, concern is with a multiplicity of entities. Although this general notion may be applied to all beings, I shall confine myself here to ideas of the origin of humankind and its implications for the structuring of society.

In some myths, a creator god attempts various experiments before achieving the appropriate creature. Usually this creature is an aristocratic form of human being — not the progenitor of all humankind. In other myths, a variety of humans derive from the destruction of different parts of a cosmic tree; in still others, this variety comes from the fertile union of different sorts of beings. In most Austronesian societies, however, a multiplicity of origins is assumed and groups as well as individuals are allowed to trace their origins as is deemed appropriate for social differentiation. The sharing of origins is socially defined and thus always circumscribed. Thus in a now classic ethnography, Michael

Young reports that the eight clans of the Kalauna of Goodenough Island emerged from the earth in a specific order "bringing with them the customs and competences by which [they] ... are still identified" (1971:29). The same description would hold for the hundreds of name-clans of the Atoni Meto of Timor, most of whom trace their separate origins to some emergence site marked by a rock and tree.

Under the influence of Islam or Christianity, some unifying of human origin accounts has occurred. The rulers of Java trace a double origin relying on genealogies of the right and left, one of which derives from the gods and heroes of Java, the other from the prophet and saints of Islam. Similarly the aristocracy of some of the domains of Roti have included Biblical figures in their own royal genealogies but such genealogies do not embrace all members of their own domain; they would deny a common origin with all of their commoner class. The introduction of new sacred versions of origin have enhanced rather than obliterated the idea of multiple origins.

The notion of multiple origins is a prime means of social differentiation. Such a notion may operate at many levels within a society. For my purposes here, I want to concentrate on the implications of this notion for the structuring of society, focusing on selected examples. I use the phrase "origin structure" as a general designation for the diversity of social formation by which Austronesians explain and order their derivation.

STRANGER KINGS, MUSLIM SAINTS AND BRAHMANA PRIESTS

Marshall Sahlins, in a well-known essay on "The Stranger-King", has called attention to the origin of the Noikoro chiefs of Fiji who trace their beginnings from a handsome stranger who is carried to the shore of Viti Levu by a shark, wanders into the interior of the island, is taken in by a local chief whose daughter he marries and becomes the founder of the ruling clan known as "The Sharks". Thus the ruler has a different origin from the rest of the population; he is a stranger, a guest, a person of the sea as opposed to the people of the land. In form, this is a classic origin narrative that is repeated in different guises throughout the Austronesian world. In Timor, the ancestor of the ruling line of Sonbai is discovered in mysterious circumstances as a resplendent youth who is taken in by the local population and elevated to ruler. The Sonbai ruler was treated like the Fijian ruler. To quote Sahlins: "he is ... immobilized: he 'just sits,' Fijians say, i.e., in the house as a woman — 'and things are brought to him'" (Sahlins 1985:91).

Another variant of this narrative can be seen in the origin of the ruling line of Termanu on the island of Roti. Here the ancestor of the ruling clan arrives from the sea and in a series of contests outwits the ancestor of the land, thereby gaining rule but without ritual authority over the earth. Thus the ruler shares a different origin from the head of the earth and this dichotomy forms the basis of the domain.

Structurally similar variants of this narrative are cited as the foundation of many of the ruling lines of the coastal states of Western Indonesia. To cite but one example, the founder of the once powerful line of the Muslim ruler-saints of Giri on the north coast of Java was washed ashore in a box at Gresik and raised by a pious widow. This figure, known originally as Jaka Samodra, "Sea Youth", became the first Sunan Giri, one of the most important purveyors of Islam on Java (Fox 1991:24-28).

Another variant of this narrative serves as one of the principal legendary charters for the structure of Bali. This legend begins with a victory by the Javanese Hindu kingdom of Majapahit in Bali and the despatch of a noble entourage led by a Brahmana priest named as Ida Dalam Ketut Kresna Kepakisan to bring civilization to the island. From this priest and his entourage come the ruling Triwangsa who continue even after the fall of Majapahit to provide the knowledge of the Hindu rituals and of statecraft that transforms the Bali Aga populations of the island. Only a minority on Bali, however, are twice-born; the charter of their origin links spiritual derivation with a historical locality, physical conquest with civilizing status and distinguishes them from the majority of the population. This enduring charter is predicated on multiple origins and the perpetuation of different statuses. Instead of being contested, it is further embellished by other charters that also claim separate origins for particular social groups (Fox in press).

A diversity of origins within the same society creates a diversity of possibilities. In many Austronesian societies, origins are conceptualized as a form of growth: derivation from a "source", "root", "base", or "trunk". In this structure, which may be graphically described as a tree, vine or climbing plant, growth is either upward or outward toward a "tip" or apical point. The Rotinese use this metaphor to describe their maternal origins as well as the structure of their clans; other populations in eastern Indonesia, such as the Weyewa of Sumba, the Mambai of East Timor or the Atoni of West Timor use a similar metaphor to describe "origin structures" of varying sorts (Fox 1971, 1980, 1988a; Kuipers 1985; McWilliam 1990; Traube 1989). The central Polynesians use the same metaphor to trace origins among different island populations; the Satawal of Micronesia to identify the matrilineal source clans on their island of origin (Siikala in press; Sudo in press).

Where this metaphor is used to describe specific groups, it would be more appropriate to refer to these groups as "ascent groups" rather than "descent groups" — an observation made some years ago by Hooper in his discussion of Tahitian social organization (1970). For these groups, social reckoning is from a base upwards, rather than from some apex downward (see Fox 1988a). Often in societies with such ascent structures, one group "grows" to prominence and it is around this group that other ascent groups cluster. Thus in Termanu on the island of Roti, one clan, Masa-Huk, of outside origin forms the base (*huk*) that gives rise to a complex set of multiple lineage branches (*ndanak*) in whose shadow other lesser clans are shaded.

Such "ascent groups", however, are only one form of origin structure among the Austronesians. Heavenly origins are also a common form of "outside origin". Groups claiming origins of this sort may more aptly be called "descent groups". The nobility in societies of southern Sulawesi — the Bugis, Makassarese and some Toraja — trace their origins to a class of heavenly beings known as the *tomanurung*, the "descenders" who contributed the white blood that distinguishes nobles from commoners. Like the rulers of Fiji, the lords of Timor, or the Triwangsa of Bali, the nobles of southern Sulawesi trace separate origins distinct from the rest of the population over whom they hold authority.

ORIGIN, NARRATIVE AND JOURNEY

Michael Young, in his account of Goodenough Island (Young 1971), describes the origin structures of the Kalauna: the separate emergence of a succession of eight clans; the establishment of pre-eminence by the second of these clans based on a knowledge of the generative rituals for the main foodstuffs; the split within this clan; the sharing and assignment of tasks to the other clans; and, finally, the account of the various events that led to the scattering of some clans and the "journey" or migration of the others from their place of origin to the present settlement, most of which, as Young explains, is told by the pre-eminent clan itself.

This account begins with multiple origins, assigns an order of precedence among the clans and pre-eminence to one clan whose internal divisions are thereafter significant. In Young's phrase, it designates the "competences" of the clans and recounts the vicissitudes of their journey through various places to the present. Each clan recounts its separate origin narrative; only the account of the pre-eminent clan contains the information that links the separate accounts to one another and explains the origins of the principal exchange institutions of the society. Finally, to the public account of each narrative is attached an esoteric component that reveals to its members alone the magical formulae of the group. These accounts, which are of evident importance to the Kalauna, are — even in their ambiguity — paradigmatic of the sort of narratives that establish an Austronesian "origin structure".

Compare these narratives of origin with those of several other societies from different parts of the Austronesian world. In a recent ethnography, E.

Douglas Lewis (1988) presents the narratives of origin of the Ata Tana 'Ai of east central Flores. These narratives are immensely complex and detailed and Lewis devotes twenty-five pages of his ethnography to outline their basic structure. They form the foundation of the domain of Wai Brama and must be recounted in ritual language at the principal ceremonial celebration of the domain. The rituals speak of a community of "ten clans plus", although in fact there are twenty-five separate clans resident within the domain.

Each clan recounts its separate origin and its particular journey into Tana 'Ai. One clan — in Lewis' words, "the source clan" — is pre-eminent. This clan possesses the narrative that integrates the other clans to it. As among the Kalauna, this clan's "history" is especially complex because its own internal division is of great significance. For the source clan of Tana 'Ai, this internal division is an ancestral elder/younger bifurcation represented by critical differences encountered in hunting together. On arriving in Tana 'Ai, the elder of the brothers assigns precedence to the ancestors of the other clans as they, in turn, arrive; the younger brother marries with these ancestors and shares out ceremonial goods and ritual duties. An ambiguous third ancestor who accompanies the two brothers at the outset takes a divergent journey and finally arrives in Tana 'Ai to become the founder of the lowest clans of the domain.

To quote Lewis: "The people of each Tana 'Ai clan conceive of themselves as making up a group by virtue of descent from ancestors named in the histories, who were the first people of the clan to arrive in the various localities occupied by the clan ... Furthermore the Ata Tana 'Ai say that each of their clans originated from a different place. Thus the histories serve to identify each clan in terms of its origins and to distinguish each clan from every other clan" (Lewis 1988:61).

Like the narratives of the Kalauna but in a more elaborate fashion, the histories of Tana 'Ai serve as the charter for the society's origin structures. In the case of the Kalauna, these structures encompass a single settlement; for the Ata Tana 'Ai, they encompass a region that forms a single ritual domain. Instances of similar narrative accounts of origins could be cited from the ethnographies of the Timor area (Renard-Clamagirand 1982; McWilliam 1990) or from Roti where such narratives establish a class system with all of the prerogatives of rule and authority. It is more instructive to consider another example, typical of its kind, where similar narratives are told at a more individual level.

The case of the Ilongot, a small-scale hunter-horticultural population in Luzon, may be taken for present purposes to represent a class of Austronesian societies often distinguished by their lack of clans or lineages from societies like the Kalauna or Ata Tana 'Ai. The household group is important in all these societies but a further scaffolding of relations is seemingly less elaborate among the Ilongot. The idiom of relationships, however, is articulated in a similar fashion.

Among the Ilongot, each household is regarded as "one trunk" (*tan tengeng*). These "trunks" form local clusters generally denoted by the names of rivers or other prominent features of their environment. The boundaries of these settlements and the affiliation of households within them is flexibly interpreted. But in each settlement, according to Michelle Rosaldo,

> there is at least a core group of closely related families who are apt to share a history of common residence, having lived in close proximity over years of intermittent movement in search of fertile lands, abundant forests, or freedom from lowland law. It is this history of coordinated moves, through times of inward-turning "concentration" and then "dispersal" toward the lowland margins of Ilongot lands, that lends a settlement its viability as an ill-defined yet generally recognized and cooperating social group (M. Rosaldo 1980:5).

Like the Kalauna and Ata Tana 'Ai, Ilongot also possess origin narratives that relate journeys of the past. Although they focus mainly on the recounted memories of their oldest living members, these narratives nevertheless articulate two distinct levels of origin. Again to quote Michelle Rosaldo:

> A history of related moves, interpreted in an idiom of bilateral kinship and reinforced by bonds of marriage, permit most members of a settlement to construe themselves as kin, who (as Ilongots express it) share a "body" (*betrang*) ... What continues over time is not a stable group but a tradition of relation (M. Rosaldo 1980:9).

Here kinship is constituted by a shared journey which includes hunting together. A tradition of such shared relationship points to still earlier origins.

> Those people who have shared in hunts, along with kin in other settlements with whom they have been wont to live at times of "concentration", will tend to see themselves as members of a single *bertan* ... *Bertan*, unlike settlements, are seen by Ilongot as timeless and discrete collections of related persons who share an origin from unknown common ancestors who once lived together "downstream", "in the lowlands", "on an island", "near a mountain" — in short, in some environment from which the *bertan* takes its name (M. Rosaldo 1980:9).

Ilongot society is composed of at least thirteen such discrete, named, and loosely localized groups. Seen from a perspective of origin structures, there is little formal difference between the Ilongot, the Kalauna or the Ata Tana 'Ai except in the way in which each of these societies reckons its path of origin through the father in the case of the Kalauna, the mother in the case of Ata Tana 'Ai or through either parent in the case of the Ilongot. In all of these societies, the sharing of a journey is part of the reckoning of social ancestry. This reckoning is enhanced by the recurrent linguistic use of terms for "path" as a common Austronesian metaphor for social relationships.

In comparing these societies, one crucial difference needs to be pointed out in the case of the Ilongot. All the *bertan* of the Ilongot recount their own separate narrative of origin; no member of a *bertan* recites a narrative that links the *bertan* to each other as a group.

TRANSFORMATIONS OF AUSTRONESIAN SOCIETIES

The three societies I have focused on were chosen purposely. In historical linguistic terms, which are relevant to this discussion, each of these societies belongs to a different Malayo-Polynesian subgroup: the Ilongot belong to the Western; the Ata Tana 'Ai to the Central; and the Kalauna to the Eastern. Together they cover a wide dispersal of Austronesian-speaking peoples. However, in the anthropological literature that has made descent and marriage the principal — if not exclusive — criteria for defining and typifying Austronesian societies, such societies as these would rarely be considered together except possibly as contrastive types.[2] My purpose in considering these three societies was to show their similarities to one another, particularly in their concern with origins as a prime marker of social identity. In doing this, I have simply attempted to take seriously precisely those features of identity that the members of these societies appear to regard as fundamentally important.

Having set the stage for an alternative understanding of Austronesian societies through a consideration of their origin structures, I now wish to extend my initial observations in a more speculative fashion. If one were to adopt a bird's eye (or perhaps better, a "satellite") view of the Austronesian societies from Madagascar to Hawaii, one might venture a few generalizations based on our current knowledge of these societies. The first of these is that the Austronesians show a range of ways in which they reckon their social origins: from fully bilateral reckoning to strict lineal reckoning. The majority of Austronesian societies, when examined closely, are neither fully bilateral nor strictly lineal. This large middle range of Austronesian societies that is neither exclusively one nor the other is, of course, what is interesting to the analyst of social organization. But for the purposes of analysis, it is better to examine the two extremes of the continuum. If, as a first approximation, one were to ask not just which societies are the most bilateral in their modes of social reckoning but where these societies are located, a crude pattern appears to emerge. These societies are found on the relatively large islands of the Austronesian world, areas of potential expansion, where land and other resources are (or, in recent historical times, were once) readily available. Thus bilateral societies are most common in the main Philippine islands but particularly in northern Luzon, Mindoro and much of Mindanao; in Borneo; large areas of Madagascar, and in Java; but bilateral reckoning is also characteristic of the early Maori of New

Zealand and of historical Hawaiians.[3] The principal mode of social differentiation in these societies is relative age (i.e. elder/younger) which may, in certain contexts, provide the means of creating an extended order of precedence (as, for example, amongst the Maori) but more generally offers an opportune line of fission, whereby the younger — or in a few cases, the elder — sibling simply moves away to found a new settlement. The founder of this new settlement thus becomes the point for a new system of local precedence (Bellwood in press). I would describe all of these systems as systems of lateral expansion.

In contrast to these societies are those that endeavour to restrict social reckoning in an ever-more-exclusive mode. Again, if one looks to the distribution of these societies, they are to be found on smaller islands, but not on islands too small to support such exclusivity, on the coastal margins of large islands where they are (or were) concerned with trading and raiding, and also among specific notable status groups in the very midst of societies with bilateral reckoning. Status is a preoccupation in these societies and it is reckoned in subtle and complex ways. Such societies are centred on a single source. Elaborate narratives of origin — and with them, exclusive genealogies — to this source are seen as a prerogative of high status. Such narratives are exclusively preserved and jealously guarded. The degree to which such exclusivity is achieved may vary as do the means to achieve precedence in such societies.

What is striking is that throughout the Austronesian world the same formal structure has been devised for achieving this exclusivity. I refer to this formal structure as a system of apical demotion.[4] In such a system, only one line retains status; and within that line, in each generation, ultimately one individual. All other individuals are automatically demoted and thus lose status relative to a single apical point. Unless they can manage to reunite their line with that of the highest status line, they continue to decrease in status. Such a society has a single source of precedence with restricted modes of reckoning relationships to this source.

Examples of societies that have developed systems of apical demotion are numerous but these systems, by their exclusivity, generally do not apply to the whole of these societies. Apical demotion is a dynastic device of an elite to distinguish itself from the majority of its own society. This form of precedence emerges within particular societies and invariably leads to an internal division, whereby one segment of society traces exclusive origins in marked contrast to a more reflexible reckoning of origins by the rest of the population.

Such systems of apical demotion are generally to be found in societies with royalty — rulers, kings, rajas, sultans and sacred chiefs — though not all such societies rely only upon apical demotion. Examples of such systems are those of the Merina aristocracy, the ruling classes of the Malay states as well as those of the former Bugis and Makassarese, or of the nobility of Mataram on

Java and of the high Balinese who claim to come from the kingdom of Majapahit. In eastern Indonesia, the ruling clans in many of the states and domains of the region — in eastern Sumba or in central Roti, for example — are predicated on systems of apical demotion. In the Pacific, the classic systems of this sort are those ruling elite of Tonga, Samoa, Tahiti and Hawaii.

As a first step, it is useful to note some of the common features of systems of apical demotion wherever they occur in the Austronesian world. With this perspective, it is possible to recognize formal resemblances between Bali and Tonga or the Merina kingdom and the Malay states. It is, however, the differences among these systems that are of equal interest. Thus within a formal system, it becomes possible to delineate specific structural differences. In systems of apical demotion, it is not the way that status is automatically diminished that is significant, but rather the variety of ways by which status, in different systems, is maintained and promoted.

Thus generally within the western subgroup of Malayo-Polynesians, a greater relative stress is placed on the husband/wife couple as a focus of status determination. Genealogies that record high status often preserve the names of marriage partners (see Bulbeck, in press, for a particularly lucid examination of the Makassarese system of apical demotion based on substantial written records of married couples). Status derives from both sides of the marriage and involves a careful balance. Further elements may add weight to this balance. Among the Merina, the first-born is a social category of particular importance. Hence the marriage of a first-born man of high rank with a first-born woman of equally high rank was the ideal device for attaining apical distinction. By contrast, in the central-eastern subgroups of Malayo-Polynesians, greater stress is focused on the brother/sister pair. A cultural ideal, muted among the Western Malayo-Polynesians, is that the brother/sister pair (or the lines of sibling differentiation that they represent) should be reunited in their offspring. Among the Central Malayo-Polynesians, the brother in this pair is accorded positive status with the result that, in structural terms, the mother's brother's line retains and confers status. Marriages tend to return to this line to maintain status. Further to the east, especially in Polynesia, greater weighting is given to the sister in this pair with the result that relations to the father's sister's line are crucial to status reckoning. Tonga represents an excellent example of this Austronesian transformation.

Another characteristic feature of systems of apical demotion relates not to the achievement of status but to what occurs when the achievement of status is blocked. Systems of apical demotion often function as systems of predatory expulsion. They regularly expel frustrated figures of high status who, by the authority of their status, can gather around themselves followers who will join them in leaving the old system and establishing a new status system elsewhere. The history of the Austronesians, especially as this history is told in elaborate oral narratives or early written chronicles, is replete with instances of predatory expulsion. The point to be made, however, is that this form of expansion is a result of "crowding" in the system. Without "crowding" — with few restrictions on resources of land and water — systems of apical demotion do not arise and expansion is more likely to occur by lateral "hiving off" of social groups of equal status.

CONCLUSIONS

In this paper, I have described a contrast between two formal systems that are to be found among the Austronesians: the one, a system of lateral expansion and the other, a system of apical demotion with concomitant predatory expulsion. As contrastive forms, these formal systems focus our attention and allow us to delineate a variety of intermediate structural forms. I would like to go a step further and link these formal systems to the more general discussion of "origin structures" with which I began this paper.

I would argue that in systems of lateral expansion, narratives of origin focus on place. In such systems, there occurs what Renato Rosaldo has called, in regard to the Ilongot, a "spatialization of time": "The cultural conception of shifting directions as one walks along a path is at once a pattern, reflecting past experiences, and a charter, guiding future projects" (R. Rosaldo 1980:59). An appropriate comparison here would be with the Atoni Meto whose history in the past two hundred years has been characterized by rapid lateral expansion that has left a complex network of chantlines outward from central west Timor. Atoni name groups (*kanaf*) trace their origins as the journey of a single name — a single entity or collective ego — who wanders through a landscape of places. Atoni history is "the path and the road" and those who recite it personalize this collective history as "my path and my road" (Fox 1988a:10-15).

I would extend this argument by noting that systems of apical demotion invariably focus on persons rather than places. Genealogical reckoning becomes crucial to these systems. Origin narratives — many of which may begin with a recitation of places — come to focus on relationships among persons, on succession and the transmission of status. From this perspective, we can begin also to note, in the narration of origins, the occurrence of a "transition to genealogy" or its reverse in some instances.

If we consider these two contrasting formal systems as modes of expansion under particular conditions and in specific environments, we can see that both have been used widely and effectively. It becomes less important to designate one as the proto-system and the other as derivative than it is to recognize both as effective means by which populations of Austronesians have spread during their long history of expansion.

NOTES

[1]   One of the chief preoccupations that I wish to set aside is the concern with a dichotomy between hierarchy and equality. Interest in this dichotomy in its most current form is associated with the work of Louis Dumont whose books, *Homo hierarchicus* (1967) and *Homo aequalis, I* (1977), have set the stage for present discussion. I would note, however, that concern with this dichotomy has a long history in Western thought and evidence from Austronesian societies has been taken up in European discussions of these issues from the time of early contact. This discussion has not, however, advanced the comparative understanding of the Austronesians, but has instead led to a pernicious dichotomization that has tended to sort Austronesian societies on one or another side of a great divide. As a result, comparisons, for example, between Iban and the Javanese, between the Buid and the Balinese, or the Ilongot and the Rotinese is hardly attempted. In a number of recent papers, I have used the concept of "precedence" not as a substitute for hierarchy, as some have interpreted it, but as an analytic category intended to crosscut the dichotomy between hierarchy and equality. It is my contention that all Austronesian societies in different and varying ways make use of precedence as a means of social and individual differentiation.

[2]   Here one must be careful to distinguish societies that insist on exclusive social reckoning from satellite societies that attempt, with great effort, to retain social links to what they regard as more prestigious sources of origin.

[3]   At the very general level at which these observations are intended, it could be argued that there is effectively little difference between a bilateral system and a two-section (or two-line system) of kinship reckoning. I have elsewhere (Fox 1988b) pointed to the structural similarities between these two systems in Austronesian terminologies. Were one to accept these similarities, then much of Timor and Fiji could also be characterized as having systems of lateral expansion.

[4]   In the analysis of Balinese social organization, Clifford and Hildred Geertz aptly describe this system as that of "sinking status". See H. and C. Geertz (1975:128-131). Clifford Geertz, in particular, develops this idea in his study of the Balinese state in the nineteenth century (Geertz 1980).

REFERENCES

Bellwood, P.
   In press Hierarchy, founder ideology and Austronesian expansion. In J.J. Fox and C. Sather (eds) *Origin, ancestry and alliance. Proceedings of the comparative Austronesian conference on hierarchy, ancestry, and alliance.*

Bulbeck, F.D.
   In press The Makassar State of Gowa. In J.J. Fox and C. Sather (eds) *Origin, ancestry and alliance. Proceedings of the comparative Austronesian conference on hierarchy, ancestry, and alliance.*

Dumont, L.
   1967   *Homo hierarchicus*. Paris: Gallimard.

1977   *Homo aequalis, I.* Paris: Gallimard.

Fox, J.J.
1971   Sister's child as plant: metaphors in an idiom of consanguinity. In R. Needham (ed.) *Rethinking kinship and marriage*, pp.219-252. London: Tavistock.
1980   Models and metaphors: comparative research in eastern Indonesia. In J.J. Fox (ed.) *The flow of life*, pp.327-333. Cambridge: Harvard University Press.
1988a   Origin, descent and precedence in the study of Austronesian societies. Public Lecture in connection with De Wisseleerstoel Indonesische Studien, 17 March 1988. Leiden University.
1988b   Possible models of early Austronesian social organization. *Asian Perspectives* 26(1):35-43.
1991   *Ziarah* visits to the tombs of the Wali, the founders of Islam on Java. In M.C. Ricklefs (ed.) *Islam in the Indonesian social context*, pp.19-38. Centre for Southeast Asian Studies. Clayton (Vic.): Monash University.
In press   Installing the 'outsider' inside: an exploration of an Austronesian culture theme and its social significance. Proceedings of The First International Conference on Austronesian Cultural Studies, Universitas Udayana, Bali.

Geertz, Clifford
1980   *Negara: the theatre state in nineteenth century Bali.* Princeton: Princeton University Press.

Geertz, Hildred and Clifford Geertz
1975   *Kinship in Bali.* Chicago: University of Chicago Press.

Gibson, T.
1990   On predatory states in island Southeast Asia. Working Paper No. 2, Comparative Austronesian Project. Canberra: Department of Anthropology, Research School of Pacific Studies, The Australian National University.

Hooper, Antony
1970   'Blood' and 'belly': Tahitian concepts of kinship and descent. In Jean Pouillon et Pierre Maranda, *Échanges et communications: mélanges offerts à Claude Lévi-Strauss à l'occasion de son 60 ème anniversaire*, Tome I. The Hague and Paris: Mouton.

Kuipers, J.
1985   When the 'tip' forgets the 'trunk': remembering and forgetting in Weyewa oral performance. Paper delivered at the Meetings of the American Anthropological Association, December 1985.

Lewis, E.D.
1988   *People of the source.* Verhandelingen van het Koninklijk Instituut voor Taal-, Land- en Volkenkunde 135. Dordrecht: Foris Publication.

McWilliam, A.
  1990   Narrating the gate and the path: place and precedence in southwest Timor.
         Unpublished PhD thesis. Canberra: The Australian National University.

Renard-Clamagirand, B.
  1982   *Marobo: Une société ema de Timor*. Langues et Civilization de L'Asie du
         Sud-Est et du Monde Insulindien 12. Paris: Société d'Études Linguistiques
         et Anthropologiques de France.

Rosaldo, M.
  1980   *Knowledge and passion*. Cambridge: Cambridge University Press.

Rosaldo, R.
  1980   *Ilongot headhunting*. Stanford: Stanford University Press.

Sahlins, M.
  1985   The stranger king; or, Dumézil among the Fijians. In *Islands of History*,
         pp.73-103. Chicago: University of Chicago Press.

Siikala, Jukka
  In press The elder and the younger — foreign and autochthonous origin and
         hierarchy in the Cook Islands. In J.J. Fox and C. Sather (eds) *Origin,
         ancestry and alliance. Proceedings of the comparative Austronesian
         conference on hierarchy, ancestry, and alliance.*

Sudo, Ken-ichi
  In press Hierarchy and routes of migration: chieftainship and ranking in the Central
         Caroline Islands. In J.J. Fox and C. Sather (eds) *Origin, ancestry and
         alliance. Proceedings of the comparative Austronesian conference on
         hierarchy, ancestry, and alliance.*

Traube, E.G.
  1989   Obligations to the source: complementarity and hierarchy in an eastern
         Indonesian society. In D. Maybury-Lewis and U. Almagor (eds) *The
         attraction of opposites: thought and society in a dualistic mode*, pp.321-
         344. Ann Arbor: University of Michigan Press.

Young, M.W.
  1971   *Fighting with food*. Cambridge: Cambridge University Press.

13

SEA NOMADS AND RAINFOREST HUNTER-GATHERERS: FORAGING ADAPTATIONS IN THE INDO-MALAYSIAN ARCHIPELAGO

Clifford Sather

This chapter discusses the non-agricultural aspects of Austronesian history and ethnography, taking the basic view that the early Austronesian colonizations might have involved a range of both food producing and foraging economies and that sharp dichotomies between the two kinds of economy are unlikely to have existed. Modern Austronesian hunter-gatherers such as the Agta and Penan cannot be seen as "fossilized" foragers from the Pleistocene, but, like the Semang, as parties to a process of symbiosis with agriculturalists which has continued for several millennia. The idea of "devolution" from a prior dependence on agriculture amongst the Penan is critically assessed and rejected. Also discussed are the historical roles of the Sea Nomads — Moken, Orang Laut and Sama-Bajau.

INTRODUCTION

Peter Bellwood (1985:205) has proposed that the first "Austronesian-speakers who expanded into the Indo-Malaysian Archipelago carried [with them] a fully agricultural economy". If this is so — and the evidence in support of the proposition is compelling — then the status of contemporary foraging groups in Island Southeast Asia, whose members speak Austronesian languages, must be seen as problematic. Clearly such groups cannot be said to have preserved in any simple or direct sense a form of adaptation ancestral to Austronesian colonization. How, then, are we to place these non-agricultural societies in the history of the Austronesian-speaking world? It is this question that I want to consider here, looking, in particular, at maritime boat nomads, groups whose mode of adaptation appears to be unique to the Indo-Malaysian Archipelago, and to rainforest hunter-gatherers, particularly those of central and western Borneo.

Much of the answer to the question I pose here hinges, I shall argue, on the role of exchange and concomitant economic diversity in the early history of Austronesian adaptation. Although others have also stressed the significance of exchange (e.g. Dunn 1975; Hutterer 1976, 1977; Peterson 1978; Urry 1981), I approach the question here, not as a prehistorian, but from the vantage point of historical ethnography, extrapolating, as it were, from the "ethnographic present" back into the past. While I have tried to draw supporting evidence, where available, from archaeology, linguistics, biology and history, much of this extrapolation is clearly conjectural.

Problems in the Ethnogenesis of Southeast Asian Hunter-Gatherers

In recent years it has come to be acknowledged that contemporary hunter-gatherers, rather than representing forms of organization that evolved during the Palaeolithic and persisted unchanged ever since, are the products of continuing evolutionary processes and, in some cases, of interaction with other populations, including agriculturalists and even, in recent times, centralized states (cf. Schrire 1984). Thus, while not denying the great antiquity of hunting and gathering, most scholars today would agree with Lewin (1988:1147) that,

> ... modern hunter-gathering is a largely post-Pleistocene phenomenon. Rather than being an adaptation ancestral to food production, it is [in effect] a parallel development.

Following from this, Headland and Reid (1989:43) apply what they call an "interdependent model" of foraging to reinterpret the situation of one group of Island Southeast Asian hunter-gatherers — the Philippine Negritos. The Negritos are of special interest because, unlike other Austronesian-speaking foragers, they appear to be biologically distinct from the Austronesian-speaking cultivators who live surrounding them. Their ancestors are therefore believed to have been present in the Philippines, and possibly elsewhere in Island Southeast Asia, prior to the arrival of the first Austronesian agriculturalists (Headland and Reid 1989: 46; see also Bellwood 1985:113). On the basis of linguistic evidence, Headland and Reid (1989:46) propose that:

> At some time in the prehistoric past, the ancestors of today's Negritos must have established ... contact with the Austronesian-speaking immigrants in the course of which they lost their own languages and adopted those of the newcomers. In order for a language switch of this magnitude to have occurred, [this contact must have been both intense and of long duration. Moreover, ... t]he linguistic data suggests that all this happened a very long time ago ... well over a thousand years in the case of the Negrito languages that are today most similar to their non-Negrito sister languages and of many thousands of years in the case of those that are least similar.

The evidence thus points to a protracted interaction between Negrito foragers and Austronesian cultivators that must have begun virtually at once, as soon as the first Austronesians arrived in northern Luzon, perhaps 4500 to 5000 years ago (cf. Bellwood 1985:120; Reid 1987). Thus, rather than representing a "static window on the Paleolithic past", Negrito society must be seen as an adaptive product of prolonged contact.

From the linguistic evidence, Headland and Reid (1989:47) go on to argue that:

The interdependence of Negritos and farming populations observable today has existed much longer than most scholars have thought. [While t]here is no question that the ancestors of the present-day [Negritos] were at one time Paleolithic hunter-gatherers, [the point to be made] is that this Stone Age life-style ended long ago, probably by the middle Holocene, and that prehistoric Negritos probably moved into the Neolithic at more or less the same time as their neighbors.

Here Headland and Reid add another element to their argument. This is a notion that the Negritos first moved into the ever-wet rainforests, the habitat with which the majority are now identified, only after they had acquired at least seasonal access to cultivated foods (see also Headland 1987; Peterson 1978; Peterson and Peterson 1977). Until then, Headland (1987) maintains, they probably occupied only the margins of the rainforest, the coastal zone and more open areas of monsoon forest and parklands. Following from this, Headland and Reid (1989:47) propose,

> that the symbiotic relationship we find today between tropical forest hunter-gatherers and farmers evolved long ago as an adaptive strategy for exploiting the tropical forest.

This argument they link to one concerning the ethnogenesis of Southeast Asian Negrito cultures generally: namely (1989:47),

> that the Negritos evolved culturally into what they are today as they moved into the forest to collect wild products to trade with agriculturalists and overseas traders.

Negrito cultures are thus an innovative product of contact and economic interaction. In this case, contact between pre-existing foragers and Austronesian farmers resulted, not only in the former borrowing the languages of the latter, but in the two becoming mutually enveloped in a symbiotic economy. One consequence of this envelopment was a kind of radial adaptation that allowed the foraging partners in the system to invade and successfully exploit what may have been, until then, a relatively unutilized habitat — the ever-wet rainforest. I will return later to consider a more general form of this argument.

First, however, it must be noted that Headland's thesis rests upon a view of the ever-wet rainforest as an inhospitable habitat incapable of supporting populations of independent foragers (1987; also Bailey *et al.* 1989). This view is by no means securely established and recently Bellwood (1993), using archaeological evidence, and Endicott and Bellwood (1991), using both ethnographic and archaeological data, have made a convincing case that self-sufficient foraging is not only possible but has historically been present, both in the prehistoric past and more recently among contemporary Batek Negrito communities living today in the ever-wet rainforests of the Malay Peninsula (see also Endicott 1984). More generally, Endicott and Bellwood (1991) conclude that, while "tropical rain forests vary in their potential for supporting human foraging", in some areas at least, "small nomadic groups of foragers can live off wild resources alone" and, indeed, have done so in the past, although "the paucity of resources" tends to make such groups opportunistic, and "one of the opportunities they are quick to take up is the opportunity to trade for agricultural produce".

Whether foragers occupied the tropical rainforests before Austronesian colonization or not, Bellwood (1985:132) argues that, in either case, if Austronesian-speakers initially arrived in the Indo-Malaysian Archipelago as cultivators, then, logically, "hunting and collecting societies", whose members now speak Austronesian languages, can have originated in one of two possible ways. They may

have either survived assimilation by, or have adapted out of [an] expanding Austronesian agricultural economy (1985:132).

In other words, they may, like the Philippine Negritos, derive from an earlier population whose members "resisted acculturation by surrounding cultivators", or they may have taken up foraging later on, after their entry into the Indo-Malaysian Archipelago, "as a result of change from an agricultural ancestry" (Bellwood 1985:132).

Except for the Philippine Negritos, all other Austronesian-speaking hunter-gatherers in Island Southeast Asia appear to be genetically indistinguishable from the agricultural populations present around them. In order to account for their presence it has been suggested for Borneo that such foragers are "devolved agriculturalists" (Blust 1989; Hoffman 1984, 1986), the descendants of Austronesian cultivators who moved into the rainforest in order to engage in the collection of forest products for trade. While this argument has gained some acceptance outside of Borneo (cf. Bailey *et al.* 1989), the ethnographic evidence supporting it has not been well marshalled, and anthropologists working with contemporary hunter-gatherers in Sarawak and Kalimantan are considerably more critical (cf. Brosius 1988, 1991; Sellato 1988). At the end of the paper I will examine some of the reasons why this is so and look briefly at several alternative arguments. Together, these point up, as we shall see, a rather more complex solution.

First, however, it is useful to consider briefly the adaptive history of the Aboriginal (Aslian) peoples of the Malay Peninsula. Although most are Austroasiatic- rather than Austronesian-speaking, the history of these groups presents us with a valuable comparison; it also interpenetrates, in more recent times, with the story of Austronesian expansion.

Benjamin, in a series of valuable papers (1979, 1985, 1986), has proposed a model for the development of the three major Aboriginal groupings of the

Malay Peninsula: 1) nomadic foragers in the north (the "Semang"); 2) sedentary swidden farmers in the central uplands (the "Senoi"); and 3) southern lowland forest collectors-for-trade (the "Aboriginal Malay").[1] His underlying argument is that (1986:5),

> the present-day array of indigenous cultures in the Peninsula [has] come about through processes of mutual dissimilation or assimilation (as the case may be) within an essentially common cultural frame.

In other words, each of these major traditions arose, Benjamin (1986:10) argues, out of a common cultural matrix, and in assuming its distinctive form, was shaped, not only by ecological forces, but also by socio-cultural choices made by its members in full awareness of the "ways of doing things" practised by the members of each of the other traditions. Each tradition thus emerged, not out of isolation or from lack of contact, but as a result of "differentiated responses to a heightened attachment to foraging, swiddening, and collection-for-trade", made by groups whose members saw "themselves, complementarily, as part of each other's environment" (Benjamin 1986:10).

Benjamin suggests that food crops began to be cultivated in the Malay Peninsula by about 5000 years ago and so made sedentism a possible option. Among these crops were both cereals and root-crops (cf. Dunn 1975; Peacock 1979). Initially, however, while allowing for a broader spectrum of subsistence modes, the Peninsula was not, Benjamin (1986:12) maintains, well-adapted to sedentary farming. Instead, its economic hallmark was diversity. Not only was there variation in crops and patterns of cultivation but also in subsistence modes themselves, which besides farming, included forest hunting-gathering, strand-foraging, fishing and trade (see also Dunn 1975). While this diversity allowed for considerable adaptive flexibility, it did not lead, initially at least, to a rapid run up of population or to the development of higher levels of socio-cultural integration. Both came only much later. Initially, Benjamin (1986:14) asserts, the social and demographic patterns of farming communities were not very different from those that continued to subsist by foraging. Indeed, he suggests that most groups probably combined both foraging and farming, much as do upland "Senoi" groups today (Benjamin 1986:13). Thus, while foragers planted crops from time to time, farmers continued to engage in hunting and gathering. In Benjamin's view, until some 2000 years ago, the Aboriginal cultures of the Peninsula, while internally diverse, remained socially and economically undifferentiated.

Here a cautionary note is in order. Almost certainly Benjamin overstates the *in situ* nature of these developments (cf. Bellwood 1993). Recent archaeological evidence points to a marked discontinuity between foraging "Hoabinhian" communities and subsequent Neolithic assemblages, indicating that cultivation, and in particular the introduction of rice-agriculture, brought about significant demographic and social organizational changes (Bellwood 1993). Moreover, agriculture appears to have entered the Peninsula from the north and was probably carried southward by Austroasiatic-speakers, including among them, very likely, the ancestors of the present-day "Senoi". Like the Philippine Negritos, the ancestors of the Semang appear to have similarly undergone an early language "switch" as a consequence of this southward expansion of agriculturalists, thus becoming Austroasiatic-speaking like their neighbours. As Bellwood (1993) notes, this tandem spread of language and agriculture appears to parallel the spread of Austronesian-speaking agriculturalists to the east. Both seemingly represent a continuous expansion of a rice cultivating population to the south, commencing about 3000 BC, with, in this instance, its ultimate products impacting on the Malay Peninsula from two opposed directions, the Austroasiatics from the north, the Austronesians from the south.

These qualifications aside, the fact that the ancestors of the Semang underwent a language "switch", and that the Austroasiatic languages now spoken in the Malay Peninsula are as highly differentiated as they are, all point, as Benjamin rightly argues, to an impressive history of local contact and development.

Later, in the south, contact with Austronesian mariners began a process of internal differentiation. Thus,

> the Peninsular coastline began to be contacted by "oceanic nomads", making available the further option of trading in forest products with outsiders ... At first these Austronesian-speaking mariners would have seemed exotic to the Austroasiatic-speaking land-dwellers, but it would not have been very long before certain parts of the Peninsula (the coastal lowlands and the south in particular) would, by cultural assimilation and intermarriage, have become an extension inland of the Austronesian world (Benjamin 1986:11).

In the northern and central regions of the Peninsula, around the same time, farming became efficient enough to allow for the emergence of a more overtly differentiated array of cultures (1986:14). Thus Benjamin suggests that while swiddeners were able to intensify their sedentism as a result, foragers, the ancestors of the present-day "Semang", became, in response, even "more nomadic ..., cutting down ... further their sedentary periods of desultory swidden-tending" (1986:14). Thus, while both sedentism and rainforest foraging had long been options, the marked differentiation of the two came about only much later, through a process of "mutual socio-cultural dissimilation" (Benjamin 1986:15).

In this process of dissimilation, different patterns of social organization were generated as each group came to emphasize what Benjamin (1986:6) calls "deliberately-constructed carriers of ecologically-related meanings and values". One example he discusses are rules of marriageability. Thus, among the foraging Semang, cross-sex avoidances, especially between siblings- and cousins-in-law, produced, Benjamin argues, "a mental image of anti-sedentism" by picturing the ideal society as one constituted of easily detachable conjugal-family groups, linked together by marriages contractible only between those who are not previously related either by consanguinity or affinity. This image, coupled with low population density, compels a "readiness to wander far and wide in search, not only of food, but of social relations" (1986:14). The result is a social organization that is both well-suited to nomadic survival, but also, through its scheme of values, one which irreversibly commits those who practise it to a nomadic mode of life. In contrast, the agricultural Senoi "switched signs" and imposed joking relations where the Semang imposed avoidance, thereby making it, not proscribed, but desirable to marry someone from the same group into which one's siblings and cousins had already married. In this way intermarrying kin groups were consolidated and a premium was placed on sedentism rather than mobility. This difference "not only proclaimed that Senoi ways were different from Semang ways", but provided a further reason for rejecting the other. In consequence,

> two quite complementary patterns of social praxis were evolved and locked into place (Benjamin 1986:15).

Finally, by the end of the first millennium AD, among the now Austronesian-speaking peoples of the southern lowlands (and in the neighbouring coastal regions of Borneo and Sumatra), petty chiefdoms became progressively "nested" within one another to form small-scale states (cf. Benjamin 1985; Wolters 1967, 1979). This process of state formation almost certainly involved boat-dwelling mariners — the peoples whose adaptation I turn to presently — who acted as "integrating information-carriers" linking together, as agents in this process, the emerging courts, subsidiary chiefs and a developing peasantry (Benjamin 1986:16).

ADAPTIVE DIVERSITY IN EARLY AUSTRONESIAN SOCIETY

In order to bring together our discussion so far, it is useful to return to the notion, introduced at the beginning of the paper, of communities enmeshed in systems of symbiotic interaction, at once interconnected but economically diverse. Here I want to suggest that such a pattern was probably an integral feature of early Austronesian society.

Current linguistic evidence places the beginning of Austronesian expansion, initially involving most likely groups from Taiwan moving south-ward into the northern Philippines, at around 5000 BP (Bellwood 1985:107-121;

Pawley and Green 1973:52-54). Bellwood (1985) has proposed a comprehensive model of this expansion based primarily on linguistic and archaeological evidence. According to this model, carriers of Austronesian languages essentially moved southward, settling the islands they encountered with an economy based on agriculture, focused initially on cereals, rice in particular, but adding as they moved southward a variety of tuber and tree crops which in some areas replaced rice as the locally dominant staples.

Without disputing this model, it should not be taken to imply that all early Austronesians were equally committed to rice agriculture. This seems unlikely. Instead, they probably included groups practising a comparatively broad spectrum of economic activities, including trade and, in addition to farming, elements of secondary foraging, hunting, fishing and marine collection (cf. Pawley and Green 1973:35-36). This is not to suggest that the early Austronesians subsisted as full-time foragers, and certainly not as rainforest hunters and gatherers. Rather, what appears to have distinguished the early Austronesians was, almost certainly, the existence of a strong maritime element and, as a concomitant of economic diversity, the presence of significant relations of exchange. Although not full-time foragers themselves, the early Austronesians almost certainly initiated, by their arrival in Island Southeast Asia, two major innovations, both of them associated with exchange, that transformed the nature of foraging in the region: namely — (1) the creation of a special niche for forest collectors-for-trade and (2) the envelopment of foraging groups with agriculturalists and others in a diversified economy.

The principal evidence that the proto-Austronesians practised rice agriculture comes from linguistic reconstructions, and most especially from the work of Robert Blust (1976). This evidence also points to economic diversity. Thus, the early Austronesians appear to have possessed a diverse technology which Blust (1976:37) describes as a "mixed picture" — "with stone tools next to iron, probably bark cloth next to textiles, root crops next to grains". While Blust (1984-5) has since revised his views somewhat, particularly in regard to iron, the picture he presents remains a complex one. Rice agriculture is certainly a major feature, but, at the same time, the evidence suggests,

> a polymorphous economic base incompatible with the somewhat rigid notion of "progress" from one exclusive level to the next (Blust 1976:37).

Economic polymorphism is also suggested by the archaeological record, incomplete as it is. Thus, Bellwood (1985:159), in discussing the gradual southward expansion of Austronesian-speakers, while stressing the propelling role of agriculture, points up the continuing presence of foraging adaptations, noting that (1985:159):

This expansion was not a geographically unified process of replacement. The hunting and gathering lifestyle has been progressively eroded but it has certainly never disappeared entirely ... Hence in recent millennia different technologies and economies could and did occur in neighbouring and contemporary sites in a mosaic-like fashion (Hutterer 1976).

Later I will suggest that, in addition to agriculture, the continuing presence of secondary foraging may, indeed, have contributed to the success of the early Austronesians as colonizers. At the same time, the envelopment of foragers in a more diversified economy may have increased the effectiveness of foraging itself, possibly drawing new groups into this niche.

Finally, while cereal cultivation appears to have been a major factor in Austronesian expansion, the Proto-Austronesians, it is equally clear, were not an exclusively land-oriented people. Thus, linguistic evidence confirms the existence of an early and well-developed maritime tradition (Blust 1976:36) and with it, very likely, a pattern of sea-going trade.

While economic diversity might not have contributed to population density, it seems likely to have encouraged a centrifugal, outward-movement of people, one consequence of which may well have been the incorporation of still greater diversity. As I will suggest later, secondary foraging probably played a role in this, facilitating both expansion and the incorporation of new crops and cultivation methods as expanding groups colonized new environments. Moreover, by holding open, initially at least, the option of a thorough-going sedentism, the early Austronesians succeeded as colonizers, pursuing a variety of adaptive strategies and adding new ones as they colonized new environments, while preserving, at the same time, the possibility of future socio-cultural complexity.

Finally, from the outset, the Austronesians must have been able, as a result of economic interaction and exchange, not only to envelop and so transform existing foragers, but also to develop and enmesh new lines of economic adaptation, including in time, new varieties of foraging particularly geared to the region's unique environments — to its ever-wet rainforests and, even more importantly, to its vast archipelagic seas.

THE PRE-EMINENCE OF THE SEA

Urry (1981) has made a powerful argument that, because of its role in communications, the sea constitutes the dominant factor in the prehistory of the Indo-Malaysian region. Geographically the archipelago consists of thousands of islands, joined by relatively shallow, warm seas ideally situated for easy communication, while, in contrast, the larger islands of the region are often difficult to penetrate, except where river systems reach inland, forming, as it were, extensions of the sea (Urry 1981:2-3).

It is not known how long the sea may have exerted this pre-eminence. But Urry suggests that its importance began to be felt by at least the end of the Pleistocene, when ocean levels altered, encouraging marine innovation (1981:4). Whatever the case, in recent historical times, despite geographical and cultural barriers, nearly all societies indigenous to the archipelago have been involved in a complex network of trading and exchange relationships. "At the centre" of this network have historically been "... those who controlled the seas, integrating communities and regions" (Urry 1981:4).

Here it needs to be pointed out that, in addition to the role of the sea in communications, the Indo-Malaysian Archipelago is also singularly rich in marine life. While Island Southeast Asia, in terms of its terrestrial fauna, comprises a zone of overlap between Asian and Australian faunal zones, in terms of its marine fauna, it is, of itself, the single primary centre of world diversity. Thus as Dunn and Dunn (1984:252) observe, while

> [T]he tropics are far richer in numbers of animals and plant species than are the temperate ... regions of the world, ... this generalization holds true for the seas at least as much as for the terrestrial realm ... [and o]f the tropical seas, ... those surrounding the mainland and islands of present day Southeast Asia are known to contain the greatest wealth of marine life ... The centre of this richness is Sundaic Southeast Asia, and Ekman's (1953:18) oft-quoted statement on this matter bears repeating here: "The further one moves away from this centre in any direction, the more the fauna appears as ... progressively impoverished ...".

Much of this richness is due to the existence of two ecosystems unique to the tropics: coral reefs and mangrove associations (Dunn and Dunn 1984:252-253). In the next section, I will touch briefly on their significance to the development of maritime foraging in the region. But here the important point is that, from early times, large numbers of people in the Indo-Malaysian Archipelago have depended on the sea for their subsistence. If the early Austronesians entered the archipelago with an already developed maritime technology, it is likely that while some groups may have abandoned seafaring to concentrate on the land, others almost certainly responded to this richness by developing even more proficient fishing and strand-gathering technologies.

While trade was undoubtedly part of the resulting marine adaptations that evolved, the second point to be made is that not all of those who engaged in maritime trade occupied positions of economic or political dominance. Coastal fishing communities, while dependent on trade, have never enjoyed high status or notable power in Southeast Asia. The "oceanic nomads" who appear to have been instrumental in the formation of the earliest historical states in the region were in many cases semi-pariahs, some of whom maintained boat-nomadism, as we shall see presently, just as hunter-gatherers ashore preserved its forest counterpart, as a means of dissimilation, a way of resisting domination and the loss of identity to neighbouring land-based societies.

All of this should not detract, however, from Urry's main argument concerning the dominance of the sea, and so of trade in early Austronesian prehistory. Initially, before the development of navigational skills, the sea must have constituted a barrier to wider integration. Thus during this early period, a mosaic of cultures would have developed, occupying different environments, and it was this rich variety of environments and human cultures that provided, Urry (1981:7) argues, the basis upon which the trade and exchange of later periods developed. It also contributed to the formation of political hierarchy. Thus he maintains (1981:7),

> the group or groups who gained some mastery of the seas and who could thus transform the barrier into a bridge, could exploit this cultural variety for their own ends. Indeed, if it were done carefully, they had the potential to dominate the whole archipelago.

The subsequent growth of trade did not spell an end to socio-cultural diversity. Indeed, as Urry notes, the experience in Southeast Asia has been that cultural distinctiveness is characteristically fostered rather than destroyed by trade. However, Urry argues that if one group dominates, then the danger exists that this domination may threaten the very diversity on which the system is based. This question of dominance and possible assimilation leads to Urry's major argument (Urry 1981:9) that the early Austronesians, even before they left eastern Asia, may have already been adapted to coastal conditions and to inter-island trade. Thus trade itself may have contributed to Austronesian expansion. Groups may have set out, in other words, seeking not only new lands to farm, but exchange goods and new communities to trade with (Urry 1981:9). As the Austronesians entered the archipelago, the geography of the region would have given a further stimulus to trade and to the development of maritime technology. Geography thus provided the "basic outline upon which ... the prehistory of the region [was later] played out".

> The pattern of islands and inland seas provided the stimulus for maritime innovation and the production of goods from the ecological and cultural diversity of the islands supplied the impetus for trade and exchange. Utilizing sea routes the whole pattern of trade and exchange and the strategies for developing producers and consumers was expanded within and beyond the archipelago (1981:23).

Ultimately this expansion drew the Austronesians westward, throughout Island Southeast Asia to the mainland, and eventually to the Indian Ocean and beyond.[2]

As a result of their control of the sea, the first Austronesians were able to spread their culture and language, assimilating pre-existing populations through their command of maritime trading networks. An example is provided by the collectors-for-trade of southern Malaya whose assimilation we described in the previous section. Thus Urry (1981:10) argues that a mass movement of people is not necessary to account for the spread of Austronesian languages. Trade seems likely to have played a part in encouraging expansion, and once the Austronesians began to penetrate the Indo-Malaysian Archipelago, the subsequent spread of Austronesian languages is likely to have been linked to trade itself, with Austronesian languages replacing the earlier languages of the area through their role as the dominant languages of trade.

Sea Nomads

Whatever its role in Austronesian expansion, there can be little doubt that the sea has shaped, in a major way, the subsequent history of the Austronesian-speaking world. In Western Austronesia the sea and immediate littoral have also been, from the beginning of historical documentation, zones of notable economic and ethnic diversity, and have included within their compass widely-scattered communities whose distinctive mode of life is characterized by various forms of boat-dwelling nomadism — peoples constituting, in short, maritime foragers.

The Southeast Asian sea nomads are divided geographically, culturally, and linguistically into three major groupings, each the product of an apparently independent history of adaptation. The first of these groupings comprises the Moken and Moklen of the Mergui Archipelago of Burma, with extensions southward into the islands of southwestern Thailand (Anderson 1890; Hogan 1972; Ivanoff 1985, 1987). The second is represented by a congeries of variously named groups, collectively referred to as *Orang Laut* (lit. "sea people"), who inhabit the islands and estuaries of the Riau-Lingga Archipelagoes, the Bantam Archipelago, and the coasts and offshore islands of eastern Sumatra, Singapore, and southern Johor (Andaya 1975; Logan 1847; Sopher 1965; Wee 1985). A northern subgroup of Orang Laut, the Urak Lawoi, occupy the offshore islands from Phuket to the Adang island group, along the southern edge of the Moken-Moklen range (Hogan 1989:1-2).[3] Finally, the third, and largest grouping consists of the Sama-Bajau, most of them maritime or strand-oriented communities, but including also small numbers of boat nomads, who together form what is probably the most widely-dispersed ethnolinguistic group indigenous to Island Southeast Asia, living over an area of some one-and-a-quarter million square miles, from south-central Philippines, eastern Borneo and Sulawesi, south and eastward through to the islands of eastern Indonesia to Flores and the southern Moluccas (Fox 1977; Geoghegan 1984; Nimmo 1972; Pallesen 1985; Sather 1975a, 1978, 1984, 1993a).

THE SAMA-BAJAU

Here I begin with the last of these groupings, the Sama-Bajau, with whom I conducted fieldwork in coastal Borneo.[4] The earliest mention of maritime peoples identifiable as Sama goes back to the 16th century. Today the Sama characteristically live in dispersed shoreline and island settlements, often surrounded and interpenetrated by those of more numerous land-based peoples. Everywhere the Sama lack political unity. In contrast to their politically-dominant neighbours, they identify themselves with a multitude of small, highly fragmented local groups, none of them sufficiently integrated or large enough to exist in its own right as an independent political entity. Most of these groups are distinguished toponymically by the name of an individual island or island cluster identified by its members as their homeland or principal area of settlement (Sather 1993b). The boat nomads are the chief exception. Without an exclusive land affiliation, nomadic groups characteristically identify themselves as the *Sama Dilaut*, the "Sea" or "Oceanic Sama" (Sather 1984:12-13, 1993a).

As a whole, the Sama are strongly associated with the littoral. In the Sulu Archipelago of the Philippines, where perhaps a half of the total Sama-speaking population lives, they predominate chiefly in the smaller coralline islands, particularly those of the northern, southern and western margins of the archipelago (Sather 1993b). On the larger, more heavily populated and mainly central islands, the Sama are greatly outnumbered by the land-based and predominantly agrarian Tausug. Historically, within the Sulu Sultanate the Sama formed a subordinate population. In the *silasila*, the Tausug genealogical histories of Sulu, the Sama are represented as the recently-arrived "guests" of ranking lines of local Tausug leaders (Saleeby 1908:156-157), a representation that reverses, as we shall see, their actual historical relationship. Traditionally, power in Sulu was based on factional politics, and local leaders, both Tausug and Sama, were joined in a loose, pyramidical network of personal allegiances that ran from village headmen and local title-bearing chiefs to the sultan at the apex of the political order (Kiefer 1972; Sather 1984:3-8).

Tributary trade was a central feature of the Sulu state. Power derived from control over trading commodities and the people who procured them. Thus, the sultan's authority was sustained by a procurement economy, articulated through personal patronage and alliance, in which labour and locally-produced commodities of trade were supplied by a variety of differentially adapted ethnic and sub-ethnic communities, including local bands of boat nomads. Within the archipelago, trade was the single unifying principle, welding together people in what was otherwise a zone of enormous cultural and linguistic diversity (Sather 1985:168-175; Warren 1979).

Through this system of procurement, shore-based Sama provided their local patrons with services as skilled seamen, boat-builders, smiths, artisans, mat-makers, potters, fishermen, and inter-island carriers and traders, while the most prestigious and independent of these groups, such as the Balangingi Sama, supplied maritime raiders and procured slaves for the Tausug markets of Jolo (Sather 1984, 1985, 1993b; Warren 1978, 1981).[5] The boat nomads, who lived in scattered bands throughout the whole of Sulu, formed, together with swidden cultivators inhabiting the coastal fringes of Mindanao and eastern Borneo, the least prestigious and lowest ranking of these groups. Historically the boat nomads acted chiefly as divers and specialized fishermen, procuring for their land-based patrons a variety of important commodities of trade, including, in the eighteenth and nineteenth centuries, tortoise-shell, *tripang*, pearls, dried fish and pearl-shell (Sather 1984, 1993a; Warren 1981:60-61). Although the boat nomads formed only a small minority of the islands' population, these commodities represented in the past a major source of Sulu's export wealth.

Lacking a territorial identity, the sea nomads, in contrast to other Sama, were without formal jural status in the Sulu Sultanate (Sather 1984:15). Among them, characteristically, each boat housed a single family. Local bands were comprised of families that regularly anchored together at the same moorage site (*sambuangan*), or at the same seasonal sites, mooring their boats in smaller family alliance groups (Sather 1985:190-194). While at anchor, family members repaired and careened their boats, traded and engaged with others in an intense round of social transactions (Sather 1976, 1984:12, 1985:171). Each local anchorage group was under the protection of a recognized leader ashore whose land-based followers enjoyed a privileged trading relationship with its members. In the past, at every level of the alliance hierarchy, individual leaders, from village headmen to the sultan, maintained armed retinues (Kiefer 1972). In a setting of endemic factional violence, rivalry and armed feuding, nomadic bands depended for their physical security on their patron's protection (Sather 1984: 14-15). Although patrons described "their" boat-nomadic clients as "property" (Sather 1984:14), these local groups were able to move relatively easily from the territorial sphere of one leader to another, and so had to be treated with some care for fear of losing their trade to rivals (Sather 1971, 1984:13-15).

Kemp Pallesen (1985) has proposed a model for the historical dispersion of the Sama-Bajau, based on a linguistic reconstruction that, extending over a millennium, highlights the role of trade and political relations in the development of maritime adaptations, including boat nomadism.

Sama-Bajau language relations are reconstructible only to the first millennium AD. Beyond that, wider affiliations are problematic (Pallesen 1985: 117).[6] By AD 800 speakers of Proto-Sama-Bajau were established in the area surrounding Basilan Straits, in the northern islands of the Sulu Archipelago and along the adjacent Mindanao coastline (Pallesen 1985:117). Language reconstruction indicates that these people were predominantly sea-oriented, but not exclusively so. Thus, evidence also points to a long familiarity with farming, iron-forging, pottery-making and weaving. Although their knowledge of the sea was more intimate than of the land, the early Sama were, by no means, a population made up entirely of boat nomads and fishermen. Instead, a marine orientation coexisted with "a significant and coherent tradition of land-oriented activity" (1985:255), indicating the presence,

> ... already at this predispersion time [of] a divergence of orientation between the land and the coastal strands ... (Pallesen 1985:117).

Reflecting this divergence, different Sama groups, from the beginning, appear to have pursued, much as they do today, various permutations of this "dual orientation", some focusing on the land, others on the strand or sea, with communities of sea nomads forming only one of a multitude of economically diverse groups (Pallesen 1985:118).

The ethnography of the Sama-Bajau is fully consistent with this reconstruction. Not only do boat-nomadic groups comprise only a small minority of all Sama-speakers,[7] but everywhere they exist within a larger cultural and linguistic matrix that includes closely related shore- and land-based communities.

When I began fieldwork in southeastern Sabah in 1964, some families making up the local community were still boat-dwelling, while others had begun a short time earlier to erect a pile-house village over the community's principal moorage site (Sather 1984:20; 1985:173-176). The community itself, however, remained largely nomadic. Thus its families continued to move between the site and dispersed over an extended fishing zone surrounding it (Sather 1976; 1985: 187-190). Although some, particularly younger, men were beginning to seek wage-work ashore, the community as a whole remained overwhelmingly maritime and entirely non-agricultural, without crops or landed property. Yet, within the community, there existed a tradition of myths in which the narrative heroes practised swidden rice-cultivation, with the myths themselves giving a technically detailed account of swiddening (cf. Sather 1975b). In addition, mediums (*jin*) conducted an annual trance-ritual called *magpai baha'u* in which conical mounds of "new rice" (*pai baha'u*) were shaped into symbolic "mountains" (*bud*). Thus, while the Bajau Laut did not themselves farm, rice and its cultivation, nevertheless, formed an integral part of the community's mythic and ritual vocabulary.

At one level, this example might be taken as a cautionary case, illustrating the danger of reconstructing the economy from the evidence of language alone. Yet at another, and perhaps more significant level, it can be said that the boat nomads, although non-cultivators, participated in a larger cultural and cognitive universe in which rice-cultivation is both present and familiar. The surrounding islands and coastline are relatively populous, and coastal and shoreline Sama villages, many of them agricultural, are seldom out of the sight of Bajau Laut fishing parties. Thus, farming is not unknown, even to the most sea-oriented Sama. Moreover, as I have described elsewhere (1984:10-11), all local Sama communities, whether sea nomads or shore-oriented groups, were historically enmeshed in a regional network of symbiotic exchange. Thus, for example, in addition to farming, some Sama communities in Semporna produced pottery for trade, including earthenware hearths carried by sea nomads aboard their boats; others offered iron-work, tortoise-shell jewellery and skilled carpentry; or supplied caulking resins and *kajang*-roofing for boats (Sather 1984:11). Locally, each of these groups constituted a named dialect community. Linguistically, each community was, and continues to be, aligned with others in continuous dialect chains. Thus, in any one region, interacting Sama, both at sea and ashore, speak mutually intelligible dialects, at once understandable, yet readily identifiable by community affiliation. Within this enmeshing network, exchange and regular contact, while fostering economic specialization, prevent groups from undergoing total dissimilation, ensuring instead that they all share in a common language and cultural tradition.

Pallesen (1985:118), in his reconstruction, sees the 10th century as the beginning of a major period of Sama dispersion. Thus, a number of sea-oriented groups probed northward, establishing ports of call around the eastern coast of Mindanao and beyond. Others settled the broad zone of mangrove swamps at the head of Sibuguey Bay. At the same time a third group, the Yakan, located on Basilan Island within the original Sama-Bajau homeland, became linguistically and socially distinct, not by sea-going migration, but, on the contrary, as a result of territorial stability, by intensifying its land-orientation, shunning the sea and becoming a settled group of inland swiddeners (Pallesen 1985:118). Today dissimilation is so complete that the Yakan are generally accepted as a separate ethnolinguistic group, distinct from other Sama-speakers (Frake 1980:325-326). Later, in the eleventh century additional sea-oriented groups spread southward, down the Sulu Archipelago. One branch eventually settled the northern and western coasts of Sabah (Sather 1993b). Another established itself along the southeastern coast of Sabah, and from there its forward advance reached the Straits of Makassar, entering eastern Indonesia some centuries before the first European penetration of the region (Fox 1977).

The turn of the millennium thus marked the beginning of a long period of Sama movement. In addition, some 700 years ago, the Sama came into first contact with the Tausug. Pallesen (1985:246-247) argues that these two events were related and that changing economic and political relations were the catalyst of both. Underlying these changes was long-distance trade with China, India and the Middle East. Pallesen (1985:247) suggests that the Sama, in probing northward, established a network of trading colonies along the rivermouths and coastlines of the islands they encountered, including Mindanao. This development, while commercial in motive, did not necessarily entail elaborate enterprise. Instead, Pallesen (1985:248) suggests,

> ... a major early element of ... trade may well have been the protein-starch exchange which underlies much economic activity in Sulu [to the present].

Salt fish is today the major source of protein for inland peoples in the Philippines and northern Borneo and dried fish has been, throughout historical times, a principal item of trade for Sama-speaking peoples and the major export commodity of Sulu.[8] Pallesen argues that this protein-starch exchange was probably a major factor in the early dispersion of the Sama. But once they had established a network of scattered bases, they were then well-positioned to take advantage of further trading developments. Thus Pallesen (1985:249) writes:

> The maritime skills of [the Sama] and the wide distribution of their settlements or ports of call would have given them an advantage in exploiting the growing trade opportunities in the centuries around 1000 AD.

By the eleventh century, Jolo Island, located at the centre of the Sulu Archipelago, emerged as the hub of this network and the primary *entrepôt* for the whole of the archipelago.

Pallesen argues that this spread of Sama colonies brought Sama-speaking traders into contact with the ancestors of the Tausug. Linguistically, Tausug is a Southern Central Philippine language. Its nearest sister language is Butuanon, spoken today in a limited area at the mouth of the Agusan River in eastern Mindanao (Pallesen 1985:125ff). Pallesen considers it probable that Sama traders established an early colony here, in order to command the local river trade, and that, through intermarriage, some returned to central Sulu, taking with them Tausug women and children. According to Pallesen (1985:265), the present Tausug population thus had its genesis in a bilingual trading community established chiefly at Jolo by Sama traders and their Tausug-speaking wives and children.

By the time this bilingual community took form, Jolo was already a major commercial centre with links to China, the central and northern Philippines, Borneo, and to other parts of the eastern and western Malay world. Taking advantage of its strategic location, this Jolo-based trading élite gained power and numerical strength, using its power not only to maintain Tausug as a distinct language, but to absorb the more settled land-based Sama then present in the larger central islands of Sulu, assimilating them linguistically and culturally. This process of assimilation continues to the present. Economic differences were thus accentuated and the remaining Sama came to be increasingly associated with the peripheral islands of the archipelago and with the more maritime sectors of Sulu's economy.

With the coming of Islam, and the emergence of the Sulu sultanate in the 14th century, the Tausug assumed formal dominance over the other peoples of the Sulu Archipelago, most of them Sama-speakers. In the process the Tausug evolved a distinctive ethnic identity by way of sealing their political and economic domination, and with the rise of the Sulu Sultanate, differences of rank, religion and power came to assume ethnic characteristics (Frake 1980; Sather 1984).

The sultanate, with its defining features of political and religious hierarchy, constituted an ethnically segmented state, with political allegiance, rank and religion all united in a single, all-embracing system of ethnic stratification (Sather 1984:3-8). Thus the Tausug, concentrated in the larger central islands of the Sulu Archipelago, where the power of the state was strongest, formed its principal agrarian population, its chief traders, and through their monopoly of aristocratic titles, the holders of its most powerful political and religious offices, including that of Sultan. By contrast, the Sama, and above all the nomadic Bajau Laut, were identified with the margins of the state, its territorial peripheries, the sea and shoreline, political clientage, lesser degrees of religious piety, and in the case of the boat nomads exclusion from the Faith altogether, as non-Muslims (Sather 1984:13-15).

Outside of the Sulu Archipelago, the southward spread of Sama-speakers throughout eastern Indonesia appears to have similarly preceded the rise of commercial polities. Again, the emergence of regional trading states marked the subordination of Sama mariners and fishermen, and the related development of maritime trading networks, in particular the *tripang* collecting industries organized under Makassar and Bugis patronage, followed closely patterns of Sama dispersion and voyaging (Fox 1977; Pelras 1972; Reid 1983:124-129).

For the Bajau Laut, sea nomadism existed, then, in a context of states and trade, including both symbiotic trade and politically-structured tributary trade directed toward international markets (Sather 1985:168-175). The boat nomads, as we know them from the nineteenth and early twentieth centuries, practised a complex, highly specialized adaptation and in no sense can they be described as "primitive" foragers. In this regard, Bellwood (1985:136) is almost certainly right to regard their way of life as a comparatively recent development.

On the other hand, it should not be forgotten that, among the Sama as a whole, communities of boat nomads appear to have emerged out of a larger, more highly diverse island and coastal population. It seems probable that boat nomads everywhere in Southeast Asia evolved from a similar matrix, appearing originally as generalized coastal foragers, but becoming increasingly specialized and trade-dependent with the rise of maritime states, a development to which their presence itself almost certainly contributed.

Through trade and political clientage, the Bajau Laut appear to have become not only trade-dependent, but also increasingly specialized in an ecological sense. Two major sources accounting for the richness of marine life in the Indo-Malaysian Archipelago are, as we noted earlier, its coral reefs and mangrove forests, both of which are unique to the tropics and particularly well-developed in Island Southeast Asia. Other littoral environments such as sandy or rocky shores are essentially the same as in other parts of the world. Each of these environments has a distinctive biota. However, as Dunn and Dunn (1984:254) observe:

> two or more such biotypes may occur together or within a small area. For example, a coral reef may fringe any type of shore, and rocks may occur in the midst of sand beaches. Such areas have a greater variety of species than has each biotype alone, and for that reason it is likely that mixed environments would be preferred as subsistence zones by peoples who exploit marine resources.

Indeed, most sea nomadic communities exploit an extended range of habitats, typically incorporating a variety of biotypes (cf. Sather 1985:183-190). However, most contemporary communities tend to concentrate on one or two primary ecosystems. Thus, in southeastern Sabah, the Bajau Laut focus most of their fishing activity on coral reefs, submerged coral terraces, associated sandy beaches and tidal shallows. They make little use of mangrove shores, except to take firewood, and avoid altogether muddy or turbid waters. Cultivated foodstuffs are obtained entirely by trade. In contrast, some Orang Laut communities, such as the Duano of east Sumatra (Sandbukt 1984:10), occupy areas of brackish mudflats and mangrove swamps and have developed a highly specialized foraging adaptation that utilizes the extremely narrow but rich resource base represented by this particular environment. As with the Bajau Laut, such specialization does not permit economic self-subsistence, and in return for littoral produce the Duano obtain virtually all of their other necessities from trade with riverine Malay horticulturalists, including cultivated foodstuffs and even their dwelling-boats.

Such specialized adaptations appear, however, to have developed from a more generalized pattern of coastal foraging. Evidence of such an early pattern has recently come to light from Bukit Tengkorak in southeastern Sabah (Bellwood 1989; Bellwood and Koon 1989). Here archaeological materials reveal a population living during the first millennium BC in a coastal setting, heavily exploiting the area's marine resources and engaged in long-distance sea trade, while at the same time exploiting also the nearby streams and coastal forests. Perhaps the most intriguing feature of this site is the presence of portable pottery hearths. These hearths, carried on boats, have historically been the hallmark of boat nomads and related maritime Sama in the region. Thus there may be a suggestive link here to the possible precursors of the later sea nomads in the region.

With the dissolution of the Sulu Sultanate, and the breakdown of procurement trade and its replacement by a monetized market for fish and other maritime products, the specialized adaptation of the Bajau Laut also broke down, leading in this century to an almost complete disappearance of boat nomadism and to the settlement of formerly nomadic communities in permanent strand villages (see Nimmo 1972; Sather 1984, 1993a; C. Warren 1983).

THE ORANG LAUT

Although culturally and linguistically very different, the situation of the Orang Laut, as we know it from the 16th through the end of the nineteenth century, was in many ways similar to that of the Sama-Bajau. Even more than Sulu, the Straits of Malacca, along the southern approaches to which the Orang Laut were very largely concentrated, were and continue to be a major cross-roads of maritime commerce. They were also the primary arena of Malay political history. Thus historians like Wolters (1967, 1979) on Srivijaya and Andaya (1974, 1975) on the Johor Kingdom have stressed the centrally important role they see the Malay-speaking Orang Laut as playing in providing the naval power and communicative links on which the hegemony of successive Malay states was based in a zone of otherwise relatively sparse population. Here, like Sulu, the sea nomads similarly emerged, together with a variety of related coastal and strand peoples, from a common cultural matrix.

With the Orang Laut, we see boat nomadism, again, embedded in a complex political order. In the seventeenth and eighteenth centuries, for example, different named groups of Orang Laut were incorporated in the Kingdom of Johor by their formalized ties to the ruler (Andaya 1974). These ties were articulated in terms of the specific corvée duties assigned to each of these groups (or *suku*). With corvées were associated degrees of status. Thus Andaya (1974:7), writing of the seventeenth century, outlines these relationships in the following terms:

> The more powerful and prestigious Orang Laut groups were associated with the larger islands or those islands which were favourably situated on major sea trading lanes, ... The duties of the Orang Laut were to gather sea products for the China trade, perform certain special services for the ruler at weddings, funerals, or on a hunt, serve as transport for envoys and royal missives, man the ships and serve as a fighting force on the ruler's fleet, and patrol the waters of the kingdom. Except in times of actual warfare when their services were needed for the fleet, the Orang Laut were usually on patrol providing protection for Johor's traders or to those wanting to trade in Johor while harassing all other shipping.

Groups such as the Orang Suku Galang, for example, comprising the upper stratum of Orang Laut, were those whose duty, as might be expected, was to provide the naval fighting force for the realm. In contrast, the corvée duty assigned to the Orang Mantang, who formed one of the lowest status groups, was to care for the ruler's hunting dogs. Later, with the breakdown of central hegemony, fighting groups like the Orang Galang appear to have transferred their allegiance to local Malay chieftains who engaged them as pirate crews. As a result, one of the consequences of the suppression of piracy in the mid-nineteenth century was a rapid sedentarization of a number of these Orang Laut groups (Sandbukt 1984:7; Sopher 1965). Today, former high status groups have generally embraced Islam and become more or less assimilated into the general Malay population, while marginal low status groups have generally continued to maintain a separate ethnicity, even after becoming sedentary fishermen.

Like the Bajau Laut, the identity and mode of life of the Orang Laut was powerfully shaped by their interaction with settled groups in a larger, hierarchically-constituted field of political and economic relations. Both groups lacked an independent political and economic existence, separate from that of their settled neighbours. Within the Malay world, this interaction appears to have been even more formally structured than it was in Sulu, where the sultanate remained, despite its formal patterning on a Malay court model, a relatively loosely structured polity (cf. Kiefer 1972). Thus the Orang Laut were divided, through their relationship to the ruler, into status groups, each differentially situated to perform specific corvée tasks, these tasks in turn associated with positions in an almost caste-like status hierarchy. To the extent that the Orang Laut functioned as marine foragers and fishermen, they were clearly, like the Bajau Laut, "professional" foragers whose very existence presupposed trade, political hierarchy and the institutions of the state.

The Moken

In comparison, the Moken offer an important contrast. If Bukit Tengkorak suggests that boat nomadism may have evolved from a more generalized form of coastal foraging, the Moken give evidence of what such an adaptation may have been like. Unlike Sulu, and even more the Straits of Malacca, the Mergui Archipelago was a comparative backwater in the past. Here boat nomads, while trading with shore people for agricultural produce, appear to have been much less subject to their political domination and were little involved in a procurement trade for external markets. Mergui therefore presents us with a form of boat nomadism as a predominantly subsistence adaptation.

Fortunately for the Moken, unlike the Bajau Laut and other boat nomadic groups, we have a comparatively detailed ethnographic literature for the late nineteenth and early twentieth century (cf. Anderson 1890; Carrapiett 1909; White 1922). While the Moken also gathered some marine and littoral produce for exchange, receiving in return cultivated staple foods such as rice, this trade was mainly seasonal and for most of the year Moken bands appear to have been largely self-sufficient. Some groups in addition planted shoreline gardens, to which they returned from time to time to harvest crops. In contrast to the Bajau Laut, the Moken made extensive use of the resources available in the interior of the larger islands of the archipelago. Here they gathered wild honey, fruit, roots and tubers and hunted wild pigs with the aid of dogs. Some communities also occupied brackish tidal estuaries and mangrove swamps, exploiting these areas, not in the highly specialized manner of the Duano, but as one of a number of varied foraging habitats.

Today many of these groups, much like rainforest hunter-gatherers, are faced with environmental loss as mangrove and coastal forests are cleared for farming, charcoal production, plantations and other kinds of coastal development (Engelhardt 1987:11-13). Thus, many former boat nomads in southwestern Thailand have been forced into an increasing reliance on inshore fishing, where they face competition and, increasingly, assimilation by established coastal populations.

From this survey it should be clear that an understanding of boat nomadism requires that it be seen historically and in a wider ecological context. As Sandbukt (1984:4) stresses,

> Because of their dispersal ... and the varying extent and significance of their historical interaction with land-based peoples, a comprehensive study of the sea nomads necessitates a region-wide perspective and one with a considerable time-depth, in addition to localized field studies.

When viewed from such a perspective, the sea nomads may be seen as associated with archipelagic environments that are, in the western Austronesian world, singularly extensive and rich in food resources. Implied is a wealth of opportunities for strand foraging and for the exploitation of inshore waters using nets, spears and other techniques, all historically employed by the sea nomads (cf. Sopher 1965). But also implied is access to the shoreline and to coastal forests which hold out still further exploitable resources, including wild plant foods capable of supplementing a protein-rich marine diet. What is suggested is a range of possible adaptive modes, and among them the possibility of a more generalized adaptation, resembling more closely hunter-gathering (rather than peasant fishing), in the sense that it involves the exploitation of a highly diverse resource base. This possibility is obscured in the case of the Sama and Orang Laut by their specialized adaptation to trade and the state.

Finally, while the role of maritime peoples in early Austronesian expansion remains unclear, Solheim (1975, 1984) has recently proposed that this role was possibly central and that it may have involved peoples ancestral to the historical sea nomads. As an alternative to the model of southward migration proposed by Bellwood and others, Solheim (1984:86) has argued that the proto-Austronesians first emerged within Island Southeast Asia itself. In this thesis, he proposes that Austric, a possible language grouping encompassing both Austroasiatic and Austronesian, was spoken throughout the whole of Southeast Asia, including Sundaland, during the late Pleistocene (Solheim 1975:152). Later, with raising sea levels, Sundaland became a zone of islands, isolating Austric speakers in the east from those of the west and north, and so producing a split between what he calls "Pre-Austroasiatic" speakers on Sumatra and the Southeast Asian mainland and "Pre-Austronesian" speakers in eastern Indonesia and the southern Philippines (1975:156). Following this split, Proto-Austronesian developed according to Solheim in Island Southeast Asia and from there was carried northward to Taiwan and South China by a developing maritime people whom he calls the "Nusantao" ("people of the island homeland") (1975:156-158).

In a more recent version of this hypothesis, Solheim (1984:81) proposes that Proto-Austronesian developed initially as a "barter language" among these early "Nusantao" mariners, who came eventually, following their northward migration, to occupy the coasts of northern Luzon, southern Taiwan and South China some time between 4500 and 5000 BC. Later Taiwan became isolated, while elsewhere along the western shores of the South China Sea, developing Austronesian languages remained in contact as a result of "Nusantao" voyaging and so diverged only much more slowly from one another. Following the isolation of Taiwan, the resulting "Proto-Malayo-Polynesian" languages were then carried southward, back through the Philippines to Borneo and from there south, east and westward, by groups of bartering "Nusantao" mariners (1975: 153; 1984:84-85).

While many elements of Solheim's hypothesis appear improbable, particularly, his account of the emergence of Proto-Austronesian, his arguments have the merit of highlighting the possible role of sea-going trade and maritime peoples in early Austronesian expansion. Indeed, Solheim sees the historical sea nomads as representing "the most direct descendants" of his "Nusantao" mariners, although,

> During the last few hundred years their status has deteriorated, bringing them to the bottom of the local pecking order instead of being, as they were around 2000 years ago, economically prosperous and the masters of their homes and livelihood, the southern and eastern seas, from Madagascar to Japan to Easter Island (Solheim 1984:86).

Here Solheim perilously telescopes a vast sweep of Southeast Asian and Pacific prehistory; he also ignores the apparently diverse origins of the sea nomads themselves and the existence of close cultural and linguistic affinities between them and related shore- and island-peoples, all suggesting a long and complex pattern of local interaction.

FOREST FORAGERS

Today, contemporary hunter-gatherers in Island Southeast Asia are associated primarily with the equatorial rainforest, an ecosystem that is believed to have expanded in the region around 10,000 BP, replacing in many regions monsoon forests and parklands (see Bellwood 1985:31-36). It is, as yet, unclear when Southeast Asian foragers began to exploit the equatorial rainforest. As indicated earlier, some have argued that this may not have taken place until after cultivated foods became available and the rainforest itself was modified as a result of agricultural clearing (cf. Headland 1987; Bailey *et al.* 1989; Peterson and Peterson 1977). The details of this argument are beyond the scope of our discussion here, but basically the contention is that "undisturbed" equatorial rainforest lacks an adequate resource base, particularly in starch foods, to support an independent foraging economy, a contention that is open, as we have seen, to serious question (see Brosius 1991; Endicott 1984; Endicott and Bellwood 1991).

For Borneo, Blust (1989) has argued on linguistic grounds that present-day foragers, being Austronesian-speakers, are the descendants of past cultivators. Similarly, Hoffman (1984, 1986) maintains that Bornean foragers are "secondary hunter-gatherers" whose ancestors were former horticulturalists who moved into the forest in order to specialize in the collection of forest products for trade. Harrisson (1949) and Seitz (1981) make similar arguments. However, anthropologists working with contemporary foraging societies in Borneo have disputed these views, particularly those of Hoffman, doing so on both conceptual and empirical grounds (cf. Brosius 1988, 1991; Nicholaisen 1976a; Sellato 1988, 1989). Without denying the significance or long history of trade in forest products, or the close economic ties that typically exist between foragers and surrounding cultivators, most have stressed the lack of a precise time-frame that tends to characterize many of these "devolution" arguments. Thus, Sellato (1989:6) notes that there are no recorded instances in Borneo of horticulturalists having become forest nomads. Instead, over the last two centuries, the observed movement has been entirely in the opposite direction, with virtually all foraging groups adopting some elements of cultivation and sedentism.

Linguistic evidence, although incomplete, also fails to support a notion of recent "devolution". Hoffman (1986:14-15) argues that adjacent, trade-connected foraging and agricultural groups speak "nearly identical languages". This, however, is not the case (cf. Brosius 1988:83-84). In Sarawak, for example, the principal foraging population, the Penan, is divided between two dialect groups which Needham (1972:177) calls the Eastern and Western Penan. Although distinct, dialects of both groups are mutually intelligible. In contrast, the settled agriculturalists with whom these groups regularly trade belong to at least twelve different language families (Brosius 1988:84). Thus, while the Penan show some degree of linguistic unity, no close linguistic relationship has yet been demonstrated between them and other major foraging populations in Borneo. Instead, the Penan are linguistically related to the Kenyah, a diverse collection of swidden cultivators. While the present Penan may thus have "devolved" from Kenyah cultivators in the past, the situation is complex, as ethnohistorical evidence strongly indicates that at least some Kenyah have adopted agriculture relatively recently as a result of contact with an expanding Kayan population (Rousseau 1990:245-246). A much stronger probability therefore exists that many, if not all, Kenyah were, like the Penan, rainforest foragers in the past (Rousseau 1990:246).

With regard to nutritional arguments, the debate concerning rainforest foragers has centred chiefly on wild yams (cf. Headland 1987). In Borneo, however, the principal source of dietary carbohydrate is not yams, but rather the starch of the wild sago palm (*Eugeissona utilis*). Dependence on wild sago not only sets Borneo foragers apart from other Southeast Asian hunter-gatherers, but seriously challenges the more general nutritional arguments against independent foraging (Brosius 1990, 1991). Closely related to this, a second feature which

> distinguishes Penan (and other Bornean foragers) from those elsewhere in Southeast Asia, ... is that whereas groups such as Agta and Semang live and forage in close proximity to agricultural settlements, Penan inhabit areas in the deep interior, usually one to four days' walk from the nearest agricultural settlements (Brosius 1991:136).

This is not to say that they live isolated from contact or trade with neighbouring longhouse people. On the contrary,

> trade is of vital importance to Penan. However, unlike most other tropic foragers, ... trade does not involve the exchange of forest products for food. Penan trade various forest products for items such as tobacco, metal, cloth, salt, and flashlight batteries, but not for food items ... With respect to food, [they] are wholly self-sufficient ... (Brosius 1991:136).

Here, as Brosius (1991:130) notes, contrary to assumptions made regarding tropical foragers elsewhere (cf. Bailey *et al.* 1989:64), the existence of a vigorous, long-established trade with settled agriculturalists does not, in itself, rule out the possibility of subsistence independence.

The *Eugeissona* palm on which the Penan and other Bornean foragers depend occurs throughout the interior of central Borneo, at a wide range of elevations, but is found in greatest concentrations on steep ridges and slopes, where it grows in dispersed groves interspersed with other forest vegetation (Brosius 1991:146). While we lack detailed quantitative data on nutrition and production, *Eugeissona* is known to be a rich source of carbohydrate and studies indicate that its starch is high in energy (350-400 kilocalories/gram) (Sellato 1989:159). Although much smaller than cultivated sago (*Metroxylon*), a single trunk yields, on average, about 4 kg of starch,[9] roughly enough to feed a single adult for a week (cf. Sellato 1989:159-60; also Anderson *et al.* 1982; Kedit 1982). To feed a band of 20-50 persons requires a weekly felling of some 15 to 20 palms.

Wild *Eugeissona* grows in dense clumps of some 3 to 6 trunks per clump, raised on a mass of aerial roots. While Borneo foragers vary considerably in social organization and settlement, basic subsistence patterns are notably similar. Typically, in processing palms, the men first fell 2 or 3 mature trunks from each clump, cutting the logs into sections, which are then carried to a stream or other water source, where the pith is reduced to flour (Langub 1989:175). This the women wash to extract the starch. Brosius (1986) and Langub (1988, 1989) have both shown how, in the case of the Penan, methods of sago extraction are designed not to interfere with the palm's natural regeneration. Thus the Penan cut only a small number of mature trunks from a single clump, never felling the entire root-stock, thus leaving the clump to sprout new trunks. In this way stands are regularly harvested on a sustained basis. After the mature sago (*nangah*) has been cut, the remaining young sago (*uvud*) is marked (*molong*) (Langub 1989:174-176). The group then moves on to a new stand of palms where the process is repeated. After 2 or 3 years, the marked trunks are mature enough to be felled and the group returns to the original stand where the individuals who marked them now claim the mature trunks for processing into starch. Thus local groups orient their movements around known palm-stands. In doing so, they follow a pattern of regular rotational re-use not entirely unlike the fallow-rotation pattern practised by established swidden cultivators with regard to parcels of secondary forest (Sather 1990).[10] The entire cycle extends over 5 or 6 years. By marking young sago, families secure for themselves rights of future harvest. These rights are respected not only within the owner's band, but between neighbouring Penan groups as well. A similar system of marking also applies to rattan, the principal item of Penan trade with outsiders. By means of this system, an orderly supply of sago, rattan and other items is thus assured and the principal forest resources on which the Penan depend are managed in a way that avoids their depletion or overuse (Brosius 1986, 1990; Langub 1988, 1989).[11]

Brosius (1991:131-132) sees in this pattern of management an important point regarding the nature of foraging generally. Foraging and agriculture are commonly treated as dichotomous modes of subsistence. "Yet", as Hutterer (1983:172-173) notes, farmers also harvest what nature produces. [And while] It is true that agriculturalists manipulate the environments from which they derive their food ... so do hunters ...

In the case of the Penan and other Borneo foragers, this manipulation significantly affects the long-term availability of the forest resources these groups exploit (Brosius 1991:131). Farmers are not alone in modifying their environments. For the Penan, too,

the effects of past human exploitation [bear directly] on the present abundance of resources. Penan actively manage the *Eugeissona* palm, and their exploitation of this resource has a further impact on [its] demography (1991:146).

With an increasing availability of cultivated foods, foragers like the Penan, Brosius observes, may abandon their traditional management of forest resources. This, together with a loss of prime habitats to agricultural settlement, may make these resources less available. As a consequence, they may

drop out of the subsistence repertoire because their management is abandoned ... Thus, contrary to the assumption that hunter-gatherers could only have occupied tropical forests with the advent of agriculture,

it is possible, Brosius (1991:133) argues, that the introduction of

agriculture itself [may have] led to the current dearth of carbohydrate resources in most tropic forest ecosystems.

Sellato (1989:154-155) argues, too, against a radical dichotomization of foraging and agriculture, noting that questions regarding the origin of Bornean foragers have been founded conceptually upon just such an opposition. By accepting this dichotomy, observers have been prevented from seeing that the result of interaction between foragers and settled food-producers has been the emergence in Borneo of relatively stable societies combining features of both lifestyles, not of short-lived communities representing "intermediate stages" of either "evolution" or "devolution". Thus, today while foragers may be in the process of becoming sedentary, the end result is by no means a complete conversion to cultivation, much less to full-time rice-agriculture. Instead, partially settled foragers usually continue to forage, often, in fact, intensifying their collection of forest products as they take up part-time cultivation for subsistence. The reason, Sellato (1989:215) argues, has to do with the importance of trade itself as a social and economic relationship.

Here, it is possible to go even further and to point out that the great majority of Bornean foragers today are neither fully nomadic nor permanently settled (Langub 1989:172). While sedentism is relatively recent for many, Bornean foragers have long displayed marked variation in social organization and settlement forms. Thus, in Sarawak, the Western Penan work sago in large task groups, while the Eastern Penan process it in smaller groups (Brosius 1990:

7). Correspondingly, Western Penan bands represent highly enduring social aggregates, characterized by long-term population stability, not the fluid social groupings generally associated with hunter-gatherers. Reflecting this stability, the Western Penan maintained what Brosius (1986:176) describes as a "two-tier settlement pattern", consisting of a main settlement, called the *lamin jau*, and a series of impermanent satellite camps, the *lamin tana*, located close to the sago stands in which families are currently working. Today, this "two-tier" system has proved highly adaptable to semi-sedentarism, including continuing forest collection-for-trade, with permanent settlements — villages and longhouses — now taking the place of the traditional *lamin jau* (Brosius 1990:4).

Similarly, upland cultivators in Borneo engage in substantial hunting, gathering and fishing, particularly in areas of expansive forest-pioneering. Here, especially in migratory situations where swidden cultivation is used as a pioneering technique to open tracts of primary forest to clearance and permanent settlement, upland cultivators enjoy both greater opportunity to forage and an increased need to retain foraging skills for survival. For the Iban, a major upland population of west-central Borneo, a significant attraction of primary-forest pioneering is the opportunity it affords for taking game, freshwater fish and wild plant foods. On the other hand, clearing the primary forest is a risky and arduous task, even with metal tools. As a result, in settled areas, as established swiddeners, the Iban, like other rainforest cultivators in Borneo, prefer to re-use the secondary forest well before its full natural succession in order to avoid the larger amounts of labour required to fell fully mature forest. Many also, like the Penan, manage stands of *Eugeissona*, both wild and planted, particularly in areas of pioneering where new and unfamiliar terrain is being brought under cultivation, as a famine food against possible crop failure.

In a more general way, it seems likely that the early Austronesians, too, as they spread southward through the Indo-Malaysian Archipelago, made similar use of foraging, particularly in extending their settlement into forested environments. Indeed, Austronesian expansion may itself have temporarily increased the value of foraging as an adjunct to agriculture. Secondary foraging may also have played a role in the domestication of new cultigens. It seems unlikely that groups narrowly focused on intensive rice agriculture would have been as inclined as those who continued to practise at least some secondary foraging to explore the wild plant resources of the new environments they came to occupy and incorporate not only new plant crops, but also, in the case of palm and tuber crops, new modes of husbandry and propagation. Finally, the early Austronesians, by enveloping foragers in a diversified economy, almost certainly made available technological innovations that rendered hunting and gathering itself more effective (Nicholaisen 1976a, 1976b). Thus, in Borneo, the Western Penan were well-known in the past as skilled iron-smiths (Needham 1972:178).

Yet iron-working derived originally from surrounding cultivators. In adopting it, the Penan used iron to produce spears and drill-bits with which to bore hardwood blowpipe shafts. The use of spears and blowpipes both enormously enhanced the effectiveness of hunting and so the productivity of rainforest foraging itself as an economic option (Brosius 1990:5-6).

In other ways as well, the dichotomization of foraging and cultivation may be misleading. Thus, subsistence systems in Borneo show a continuum of stable combinations of rice agriculture, domesticated sago and tuber cultivation, orchard crops, forest foraging, hunting, fishing and marine collection. Rice itself is grown by means of an almost infinite variety of methods. Upland peoples are often characterized as swidden cultivators. However, in Sabah and northern Sarawak many practise irrigated forms of cultivation, some of which are highly distinctive (cf. Talla 1979:309ff.), suggesting a long history of local development. Similarly swidden systems are themselves diverse, not surprisingly so considering the great variety of terrains and cultural settings in which swiddening is practised. Moreover, swidden cultivation is almost never the sole method of farming employed by upland peoples. Thus, in western and central Borneo, swidden cultivation is regularly combined with a variety of intermediate systems known in Sarawak as *padi paya* or "swamp-rice" cultivation. *Padi paya* agriculture combines elements of both swiddening and irrigated farming (cf. Pringle 1970:26-27).[12] Thus cultivation begins in the same way as dry-rice farming with cutting, drying and burning, but farms are typically cleared from naturally fooded plots and as in irrigated systems, planting is typically done in seedbeds with seedlings usually transplanted into prepared fields.

In this connection, Sellato (1989) offers an alternative interpretation of the role of foragers in the Austronesian settlement of Borneo. He suggest that initially pre-Austronesian groups occupied the coastline and areas of inland and riverine rainforest before the first Austronesians arrived bringing with them a developed agricultural economy. While these newcomers almost certainly brought rice, Sellato argues that without metal tools, they were unlikely to have been able to extend rice agriculture into the interior rainforests of the island with any degree of effectiveness.[13] Indeed, Sellato argues that the extensive opening of the interior of Borneo to swidden rice-cultivation came about only with the massive proto-historic migrations of groups like the Kayan, Iban and Ngaju Dayaks, all of whom expanded largely through areas previously occupied by only scattered populations of forest foragers. For the Iban, these migrations began in the mid-16th century and involved the settlement of areas inhabited chiefly by Bukitan and Ukit foragers and, in the lower river valleys and estuarine lowlands, by small communities of sago-cultivators (cf. Sandin 1967). Sellato thinks it likely that the early Austronesians were chiefly foragers rather than cultivators. In this, he appears to slip into the same dichotomizing argument he criticizes in others. More likely, they practised both cultivation and foraging. Some groups appear to have remained coast-bound, practising a mixed economy of forest foraging, fishing and horticulture — cultivating sago, fruit trees and tuber crops, and possibly, on a small-scale, swamp-rice. A few, living in the interior headwaters, subsisted as full-time foragers. Only later did swidden agriculturalists spread inland, through the interior of Borneo, bringing with them a permanent system of inland forest cultivation.

Finally, foraging groups, over much of central, southern and western Borneo, have historically maintained some degree of contact with one another (Sellato 1989:153ff.).[14] In addition, they have also maintained long-term trading ties with surrounding longhouse communities. For centuries, probably millennia, trade has been a major feature of the economy of the Penan and other Borneo foragers. In a regional perspective, these groups have long occupied a specific niche in the interior economy, acting as the major source of forest products traded to riverine longhouses and so to the coast (Brosius 1990:6). Historically, this trade shaped important features of longhouse society in many parts of Borneo, including social ranking and external relations with coastal sultanates. But, while trade has played a significant role in the lives of the Penan and their neighbours, it does not, in itself, "explain" the existence of forest foragers in Borneo.

> Traditionally, [the] Penan depended on longhouse peoples, particularly aristocrats, to act as mediators with the outside world and to serve as the conduit by which both information and material goods reached them. The traditional type of relationship existing between Penan and longhouse aristocrats was multi-dimensional in that longhouse peoples provided not just trade goods ... but other types of "services" as well (1990:6).

Trade, important as it was, did not, however, involve subsistence inter-dependence (1990:6). Thus, foodstuffs were not, for either party, an item of trade. Finally, traditional trading ties were formed primarily with stratified societies. This is because, Sellato (1989:224) argues, egalitarian peoples like the Iban historically engaged in forest collection-for-trade themselves. As a result, when they encountered competing foragers, they tended either to absorb or displace them rather than engage them as trading partners. With stratified groups, trade was, and remains, largely monopolized by upper stratum families, whose economic position it enhances, while stratification itself prevents the easy assimilation of outsiders, thereby allowing trading relations to be maintained on a long-term basis without foragers losing their separate identity (cf. Sellato 1989: 224). Today, these traditional trading ties are breaking down as forests disappear and roads, timber camps and permanent market settlements increasingly penetrate the territories of former nomads.

In conclusion, the evidence from Borneo suggests that Austronesian settlement involved, initially, neolithic populations possessing a diverse economy combining secondary foraging, hunting and fishing with varied forms of horticulture, including the cultivation of sago, fruit and tuber crops, as well as rice, with individual groups radiating, as they settled the island, into a multitude of local economic niches. Even rice cultivation appears to have undergone diversification in Borneo. Thus, while some groups appear to have adapted to the Bornean rainforest as relatively self-contained foragers; others took up a mixed economy combining forest-collection-for-trade with farming; while a fully-developed system of swidden rice-cultivation, rather than being a "primitive" adaptation that early on in its settlement history opened the interior of the island to both horticulturalists and forest foragers alike, may have developed as a relatively late florescence.[15]

CONCLUSION

Foraging economies existed in Island Southeast Asia, including Borneo and the Philippines, long before the spread of Austronesian-speaking peoples. On this point, the archaeological record is clear. But, with the arrival of the Austronesians, the nature of these economies was almost certainly transformed. Foragers were enveloped with agriculturalists and others in networks of symbiotic exchange. One consequence of this envelopment may well have been an expansion of foraging itself, now by Austronesian-speaking peoples, into a variety of previously unexploited or little utilized ecosystems, including possibly the ever-wet rainforest. More likely, rainforest foraging was already practised, but was intensified by trade and made more effective as a result of contact with settled, technically advanced agricultural populations.

Another expansion was almost certainly into the coastal foreshores and sheltered offshore waters and reefs. Here, however, the development of an early foraging tradition is still largely conjectural. While maritime technologies clearly played a part in the spread of the Austronesians, whether boat-nomadic groups were involved or not is far less certain. More probably, as Bellwood suggests, maritime specializations developed out of the process of expansion itself. And as Urry argues, the geography of the Indo-Malaysian Archipelago itself would have been a powerful stimulus to such a development. What we do know is that, by the time of European penetration, maritime foragers were already widely dispersed throughout much of Island Southeast Asia, some of them, like the Sama-Bajau, phenomenally so. How long the ancestral traditions to these historical forms of boat nomadism may have been present is uncertain, although evidence for the Sama-Bajau suggests that scattered groups of sea nomads may have emerged by as much as 1000 years ago, perhaps earlier. Whatever the case, maritime boat people contributed in a major way to later Austronesian history, particularly to the early development of maritime trading states and to the networks of communication and long-distance commerce on which these states were founded.

NOTES

[1] The latter Benjamin sees as antecedent to an emergent "Malay" tradition (1985: 226).

[2] It also drew them eastward as well, of course, into Oceania.

[3] The Moken and Orang Laut (including the Urak Lawoi) have sometimes been treated as if they constitute a single ethnolinguistic group (e.g. Lebar 1964). This, however, is not the case. Hogan (1989:2-4) discusses the linguistic relationship between the two groups. The Orang Laut are Malay-speakers and the cognate ratio between Moken-Moklen and Malay is only 44.51 to 45.60 per cent (Hogan 1989:3). The cognate ratio with Sama-Bajau is probably even lower, and it is significant therefore that these three sea nomadic groups, while all Austronesian-speaking, are only very remotely related to one another. Benjamin (pers.comm.) has suggested that the Aslian languages of the Malay Peninsula show evidence of contact with an earlier Austronesian language, prior to Malay, and has plausibly hypothesized that Moken may represent a continuing form of this language, surviving today as a northern outlier. More recently, Benjamin (1990) has suggested that the Moken themselves may have originally been Austroasiatic-speakers, who, living in a coastal setting, underwent an early language shift to Austronesian.

[4] In the Semporna District of southeastern Sabah, Malaysia, in 1964-65, and more briefly, 1974 and 1979. *Sama* is the principal autonym used by most members of this group to refer to themselves; Bajau, Bajao, etc. is the chief exonym (see Sather 1993a and 1993b for a discussion).

[5] Early sources relating to the history of Sulu suggest an original dual governance, with complementary land and sea authorities. Thus the Balangingi and other Sama groups provided the naval forces of the sultanate. Later Tausug historiography has tended to obscure the importance of Sama mariners in the formation of the state, but there is evidence to suggest that they played a critical role, much like that of the Orang Laut in the rise of the first Malay states discussed presently.

[6] Pallesen (1985:245) suggests, however, that Sama-Bajau is probably an Indonesian rather than a Philippine-related language family. He also suggests that it may have originated as a maritime creole.

[7] Although overall population figures are not available, throughout the period 1964-74, the *Sama Dilaut* constituted slightly more than 5 per cent of the total Sama-speaking population of the Semporna District.

[8] Dried fish, supplied by Orang Laut fishermen, was also a significant item of export trade in the early Malay states that developed in the Straits of Malacca (cf. Pallesen 1985:249).

[9] As compared to some 150 kg for cultivated sago in Sarawak (Sellato 1989:159).

[10] The swiddening cycle is, of course, of longer duration and involves the temporary destruction and burning of the forest cover. It may be worth noting that among the long-established Saribas Iban, upland swiddeners who regard themselves as quintessential rice-cultivators, a root-stock metaphor (*pugu'*) is commonly used in prayers and invocation to describe a family's total store of rice seed and its collective powers of increase.

[11] Brosius (1990:3) glosses *molong* as "to preserve or foster". The concept also applies to fruit trees. In Borneo similar systems of marking, applying to trees and other valued forest resources, are also employed by longhouse cultivators, including the Iban (see Sather 1990).

[12] To highlight its intermediate status, Pringle (1970:27), writing specifically of the Iban, suggests that we might add to the familiar "wet" and "dry", the terms "damp rice". It is significant to note that *paya* cultivation is practised in the original Kapuas homeland of the Iban and was introduced with the first Iban migrations to the Batang Lupar and Saribas river systems in Sarawak. Thus, in Sarawak, *padi paya* cultivation would seem to have an antiquity equal to that of swiddening among the Iban. Despite the general association of the Iban with swidden cultivation, among some regional groups, e.g. the Balau Iban, *padi paya* culture forms the dominant system of rice cultivation.

[13] Hutterer (1983) makes a similar argument for tropical rainforest cultivation generally. Thus, he argues that in such environments "major environmental modifications are far more difficult to achieve and require a relatively highly developed technology ... [including] metal tools" (1983:180, 186). This difficulty may partially account for the highly developed state of indigenous iron metallurgy in Borneo, including the traditional smelting of iron ore by tribal groups such as the Kayan (Christie 1988).

[14] The rainforests of northern Borneo have never, in historical times, been occupied by populations of hunter-gatherers. Thus, in Sabah there are no indigenous populations comparable to Sarawak's Penan, Bukitan, Sihan, Ukit and others. However, cave sites in eastern Sabah were occupied by prehistoric foragers beginning by at least 18,000 BP (Bellwood 1988). What became of the descendants of these early hunter-gatherers, or how they might be related to contemporary foragers in other parts of Borneo, remains an unresolved question.

[15] Botanically dryland varieties of rice appear to be a more recent evolution, pointing, in general, to the priority of wetland rice culture (cf. Chang 1984:71).

REFERENCES

Andaya, Leonard
    1974   The structure of power in seventeenth century Johor. In Anthony Reid and Lance Castles (eds) *Pre-colonial state systems in Southeast Asia: the Malay Peninsula, Sumatra, Bali-Lombok, South Celebes*, pp.1-11. Kuala Lumpur: Monographs of the Malaysian Branch of the Royal Asiatic Society, No. 6.

1975   *The kingdom of Johor, 1641-1728.* Kuala Lumpur: Oxford University Press.

Anderson, G.
1890   *The Selungs of the Mergui archipelago.* London: Truber and Co.

Anderson, J.A.R. *et al.*
1982   *Gunung Mulu National Park, Sarawak: a management and development plan.* London: Royal Geographic Society.

Bailey, Robert C., Genevieve Head, *et al.*
1989   Hunting and gathering in tropic rain forest: is it possible? *American Anthropologist* 91:59-82.

Bellwood, Peter
1985   *Prehistory of the Indo-Malaysian archipelago.* Sydney: Academic Press.
1988   *Archaeological research in South-Eastern Sabah.* Kota Kinabalu: Sabah Museum Monograph, 2.
1989   Archaeological investigations at Bukit Tengkorak and Segurong, Southeastern Sabah. *Bulletin of the Indo-Pacific Prehistory Association* 9: 122-162.
1993   Cultural and biological differentiation in Peninsular Malaysia: the last 10,000 years. *Asian Perspectives* 32:37-60.

Bellwood, Peter and Peter Koon
1989   'Lapita colonists leave boats unburned!' The question of Lapita links with Island Southeast Asia. *Antiquity* 63:613-622.

Benjamin, Geoffrey
1979   Indigenous religious systems of the Malay Peninsula. In A. Becker and A. Yengoyan (eds) *The imagination of reality: essays in Southeast Asian coherence systems,* pp.9-27. Norwood: Ablex Publishing.
1985   In the long term: three themes in Malayan cultural ecology. In Karl L. Hutterer, A. Terry Rambo and George Lovelace (eds) *Cultural values and human ecology in Southeast Asia,* pp.219-278. Michigan Papers on South and Southeast Asia, No. 27, Center for South and Southeast Asian Studies. Ann Arbor: University of Michigan.
1986   Between Isthmus and Islands: reflections on Malayan Palaeo-sociology. Department of Sociology, Working Paper No. 71. Singapore: National University of Singapore.
1990   Ethnohistorical perspectives on Kelantan's prehistory. In Nik Hassan Shuhaimi (ed.) *Kelantan zaman awal: kajian arkeologi dan sejarah di Malaysia.* Kota Bharu: Muzium Negara Kelantan.

Blust, Robert
1976   Austronesian culture history: some linguistic inferences and their relations to the archaeological record. *World Archaeology* 8:19-43.
1984-5 The Austronesian homeland: a linguistic perspective. *Asian Perspectives* 26(1):45-69.
1989   Comments. *Current Anthropology* 30:53-54.

Brosius, J. Peter
1986   River, forest and mountain: the Penan Gang landscape. *Sarawak Museum Journal* 36:173-184.
1988   A separate reality: comments on Hoffman's *The Punan*. *Borneo Research Bulletin* 20:81-106.
1990   Penan hunter-gatherers of Sarawak, East Malaysia. *AnthroQuest* 42:1-7.
1991   Foraging in tropical rain forests: the case of the Penan of Sarawak, East Malaysia. *Human Ecology* 19:123-150.

Carrapiett, W.J.S.
1909   *The salons*. Rangoon, Burma: Ethnographic Survey of India No. 2.

Chang, Te-Tzu
1984   The ethnobotany of rice in Island Southeast Asia. *Asian Perspectives* 26 (1):69-76.

Christie, Jan
1988   Ironworking in Sarawak. In J.W. Christie and V.T. King (eds) *Metal-working in Borneo*, pp.1-27. Occasional Paper, 15. Centre for South-East Asian Studies, The University of Hull.

Dunn, F.L.
1975   *Rain-forest collectors and traders: a study of resource utilization in modern and ancient Malaya*. Monographs of the Malaysian Branch, Royal Asiatic Society, No. 5.

Dunn, F.L. and D.F. Dunn
1984   Maritime adaptations and exploitation of marine resources in Sundaic Southeast Asian Prehistory. In Pieter van de Velde (ed.) *Prehistoric Indonesia: a reader*, pp.244-271. Dordrecht: Foris Publications.

Ekman, Sven Petrus
1953   *Zoogeography of the sea*. London: Sidgwick and Jackson.

Endicott, Kirk M.
1984   The economy of the Batek of Malaysia: annual and historical perspectives. *Research in Economic Anthropology* 6:29-52.

Endicott, Kirk and Peter Bellwood
1991   The possibility of independent foraging in the rain forest of Peninsular Malaysia. *Human Ecology* 19:151-186.

Engelhardt, Richard
1987   Forest-gatherers and strand-loopers: econiche specialization in Thailand. Unpublished paper, The Siam Society Symposium, Enduring Autochthonous Adaptations.

Fox, James
1977   Notes on the southern voyages and settlements of the Sama-Bajau. *Bijdragen tot de Taal-, Land- en Volkenkunde* 133:459-465.

Frake, Charles O.
1980   The genesis of kinds of people in the Sulu Archipelago. In *Language and cultural descriptions: essays by Charles O. Frake*, pp.311-332. Stanford: Stanford University Press.

Geoghegan, William H.
1984   *Sama*. In Richard V. Weekes (ed.) *Muslim peoples: a world ethnographic survey*, Vol. 2, pp.654-659. London: Aldwych Press.

Harrisson, Tom
1949   Notes on some nomadic Punans. *Sarawak Museum Journal* 5:130-146.

Headland, Thomas N.
1987   The wild yam question: how well could independent hunter-gatherers live in a tropical rain forest ecosystem? *Human Ecology* 15:463-491.

Headland, Thomas and Lawrence Reid
1989   Hunter-gatherers and their neighbors from prehistory to the present. *Current Anthropology* 30:43-51.

Hoffman, Carl
1984   Punan foragers in the trading networks of Southeast Asia. In C. Schrire (ed.) *Past and present in hunter gatherer studies*, pp.123-149. London: Academic Press.
1986   *The Punan: hunters and gatherers of Borneo*. Ann Arbor: UMI Research Press.

Hogan, David
1972   Men of the sea: coastal tribes of south Thailand's west coast. *Journal of the Siam Society* 60:205-235.
1989   *Urak Lawoi': basic structures and a dictionary*. Pacific Linguistics Series C No. 109, Canberra: Department of Linguistics, Research School of Pacific Studies, The Australian National University.

Hutterer, Karl
1976   An evolutionary approach to Southeast Asian cultural sequence. *Current Anthropology* 17:221-241.
1983   The natural and cultural history of Southeast Asian agriculture: ecological and evolutionary considerations. *Anthropos* 78:169-212.

Hutterer, Karl (ed.)
1977   *Economic exchange and social interaction in Southeast Asia*. Ann Arbor: University of Michigan Center for South and Southeast Asian Studies.

Ivanoff, Jacques
1985   L'epopée de Gaman: conséquences des rapports entre Moken/Malais et Moken/Birmans. *Asie du Sud-Est et Monde Insulindien* 16:173-194.
1987   Le concept de société "à maison" confronté aux contradictions des cultures moken et moklen. In C. Macdonald (ed.) *De la hutte au palais: sociétés "à maison" en Asie du sud-est insulaire*, pp.109-131. Paris: Editions du Centre National de la Recherche Scientifique.

Kedit, Peter M.
  1982   An ecological survey of the Penan. *Sarawak Museum Journal* 30:225-279.

Kiefer, Thomas
  1972   The Tausug polity and the sultanate of Sulu: a segmentary state in the southern Philippines. *Sulu Studies* 1:19-64.

Langub, Jayl
  1988   The Penan strategy. In Judy Sloan Denslow and Christine Padoch (eds) *People of the tropical rain forest*. Berkeley: University of California Press.
  1989   Some aspects of life of the Penan. *Sarawak Museum Journal* 40(3):169-184.

Lebar, Frank *et al.*
  1964   Mowken. *Ethnic groups of mainland Southeast Asia*, pp.263-266. New Haven: Human Relations Area Files Press.

Lewin, Roger
  1988   New views emerge on hunters and gatherers. *Science* 240:1146-1148.

Logan, J.R.
  1847   The Orang Sletar of the rivers and creeks of the old strait and estuary of the Johore. *Journal of the Indian Archipelago and Eastern Asia* 1:295-298.

Macdonald, C. (ed.)
  1987   *De la hutte au palais: sociétés "à maison" en Asie du sud-est insulaire.* Paris: Editions du Centre National de la Recherche Scientifique.

Needham, Rodney
  1972   Penan. In Frank LeBar (ed.) *Ethnic groups of insular Southeast Asia*, Vol. 1, pp.176-180. New Haven: Human Relations Area Files Press.

Nicholaisen, Johannes
  1976a   The Penan of Sarawak: further notes on the neo-evolutionary concept of hunters. *Folk* 18:205-236.
  1976b   The Penan of the seventh division of Sarawak: past, present and future. *Sarawak Museum Journal* 24:35-61.

Nimmo, H. Arlo
  1972   *The sea people of Sulu*. San Francisco: Chandler.

Pallesen, A.K.
  1985   *Culture contact and language convergence*. Manila: Linguistic Society of the Philippines.

Pawley, Andrew and Roger Green
  1973   Dating the dispersal of the Oceanic languages. *Oceanic Linguistics* 12:1-67.

Peacock, B.A.V.
  1979   The later prehistory of the Malay Peninsula. In R.B. Smith and W. Watson (eds) *Early South-East Asia: essays in archaeology, history and historical geography*, pp.199-214. Oxford: Oxford University Press.

Pelras, Christian
1972   Notes sur quelques populations aquatiques de l'Archipel nusantarien. *Archipel* 3:133-168.

Peterson, J.T.
1978   Hunter-gatherer/farmer exchange. *American Anthropologist* 80:335-351.

Peterson, J.P. and W. Peterson
1977   Implications of contemporary and prehistoric exchange systems. In J. Allen *et al.* (eds) *Sunda and Sahul*. London: Academic Press.

Pringle, Robert
1970   *Rajahs and rebels: the Iban of Sarawak under Brooke rule, 1841-1941*. New York: Macmillan.

Reid, Anthony
1983   The rise of Makassar. *Review of Indonesian and Malaysian Affairs* 17:117-160.

Reid, Lawrence
1987   The early switch hypothesis: linguistic evidence for contact between Negritos and Austronesians. *Man and Culture in Oceania* 3:41-59.

Rousseau, Jerome
1990   *Central Borneo: ethnic identity and social life in a stratified society*. Oxford: Clarendon Press.

Saleeby, Najeeb
1908   *The history of Sulu*. Manila: Philippine Bureau of Science, Division of Ethnography Publications, Vol. 4, Part 2.

Sandbukt, Oyvind
1984   The sea nomads of Southeast Asia: new perspectives on ancient traditions. *Annual Newsletter of the Scandinavian Institute of Asian Studies* 17:3-13.

Sandin, Benedict
1967   *The sea Dayaks of Borneo before white Rajah rule*. London: Macmillan.

Sather, Clifford
1971   Sulu's political jurisdiction over the Bajau Laut. *Borneo Research Bulletin* 3:58-62.
1975a   Bajau Laut. In Frank LeBar (ed.) *Ethnic groups of insular Southeast Asia*, Vol. 2, pp.9-12. New Haven: Human Relations Area Files Press.
1975b   Seven fathoms: a Bajau Laut narrative tale from the Semporna district of Sabah. *Brunei Museum Journal* 3(3):30-40.
1976   Kinship and contiguity: variation in social alignments among the Semporna Bajau Laut. In George Appell (ed.) *The societies of Borneo*, pp.40-65. Washington, D.C: Special Publication of the American Anthropological Association, no. 6.
1978   The Bajau Laut. In Victor King (ed.) *Essays on Borneo societies*, pp.172-192. Hull Monographs on Southeast Asia, 7. London: Oxford University Press.

1984   Sea and shore people: ethnicity and ethnic interaction in southeastern Sabah. *Contributions to Southeast Asian Ethnography* 3:3-27.

1985   Boat crews and fishing fleets: the social organization of maritime labour among the Bajau Laut of southeastern Sabah. *Contributions to Southeast Asian Ethnography* 4:165-214.

1990   Trees and tree tenure in Paku Iban society: the management of secondary forest resources in a long-established Iban community. *Borneo Review* 1 (1):16-40.

1993a   Bajau. In David Levinson (ed.) *Encyclopedia of world cultures*, Vol. 5. New Haven: Human Relations Area Files Press.

1993b   Samal. In David Levinson (ed.) *Encyclopedia of world cultures*, Vol. 5. New Haven: Human Relations Area Files Press.

Schrire, Carmel (ed.)
1984   *Past and present in hunter-gatherer studies*. London: Academic Press.

Seitz, S.
1981   Die Penan in Sarawak und Brunei: Ihre kulturhistorische Einordnung und derzeitige Situation. *Paideuma* 27:275-311.

Sellato, Bernard
1988   The nomads of Borneo: Hoffman and "devolution". *Borneo Research Bulletin* 20:106-120.

1989   *Nomades et sédentarisation à Bornéo*. Paris: Éditions de l'École des hautes études en sciences sociales.

Solheim, Wilhelm II
1975   Reflections on the new data of Southeast Asia prehistory: Austronesian origin and consequence. *Asian Perspectives* 18(2):146-160.

1984   The Nusantao hypothesis: the origin and spread of Austronesian speakers. *Asian Perspectives* 26(1):77-88.

Sopher, David
1965   *The sea nomads: a study of the maritime boat people of Southeast Asia*. Memoirs, No. 5. Singapore: National Museum.

Talla, Yahya
1979   *The Kelabit of the Kelabit Highlands, Sarawak*. Provisional Research Report, No. 9. Penang: School of Comparative Social Sciences, Universiti Sains Malaysia.

Urry, James
1981   A view from the west: inland, lowland and islands in Indonesian Prehistory. Unpublished paper presented at the 51st ANZAAS Congress, Brisbane.

Warren, Carol
1983   *Ideology, identity and change: the experience of the Bajau Laut of East Malaysia, 1969-1975*. South East Asia Monograph Series No. 14. Townsville: James Cook University.

Warren, James F.
    1978   Who were the Balangingi Samal? Slave raiding and ethnogenesis in nineteenth-century Sulu. *Journal of Asian Studies* 37:477-490.
    1979   The Sulu Zone: commerce and the evolution of a multi-ethnic polity, 1768-1898. *Archipel* 18:133-168.
    1981   *The Sulu Zone, 1768-1989*. Singapore: Singapore University Press.

Wee, Vivienne
    1985   Melayu: hierarchies of being in Riau. PhD dissertation, Canberra: The Australian National University.

White, Walter
    1922   *Sea Gypsies of Malaya*. London: Seeley, Service.

Wolters, O.W.
    1967   *Early Indonesian commerce: a study of the origins of Srivijaya*. Ithaca: Cornell University Press.
    1979   Studying Srivijaya. *Journal of the Malaysian Branch of the Royal Asiatic Society* 52(2):1-32.

14

EXCHANGE SYSTEMS, POLITICAL DYNAMICS, AND COLONIAL TRANSFORMATIONS IN NINETEENTH CENTURY OCEANIA

Nicholas Thomas

This chapter characterizes Oceanic exchange regimes in terms of a continuum. It is suggested that there are a number of broadly parallel axes of difference along which very diverse exchange systems can be ranged. At one end are forms of exchange that typically transact like against like, that deploy quantity rather than qualitative rank difference, that often are based on food rather than valuables and are also articulated with brideservice rather than bridewealth.

These systems are also typically localized rather than regionally extensive, they exist within societies which are not economically specialized, they are characterized by intense and unstable competition, and values are generally non-convertible, that is, life and valuables circulate in distinct spheres and cannot be written off against one another. This regime of non-convertibility is epitomized by the Marquesas in Polynesia and many Austronesian and non-Austronesian New Guinea societies. The exchange regimes characterized by convertibility, regional differentiation, the use of valuables and categorically hierarchical relations are epitomized by Fiji.

While such a schematic analysis requires many qualifications, the broad continuum is important for the colonial histories in which indigenous systems are caught up. In general, "non-conversion" regimes are less able to exploit and incorporate the new possibilities for external and internal exchange that contacts with traders, missions, and the like, enable. Although there is a brief period of political efflorescence in the early nineteenth century in eastern Polynesia, the pattern is one of political decline, that contrasts sharply with the continuing dynamism of "value conversion" systems such as Fiji.

INTRODUCTION

Elaborate exchange systems have always been conspicuous features of Austronesian societies, and travellers' accounts frequently feature extended descriptions of activities described as trading or feasting. Even in relatively casual or shallow descriptions, it is often apparent that the practices witnessed were not merely economic transactions or ceremonies in a narrow sense, but events linked with kinship economies, with social reproduction as well as utilitarian traffic, that were often also evidently arenas for political competition. Twentieth-century anthropology, particularly with respect to Oceania, extended these observations to a dramatic extent and made them the basis for fundamental theories of "the gift" and of reciprocity: while Marcel Mauss's work was crucial theoretically and heavily dependent upon Pacific cases, Malinowski's account of "the *kula*" became an ethnographic classic.

In some ways, however, the very prominence of these studies hindered an extended comparative understanding of Oceanic exchange. Malinowski's texts, used again and again in teaching general anthropology courses, were decontextualized from the region that they dealt with and instead taken to illustrate general theses concerning reciprocity; "the Kula Ring" was paradoxically considered a unique system, yet also one that revealed fundamental aspects of human sociality, at least in its non-modern forms. Even a recent theorist can observe that the kula is "one of the most extraordinary phenomena for which anthropologists have been called upon to account" (Miller 1987:60). Discussion of this kind overlooked the extent to which the kula was articulated with other exchange systems along the northern coast of New Guinea and around southeast Papua, and the fact that certain other systems in the region, which also featured shell valuables, involved similar transactions, even though the exchange-paths did not constitute a circle. Paradoxically, also, most research on the kula has dealt with its manifestations in ethnographic localities and raised questions concerned with the representations of value, mortuary exchange, and other topics, within those sites, without actually attempting to grasp the regional properties of the system or its dynamics at that supra-local level.

This chapter does not review the anthropological literature on exchange in Oceania, or interpretations of the kula specifically (but see Specht and White 1978; Leach and Leach 1983; Macintyre and Young 1983; Gardner and Modjeska 1985; Keesing 1990; Thomas 1991). It instead attempts, in a very provisional way, to address the comparative agenda that seems to have been marginalized by the focused character of ethnographic research. I suggest some principles that could form the basis of a typology of Oceanic exchange systems, not with the intention of producing any static classification, but rather to suggest how significant differences in exchange made a difference at the level of political dynamics, that is, the capacities of particular social forms to expand, to generate stable relations of dominance and to be reproduced over long periods of time. These points are illustrated through reference to the indigenous systems, in so far as they can be reconstructed on the basis of ethnohistoric evidence from the contact period, in the western Solomon Islands, Fiji, and eastern Polynesia. It would not be adequate, of course, if such a discussion, based on evidence concerning societies undergoing transformation attendant upon European contact, was restricted to postulates concerning an imagined pre-contact order; it is more satisfactory, and quite feasible, to use this information to postulate processes (rather than states) and to examine the differing ways in which particular forms of indigenous exchange were able to accommodate or respond to engagement with European trade. Indeed, the significance of discriminating among the variety of indigenous systems might be seen to arise from the better understanding they afford of the various histories of contact and colonialism.

PATTERNS OF DIFFERENCE

As has been noted, exchange is conspicuous in most Oceanic societies but does not everywhere have the same character. In some instances the events which observers found remarkable or which have been documented in scholars' accounts were presentations of food that appeared to have no links with any larger or regional trade system; in other cases, they were exchanges of valued artefacts — sometimes women's products such as mats, sometimes products of male woodcarving or stone work, otherwise shell valuables — that depended directly on wider transacting networks. These could, of course, exist together, and do not, in any case, exhaust the whole social field of exchange in any particular society; in addition to the collective events which were often of greatest interest to outside observers, exchange takes place in a more quotidian and domestic fashion and also in various secret ways — the services of sorcerers, for instance, may be purchased with valuables or in exchange for other services. Despite the great degree of diversity and the heterogeneous forms of exchange which may exist within particular societies, there are major axes of difference across which systems can be ranged. These relate particularly to the possible forms of substitution entailed in varieties of exchange and can be expressed by the following contrasts:

like-for-like <---> like-for-unlike
quantity <---> quality
food <---> valuables
brideservice <---> bridewealth
localized <---> regionally-extensive
regional non-differentiation <-----------------------------> regional differentiation
competition <---> hierarchy
values non-convertible <---> value conversions

There are two important general points about these terms; first that they can only be useful once they are contextualized, as I shall proceed to do; clearly hierarchy and competition are not generally mutually antithetical, but in the context of exchange practices a particular juxtaposition can be made. Secondly, the several different continua frequently cannot be correlated, such that a case manifesting several attributes to the arrows' left may display other features or emphases that stand more to the right: an exchange system that proceeds mainly on a like-for-like basis is not necessarily found in a society in which brides are compensated for by labour rather than wealth items. Hence, initially, these are descriptive rather than theoretically informed discriminations, but I will suggest that there is a significant underlying contrast, amenable to being explained and elaborated upon in a relatively economical way. Before taking this non-ethnographic approach further, the terms of these contrasts need to be elucidated further.

Like-for-like refers to exchange in which things of the same kind move in both directions, though typically at different times. For example, a group that has given pigs later receives pigs. Like-for-unlike entails movement of, say, food against valuables, or valuables of different kinds (or more importantly perhaps, of different rank or status) against each other. The first form of exchange almost necessarily turns upon quantity rather than quality, in the sense that there are primary media of exchange, such as live animals, and what is at issue are the volumes presented; while the second principle turns upon qualitative difference, on the specific associations of particular categories of things. Irrespective of the principles of exchange, the properties of dominant media are highly significant, in the sense that cooked or prepared foods, for instance, generally cannot have value for the receivers beyond the point of consumption; they cannot be recirculated as further gifts in the way that semi-perishable or non-perishable items such as mats and shell valuables can be. An exchange system based in food, in principle, does not afford much scope for accumulation and this also implies constraints on political dynamics.

These constraints cannot, however, be understood as crudely material or environmental factors. From the perspective of political economy, the most crucial issue is the extent to which it is possible for one sort of objectified value (in food, for instance) to be converted into another (in valuables, relations, persons, or services). The greater the range of possible conversions, the greater the scope for political actors to mobilize resources of different kinds and obtain strategic advantages over other competing groups, and the more scope, in particular, for the development of complex regionally-differentiated exchange systems in which some groups have central and others peripheral statuses. Where scope for value-conversion is limited, on the other hand, political competition is not necessarily less intense, but tends to take a more localized form and be articulated with unstable and localized hierarchies rather than regionally-extensive confederacies. For Papua New Guinea, this issue has been analysed particularly with reference to the difference between bridewealth and bride-service marriage compensation systems: the latter exemplify the principles that persons or labour can only be recompensed by persons or labour; such societies are typically characterized by restricted exchange and in extreme cases by high incidences of direct sister exchange. This logic does not apply merely to marriage, but also in other domains such as compensation for killings in warfare;

in bridewealth societies, deaths need not be avenged by further deaths but can be recompensed through payments of valuables, just as the wife is paid for in objects rather than services (Wood in press; Modjeska 1982; Godelier 1986; Godelier and Strathern 1991; see also Jolly 1991 for Vanuatu). These analyses and debates have been problematic partly because links have been made between a variety of distinct phenomena; in the Highlands case, there has been particular stress on correlating limited scope for substitution (what I have called non-conversion) with leadership by "great men", that is by figures such as warriors and shamans, and on the other hand between high-substitution systems and "big men" who are first and foremost masters of ceremonial exchange.

Here I focus less on leadership and marriage and more on the major forms of ceremonial exchange; without attempting to theorize whole systems of social reproduction, I suggest that the issue of substitution makes crucial differences both for the expansive potentialities of indigenous social forms and for their responses to external contact — which in some cases can mean contact with other indigenous systems, as well as with the European-based world economy. Fiji and the New Georgia group exemplify systems in which elaborate value conversions were possible, while the Marquesas in eastern Polynesia, though not a typical Oceanic chiefdom from most perspectives, illustrates the political dynamics of a non-conversion system. So far as Fiji is concerned, it is worth differentiating the expansive and politically stratified confederacies of the coastal parts of the large island of Viti Levu, and the eastern parts of the archipelago as a whole, with the more localized societies of the interior of Viti Levu. Though both cases were arguably equally substitution-oriented, the more limited articulation with external exchange in the interior had important ramifications. The systems can only be sketched out in the most cursory way here, but more detailed accounts are readily available (for the Marquesas, see Robarts 1974, Dening 1980, and Thomas 1990; for early Fiji, see Williams 1858 and 1931, and Sahlins 1985; for twentieth century Fiji, see Sahlins 1962, Belshaw 1964, Toren 1990, and Thomas 1991; for New Georgia, see Hocart 1922, 1931, n.d.).

THE MARQUESAS

At the end of the eighteenth century, Marquesan society was characterized by intensely competitive and unstable relations between the populations of particular valleys, which were usually referred to as "tribes" by most observers and ethnographers. Within most parts of the group, "tribes" were understood to be descended from one or the other of a pair of antagonistic brothers and thus fell into two divisions. Though these were not exogamous and were not internally unified in any continuous or politically consequential fashion, major conflicts were usually between groups in opposing divisions, who also met in aggressive competitive feasts. As was the case in parts of the western Pacific, there were structural continuities and analogies between warfare and the competitive exchange that has been dubbed "fighting with food" (Young 1971).

Although there were a variety of forms of feasts and exchange-events, some of which were primarily commemorative, the usual form seems to have involved a major presentation of prepared food, in the form of cooked pork and preserved breadfruit, which was consumed by the receiving group on the feasting ground (the *tohua*), which sometimes took them a number of weeks or, reputedly, even months. At some subsequent date, the receivers would stage a reciprocating prestation, at which they would attempt to offer more cooked food; what was transformed by these gifts was a balance of shame and prestige, rather than a political relationship that had some content distinct from the competitive context itself, or a material economic relationship. Though the receiving group of course acquired food that supplemented their own production, they gained little that they could take away or turn to other purposes and the relationship produced was one of differentiated status, rather than hierarchy in any strict sense: the "winning" group had it over the "losing" one, but this supremacy might only be temporary and effected no permanent difference of rank. This was, therefore, a like-for-like system, in which the quantities rather than the qualities of the stuff exchanged were crucial, which was competitive, and which prompted efforts to expand production of what could be offered, but which was not transformative, in the sense that the outcomes of exchange events — however ignoble a particular group's "defeat" — did not produce a relationship of vassalage or some other form of regional political dominance. It was also a system which operated on the basis of one-to-one relations between groups rather than systemically integrated series, even though each group engaged in competitive feasts with more than one enemy/exchange partner. That is, while group A might engage in rivalrous exchange with several others, B, C, and D, each of these relations took the same form:

event 1)   A ------------------ quantity x --------------------> B
event 2)   B ------------------ quantity x + ------------------ > A
event 3)   A ------------------ quantity x ++ ------------------ > B

Any ideal sequence would rarely be realized, because the groups might at any time shift from the feasting register to that of warfare — either for their own reasons or through implication in some conflict of their allies — and the outcome of this military encounter would displace whatever balance of prestige or shame arose from the feasting cycle. The fact that this schema is remote from any particular sequence of events, and of course neglects the nuances of practical competition, does not however alter the point that this mode of exchange is disconnected from a political dynamic which produces definite regional hierarchy, or stable relations of the quasi-feudal type, that, from somewhat different theoretical perspectives, both Valerio Valeri (1985) and Jonathan Friedman (1981) have found to be characteristic of most eastern Polynesian societies.

What is conspicuous about this sort of system is in fact the degree to which various forms of exchange are insulated from one another: while there were numerous kinds of specialized production in the Marquesas and a trade in articles that were only found in certain localities, such as certain feathers used in ornaments, this was not linked with the ceremonial exchange that has been described, which did not feature like-for-unlike transactions. On the other hand, while marriage was of great political importance as a means of establishing or securing alliances, it did not produce an exchange relation or a rank order of any particular type; that is, there was no general rule that wife-takers ranked higher than wife-givers, or vice versa; in fact the content of particular relationships, produced through marriage or other links such as adoption, was highly mutable and dependent upon the practical deployment of links. Relationships between populations were thus characterized by equality in a formal sense, by reciprocal competitive presentations and by restricted exchange of spouses and children for adoption. The marked inequalities that existed derived from military strengths, productive capacities, and, in the contact period, from differential access to trade goods; they were not generated structurally.

FIJI

While Marquesan societies were, in the terms of my polarities, "non-conversion" systems — though they were nevertheless very different from the "non-conversion" systems that might be identified elsewhere, such as in Papua New Guinea — Fiji did and in many ways still does exemplify the opposed type, being characterized by great scope for value-conversion, by exchange entailing like-for-unlike transactions and by hierarchical ranking rather than competitive inequality.

The main occasions for ceremonial exchange in Fiji were known generically as *solevu*; though of diverse kinds, these mostly either marked some life crisis event — betrothal, marriage, birth, presentation of children to their mother's people, death, and so on — or recompensed some service or assistance in warfare or need of some other kind. The substance of these presentations were *iyau*, valuables or manufactured articles for exchange, which in particular localities might consist mainly of pots (where local styles gave signatures to particular forms), wooden articles such as headrests or kava dishes, barkcloth (again usually of a particular, locally recognizable type), mats, and, in the post-contact period, a variety of introduced goods, particularly kerosene, items of household furniture, and manufactured fabric. Often accompanied, at least now, by live pigs and cattle, these presentations were encompassed in gifts of whale teeth, which were the focus of formal speeches and were handed between the senior men of giving and receiving groups. These teeth, *tabua*, were the "heaviest" and "most chiefly" of valuables, were the substance of any important request or gift of atonement, and were strongly identified with women, not in the sense of standing for them symbolically, but in the sense that they figured as the proper exchange objects through which alliance was initiated and periodically expressed. Those presenting valuables at *solevu* were generally immediately given a feast (*magiti*), which figured as the acknowledgement of the prestation rather than as a counter-prestation or reciprocation.

Although some kinds of *iyau ni vanua* — the valuables of a particular land or polity — were the singular products of particular groups; other kinds, such as mats, were widely distributed and carried no local signature. However, there was a basic element of differentiation in the system that arose from the fact that any particular prestation did not recompense a previous offering of *iyau* but related to debts associated with kinship which were expressed rather than eradicated by presentations, and debts arising from assistance or from other activities. While it would in some ways be wrong to suggest that women were convertible into whale teeth or valuables generally — since their presentation produced a manifold state of indebtedness that had to be addressed in a variety of behavioural ways rather than a particular debt that could be repaid — this was a conversion-oriented system in the sense that its prestations were structured by difference, that is, by the matching of things against each other in a fashion that produced or displayed relationships. While the sheer quantity of food and manufactured articles presented was of course important, it was of less structural significance than the oppositions between particular kinds of things, and particularly between activities and relationships on one side and objects on the other.

In upland Fiji, the most prominent feature of alliance relationships was enduring indebtedness to the wife's people, or to the mother's side, from the point of view of the offspring. This was (as it still is) marked by substantial presentations of whale teeth and other valuables at various stages of betrothal and marriage, but was further expressed in presentations on the birth of the first child, on the occasion that children were presented to their mother's people, and particularly on their deaths when whale teeth would flow back marking the enduring debt of substance to the maternal uncle. Because marriage exchange was generally restricted, the ranking implied at particular moments in alliance relations was generally equivalized through reciprocity. Hence an economy of kinship was articulated through the movement of *iyau* with a system of specialized trade in paths of alliance that entailed a dense mesh of obligation mutual indebtedness and political and military reciprocity. These links, then, were significant during warfare as they were in the Marquesas but with the important difference that valuables could be converted into assistance and services of various kinds; whale teeth could even be seen as a kind of capital available for strategic investment with different people or in different kinds of operations (in marriage, or in paying for assassinations).

This upland Fijian system can be understood, despite the restricted character of the exchange, as a relation entailing a series of groups (A, B, C) and a variety of valuables (r, s, t, u, v, etc.).

```
A <========> B <========> C <========> D
   women          women          women


A <----------------------B <---------------------- C <-------------------- D
      r                       s                       t


A ----------------------> B ---------------------> C ----------------------> D
      u                       v                       w
```

All of this was founded on a paradigmatic transaction:

```
A ==== gives wife ===========> B
  <---------- receives whale tooth ------------------------
```

The picture is of course more complicated, because each polity would offer to another not only its own singular *iyau*, but often an accumulation, drawn partly on its own production and partly on material that was drawn in from outside; there was no stipulation that *iyau* had to be manufactured by the presenting group. While this sketch could be considerably elaborated upon, it is the basic principle that I want to draw attention to here, that the open-ended character of the system and the differentiated character of valuables make it highly receptive to new items and extended exchange relations, which become directly articulated with the reproduction of local affinal relations.

In coastal and insular Fiji this system existed in a more regionally and hierarchically differentiated form. The distinction is marked particularly by a difference in the character of the all-important *vasu* relationship, that is, the relation between sister's son and mother's brother, or, among chiefs, between a man's place and that the whole domain of his maternal uncle. While the *vasu* relationship, in upland Fiji, certainly has a special character, it does not and did not have the feature which struck the attention of various commentators on Fijian society from Williams to Hocart: the right of the *vasu* to appropriate property from the mother's people, and specifically from anywhere within the domain of a chiefly uncle. In the centralized confederacies of Bau, Rewa,

Cakaudrove, and Lau — to mention only the most important — *vasu* relations provided a context for tribute payments, since lesser chiefs anxious to forge alliances with the paramount families gave their daughters in marriage, thus providing for offspring able to liberally appropriate pigs, valuables, canoes, or virtually anything else, from their home domains. The content of the *vasu* relation was not uniform and although it is generally stated as a categorical entitlement in ethnographic accounts, those who were *vasu* to the central places such as Bau could not appropriate in an unrestrained way, although some sources suggest that their relationship was a means through which Bauan wealth was dispersed, thus making the polity a fount of prosperity for its subjects. There is also, however, some evidence that Bauans reversed the relationship as they became more powerful, such that *vasu* were expected to *bring* property rather than take it away; this could only have been true of thoroughly subordinated subjects; relatively powerful allied groups certainly also paid tribute, but relations had a more reciprocal character, as is apparent from Williams' account of the visit of the Bauan paramount Cakobau to Lakeba, central place of the Lauan polity in eastern Fiji. While the Bauans received a particularly large canoe which was being manufactured probably with the assistance of Tongan craftsmen on the island of Kabara, they also brought some goods with them — "two handsome spears, more than 30 clubs wrapped in fine cynet, 20 whales' teeth, an immense root of yangona [kava] and several hundred fathoms of *lichi* or *masi* [barkcloth] from Kandavu" (Williams 1931:162-166). Only a few months earlier, however, another major presentation had taken place, associated with the presentation of the chief's daughter as another bride for Cakobau's father, Tanoa: the party took "an immense new canoe, 15 large packages of native cloth ... 7 large balls of cynet, 10 whales' teeth of from $1\frac{1}{2}$ to 4 lb. weight" (*ibid.*:145). It was quite fundamental to Fijian polities that property of this kind did not remain with the receivers, but could be deployed in a great variety of ways to solicit a marriage, to secure military assistance, for redistribution within an elite, to consolidate a particular faction's power base, and so on.

While a great deal more could be said about the functioning and history of this system, the contrast with eastern Polynesia should be apparent: hierarchical relations in Tonga and Samoa as well as Fiji were indissociable from relations of exchange and alliance; in eastern Polynesia, on the other hand, dominance was grounded in "theocratic feudalism" and, where it was contested and insecure, as in the Marquesas, what was crucial was production of food and pigs, not access to or control over exchange.

EVOLUTIONARY AND NON-EVOLUTIONARY MODELS

My main concern in this essay is to show how these two crude types — value conversion and non-conversion systems — respond quite differently to colonial contact in its early typically Oceanic form of trade with European ships seeking provisions and commodities such as sandalwood, tortoise-shell, and *bêche-de-mer*. Before discussing these histories, however, it is important to raise a larger issue about how these systemic types are thought to be associated. This is necessary in part because my substitution/non-substitution opposition is drawn from debates about New Guinea Highlands societies where analysis has usually been frankly or explicitly evolutionist. Feil, in particular, suggests that western highlands societies are more evolved than those of the east (1987), and Godelier (1986, 1991) assumes that big man societies develop out of great men rather than vice versa. Although the analyses have undergone a good deal of refinement (Lemonnier 1990) and have been criticized in various ways (Strathern 1990), it is not clear that there is any positive formulation of a multilinear or cyclical transformational model that actually replaces a logic of from-to. The evolutionary view becomes particularly problematic if a broader range of Oceanic societies are considered since the Marquesas on the basis of some traditional criteria would have to be seen as a relatively "evolved" society: craft specialization was elaborate, there was hereditary leadership, notable inequality and so on. The Tongan and Hawaiian kingdoms are often classed together as the most developed and stratified Polynesian societies; in opposition to this evolutionary view, both Friedman (1981) and I (Thomas 1989) have emphasized not the degree of centralization or hierarchization from which perspective they may well be similar but instead the form of hierarchical reproduction which is distinctly different.

An alternative view could note the strong correlation between substitution or conversion systems and external exchange; the groups in which there is the most elaborate scope for conversion, say of services and kinship debts of various kinds into shell valuables, were also most densely associated with external trade: this is notable, for instance, for the Tolai, in New Georgia, in western Polynesia and in parts of the Massim region. On the other hand, the groups in which the life-for-life principle is most rigorously applied are also those excluded from wider exchange relations, such as the Umeda, the Kamula, and the Baining. This may not be true to the same degree of the Baruya, but they are not, in any case, on an extreme point of the continuum. If a regional-systemic perspective is adopted, it appears that the character of internal exchange is dependent on external articulations (cf. Gell 1992); this appears to be true, at least in a gross sense, where a wide range of cases rather than only the societies of the eastern and western highlands are considered. But my interest is not in proposing that it would be ultimately useful or informative to trace precise correlations on this point. The implication is rather that if the extent to which value conversions can be effected is linked with external exchange, then the systemic characteristics of particular societies can be related to the dynamics of regional trade systems rather than to some hypothetical and unilinear evolutionary index. Groups that were not in the early contact period engaged in trade may well have earlier been integrated into wider systems and were subsequently excluded for military reasons or because the nature of trade changed — the demands for certain articles may have ceased; routes may have shifted. While little will ever be known about such developments, it can safely be said that there were many changes — in demography, in production systems, in material culture — over time, that would have implied different configurations in trade routes. This would, in itself, imply the possibility of change in both directions — toward great men systems as well as from them — but would only be part of a broader processual model that privileged the variety of possible systemic forms and transformations rather than evolutionary direction.

INDIGENOUS SYSTEMS AND COLONIAL HISTORIES

No-one with a general knowledge of the Pacific today can fail to be struck by the differences between western and eastern Polynesia. Superficially, people appear to be more "westernized" in the east; this perception might be challenged in various ways, but it is true that there is little continuity between indigenous forms of social organization and hierarchy and almost no perpetuation of traditional ceremonies or of life crisis activities on anything but the most restricted domestic scale. What is particularly notable is the fact that throughout French Polynesia the traditional aristocracy is virtually invisible — in most places claims to chiefly status would be rarely if ever enunciated — while in Fiji, Tonga, and Samoa, on the other hand, indigenous rank systems have not only survived but been extended and entrenched under colonial rule, while chiefly elites are influential if not securely dominant in national politics.

This difference obviously owes a good deal to the colonial history itself; Tonga was under British tutelage rather than formal administration; in Fiji the indirect rule approach did much to codify and rigidify customary hierarchies and land-holding, as has often been noted. The French assimilationist approach, on the other hand, virtually swept the Tahitian aristocracy aside and refrained from any elaborate investigation or administrative use of customary social organization; the Americans in Hawaii and the Chileans in Rapanui behaved in a similar fashion. It is notable, however, that the divergence in response and development is conspicuous at quite an early point, even before the French annexed the Marquesas in 1842 and white settlers moved into Fiji in large numbers in the 1860s, prior to secession in 1874. In one case, what is manifest is decline — severe depopulation, a breakdown of traditional hierarchical forms and ceremonial activities. In the other, in Fiji, what is conspicuous is an effloresence of political and military activity and a period of great expansiveness and dynamism, particularly so far as the Bauan confederation is concerned.

In the Fijian case, it is important to note that the key valuables for transactions today, as in the nineteenth century, namely whale teeth, were probably in the most limited circulation prior to the visits of European traders (although this point is not mentioned by most ethnographers who simply regard the teeth as the paradigmatic traditional valuable). It is popularly stated in Fiji that the "original" *tabua* were not whale teeth, but were made of some kind of ironwood; this may well be true, although some teeth very likely came into Fiji via Tonga where whales were occasionally stranded. There was very little significant contact between Fijians and whites before 1800 — though an epidemic of dysentery occurred as a result of a shipwreck — but after 1801 sandalwood was discovered and sought after intensively in the period up to about 1814, when it had essentially been exhausted. William Lockerby, who resided in the islands in 1808-9 and who interpreted and facilitated trade, prepared a sort of guide to traders, including navigational directions, some Fijian vocabulary, and notes on reliable and not so reliable chiefs:

> the Articles of Traid to pleas the Natives are Ivory Iron Work such as Tools the best plan is to carry a forge with you & make the tools to sute them knives & scisors Beads they are very fond of — White shels & Cloth the two latter are to be got At the Islands to windward of MyGoro [Koro] should you tutch their however Ivory is the Most Vallable Article Made in the form of a Whales Tooth and those of them that is possessd of any of them lays them up as graet riches as porshens for their Daughters & Making peace with their offended Supirurs etc. ([1972]:184).

Lockerby's assumption here is that ivory in some other form would be obtained and cut to resemble whale teeth; later, when whaling was being conducted extensively in the Pacific, mainly by American ships from New England ports and some English vessels, it was easier to obtain the actual whale teeth. After sandalwood became exhausted, trade contracted for a few years but soon developed again around different products for the Manila and Canton markets — *bêche-de-mer* and tortoiseshell. But because the routes of these vessels often did not intersect with those of the whalers, the teeth were obtained through rather circuitous paths. Whale ships frequently called at the island of Rotuma to the northwest of Fiji for provisions, and although the Rotumans did not themselves use whale teeth as valuables, they took these to exchange with the traders active in Fiji ("This island is a great resort for whalers from whom the natives obtain their whales' teeth"). Trade took place both directly and through white middlemen resident on Rotuma. Tobacco, which was conveniently light and compact in relation to its value, was given in return; it was said to be "worth almost its '*weight in gold*' at this place" (Cheever MS:23 June 1834). At about the same time Tahiti similarly became a port through which teeth were effectively transhipped:

> I understand that Vandervort gave a great price for a few whales teeth here ... The people here natives and all have found out that teeth are valuable & ask a monstrous price for them — one large tooth that might weigh say 2 lbs. they wanted a dollar for — the Emerald was well supplied with that article of trade which are in great demand among Feejee-men (*ibid.*:5 August 1834).

This is indicative of the manner in which quite localized developments in exchange and in transactions between islanders and Europeans had broad ramifications that had effects on other islands great distances away.

To turn more specifically to transactions associated with *tabua* in Fiji, and their implications, it must be appreciated that the conduct and organization of trade was essentially upon Fijian terms to which foreigners were obliged to adapt. This was apparent even at the level of language use: the owner of a ship could presume in his instructions to the captain to stress that "it should be your first object to acquire a knowledge of their language" (Phillips MS). So far as transactions and the organization of collecting *bêche-de-mer* was concerned, the cooperation of chiefs was indispensable. *Tabua* were used, not so much in payment for *bêche-de-mer* as in ritualized presentations to chiefs made routinely upon arrival at a place and at certain other times. Trade was a two-level process: periodic high-value gifts to chiefs were a precondition for any economic engagement at all, while *bêche-de-mer* and tortoiseshell were reciprocated more directly to producers, and usually with guns, associated supplies (such as powder) and iron implements.

Although it is difficult to estimate in any precise way the *total* number of muskets and other goods which were imported, lists from certain ships are available. Eagleston's trade, consisting of guns and many other "notions" (smaller articles such as beads) had cost $3000; this included one lot of four hundred muskets, but it is not clear whether these were the only ones on board (Eagleston MS:250, 289). It appears to have been not uncommon to carry four to six hundred pounds (weight) of whales' teeth, which, at about two pounds each, represented two to three hundred *tabua*. The profits from the sandalwood trade had been very high and even for the later period Eagleston frequently noted the "small cost" of what was received — "I bought nine head of beautiful tortoiseshell weighing thirty pounds; worth in the States $360. I paid for same three muskets that cost $1.25 each" (*ibid.*:282). However, the volume of what was given to Fijians was also very considerable, and the consequences of the introduction of huge quantities of guns and other goods have occasioned debate.

In most discussions so far *tabua* have been neglected; the emphasis of most earlier writers and a few recent scholars has been the consequences of imports of guns, while some others have stressed continuity despite contact and the persistence of "paths of the land".

Whales' teeth probably substituted for the range of uses of prior forms of *tabua*; as was noted, this was a very wide range of ceremonial contexts, including installations to chiefly titles, at mortuary ceremonies and presentations of children to their maternal kin; from the start they were certainly used, as Lockerby noted, in marriage, which was indissociable from regional political relations. *Tabua* were also used to request and acknowledge assistance in political trouble and war, and thus figured prominently in exchanges between chiefs and those referred to as the "teeth" or the "edge" of the land — the warrior-subjects who stood in a protective but privileged relationship to the sacred titleholders. In 1834 George Cheever witnessed a ceremony after a battle between Bau and Rewa where a Bauan man of chiefly rank had been killed. The warriors brought the body "ornamented with a white flag" to Rewa and after performing a chant seated themselves respectfully while the "king" presented them with spears, "about 100 fathom of Tapper", and presented a *tabua* to the man who had actually killed the chief. After receiving their gifts the warriors reasserted their loyalty in a ritual manner by striking their clubs in the ground (Cheever MS:21 May 1834). Ordinary relations of this type would no doubt have been consolidated by the capacity of chiefs — who were virtually the sole recipients of whales' teeth from traders — to draw on new supplies of valuables.

The use of *tabua* in more singular cases of political upheaval is exemplified by two cases, both involving violent conflict within élite families. In the early 1830s bad relations developed between Tabaiwalu, then the paramount chief of Rewa, and his son Koroitamana; ill-feeling was generated, as was typical, by rivalries between co-wives and their sons; the latter were, of course, potential and competing successors to the title. The conflict gradually escalated until Koroitamana, confident that he would be supported by a number of high-ranking men and warriors, assassinated his father. However, the chief's principal wife, Adi Dreketi, successfully deceived the people of the town, leading them to believe that her husband was still alive but very weak and that he wanted his son killed. A meeting took place at which the general opinion was reputedly that Koroitamana's conduct had been justifiable and provoked, but many also "feared the wrath of the king, in case he should recover". Hearing of the uncertainty, the "queen" settled matters by taking "some whales' teeth and other valuables and presented them herself to the chiefs, saying they were sent by the king to purchase the death of his son". Whether the general belief actually was that the king was still alive is not clear; in any event, it was not long before Koroitamana was clubbed (Thomas 1986).

A case which had much wider ramifications for the polities of central and eastern Fiji in the 1830s was the "coup" — Fijians do make the analogy with the military takeovers of 1987 — against Tanoa, the paramount chief at Bau. There are various interpretations of precisely why dissent within Bau came to a head, which need not be reviewed here; a faction based around his half-brothers seized power, and Tanoa was fortunate to escape assassination himself, but was exiled to Somosomo between 1832 and 1836. From this base, and subsequently from Rewa, he began to build up his support amongst the people subject to Bau, but the process which was perhaps more crucial for his return to power was recovering the internal support of the Bauan clans. This was effected by his son, Seru (subsequently known as Cakobau), particularly through a steady stream of gifts of *tabua* to the Lasakau group, who played a crucial role in a brief but decisive fight which actually displaced the rebel side (Waterhouse 1866; for further discussion and references, see Thomas 1986).

This remarkable capacity of the Fijian system — or at least of the chiefs of the first half of the nineteenth century — to absorb and put to use a new set of trading relations and imports might be taken to attest to a general theoretical principle about the capacity of local systems to appropriate introduced goods. While I have elsewhere argued that it is certainly important to recognize the processes of selective indigenous recognition and use of foreign contact, and to insist upon the historically particular character of the form of appropriation, here, however, it seems more important to emphasize the singularity of the Fijian system, which, as we have noted, is distinguished by the possibility of a wide range of conversions between services, valuables, debts, assistance and, not least, spouses. The fact that, paradigmatically, the whale's tooth stood for a woman meant that it was a signifier for and a means to an open-ended kin path of debt and exchange. As in any other system, marriage created a broader set of relations, but in the Fijian case these had distinctive political potential.

Moreover, and equally importantly, there was no contradiction between this positive process of deploying imports for political purposes and the production of what was to be extracted. The resources which the traders wanted were mostly not significant for Fijians. There is no suggestion that *bêche-de-mer* was eaten by Fijians; if so, it could only have been marginal to a diversified subsistence base. Curiously, tortoiseshell, which was used extensively in some Pacific material cultures, did not feature much in Fijian ornaments or regalia and sandalwood also was either not used at all or very insignificant. Although the preparation of *bêche-de-mer* did involve substantial commitments of labour, the activities were not unlike the collective efforts associated with certain projects such as canoe building, warfare, or preparing for ceremonies in areas away from one's home village. Fijians did not, in any case, agree to work continuously if there were other things that they wanted to do, and in some cases traders could do nothing but feel frustrated for some days or weeks when something exciting like fighting or a large ceremony took their workers away. It was also, of course, necessary to provision trading vessels but their relatively limited demands were met by different groups over quite a wide area — the scatter of islands in central Fiji, the Lau group and the coasts of Viti Levu and Vanua Levu — and could easily be accommodated. This was so because the ceremonial economy in Fiji was already developed to an enormous extent: there were many forms of intensive irrigated horticulture and food was routinely produced to be offered up for ceremonial exchange — in some areas specifically for barter through specialized production networks. When accounts are read of feasts at which many thousands of yams or taro and dozens or occasionally hundreds of pigs and turtles were presented, it is not difficult to imagine the smaller needs of ships being relatively easily dealt with.

This is not to say that there were not problematic longer-term ecological consequences; for instance, Ward has pointed out that the quantity of firewood required to smoke and cure the *bêche-de-mer* was enormous and must have reduced coastal forests around Bau and those other parts of Vanua Levu which supplied the "fish" considerably. Over-collection diminished supplies of *bêche-de-mer*, while sandalwood was virtually obliterated in a short period. However, from a shorter-term perspective — usually the only one in which economies have a rationality — there was a good deal of compatibility between the interests of traders and the Fijians. The indigenous ceremonial economy did not depend upon goods which were being extracted to any excessive extent, while what was introduced was of considerable cultural and political use.

The contrast with the Marquesas is marked. While sandalwood was extracted early, by the 1820s and 1830s, the trade essentially consisted in exports of pork and other food in return for guns and related supplies. However, as we have seen, the Marquesan system did not function through value conversions in a manner at all similar to Fiji. Although there was a certain amount of internal barter, this was not the basis for relations of prestigious social value; inequalities were instead worked through and expressed in competitive presentations of food; these were connected closely with matters of the greatest ritual consequence, such as the commemoration of powerful shamans and chiefs. The estimation of individuals and groups was intimately connected with the capacity to stage such events, and to consume what was received.

More fundamentally, there was a direct contradiction between what ships wanted to take away and the basis of the Marquesan competitive feasting system. Pork was not only a crucial element of this political "fighting with food" but was also of ritual importance: certain animals were raised specifically for commemorative feasts for many ordinary people, as well as renowned chiefs and shamans. And there may not have been much scope for diverting beasts from feasting to trade: the evidence is not good, but it seems that there were never particularly considerable numbers of pigs in the islands. Supplying ships would thus certainly have undermined the other competitive and religious activities.

There are many travel books and official and missionary letters which convey a sense of disillusionment and apathy amongst Marquesans after the French annexation, and in especially intense and tragic terms in the late nineteenth and early twentieth centuries. Rather than repeating verbose and patronizing accounts of cultural despair, it is worth trying to specify precisely what it was about colonial contact in this case — in addition to the drastic character of disease and depopulation — which engendered such acute social and cultural decline. It may be that the conjunction of the form and purposes of indigenous exchange, together with traders' demands, made it impossible to conduct certain ritual activities properly and at the same time diminished the status of the prominent people who had formerly focused their energies upon organizing such events. The dispersed and ineffective character of resistance at the time of French annexation is linked with the undermining of indigenous institutions, and to some extent to the character of those institutions, prior to contact.

While the account presented here is sketchy, its aim is to establish the possibility for a kind of processual, comparative analysis. This aims to avoid focusing exclusively either on static constructs of indigenous systems, supposedly occupying some imaginary time that is at once pre-colonial yet accessible to our vision, or on the other hand on colonial histories in which it is assumed that colonizers play the dominant role. Of course it would be foolish to understate the military and economic superiority of colonizers, but what I have tried to show here is that quite divergent paths of colonial history can be understood to have arisen partly on the basis of differences between the indigenous systems. I am not trying to advance a general argument that substitution-oriented exchange regimes in Oceania always fared better than non-substitution regimes; it is clear in some cases, such as New Georgia, that the violence of colonialism could obliterate indigenous dynamism if, for whatever reason, administrators opted for a repressive strategy. Contingencies are always significant; under other circumstances, there might have been a less destructive accommodation between indigenous society and external trade in the Marquesas, but it so happened that what were perceived to be military imperatives led the islanders to give away a supply of protein at a time of disease and intermittent famine — when they needed that food most. That is all too reminiscent of later colonial histories in other parts of the world.

CONCLUSION: THE DISTINCTIVENESS OF AUSTRONESIA

While Oceanic forms of exchange — encompassing kula-type trade partnerships, collective prestations of ranked valuables, competitive feasts and transactions closer to the old stereotype of utilitarian barter — are bewilderingly diverse, there can be no doubt that the prominence of exchange, in whatever form, is a pervasive and fundamental feature of these Austronesian societies. Even in eastern Polynesia, where regional trade is limited and in some cases non-existent, localized competitive reciprocity was, as we have seen, central to the production, reproduction and transformation of hierarchical relationships. In western Oceania, however, it is also notable that the non-Austronesian societies of New Guinea were similarly exchange-oriented; this is true not only of the coastal regions which can be seen to have been heavily influenced by Austronesian populations, but also of the highlands, where there can hardly have been direct contact. This general congruence has permitted many anthropological discussions to ignore the Austronesian/Papuan distinction and argue comparatively about "Melanesian" exchange, without reference to the linguistic and prehistoric differences. While this approach, like the earlier treatment of Melanesian leadership in terms of a generalized big man model, seems inadequate, I too have found terms developed for the analysis of highlands societies relevant, in adapted form, to the wider range of Oceanic variation. The parallels between Papuan and Austronesian forms present scholars with a peculiarly difficult problem: is it most likely that the two populations were autonomously similar in this respect; or should exchange systems in the highlands be seen as a long-distance product, though obviously one that is locally incorporated, of ramifying and expansive coastal exchange; or should forms such as the *moka* and *tee* be considered simply as independent developments, which very likely postdate the Austronesian settlement of coastal New Guinea and adjacent archipelagoes, but which have no particular connection with or dependence upon that change in the less immediate social environment? Any responses to such questions would, of course, be highly speculative; they would also be tentative because there are few models for addressing problems of such an order in either prehistory or anthropology: the first discipline's interest in social processes is too limited, while that of the second in longer-term transformations has been equally attenuated. Given the evident expansiveness of exchange in many Austronesian societies, it would however seem worth exploring the possibility that these dynamics are inherently expansive and invasive and that in the longer run the movements of objects such as pearlshells may have effected the transposition of Austronesian forms of sociality, well beyond the apparent geographic and linguistic Austronesian boundaries.

REFERENCES

Belshaw, C.S.
   1964   *Under the ivi tree: society and economic growth in rural Fiji*. London: Routledge and Kegan Paul.

Cheever, G.
   1834   *Fiji bêche-de-mer trade. Log of the Emerald*. Microfilm M97, Peabody Museum, Salem, Massachusetts. [Copy held in Division of Pacific and Asian History Library, Research School of Pacific and Asian Studies, The Australian National University, Canberra.]

Dening, Greg
   1980   *Islands and beaches. Discourse on a silent land: Marquesas 1774-1880*. Honolulu: University of Hawaii Press.

Eagleston, J.H.
   1831-36 *Fiji bêche-de-mer trade. 'Ups and downs through life'*. Microfilm M97, Peabody Museum, Salem, Massachusetts. [Copy held in Division of Pacific and Asian History Library, Research School of Pacific and Asian Studies, The Australian National University, Canberra.]

Feil, Daryl
   1987   *The evolution of Papua New Guinea Highlands societies*. Cambridge: Cambridge University Press.

Friedman, Jonathan
   1981   Notes on structure and history in Oceania. *Folk* 23:275-295.

Gardner, Don and Nicholas Modjeska (eds)
   1985   Recent studies in the political economy of Papua New Guinea societies. Special issue, *Mankind* 15(2).

Gell, Alfred
   1992   Inter-tribal commodity barter and reproductive gift exchange in old Melanesia. In Caroline Humphrey and Stephen Hugh-Jones (eds) *Barter, exchange and value*, pp.142-168. Cambridge: Cambridge University Press.

Godelier, Maurice
   1986   *The making of great men*. Cambridge: Cambridge University Press.
   1991   An unfinished attempt at reconstructing the social processes which may have prompted the transformation of great-men societies into big men societies. In M. Godelier and M. Strathern (eds) *Big men and great men: personifications of power in Melanesia*, pp.275-304. Cambridge: Cambridge University Press.

Godelier, Maurice and Marilyn Strathern (eds)
   1991   *Big men and great men: personifications of power in Melanesia*. Cambridge: Cambridge University Press.

Hocart, A.M.
1922   The cult of the dead in Eddystone of the Solomons. *Journal of the Royal Anthropological Institute* 52:71-112, 259-305.
1931   Warfare in Eddystone of the Solomon Islands. *Journal of the Royal Anthropological Institute* 61:301-324.
n.d.   Trade and money. Manuscript in Hocart Papers, Alexander Turnbull Library, Wellington, New Zealand.

Jolly, Margaret
1991   Soaring hawks and grounded persons: rank and gender in north Vanuatu. In M. Godelier and M. Strathern (eds) *Big men and great men: personifications of power in Melanesia*, pp.48-80. Cambridge: Cambridge University Press.

Keesing, Roger
1990   New lessons from old shells. In J. Siikala (ed.) *Culture and history in the Pacific*, pp.139-163. Helsinki: Finnish Anthropological Society.

Leach, Edmund and Jerry Leach (eds)
1983   *The kula: new perspectives on Massim exchange*. Cambridge: Cambridge University Press.

Lockerby, William
1972   Directions for the Feegee Islands [*c*.1811], E. Dodge (ed.). *Journal of Pacific History* 7:184.

Macintyre, Martha and Michael Young
1983   The persistence of traditional trade and ceremonial exchange in the Massim. In R.J. May and Hank Nelson (eds) *Melanesia: beyond diversity*, pp.207-222. Canberra: Research School of Pacific Studies, The Australian National University.

Miller, Daniel
1987   *Material culture and mass consumption*. Oxford: Basil Blackwell.

Modjeska, Nicholas
1982   Production and inequality: perspectives from central New Guinea. In A. Strathern (ed.) *Inequality in New Guinea Highlands societies*, pp.50-108. Cambridge: Cambridge University Press.

Phillips, Stephen C.
1830   Letter to Eagleston. In J.H. Eagleston, *Fiji bêche-de-mer trade. 'Ups and downs through life'*. Microfilm M97, Peabody Museum, Salem, Massachusetts. [Copy held in Division of Pacific and Asian History Library, Research School of Pacific and Asian Studies, The Australian National University, Canberra.]

Robarts, Edward
[1974] *The Marquesan journal of Edward Robarts*. Gregory M. Dening (ed.). Canberra: Australian National University Press.

Sahlins, Marshall
  1962   *Moala: culture and nature on a Fijian island*. Ann Arbor: University of
          Michigan Press.
  1985   *Islands of history*. Chicago: University of Chicago Press.

Specht, Jim and J. Peter White (eds)
  1978   Trade and exchange in Oceania and Australia. Special issue, *Mankind*
          11(3).

Strathern, Andrew
  1990   Which way to the boundary? *American Ethnologist* 17:376-383.

Thomas, Nicholas
  1986   *Planets around the sun: dynamics and contradictions of the Fijian
          matanitu*. Sydney: Oceania Monographs.
  1989   *Out of time: history and evolution in anthropological discourse*.
          Cambridge: Cambridge University Press.
  1990   *Marquesan societies*. Oxford: Clarendon Press.
  1991   *Entangled objects: exchange, material culture, and colonialism in the
          Pacific*. Cambridge, Mass.: Harvard University Press.

Toren, Christina
  1990   *Making sense of hierarchy*. London: Athlone Press.

Valeri, Valerio
  1985   The conqueror becomes king: a political analysis of the Hawaiian legend of
          'Umi. In A. Hooper and J. Huntsman (eds) *Transformations of Polynesian
          culture*, pp.79-104. Auckland: The Polynesian Society.

Ward, R.G.
  1972   The bêche-de-mer trade. In R.G. Ward (ed.) *Man in the Pacific Islands*.
          Oxford: Oxford University Press.

Waterhouse, J.
  1866   *The king and people of Fiji*. London: Wesleyan Conference Office.

Williams, Thomas
  1858   *Fiji and the Fijians*. London: Heylin.
  [1931] *The journal of Thomas Williams, missionary in Fiji, 1840-1853*. G.C.
          Henderson (ed.). Sydney: Angus and Robertson.

Wood, Michael
  In press *The substance of sociality: kinship and exchange amongst the Kamula*.
          London: Harwood Academic Publishers.

Young, Michael W.
  1971   *Fighting with food*. Cambridge: Cambridge University Press.

15

INDIC TRANSFORMATION: THE SANSKRITIZATION OF *JAWA* AND THE JAVANIZATION OF THE *BHARATA*

S. Supomo

This chapter gives an account of the earliest Indian contacts with Indonesia according to first millennium AD inscriptions from East Kalimantan and Java. It discusses the changes which occurred in social, religious and political organization, particularly in Java, as a result. The dissemination of literacy into Indonesia is examined in detail and a comparison is made of the rather limited literary output of Śrīwijaya (Sumatra) and the flowering of literature in Hindu-Buddhist Java. The Javanese not only adopted many literary works of Indian origin, but also transformed them in the process.

INTRODUCTION

Although contacts between the western mainland of Southeast Asia and India had existed since prehistoric times, it was only in the beginning of the Christian era that the Sanskrit civilization of India began to spread more rapidly across the Bay of Bengal into the western parts of the Austronesian world. The exact circumstances will probably remain unknown, but the following factors have been most often mentioned as the main causes of this new development.

The first was the expanding international trade which, from about 2000 years ago, greatly increased the number of traders and adventurers voyaging from India to Southeast Asia, and vice versa. Navigational skills were, after all, one of the characteristics that the Austronesians had possessed since prehistoric times. The existence of a Western Malayo-Polynesian language in Madagascar, which shows Sanskrit borrowings via Malay, is clear evidence that Austronesians had sailed as far as the east coast of Africa shortly after the introduction of Sanskrit words into Southeast Asia (Adelaar, this volume). Later evidence from Chinese accounts shows that the western Austronesians continued to supply transport facilities for merchants and cargoes from many parts of maritime Asia.

The second factor was the transformation of Buddhism into a world religion and the revival of the Hindu cult, especially the emergence of the *bhakti* movement (devotion to a personal God), which gave the impetus for Buddhist monks and Hindu Brahmans to travel to foreign countries to disseminate their faiths. It is now generally agreed that, while it may not be possible to disregard completely the possibility that the princes and warriors (*kṣatriya*) and the traders (*vaiśya*) might have played a significant part in the process of the spread of the Indian influence, it was the *brahmaṇa* (that is, the Hindu and Buddhist learned men) who were the main disseminators of the Sanskrit civilization in the region.

By the third century AD, kingdoms organized according to the Indian conception of royalty had begun to appear in certain parts of Southeast Asia, first in the mainland and then slightly later in the Indonesian archipelago. The rulers of these kingdoms embraced the Indian religions, either Buddhism or Hinduism, and adopted Sanskrit as their official language, at least for ritual purposes. Sanskrit literature, especially the Mahābhārata and Rāmāyaṇa epics and the Pūraṇas, provided mythological resources.

THE EARLIEST INDIC STATE: KUTAI

The oldest known inscriptions of the Indonesian archipelago are those on seven stone pillars, or *yūpa* ("sacrificial posts"), found in the area of Kutai, East Kalimantan, some twenty miles from the Makassar Straits. Written in the early Pallava script, these Sanskrit inscriptions were erected to commemorate sacrifices held by a King Mūlawarman, and are datable on palaeographical grounds to the second half of the fourth century AD (Vogel 1918; Chhabra 1965:50-52, 85-92; de Casparis 1975:14-18). They are only short inscriptions — in all no longer than 50 lines, the longest consisting of only three stanzas of four lines each — but they are the most important evidence that we have that testifies to the emergence of an Indianized state in the Indonesian archipelago prior to AD 400.

The inscriptions do not mention the name of this kingdom, but we have the names of three generations of rulers from one of them. They are Mūlawarman, the reigning king, who is styled the "lord of kings" (*rājendra*); his father Aśwawarman, entitled the "founder of the dynasty" (*vaṇśa-kartr*); and his grandfather Kuṇḍungga, the "lord of men" (*narendra*). It is generally agreed that Kuṇḍungga is not a Sanskrit name, and therefore he was most likely a native of the land. The fact that Kuṇḍungga's name is of native origin while both his son and grandson had Sanskrit names seems to indicate that it was not Kuṇḍungga, but his son Aśwawarman who was the first of his line to adopt the Hindu cult and was probably also the founder of the "new" kingdom based on the principles of the new faith. Accordingly, Aśwawarman was called the "founder of the dynasty" by later generations, and in the inscription he was appropriately likened to *aṅśuman*, "the sun", who was the mythical founder of the solar race of India (Chhabra 1965:51).

The inscriptions do not mention whether Aśwawarman embarked on a policy of expanding his influence to the surrounding areas, as was customary for the founder of a dynasty, but there is no doubt that his son launched such a policy. In one of the inscriptions Mūlawarman is said to have "conquered other kings in the battlefield, and made them tributaries, as did king Yudhiṣṭhira". This is no doubt a reference to the *digvijaya* episode in the Mahābhārata (Book 2), which describes the conquest of various countries in all directions by the Pāṇḍawas, after which the *rajaśuya* sacrifice was performed and Yudhiṣṭhira became the world ruler. And so, while his grandfather was only designated as a *narendra* ("lord of men") in the inscription, Mūlawarman was styled a *rājendra* ("lord of kings"), with all the neighbouring rulers paying tribute to him.

But who were these other kings who were conquered in the battlefield by Mūlawarman? Were they, like Mūlawarman himself, also rulers of Indic states, or were they chieftains of tribal communities in the surrounding areas? Obviously we are not in a position to give definite answers to such questions but, until new evidence is found which proves otherwise, it seems likely that they were the latter. Whereas in Kutai there are findings of various archaeological remains such as Hindu and Buddhist images, there has been no evidence, from inscriptions or from Chinese sources, which indicates that other kingdoms existed in the area. In the inscriptions those "other kings" are called *pārthiva*, and Kulke has suggested, on the basis of the etymology of this Sanskrit word, that they were landholders, comparable to the *rakai* of the Old Javanese inscriptions (Kulke 1990:6). We do not know what happened to this Kutai kingdom after the issuing of Mūlawarman's inscriptions, but it might have declined soon afterwards and those *pārthiva* might then have regained their former status as chiefs of independent tribal communities.

Some sort of a kingdom or a chiefdom did, however, apparently continue to exist in the region, as we find the name Tuñjung Kute as one of the *maṇḍalika-rāṣṭra* ("ring-kingdoms") under the "protection" of Majapahit, which are enumerated in cantos 13 and 14 of the fourteenth-century Old Javanese poem Nāgarakṛtāgama (Pigeaud 1960-63. "Tuñjung Kute" occurs in stanza 14.1). There seems to be no doubt that this Tuñjung Kute must have been the ancient name of present-day Kutai, because the name occurs in the list of the *maṇḍala* located in the island of Tañjung-nagara, i.e. Kalimantan. (For a discussion on the concept of *maṇḍala* in early Southeast Asia, see Wolters 1982:16ff.) It is even possible that Tuñjung Kute or one of its synonyms was the name of Mūlawarman's kingdom. If the name Kute (Kutai) is still used in present-day Indonesia, there seems to be no strong reason why the name that appears in this poem could not be that of the same kingdom that existed earlier.[1] Many names of villages, districts, and kingdoms found in the inscriptions survive to the present, often with only slight modification.

THE SANSKRITIZATION OF *JAWA*

A similar case which shows the emergence of another Hinduized state in Indonesia is provided by the oldest dated inscription from Central Java, found in Canggal, a village in the region of Kedu (Sarkar 1971-72:I, 15-24). This Sanskrit inscription tells us about the foundation of a *lingga*, the phallic symbol of God Śiva, by a King Sañjaya in AD 732. It also mentions his father, named Sanna or Sannāha, who had "in the fullness of time, gone to enjoy happiness in the heaven which is the accumulated results (of his meritorious deeds)".[2] Since Sannāha, despite its spelling, is not a Sanskrit word, it seems reasonable to suppose that it was a Sanskritized Javanese name. We have a similar case in the name of Sañjaya's successor. His Javanese name, as it appears in the Old Javanese Mantyasih I inscription of AD 907, was Panangkaran, but in the Sanskrit Kalasan inscription dated 778 his name appears in its Sanskritized form as Paṇaṃkaraṇa (Sarkar 1971-72:II, 64-81; I, 34-40).

Some geographical names may also appear in Sanskrit forms. Thus the name Tārumā, mentioned in the fifth century inscriptions found in western Java, may have been a Sanskritized form of an indigenous name related to *tarum*, "indigo" (Gonda 1973:77). Another example is Yava which according to Gonda "forms a vexed question". The name Yavadvīpa, "Island of Barley", for Java and Sumatra, probably even for Kalimantan, was already known in early Sanskrit literary works (Wheatley 1961:177-179). But since barley is grown in neither island, Gonda (1973:348-350) argues that the original name was *Jawa*, which was a word for "Indonesian, indigenous" and could have applied to both Java and Sumatra, to their inhabitants, products, languages, etc. Indian navigators and colonizers interpreted the word, by way of popular etymology, as *yava-*, "abundance of barley" and named the island accordingly. Then, under the Sanskritizing tradition, the new name "Yava" returned to Java as we find it in the Canggal inscription.[3]

Since Sannāha apparently did not have a Sanskrit name it seems very likely that Sañjaya, like Aśwawarman of the Kutai inscription, was the first of his line to adopt the Śivaite cult, establish a "new" kingdom, and assume a Sanskrit name. Like Aśwawarman he was regarded as the founder of the dynasty by later generations, as is evident from the Mantyasih I charter. This is an Old Javanese inscription issued by King Balitung in AD 907, in which Sañjaya's name appears at the head of a list of eight successive rulers of Mataram. Significantly, in this charter he is simply entitled *rakai* Mataram *sang ratu* Sañjaya, while all the other rulers are recorded with a more exalted title, *śrī mahārāja*, e.g. *śrī mahārāja* Panangkaran, *śrī mahārāja* Panggumulan, etc.

However, Sanna himself was also a ruler. This is clear from the Canggal inscription which tells us that he, "by means of conciliation and gift, ruled the subjects in a proper way, out of attachment, just like a father (taking care of) the child from his very birth" (verse 8c). In the context of the organization of communities in ancient Java, the choice of the simile "like a father (taking care of) the child" to describe the relationship between the ruler and the subjects seems to be very apt. As is known from the Old Javanese inscriptions, the smallest indigenous community in ancient Java was the *wanua* ("village, settlement"). Its inhabitants, especially those born there, were called *anak wanua* or, from the end of the tenth century, *anak thāni* ("children of the village"). They were probably the descendants of the original founders of the village concerned. The *wanua* was governed by a board of elders presided over by the first among equals, the *rāma*, the primary meaning of which was "father" (van Naerssen 1977:37; de Casparis 1990:62, note 6). By using such a simile, the author of the inscription might have intended to indicate that Sanna was a *rāma*, or, if he were not one, that he governed his subjects in the manner proper to a *rāma*.

The latter seems to have been more likely. We know from the inscription Mantyasih I that his son Sañjaya was a *rakai*, one level higher than a *rāma* in the social hierarchy of ancient Java. A *rakai* was the head of a territorial unit called *watak* or *watĕk* ("group"), which consisted of several *wanua*. The *rakai*-ship must have had its origin in prehistoric times. As van Naerssen has argued, with the introduction of wet-rice cultivation a more complicated system of irrigation was required and co-operation by the several *wanua* which depended on water of the same river or its tributaries therefore became necessary. Such an irrigation system needed a head whose authority reached beyond that of a single *wanua*, and so a leader, *rakai*, was elected from among the *rāma* (van Naerssen 1977:37). It appears from the inscriptions, however, that in most cases the villages belonging to the same *watĕk* had become so dispersed that they no longer formed a contiguous territorial unit. By the tenth century a *watĕk* might have comprised villages that were located in different parts of central and/or eastern Java, and the names of the well-known *watĕk* such as Hino, Halu and Sirikan gradually lost their original territorial connotation.[4]

It has been suggested that the word *rakai* or *rake* was derived from *raka*, meaning "older brother" (Stutterheim 1933:165; van Naerssen 1977:37). Such an explanation, however, is now no longer acceptable. It has been pointed out that the word *raka* "never occurs in the inscriptions with the meaning of 'older brother', nor with any other meaning" (Barret Jones 1984:93), and the form *raka i* is not in fact found in any original inscriptions (de Casparis 1990:56). Moreover, considering that ranking based on age is a very important principle among Austronesian peoples, one would expect that a kinship term indicating an older age group than "father" would be used to denote a position higher than *rāma*. It seems more likely, therefore, that the word *rakai* and variants such as *rake, reke* and *raki*, is related to *ra-(ka)ki* or *ra-kya*, the primary meaning of which is "elder, grandfather".[5]

The highest authority in the autochthonous hierarchical system of ancient Java was the *ratu*. As far as we can see from the inscriptions, while *rakai* apparently no longer had direct relationships with the *wanua* from which they or their ancestors came, a *ratu* still maintained close ties with his own *watĕk*, as is evident from the use of his *rakai* title beside his *ratu* title. Thus, as we have seen, Sañjaya is recorded as *rakai* Mataram *sang ratu* Sañjaya in the Mantyasih I charter. Since Sannāha, as we shall see below, was also a *ratu*, it seems reasonable to suppose that he himself was also a *rakai* like his son.

The word *ratu*, or its cognates, is found in many languages which belong to the Austronesian language family with a variety of meanings, such as Tagalog *dāto* ("high priest"), 'Toba Batak *datu* ("sorcerer"), Malay *datok* ("head of a kin group"), and Fijian *ratu* ("title of rank before names of males who are chiefs"). Based on these various meanings, Blust (1980:216-217) suggests that the Proto-Austronesian **datu* had at least four components of meaning, namely: (1) political leader, chief; (2) priest, custodian and administrator of customary law, medical practitioner; (3) aristocrat, noble; and (4) ancestor, grandfather, elder.

Thus the Old Javanese *ratu*, like *rāma* and *rake* (or *rakai*), may have developed from a kinship term meaning "ancestor, grandfather" to mean "political leader, chief". In terms of ranking *rāma* ("father") was head of the smallest unit, the *wanua*; *rake* ("elder, grandfather") was head of the *watĕk*; and *ratu* ("grandfather, ancestor") was the highest in the hierarchal system.

Since Sañjaya was given Sanskrit titles meaning "king", i.e. *narapati* and *rāja*, in the Canggal inscription (in verses 1 and 11 respectively), it is obvious that the author of the inscription, and most likely local Sanskrit scholars in general, considered *ratu* as the equivalent of Sanskrit *rāja*, "king". In this meaning *(sang) ratu* also occurs frequently in the Old Balinese inscriptions, especially during the reign of Ugrasena (915-39) (Damais 1949:29; Goris 1954:II, 296). *Dātu* also occurs in the Old Malay inscriptions of Śrīwijaya, probably with the meaning of "governor of provinces", but *kadātuan*, significantly, was used for "royal residence" (de Casparis 1956:38, 345), resembling Old Javanese *kadatwan* ("royal residence, kingdom") and Modern Javanese *kraton*.

Like Sañjaya, Sannāha was also entitled *rāja* in the Canggal inscription (verse 8). So, he too must have been a *ratu* during his lifetime. In fact, he may have been the descendant of a long line of *ratu*, as the inscription specifically says that he was *rājogrodagrajanmā*, that is "a king of a very noble lineage". Likewise, Kuṇḍungga of the Kutai inscription must also have been a *ratu*, or whatever word was used in Kutai at that time to denote "political leader, chief", for in the inscription he was called a *narendra*, which is synonymous with Sañjaya's designation as *narapati* ("lord of men").

We may thus conclude that both Aświawarman in Kutai and Sañjaya in Mataram did not actually found new kingdoms or principalities, but merely transformed the old established *kaḍatwan* into new *rājya*. It is moreover evident from the great number of official titles occurring in the Old Javanese inscriptions, the overwhelming majority of which are non-Indian and non-Sanskritic (Sarkar 1971-72:I, xix), that the new kingdom was largely a continuation of an older one.

The establishment of these new kingdoms obviously took place only after their rulers had decided to adopt Hinduism. Although it is often said that one is Hindu *only* by birth, the process of "Hinduization", which is sometimes given the more general term "Indianization" or "Sanskritization" (Hall 1981:12; Coedès, 1968:15-16; Mabbett 1977) seems to have occurred throughout the long history of India and still continues to occur (Srinivas 1966:1; Coedès 1968:25). It has been pointed out by Srinivas (1989:63) in this context that it was the second *varṇa*, the *kṣatriya*, that "seems to have been the one most open, accommodating all kinds of groups, indigenous as well as alien, the only necessary qualification being the effective possession of political power". For the elevation of a native chief to the level of *kṣatriya* the Brahmanic rite of *vrātyastoma* must have been performed by Brahmans. Accordingly, in areas where there was no established Brahman the chief either had to import some from outside — offering them gifts of land and other inducements — or even create them himself from amongst ambitious local groups (Coedès 1968:24; Srinivas 1989:63).

Perhaps in order to show that one had the necessary qualifications — the effective possession of political power — it seems to have been mandatory to announce one's conquest of surrounding areas in inscriptions. Thus we read, for instance, that Mūlawarman had "conquered other kings in the battlefield, [and] made them his tributaries" (Kutai inscription), and that Sañjaya had overthrown many "circles of feudal lords" (Canggal inscription).

As far as the need for the Brahmans to perform the necessary rites is concerned, the Kutai inscriptions explicitly tell us that the sacrifices held by Mūlawarman were performed by Brahmans who "had come there". At this early stage of the Sanskritization of the Indonesian archipelago they were likely to have been Indian Brahmans, but it is also possible that they were Austronesians who had acquired a priestly education in India and who came from other parts of the country for special occasions. Whatever the case, they must have come there on the invitation of the king, who then rewarded them with religious gifts, land and great wealth (up to twenty thousand and probably forty thousand cows are mentioned in the inscriptions — though the numbers were most likely exaggerated). Some may have left soon after the events, but a number of them must have decided to stay, forming the nucleus of a growing number of indigenous learned men. A Chinese record tells us that in the kingdom of P'an-p'an (fifth century AD) "are numerous brahmans come from India in search of wealth. They are in high favour with the King" (Wheatley 1961:49).

It is clear from the above examples of the Hinduization of Kutai and Mataram that Hinduism — or Buddhism in cases where the rulers, for one reason or another, preferred the Buddhist monks — was disseminated by Brahmans invited there by the local rulers, and that these religions spread principally among the limited circles of members of the royal courts. It was, as Coedès (1968:33) puts it, "essentially an aristocratic religion which was not designed for the masses". And, like the "new" kingdom which still retained many of the essential parts of the old system, the new cult also contained many autochthonous religious beliefs. Thus one could point out, for instance, that behind the new Indian *deva* there was the ancient Javanese *hyang*, Old Javanese for "deity" (indeed the new deities were given the honorific *hyang*, e.g. *hyang* Śiwa, *hyang* Wiṣṇu); that Śiwa was easily accepted as the highest God because, as the son-in-law of Mount Himalaya, he could be related to ancient worship of the Great Mountain; that the Javanese *caṇḍi* ("temples") can be identified as successors of the terraced religious sites of prehistoric times; or that the best known Javanese Buddhist monument, Borobudur, can only be understood properly in the light of ancestor worship (de Casparis 1950:188; Holt 1967:35-38).

It is clear, then, that the adoption of the Indian concept of kingship and various forms of Sanskritic culture and Indian religions did not lead to fundamental changes *throughout* the Indonesian political and social order.[6] The sheen of these imported religions and cultural forms, to borrow a much quoted metaphor, "is a thin and flaking glaze", under which the whole of the old indigenous forms has continued to exist (van Leur 1967:95).

Nevertheless, significant changes *did* occur as the result of the penetration of the Sanskritic culture into the western parts of the Austronesian world. There seems to be little doubt that Sanskritization provided the necessary ingredients to enable the local cultures, especially those that had had more intensive contacts for a lengthy period of time, to produce cultural manifestations distinctly different from those of other Austronesian people who had no direct contacts with Sanskritic culture. Without the infusion of the Indian conception of royalty, it is extremely doubtful whether local polities with the relatively small-scale systems of political integration and ranking which were the common features of prehistoric Austronesian societies, could have developed into "true states with specialised bureaucracies and the powers to maintain allegiance by force" (Bellwood 1985:146-148). And without the foundation of such states it is very unlikely that religious monuments on the scale of the universally acclaimed temples of Borobudur and Prambanan — or even the smaller ones, the remains of which are scattered all over central and eastern Java as well as in many other places outside Java — could ever have been built.

THE SPREAD OF LITERACY

Another heritage which the Indonesians would never have had without Sanskritization is of course the Indian-based writing system and written literature derived from, or inspired by, Sanskrit literary works. This script and the literature are without doubt the most enduring elements of the adopted Indian culture.

Written literature, like Buddhism and Hinduism, entered the Malayo-Indonesian archipelago through the main gates of the *kraton* (palaces). Merchants may have introduced Indian script for the first time, perhaps inadvertently, when they brought merchandise such as seals, rings and other precious objects, engraved with Sanskrit names, into a trading port. Thus, for instance, different types of Brahmi script (datable from the second to the fifth century AD) engraved on such precious objects have been discovered at Oc Eo, the site of an ancient trading port in southern Vietnam (Coedès 1968:7; de Casparis 1975:12), while a type of Brahmi or Kharoshthi script datable from the third century BC to the fourth century AD inscribed on the body sherd of an open dish-like vessel was recently found at Sembiran on the northern coast of Bali (Ardika and Bellwood 1991:225-226). More systematic dissemination of literacy, however, must have been carried out by the Hindu Brahmans and the Buddhist monks, for whom the study of books was always a significant part of daily activities. We read in a Chinese record, for instance, that in the third century kingdom of Tun-sun (in the Malay peninsula) there were more than a thousand Brahmans. The record tells us that they did "nothing but study the sacred canon, bathe themselves with scents and flowers, and practise piety ceaselessly by day and night" (Wheatley 1961:17). Those Brahmans came to certain kingdoms by invitation of the kings, then for one reason or another decided to stay and become *guru*. People would have gathered to hear their teachings and to study under their personal guidance.

In the beginning, disciples must have been limited to a small number of people, drawn mainly from what Srinivas (1989:63) calls "some ambitious local group" who aspired to become Brahmans, and probably also from other members of the royal courts. This constituted the nucleus of the local learned men. Proficiency in the Sanskrit language and literature must have been one of the primary requirements for those aspiring to be allowed into those elite groups. This is evident from the earliest inscriptions found in the archipelago — from Kutai (around AD 400), western Java (fifth century) and central and eastern Java (seventh and eighth centuries) — all of which are written in Sanskrit, using Sanskrit metres, and are either religious or eulogistic in nature. Comparing the Kutai inscriptions with those found in India, Vogel (1918:216-218) says that the former indicate "a very fair knowledge of Sanskrit", and that as far as metrical exigencies are concerned they are "irreproachable".

It was among such small groups of learned men that literacy evolved, slowly at first, but gradually gaining momentum and spreading to the wider circles of society. The importance of writing as a medium of communication must have soon been recognized by the rulers. Using writing, a king would be able to put his orders in a concrete, visible form, transportable to a distance, so that he would always be symbolically present among his subjects. As a Javanese author of an inscription dated 1296 expresses it, "They [the receiver of the 'supreme favour of His Majesty the King' and his descendants] will keep the Sacred Royal Order as physical protection: this charter sealed with the emblem of Kṛtarājasa Jayawardhana, to be written down on one of the three kinds of material, bronze, *ripta* (palm-leaves?), or stone; [is] to be worshipped once a year, placed under a yellow parasol, to the accompaniment of music, as though it were the king himself" (de Casparis 1975:7).

While literacy by itself would not necessarily result in the increased political power of the king and the expansion of the state, it would no doubt facilitate effective control of the whole realm. A local power, or even a regional kingdom, may be able to do without it, but for an imperial kingdom, literacy must be a crucial factor in maintaining its territorial integrity.[7] As Gough (1968: 71) argues, "It does seem improbable, that centralized states containing more than about a million people can exist, or can hold together easily, without some use of writing for political administration". While the number of one million may be somewhat arbitrary, there seems to be little doubt that writing "provides a reliable method for transmitting information between the centre and the periphery, and hence mitigates the fissive tendencies of large empires" (Goody 1968:1-2).

Thus by the seventh century literacy appears to have spread to wider circles of the population. A Chinese record says that in the kingdom of P'an-p'an (located in the Malay peninsula): "The people *all* learn the brahmanical writings and greatly reverence the law of Buddha" (Wheatley 1961:48). Although it seems very unlikely that the whole population of P'an-p'an was really literate, the accounts indicate a certain degree of widespread literacy in that kingdom and probably in some other parts of the Malayo-Indonesian archipelago as well. We know from other Chinese accounts that in the seventh century, Holing (Walaing in central Java) and Fo-shih (Śrīwijaya in southern Sumatra) were famous centres of Buddhist learning. Chinese travelling to, or returning from, a pilgrimage to India often stopped there, and sometimes stayed for a considerable length of time, during which they may have studied Sanskrit grammar and copied or translated religious texts, sometimes under the guidance of local scholars (Coedès 1968:79-82).

ŚRĪWIJAYA: A CENTRE OF LEARNING?

For a communication to be effective, the language of the message sent by a speaker obviously has to be properly understood by those for whom the message is intended. Writing as an instrument of communication would be of no use if the language represented by these signs were incomprehensible to readers. Hence the spread of literacy would inevitably bring the vernacular languages of the texts into prominence.

It was not a coincidence, therefore, that some of the oldest inscriptions written in any vernacular of the Austronesian language family were issued by the rulers of Śrīwijaya, the first known imperial kingdom of the region, whose suzerainty at the peak of its power was widely acknowledged in the western parts of the Malayo-Indonesian archipelago, so much so that one of its rulers, writing to the Sung emperor in 1017, proudly referred to himself as "the king of the ocean lands" (Wolters 1970:1).

Six inscriptions from early Śrīwijaya (dated between AD 682 and 686) have so far been found in areas of southern Sumatra — three in Palembang, one in upper Jambi, one on the island of Bangka and another in Lampung — and these probably indicate the extent of the area under its effective control at this early stage of its long history (Coedès 1968:82-85; van Naerssen 1977:31-36). All these inscriptions are written in Old Malay, using a later type of Pallava script which is related to the script used in the Kutai inscriptions. Some adaptations were of course required. For instance, although the alphabet used for Sanskrit possessed many more signs than required for representing Old Malay and other Austronesian languages, it does not have a symbol for the phoneme ĕ. To overcome this problem, the Śrīwijayan scholars simply used the "zero mark", using the two consonants between which the ĕ was pronounced as a ligature, e.g. writing *tmu* for *tĕmu* ("to meet"). Whoever worked out these adaptations must have been scholar(s) of some influence, for most of the principles used in the writing of the early Śrīwijaya inscriptions continued to be used by later generations of scribes of Old Javanese and Old Balinese inscriptions and manuscripts.[8]

At about the same time as the inscriptions were issued, a well-known Chinese pilgrim, I-tsing, stopped in Śrīwijaya for six months in 671 to study Sanskrit grammar while on his way to India, and for another four years between 685 and 689, during which time he copied and translated Buddhist texts into Chinese. In his memoirs I-tsing tells us that: "In the fortified city of Fo-shih, there are more than a thousand Buddhist priests whose minds are bent on study and good works. They examine and study all possible subjects exactly as in Madhyadeśa [India]" (Coedès 1968:81; Takakusu 1966:xxxiv). I-tsing even tells us that while he was in Śrīwijaya, Śākyakīrti, one of the four most distinguished Buddhist scholars at that time, was residing there (Takakusu 1966:184). It is clear from I-tsing's accounts, and confirmed by the inscriptions, that by then Śrīwijaya was not only an established kingdom with considerable power over both sides of the Straits of Malacca, but was also a famous centre of learning.

In such an environment it is reasonable to expect that some sort of Old Malay literature must have developed in the *kadatuan* of Śrīwijaya. If I-tsing was able to complete "a new translation of Śūtras and Śāstras" into Chinese during his stay in Śrīwijaya, one would expect that the Malay scholars would have done the same into Malay, or even produced original literary works. No such works, however, have come down to us. This is perhaps not surprising, considering that Śrīwijaya did not have its "Bali", the small, insulated island to which Old Javanese literature owes its survival to the present day. But even in later Malay literature — the product of the Malay courts of Malacca and its successors, which claimed to be the heir to the Śrīwijayan cultural tradition (Wolters 1970, 1982:22-24) — we cannot find any traces of written Old Malay literature. On the contrary, it is evidence of the influence of the Old Javanese cultural tradition that we find in later Malay literature. Of the half a dozen or so works listed in Chapter III (The Hindu Period) of Winstedt's *A History of Classical Malay Literature*, most are derived from Javanese sources such as the twelfth century Old Javanese poems Bhāratayuddha and Bhomakawya (Bhomāntaka), and others from the oral tradition, e.g. the Hikayat Seri Rama (Winstedt 1977:24-27).[9]

Now, apart from the absence of any trace of Old Malay literary works, we also find hardly any architectural remains from the Śrīwijaya period. One explanation usually offered for this is that, despite its fabulous wealth, as a maritime power Śrīwijaya did not possess the necessary manpower to build great edifices comparable to, say, the Borobudur; whereas the agricultural states of Java, with their "administrative machinery expanding in patrimonial, bureaucratic forms", were able to mobilize the needed manpower from the docile peasantry (see e.g. van Leur 1967:96-97).

It seems more likely, however, that lack of manpower was not the main reason for this apparent absence of building activities in Śrīwijaya throughout its long history. Had the rulers of Śrīwijaya had the inclination to build large religious monuments there seems little doubt that they would have been able to obtain the necessary manpower to build them. We know from the Kedukan Bukit inscription of AD 683, for instance, that the king had an army of more than twenty thousand soldiers at his disposal to accompany him on his *siddhayātrā* (a journey to obtain supernatural prowess). As Hall has pointed out, an emphasis on the maritime aspect of Śrīwijaya, while in the main correct, tends to neglect the important relationship between the Śrīwijaya ports and their hinterland, from which this large force of twenty thousand soldiers could have been recruited (Hall 1985:79-80). We also know from the writing of the Arab geographer Mas'ūdi (dated AD 995) that the kingdom of the islands of Zābag (among which were "Kalah and Sribuza and other islands in the China Sea") had "an enormous population and innumerable armies". "Even with the fastest vessel", Mas'ūdi says, "no one can tour these islands, all of which are inhabited, in two years" (Coedès 1968:131).

Lack of manpower, therefore, can not be used to explain why there are hardly any architectural remains from the whole Śrīwijaya period, spanning at least four centuries (from the seventh to the eleventh century), or even seven centuries (to the fourteenth century). Considering the fact that there are also no traces of literary works from this great empire, the conclusion seems to be that either the greatness of Śrīwijaya is merely another myth, comparable to that of Prapañca's Majapahit (Supomo 1979), or that the rulers of Śrīwijaya had entirely different priorities from those of their Javanese counterparts. That is, to quote Coedès:

> After having become a great economic power, Śrīvijaya seems to have neglected the spiritual values that attracted the Chinese pilgrim I-ching there in the seventh century. In fact, while the Javanese kings were covering their island with religious buildings, the Śrīvijayan sovereigns were preoccupied with superintending the traffic straits rather than building lasting monuments, and they have left us only insignificant brick towers and a very small number of inscriptions (1968:131; cf. van Leur 1967:106-107).

"TEMPLES OF LANGUAGE" IN ANCIENT JAVA

The Javanese rulers, however, did not only cover their island with *caṇḍi śilā*, "temples of stone", but they also commissioned scores of poets and other literati to create what they called *caṇḍi bhāṣa*, "temples of language".[10] Building "language temples" turned out to be a wiser decision than covering the whole of Yawabhūmi with "stone temples", and even more so than hoarding fabulous wealth as the rulers of Śrīwijaya did in Suwarṇabhūmi ("Land of Gold", i.e. Sumatra).

The oldest known dated Old Javanese inscription is from AD 804, that is almost one and a half centuries after the Old Malay inscriptions of Śrīwijaya. But, unlike Śrīwijaya where no more Old Malay inscriptions were apparently issued, hundreds of Old Javanese inscriptions have been found in Java, covering a period of more than six centuries. Since there must have been some connection between the level of literacy and the issuing of charters in the vernacular language, the abundance of the Old Javanese inscriptions must be an indication of the extent of literacy in ninth-century Java. This is perhaps only to be expected. During the seventh century, Walaing (Chinese: Holing) was apparently already such a famous centre of learning that a Chinese scholar went there to translate Buddhist texts into Chinese under the guidance of a Javanese *guru*. The erection of the Buddhist Borobudur and the Śivaite Prambanan temple complexes, probably during the first half of the ninth century (Soekmono 1979: 457-472; de Casparis 1956:309-311), shows that the dynastic changes that occurred in central Java after Sañjaya's accession to the throne did not diminish the importance of the region as a centre of learning. The thousands of bas-relief sculptures of Borobudur, which are based on various Buddhist texts (Krom 1927; Bernet Kempers 1980), and those of Prambanan based on a version of the Rāma saga (Stutterheim 1989), are clear testimony of continued vigorous study of literary texts.

It is not surprising, therefore, that the oldest "temple of language" that has come down to us, the Rāmāyaṇa *kakawin*, was also the product of the central Javanese period.[11] Surprisingly, this poem is based neither on the best-known version of the Rāma sagas, namely Valmiki's epic, nor on the version depicted in the bas-reliefs of Prambanan temple, but on the *Rāvaṇavadha*, "The slaying of Rāvaṇa", a sixth or seventh century poem by an Indian poet named Bhaṭṭi. The choice of Bhaṭṭi's poem, rather than Valmiki's epic, to serve as the poet's model in writing his poem, is remarkable. For the latter is not only the best-known version of all the Rāma sagas, but its language is also much easier than that of the former. Bhaṭṭi himself says of his work that this poem "can be understood only by a commentary; it suffices that it is a feast for the clever and that the stupid come to grief in it as a result of my love for learning" (Keith 1956:116). Whatever reasons prompted the choice, however, the completed result was without doubt a masterpiece, the gem of all that has been produced by the Old Javanese *kawi*, "poets". To later generations it became the *ādikakawin*, that is the first and foremost among the Old Javanese poems (Hooykaas 1958). It is also testimony of the high level of scholarship that must have existed in central Java at that time. The poet's ability to grapple with a text which posed so many problems clearly shows that his knowledge of Sanskrit must have been considerable and that he must have had complete mastery of his own language to have been able to render this difficult Sanskrit prototype satisfactorily. With the creation of both temples of stone and of language of the magnitude of the Borobudur and the Old Javanese Rāmāyaṇa, it is no wonder that Java of the ninth century continued to attract people from other countries. An inscription from Champa, for instance, tells us that a high official from what is today the central coast of Vietnam went on a pilgrimage to Java "to acquire the magical science". "The pilgrim's quest", comments Wolters (1982:27), "may epitomise Java's reputation for possessing esoteric knowledge".

The obvious advantage of the "temple of language" over "temple of stone" is of course its transportability. Once completed, a book, or more likely its copies, could be transported to the remotest part of the country. Even in those days it was apparently not uncommon to purchase books and build up some kind of a library in one's residence in the countryside. Prapañca tells us in the Nāgarakṛtāgama 29.2 that his friend, Kṛtayaṣa, who lived in a village some distance from the capital, used to occupy himself "with the appraisal of kīrti (valuable) books. Having been bought they were well taken care of, put into safe keeping" (Pigeaud 1960-63). In fact, one does not have to transport literature in its physical form to convey its message. Once its contents have been mastered, one can leave the book aside and relay its message orally to audiences anywhere. In this manner, throughout the long history of Sanskritization, literature became the most potent instrument in the dissemination of the Sanskritic culture. The Mahābhārata and the Rāmāyaṇa epics in particular played a crucial role in spreading this culture from the confined walls of the kraton to the countryside. As Srinivas (1989:61) observes in the context of Sanskritization in India, the epics "have not only transmitted to the people a knowledge of the great gods of Hinduism and certain basic theological ideas, but have also helped to spread common culture throughout the century. The epics, and the innumerable stories included in them, constitute the foundation of the literature in every Indian language. The fact that the institution of harikatha, or public reading of the epics and the Purāṇas by trained masters of the art, was a popular pastime made it possible for Sanskritic Hinduism to reach even the illiterate masses."[12]

The earliest evidence of the penetration of the Sanskrit epics into rural areas is found in the Sangsang copper plate inscription issued in the name of King Balitung in AD 907 to confirm the granting of freehold to the monastery of Dalinan (Sarkar 1971-72:II, 85-98). To celebrate what must have been the most important event of the year, if not of decades, for the whole region, a variety of performances was given on that occasion. Apart from singing (mamidu), dancing (mangigal), a Kicaka dance, play-acting (mamirus) and clowning (mabañol), the inscription also mentions a wayang performance (mawayang) of the story of

"Bhīmaya-kumara", and a recital (*macarita*) of the "Bhīma-kumara" and "Rāmāyaṇa" stories. Both "Kicaka" and the "Bhīma-kumara" obviously refer to a certain episode from the Wirāṭaparwa, the fourth book of the Mahābhārata (Zoetmulder 1974:208-209). Since there is no evidence that a Javanese translation or adaptation of the Mahābhārata already existed at that time, it seems likely that the narrator of the Bhīma-kumara episode recited a Sanskrit text, and then, as in a *harikatha*, explained it to his audience in Javanese. The *mabasan* in present-day Bali, in which people gather to listen to a recital of an Old Javanese poem and its interpretation in Balinese, no doubt originated from this kind of *macarita*.

THE JAVANIZATION OF THE *MAHĀBHĀRATA*

It was some ninety years after the aforementioned *macarita* that the rendering of the Mahābhārata into Javanese was undertaken under the patronage of King Dharmawangśa Těguh (AD 990-1016) — about sixty years after the centre of power had moved from the central to the eastern part of the island. A most important event in relation to the rendering of the epic was a *macarita* at Dharmawangśa's court where people gathered to listen to a recital of the Wirāṭaparwa for "one month minus one evening" — commencing on 14 October and ending on 12 November 996. The importance of the occasion is evident from the fact that the king himself attended all the sessions, except for one, "when the king was prevented by other affairs" (Juynboll 1912:97-98; Zoetmulder 1974:95). It is very likely, therefore, that this was the first recital — some kind of a première, as Zoetmulder suggests — of the first completed rendering of one of the eighteen books of the Mahābhārata. It is true that the Wirāṭaparwa is not the first book of the Mahābhārata but, as Raghu Vira points out, "the Mahābhārata reciters commenced their sessions with the Virāṭa and not with Ādi [the first parvan]", because "the Virāṭa is one of the shortest of the major parvans, full of action and excitement" (Raghu Vira 1936:xvii). Of the eighteen books that constitute the Mahābhārata, only nine *parwa*, including the Wirāṭaparwa, have come down to us. Whether these nine were the only completed *parwa*, or other *parwa* had been written but later lost, is a question that is difficult to answer satisfactorily. In any case, in Old Javanese usage the term *parwa* includes not only the eighteen *parwa* of the Mahābhārata, but also the Old Javanese Uttarakaṇḍa, the final part of Valmiki's epic which is not found in the Old Javanese Rāmāyaṇa.

In the introductory section of the Wirāṭaparwa we find an expression used by the anonymous writer to indicate the aim of his undertaking, namely *mangjawākěn Byāsamata* — literally "to 'Javanize' Byāsa's thought". Another expression occurring in the epilogue is *pinrakṛta*, a passive form of *mrakṛta*, "to render (the story) into the vernacular". It is clear from comparing the Wirāṭaparwa and the other *parwa* with their Sanskrit originals that they are not translations, but rather adaptations of the latter. It is true that many passages in the *parwa* are in fact literal translations from the Sanskrit texts, but in general the Javanese writers merely present an abbreviated form of the metrical epic in Old Javanese prose which faithfully follows the epics in essence. Except for a few lines in the prologues and epilogues, the *parwa* writers did not insert any additions, nor make significant changes which would point to an independent attitude in their handling of the sources.

The writing of the *parwa* was not, however, the end of the "Javanization" of the Indian epics. It was soon followed by another process of "Javanization", which became apparent in the East Javanese *kakawin* and other literary products from the same period. Writing *kakawin* around themes taken from the *parwa* was undoubtedly a most popular exercise for East Javanese poets and, after the fall of Majapahit, for Balinese poets as well. The list of *kakawin* in Pigeaud's catalogue shows that more than half of them have heroes and heroines from the Indian epics as their main characters (Pigeaud 1967:157-197). There is, however, a big difference in the way the epic materials are handled in the *kakawin* and in the *parwa*. In the *kakawin* the "Javanization" was more than just substitution of a vernacular for Sanskrit as in the *parwa* and, to a lesser degree, the Old Javanese Rāmāyaṇa. It involved a more fundamental change: the transposition of what were basically still Indian narratives into a Javanese setting. All the names of the kingdoms and places where the stories take place, and those of the heroes and the heroines of the stories are, to be sure, Indian, and are known from the Indian epics. Thus we find, for instance, that in the twelfth century Bhāratayuddha *kakawin* the Pāṇḍawas and the Korawas are fighting their final fraternal war for the kingdom of Hāstina in the field of battle at Kurukṣetra, and that in the fourteenth century Arjunawijaya *kakawin*, Arjuna Kartawīrya is fighting a fierce battle against Rāwaṇa on the banks of the Narmada river. Yet, as Zoetmulder remarks:

> In spite of this, one cannot but be struck by the fact that these stories are placed in a setting that is definitely Javanese when reading the *kakawins*. Under the guise of Sanskrit personal and place names the poet is presenting a picture of his own country and his own society. These men and women with their Indian names are essentially Javanese, acting like Javanese, thinking like Javanese and living in a Javanese environment (1974:187-188).

It is thus possible for a poet to compose a poem woven around a theme taken from a *parwa*, but in fact telling the story of a Javanese king. For instance, the Arjunawiwaha (Arjuna's wedding), a *kakawin* written by *mpu Kaṇwa* around AD 1030, is generally accepted as being an allusion to the life story of King Erlangga, a ruler of the kingdom of Kahuripan, who was the poet's patron (Berg

1938). Likewise, other poets may have written *kakawin*, with certain princes, most likely their patrons, in mind (Robson 1983:302-309). Their contemporaries would no doubt have been able to identify the heroes and heroines of the *kakawin* with their princes and princesses, but without the benefit of knowing the life story of those princes and princesses it would have been impossible for later generations (and certainly for us) to know to whom the poets alluded. Not that that really mattered to them. In fact, it is very unlikely that readers of the Arjunawiwaha from, say, Kaḍiri of AD 1150, would have identified Arjuna with Erlangga, who by then had been dead for about a century. It seems most likely that those readers would have identified Arjuna with King Jayabhaya, the contemporary ruler of Kaḍiri. Likewise, readers of two centuries later would have identified him with King Rājasanāgara, the great ruler of fourteenth century Majapahit. In short, Arjuna and all the great heroes and villains of the Great Bhāratas and other Indian literary works continued to be related to contemporary Javanese life throughout the centuries. In this way Old Javanese literary works remained part of daily rituals for many centuries after the first "temple of language" was erected more than a thousand years ago — and in fact continue to be so in present-day Bali.

Creating "temples of languages" was a wiser decision of the Javanese rulers than building "temples of stone", and even more so than erecting "temples of gold". Long after the fabulous wealth accumulated by the Śrīwijayan rulers had vanished, both stone and language temples continued to function as refuges where devotees came to seek protection and blessings from the Lord. And long after all those hundreds of stone temples that covered the island of Java were in ruins — destroyed by earthquakes, volcanic eruptions or sheer neglect — and then fell into disuse and were abandoned when Islam came, quite a number of Old Javanese literary works continued to be in demand as a source of ethical and spiritual guidance in the Moslem Javanese *kraton* and for the Javanese population in general. Their Modern Javanese versions were, and are, even more popular than those derived from Islamic sources. It is certainly instructive to note that while Chandi Borobudur, undoubtedly the largest and the most majestic of all the "temples of stone", was buried under thick mud and tropical growth by the early nineteenth century (Soekmono 1976:5), Raffles was able to testify that at that time the Bhāratayuddha, one of the best known Old Javanese literary works, was "the most popular and celebrated poem in the [Javanese] language" (1965:410). It is still so in Bali today, where people still "meditate" inside all those "temples of language".

NOTES

[1]   A somewhat similar case is Malyāng, a small principality in north-western Cambodia during the seventh century which, according to Wolters (1982:3), disappeared from the records after the late eighth century but reappeared in the late twelfth century as a rebellious area when Angkor was sacked by the Cham in 1177.

[2]   This is according to Sarkar's interpretation (1971-72:I, 15-24, note 43). For a different interpretation, which says that Sañjaya was the son of Sannāha's sister, see Chhabra (1965:48) and Coedès (1968:87).

[3]   Other scholars, such as Kern, Rouffaer and Krom, argue that since Sanskrit *yava* could also apply to cereal products in general, *Yava* may have derived from *jawawut*, a Javanese word for "millet", which is an ancient cultigen in Java (see Gonda 1973:349).

[4]   For recent studies on *rakai* and *watak*, and local government in ancient Java in general, see for example Barret Jones (1984), de Casparis (1990) and Wisseman Christie (1983, 1990).

[5]   See Barret Jones (1984:93), Zoetmulder (1982), under *rake, kaki, ki, kya* and *kyayi*. The element *ke* or *ki* is probably related to Proto-Austronesian **aki*, which may refer to "grandfather" (Blust 1980:219).

[6]   A brief survey of Javanese terms of kinship also clearly shows that "the old Javanese kinship system is entirely Austronesian and, in its basic conceptions, shows little if any Sanskrit influence" (Fox 1990:325).

[7]   For the process of state formation through three successive phases, i.e. local, regional and imperial, see Kulke (1990).

[8]   For a detailed description of the so-called Later Pallava script and the adaptation required for the writing of Old Malay inscriptions, see de Casparis (1975:20-27).

[9]   My colleague Dr Virginia Hooker has kindly drawn my attention to various pre-Moslem motifs occurring in Malay literature, such as "the foam princess" and "the bamboo princess", but I believe that they are motifs from the pre-Hindu period and more likely to have been transmitted to later Malay literature through the oral tradition.

[10]   The term *caṇḍi bhāṣa* occurs, for instance, in the Arjunawijaya (1.2): "The purpose of my praise to the Lord is to implore Him to pay heed to the reverential homage of one who devotes himself to poetry, so that he may achieve the perfect goal he set himself in writing — this is what I implore, as I build my *temple of language on my writing board*" (Supomo 1977). For the conception of *kakawin* as "language temple", see Zoetmulder (1974:173-185).

[11]   The dating is uncertain. The first quarter of the tenth century is generally accepted as the most likely date of its composition (see Zoetmulder 1974:230-231), but more recently Robson (1980, 1983) argues that it should be assigned to the middle of the ninth century.

[12]   In a *harikatha* the priest reads and explains a religious story to his audience. Each story takes a few weeks to complete, the audience meeting for a few hours every evening in a temple. The faithful believe that such listening leads to the acquisition of spiritual merit (Srinivas 1956:485).

REFERENCES

Ardika, I.W. and P.S. Bellwood
1991   Sembiran: the beginnings of Indian contact with Bali. *Antiquity* 65:221-232.

Barret Jones, A.M.
1984   *Early tenth century Java from the inscriptions: a study of economic, social and administrative conditions in the first quarter of the century.* Verhandelingen van het Koninklijk Instituut voor Taal-, Land- en Volkenkunde 107. Dordrecht-Holland: Foris Publications.

Bellwood, P.S.
1985   *Prehistory of the Indo-Malaysian archipelago.* Sydney: Academic Press.

Berg, C.C.
1938   De Arjunawiwaha, Er-langga's levensloop en bruiloftslied? *Bijdragen tot de Taal-, Land- en Volkenkunde* 97:19-94.

Bernet Kempers, A.J.
1980   The reliefs and the Buddhist texts. In *Proceedings of the International Symposium on Chandi Borobudur*, pp.92-105. Tokyo: Executive Committee for the International Symposium on Chandi Borobudur.

Blust, R.
1980   Early Austronesian social organization. *Current Anthropology* 21:203-247.

Casparis, J.G. de
1950   *Inscripties uit de cailendra-tijd.* Bandung: A.C. Nix.
1956   *Prasasti Indonesia II: selected inscriptions from the 7th to the 9th century A.D.* Bandung: N.V. Masa Baru.
1975   *Indonesian palaeography: a history of writing in Indonesia from the beginning to c.A.D. 1500.* Leiden: E.J. Brill.
1990   Some notes on relations between central and local government in ancient Java. In D.G. Marr and A.C. Milner (eds) *Southeast Asia in the 9th to 14th centuries*, pp.49-63. Singapore: Institute of Southeast Asian Studies and Canberra: Research School of Pacific Studies, The Australian National University, Canberra.

Chhabra, B.Ch.
1965   *Expansion of Indo-Aryan culture during Pallava rule* (as evidenced by inscriptions). Delhi: Munshi Ram Manohar Lal.

Coedès, G.
1968   *The Indianized states of Southeast Asia.* Canberra: Australian National University Press.

Damais, L.C.
1949   Epigrafische aantekeningen: centraal gezag of koninkrijkjes? *Tijdschrift voor Indische Taal-, Land-, en Volkenkunde* 83:1-26.

Fox, J.J.
1990   The ordering of generations: change and continuity in Old Javanese kinship. In D.G. Marr and A.C. Milner (eds) *Southeast Asia in the 9th to 14th centuries*, pp.315-326. Singapore: Institute of Southeast Asian Studies and Canberra: Research School of Pacific Studies, The Australian National University.

Gonda, J.
1973   *Sanskrit in Indonesia*. New Delhi: International Academy of Indian Culture. [2nd ed.]

Goody, J.
1968   Introduction. In J. Goody (ed.) *Literacy in traditional societies*, pp.1-26. Cambridge: Cambridge University Press.

Goris, R.
1954   *Prasasti Bali*, 2 vols. Bandung: N.V. Masa Baru.

Gough, K.
1968   Implications of literacy in traditional China and India. In J. Goody (ed.) *Literacy in traditional societies*, pp.70-84. Cambridge: Cambridge University Press.

Hall, D.G.E.
1981   *A history of South-east Asia*. 4th ed. London: Macmillan.

Hall, Kenneth R.
1985   *Maritime trade and state development in early Southeast Asia*. Honolulu: University of Hawaii Press.

Holt, Claire
1967   *Art in Indonesia: continuities and change*. Ithaca: Cornell University Press.

Hooykaas, C.
1958   *The Old Javanese Rāmāyaṇa: an exemplary kakawin as to form and content*. Verhandelingen der Koninklijke Nederlandse Akademie van Wetenschappen, Afdeeling Letterkunde, vol. 65, no. 1.

Juynboll, H.H.
1912   *Wirāṭaparwa: Oudjavaans prozageschrift*. 's-Gravenhage: Koninklijk Instituut voor Taal-, Land- en Volkenkunde, Martinus Nijhoff.

Keith, A.B.
1956   *A history of Sanskrit literature*. London: Oxford University Press.

Krom, N.J.
1927   *Barabudur: archaelogical description*. 2 vols. The Hague: Koninklijk Instituut voor Taal-, Land- en Volkenkunde, Martinus Nijhoff.

Kulke, H.
1990   The early and the imperial kingdom in Southeast Asian history. In D.G. Marr and A.C. Milner (eds) *Southeast Asia in the 9th to 14th centuries*, pp.1-22. Singapore: Institute of Southeast Asian Studies and Canberra:

Research School of Pacific Studies, The Australian National University.

Leur, J.C. van
1967   *Indonesian trade and society: essays in Asian social and economic history.*
         The Hague: W. van Hoeve Publishers.

Mabbett, I.W.
1977   The 'Indianization' of Southeast Asia: reflection on the historical sources.
         Journal of Southeast Asian Studies 8:143-160.

Naerssen, F.H. van
1977   The economic and administrative history of early Indonesia. In F.H. van
         Naerssen and R.C. de Iongh (eds) *The economic and administrative history
         of early Indonesia.* Leiden: E.J. Brill.

Pigeaud, Th.G.Th.
1960-63 *Java in the fourteenth century: a study in cultural history*, 5 vols. The
         Hague: Koninklijk Instituut voor Taal-, Land- en Volkenkunde, Martinus
         Nijhoff.
1967   *Literature of Java: catalogue raisonné of Javanese manuscripts in the
         Library of the University of Leiden and other public collections in the
         Netherlands*, vol. I. The Hague: Koninklijk Instituut voor Taal-, Land- en
         Volkenkunde, Martinus Nijhoff.

Raffles, T.S.
1965   *The history of Java.* Kuala Lumpur: Oxford University Press [reprint of
         1817].

Raghu Vira
1936   *The Virāṭaparvan, being the fourth book of the Mahābhārata.* Poona:
         Bhandarkar Oriental Research Institute.

Robson, S.O.
1980   The Rāmāyaṇa in early Java. *South East Asian Review* 5:5-19.
1983   Kakawin reconsidered: toward a theory of Old Javanese poetics. *Bijdragen
         tot de Taal-, Land- en Volkenkunde* 139:291-319.

Sarkar, H.B.
1971-72 *Corpus of the inscriptions of Java*, 2 vols. Calcutta: Firma K.L.
         Mukhopadhyay.

Soekmono, R.
1976   *Chandi Borobudur: a monument of mankind.* Assen/Amsterdam: van
         Gorcum.
1979   The archaeology of Central Java before 800 A.D. In R.B. Smith and W.
         Watson (eds) *Early South East Asia: essays in archaelogy, history and
         historical geography*, pp.457-472. New York: Oxford University Press.

Srinivas, M.N.
1956   A note on Sanskritization and westernization. *The Far Eastern Quarterly*
         15:481-496.
1966   *Social change in modern India.* Berkeley: University of California Press.

1989   *The cohesive role of Sanskritization and other essays.* Delhi: Oxford University Press.

Stutterheim, W.
1933   Iets over raka en rakryan naar aanleiding van Sindok's dynastieke positie. *Tijdschrift voor Indische Taal-, Land- en Volkenkunde* 73:159-171.
1989   *Rāma-legends and Rāma-reliefs in Indonesia.* New Delhi: Indira Gandhi National Centre for the Arts/ Abhinav Publications [translation of 1925].

Supomo, S.
1977   *Arjunawijaya: a kakawin of mpu Tantular.* The Hague: Koninklijk Instituut voor Taal-, Land- en Volkenkunde, Martinus Nijhoff.
1979   The image of Majapahit in later Javanese and Indonesian writing. In A. Reid and D.G. Marr (eds) *Perceptions of the past in Southeast Asia,* pp.171-185. Singapore: Heinemann Educational Books (Asia).

Takakusu, J.
1966   *A record of the Buddhist religion as practised in India and the Malay Arhipelago (A.D. 671-695) by I-tsing.* Delhi: Munshiram Manoharlal. [reprint of 1896].

Vogel, J.Ph.
1918   The yūpa inscriptions of King Mūlavarman from Koetei (East Borneo). *Bijdragen tot de Taal-, Land- en Volkenkunde* 74:216-218.

Wheatley, P.
1961   *The golden Khersonese: studies in the historical geography of the Malay Peninsula before A.D. 1500.* Kuala Lumpur: University of Malaya Press.

Winstedt. R.O.
1977   *A history of classical Malay literature.* Kuala Lumpur: Oxford University Press (Oxford in Asia Historical Reprints edition).

Wisseman Christie, J.
1983   Raja and rama: the classical state in early Java. In L. Gessick (ed.) *Centres, symbols and hierarchies: essays on the classical states of Southeast Asia,* pp.9-44. Yale University Southeast Asia Studies: Monograph Series 26.
1990   Negara, mandala, and despotic state: images of early Java. In D.G. Marr and A.C. Milner (eds) *Southeast Asia in the 9th to 14th centuries,* pp.65-93. Singapore: Institute of Southeast Asian Studies and Canberra: Research School of Pacific Studies, Australian National University, Canberra.

Wolters, O.W.
1970   *The fall of Śrīvijaya in Malay history.* London: Lund Humphries.
1982   *History, culture, and region in Southeast Asian perspectives.* Singapore: Institute of Southeast Asian Studies.

Zoetmulder, P.J.
1974   *Kalangwan: a survey of Old Javanese literature.* The Hague: Koninklijk Instituut voor Taal-, Land- en Volkenkunde, Martinus Nijhoff.
1982   *Old Javanese-English dictionary.* 's-Gravenhage: Koninklijk Instituut voor Taal-, Land- en Volkenkunde, Martinus Nijhoff.

16

CONTINUITY AND CHANGE IN THE AUSTRONESIAN TRANSITION TO ISLAM AND CHRISTIANITY

Anthony Reid

Commercial links and a common orientation towards maritime trade continued to bind Southeast Asian Austronesian communities together in historical times, and the spread of Islam is regarded as a consequence of these cultural ties. Islam required many changes in traditional Austronesian social and religious practices, as did Christianity, but the strength of Austronesian tradition, reinforced greatly by the continuing use of the Austronesian languages as vernaculars, imposed a two-way dialogue on the process.

AUSTRONESIAN BOUNDARIES

A Samoan deposited in (say) Madura might well conclude that it was Islam that most profoundly distinguished Indonesian culture from his own. In dress, diet, naming, social and domestic relations as well as belief and ritual, Islam has taken the majority of today's Austronesians in a distinctive direction. In consequence they would probably see less reason to identify with our Samoan than with non-Austronesian Muslims in South and West Asia. One might reasonably conclude that the conversion by 1650 of most lowland areas of the archipelagoes we now know as Indonesia and the Philippines to Islam or Catholicism had created the most fundamental cleavages between Austronesians. From these transitions, however initially qualified, there was no going back. No subsequent influence from Holland, China, Britain, Japan or America could ever overturn these identities as Muslim or Catholic, whatever they were held to mean in different times and places.

This would, however, be only part of the story. The two proselytizing scriptural religions were by no means the only, nor even the first, of the consequences for Southeast Asia's Austronesians of proximity to the great Eurasian land mass. Others have spoken eloquently of the transitions wrought in Southeast Asia by Sanskrit terminology and Indian political and philosophical ideas, as these were selectively adapted by Austronesians. I want to draw attention also to the commercial and diplomatic connectedness within and beyond Southeast Asia which predated and underlay the advance of Islam among Austronesians.

When the ancestors of the Polynesians struck out to the east of the Indonesian Archipelago, they sailed off the edge of the known world. For more than a thousand years before the eighteenth century exploration of the Pacific, the Austronesians who remained in Southeast Asia were significant players in a series of interlocking trade networks which stretched from eastern Indonesia to China and Japan in the north and to Portugal and Ireland in the west. We know this not so much from the ambiguous geographical information of Ptolemy and his Chinese contemporaries as from the arrival of the products of eastern Indonesia in the markets of the world.

Only after their arrival in Southeast Asia did Europeans discover just where the spices they had been seeking came from:

> The Malay merchants say that God made Timor for sandalwood and Banda for [nutmeg and] mace and Maluku for cloves, and that this merchandise is not known anywhere in the world except in these places (Pires 1515:204).

These points marked precisely where the southeastern boundary of the Eurasian world-system lay. Cloves, nutmeg and sandalwood were sent to the north and west in small quantities from as early as Roman and Han times. Records of shipments reaching Europe are continuously available from only the tenth century, and they show a trickle of nutmeg and clove rising to a steady stream at the end of the fourteenth century. Austronesians, with intermittent stimulus from Chinese, were the carriers of these spices around the archipelago, to *entrepôts* such as Sri Vijaya, Melaka, Patani and Banten. By travelling frequently as far as Maluku and Timor, they kept these peripheries on the known map of world commerce.

Beyond that, to the east and south, lay darkness. In the perspective of Asian traders the Indonesian Archipelago represented "the outer edge of the world" (Pinto 1578:393; also Wolters 1970:23-24). Of course there was some exchange across the Arafura and Timor seas, with a few slaves and birds of paradise from New Guinea and the surrounding islands being traded as far as Java. In comparison with the intense commercial interest focused on Maluku and Timor, however, the low level of interaction beyond is extraordinary.

Austronesians were among the great sailors of Asia, and their involvement in maritime commerce was one of the themes that maintained a sense of common interest among seemingly culturally diverse Austronesians. As well as carrying their own produce into world markets, Austronesians commanded all the sea routes between east Asia and the rest of Eurasia. Whether shipping passed through the Melaka or the Sunda or the Lombok and Makassar Straits; whether portages were made across the Malay Peninsula from Melaka, from Kedah or from Tennasserim; whether traffic to and from China took on water and supplies along the Cham coast of Indochina and the east coast of the Malay

Peninsula, or in the Philippines and eastern Borneo, or along the west coast of Borneo and Java; Austronesians were directly involved. In the long and often intense commercial and diplomatic relationship between Southeast Asia and China it was Austronesians who took most of the initiatives, at least until the southern Sung dynasty (1127-1279) stimulated the creation of a Chinese sea-going fleet (Wolters 1970:19-42). The Malay culture hero, Hang Tuah, was appropriately depicted sailing, trading and fighting for his king in China, India and the Middle East as well as Java and Siam. While the Malayo-Muslim maritime tradition is well known, it is worth recalling Dampier's praise also for still-Hindu Chams, one of whose vessels he encountered in the Gulf of Siam in 1687:

> They were of the idolators, Natives of Champa, and some of the briskest, most sociable, without Fearfulness or Shyness, and the most neat and dexterous about their Shipping, of any such I have met with in all my Travels (Dampier 1697:272).

How else than through this common commitment to maritime commerce does one explain the curious ways in which Malays, Javanese, Chams and Tagalogs were tied to each other? Champa and Majapahit exchanged royal princesses and diplomatic missions in the fourteenth century, and a Cham king chose Java as his refuge from Vietnamese pressure on the Cham capital in 1318 (Robson 1981:276). Both Malay and Javanese traditions make much of the Cham connection. The *Sejarah Melayu* (1612:135) claims that a ruler of Champa journeyed to Majapahit to make his homage, fathering there a child by a Majapahit princess. This child grew up to become the penultimate ruler of Champa before the capital, Vijaya, fell to the conquering Vietnamese.

Javanese tradition asserts that it was through a Cham princess married to the king of Majapahit, and her brother Raden Rahmat, that Islam entered the Javanese court. To complete the Austronesian triangle, Rahmat took as his wife a lady of Tuban named Nyai Ageng Manila — perhaps evidence of Philippine birth (*Babad Tanah Jawi*:20-21). Although there were certainly Muslims in Champa in the fifteenth century, the Cham ruling class was still Hindu at the time of the Vietnamese conquest of Vijaya (Qui Nhon), which Vietnamese sources date to 1471. The Malay royal chronicle claims that the Hindu aristocrats who fled the Vietnamese took refuge not in nearby Hindu-Buddhist Cambodia but among Muslim fellow-Austronesians in Melaka and north Sumatra (*Sejarah Melayu* 1612:136-137). The king of Champa, with his capital further south in Phanrang, remained a Hindu until at least 1607, but he was nevertheless closely allied with Malay Johor against Vietnamese, Khmer and Portuguese (Matelief 1608:120-121; Manguin 1979:269).

The Cham diaspora of traders, warriors and refugees in the sixteenth and seventeenth centuries was Muslim or in process of becoming so. Muslim Chams were among those battling the Portuguese in the South China Sea and aiding Demak's holy wars in Java in the sixteenth century, and helping even distant Makassar in the seventeenth (Pinto 1578:107, 386; *Sja'ir Perang Mengkasar*: 146-147). Malays and Chams were so closely aligned during the conflicts of seventeenth-century Cambodia that their Iberian enemies thought they were one people.

The first European reports on the Tagalogs classify them as "Luzons" (Port. *Lucoes*), a nominally Muslim commercial people trading out of Manila, and "almost one people" with the Malays of Brunei (Pires 1515:134). One of these Luzons commanded the Brunei fleet in 1521 (Pigafetta 1524:58-59), and another was named head (*temenggong*) of the Malays remaining in Melaka after the Portuguese conquest in 1511 (Pires 1515:134, 281). As well as their substantial trade with Melaka, the Luzons were collecting sandalwood in Timor when Magellan's ship reached there (Pigafetta 1524:94), no doubt to supply the Chinese trade. Luzons were well represented in the polyglot Muslim fleets which did battle with the Portuguese in the South China Sea during the sixteenth century, and one of them held Aru (northeast Sumatra) for the crusading Sultan of Aceh in 1540 (Pinto 1578:49, 107, 112). Pinto, our source for much of this, also mentions Luzons among the anti-Muslim warriors of the Batak king, in 1538 (*ibid.*:26), suggesting they could be mercenaries valued by all sides. Luzons disappear from descriptions of the archipelago after the Spanish conquest of Manila in 1571, presumably assimilating to the Malay diaspora.

We should also recall the intermingling of Javanese and Malays, especially in Melaka where the *Hikayat Hang Tuah* admitted that the Malays were all "half-Javanese" (Winstedt 1969:38), and where the royal chronicle was studded with Javanese passages. The very categories *Jawah* and *Jawi* referred as frequently to Sumatra or Malays as to Javanese until European labels began to prevail. More surprisingly, Madagascar's interaction with the Indonesian Archipelago was still remembered in the sixteenth century, when the Portuguese found there "many brown and Javanised natives who say they are descended from them [Javanese]", which they attributed to Javanese seafarers having traveled across the Indian Ocean (Couto 1645, IV, iii:169).

It appears, then, that commercial links and a common orientation towards maritime trade continued to bind the Austronesians who "remained behind" on the fringes of Eurasia to each other, in advance of and apart from Islam or Christianity. The spread of Islam to most of the Austronesians of Southeast Asia can be seen as a consequence as much as it was a cause of this common involvement in maritime commerce.

ISLAMIZATION AS CHANGE

The initial threshold of entry into the house of Islam was deliberately low — to recite the *shahada* ("there is no god but God and Muhammad is His Prophet"); to undergo circumcision; and to abandon the consumption of pork. Understanding of the message of Islam could come later. In urging de Houtman to take the simple step which would save his life in Aceh, even if he could not appreciate the body of Islamic doctrine, a Muslim scholar there used the image of a master shipwright who had first to lay down the keel of the ship though he could not yet see the whole pattern of the vessel (a metaphor more appropriate to Austronesian than to Dutch shipbuilding) (de Houtman 1601:99). It was these external symbols of adherence to the faith which were held to be the essential requirements of entry. No internal assent to a creed or confession of past errors was called for. Europeans who encountered peoples recently converted, like the "Lutao" of Mindanao and northern Maluku, often thought these externals were all there was:

> Never is a Lutão found who has not been circumcised, or one who eats pork — and it is this which constitutes their Mahometanism ... for they do not know what the Koran is (Diaz 1718:321; cf. Legazpi 1569:60-61).

A Muslim source, the *Hikayat Patani* (75) also made the point about the first Patani ruler to adopt Islam: "He gave up worshipping idols and eating pork, but apart from that he did not alter a single one of his *kafir* habits".

This pattern has led many authors to see conversion as an inappropriate term for the first steps towards Islamic faith. Merle Ricklefs (1979) depicted Islamization not as a step but as an ongoing journey in "Six centuries of Islamization in Java". This should not be taken to mean, however, that change was imperceptible, steady, or unidirectional. Rather, I would argue, it was made up of numerous conversions to the external ideal and almost as many reversions towards the bedrock of Austronesian habits. Changes were profound, and the first step often the most profound. The cost of entry into Islam should not be minimized by a modern sensibility which sees religion as a matter of personal conviction and piety. It involved a change of identity symbolized by the abandonment of the pig-eating which had provided Austronesians with not only their major meat source but also the stuff of sacrifice and feasting.

Pig-eating was a major obstacle to conversion in all the cases for which there is first-hand evidence. In South Sulawesi Bugis and Portuguese sources agree that Islam failed to make headway in the sixteenth century because of its ban on pork and other foods (Dias 1559:306; Noorduyn 1955:105-106). A pious legend had one Makassarese chief threatened with *jihad* declare that he would not accept Islam even if rivers flowed with blood, as long as there were pigs to eat in the forests of Bulo-bulo. Of course that very night the pigs disappeared by divine intervention (Matthes 1943:257-258). Even when rulers were convinced of the need to convert, they often asked for a grace period during which they could have a mighty feast of all their domestic pigs (Jones 1979:148; Volkman 1985:21).

In the period 1540-1640 the boundary of Islam became particularly clear as a result of the military and commercial struggle with Portuguese and Spanish Catholics. Acceptance of Islam came to be seen as a test of political loyalty; non-Muslim ethnic groups were seen not simply as latent Muslims but as actual or potential enemies; the state greatly increased its commitment to upholding orthodoxy. This period of conscious competition was one of such profound religious change that it might rightly be labelled not only conversion, but revolution. That sharp boundary of the house of Islam softened when the Dutch (and later English) insulated Southeast Asia from both counter-reformation Catholicism and international Islam, and divorced the religious contest from the economic one. The tendency grew to accept existing Austronesian society as Islamic rather than seek to change it (Reid 1993).

The discontinuity represented by Islam in that period of rapid change was most obvious to outsiders in matters that bore on identity — dress, speech, deportment and diet. There were, however, two areas in which Islam (and in different degrees Christianity) represented an even more fundamental challenge to Austronesian values. In its attitude to both sexuality and death Islam offered so basic an opposition to the ways of understanding the world that tensions persist until today, even though major changes were already evident from the sixteenth century.

Austronesian religion had understood the cosmos in terms of dualities in which both male and female elements were essential. Women had crucial ritual and religious roles, especially in mediating between humans and spirits. Islam and Catholic Christianity by contrast were carried by male religious specialists ministering to a deity identified as male. Spiritually talented and ritually experienced women could not find a place in the new religion to match that which they had played in the old.

It must have seemed to many women that Islam was a male ritual activity not relevant to women. Women in the Philippines were not given the option of ignoring Catholicism in this way, however, since the Spanish friars tended to seek out and persecute female shamans where Muslims were more inclined to ignore them (Schumacher 1979:72-73; Chirino 1604:302-305). Resistance to Islam in South Sulawesi appears to have had support from a few aristocratic women. Women of ordinary birth, however, were probably under little pressure to abandon domestic ritual activity, and even shamanistic healing. The chief evidence for this is less in the sources than in Southeast Asian religious practice, where such activities survived surprisingly well until this century. There is a curious story in the *Babad Lombok* (1979:17-19), however, that when all the men of Lombok submitted to a superior Javanese force and agreed to be circumcised, the women did not. Fearful that the women's refusal to convert would enrage the Javanese, the ruling circle moved their capital away from the coast and back to the ancient Hindu capital, though their commitment to Islam remained.

The struggle of Islam to impose a radically different sexual morality on Austronesians was a long one, with rapid changes in periods of orthodox emphasis but also inevitable compromise with the autonomous position of Austronesian women. Women had been accustomed to initiating divorce with little stigma attached. In the Philippines one high-born lady protested to a Spanish missionary that "it was a hard thing if unhappy with one's husband one could not leave him, as was the custom among them" (Chirino 1604:313). Unlike Catholicism, Islam of course permitted divorce, but only in terms of repudiation (*talak*) of the woman by the man. This formula was incorporated into local law codes as a legal option (*Undang-undang Melaka* 1976:132-133), but since women continued to be economically self-sufficient the frequency of divorce initiated by women was almost unparalleled. As an Arab visitor complained, the Malays "do not treat divorce as a religious act" (Ibn Majid 1462:206).

Adultery was already punished in very varied ways before Islam, and the harsh Islamic punishments for *zina* were adopted by the élite of some trading cities in the seventeenth century. Around 1600 foreigners witnessed the death penalty being publicly administered to élite youngsters in Patani, Aceh and Brunei — something much less common two centuries later. For rape and adultery the local law codes frequently added the much harsher Islamic penalties at the end of a passage setting out the system of moderate fines preferred by local custom (Reid 1988:156-158). In all these respects, there appears to have been a dramatic lurch towards Islamic norms during the period of conversion, followed by a reversion towards an accepted compromise with Austronesian reality.

Dress in public was one of the quickest things to change with Islam, as with Christianity. Bare breasts, penis inserts, tattoos and long male hair all disappeared very quickly in favour of what we now see as standard Indonesian/ Malay dress of *sarung* and *kebaya* (chemise). Again the initial change was particularly dramatic. In Makassar city only fifty years after the conversion to Islam women were sometimes "entirely covered from head to foot, in such fashion that not even their faces can be seen" (Rhodes 1653:207). In Banten in the same period Arab-style dress became common (Schrieke 1957:242). Such un-Austronesian phenomena disappeared, however, along with the large Islamic merchant cities in the late seventeenth century.

Islam was even more uncompromising in its condemnation of idolatory, and for this reason required that the dead be buried quickly and simply, in complete contrast to Austronesian tradition. Change in the externals of funerary practice was achieved astonishingly quickly. Burial sites of the tenth to sixteenth centuries have yielded valuable ceramics and gold items, buried with the dead in the Philippines and eastern Indonesia to ensure a comfortable passage to the afterlife. These end abruptly with the coming of Islam and Christianity. The elaborate feasting, designed to ensure the deceased endured this most dangerous transition and would not return to torment the living, was modified into a relatively simple burial.

One of the major appeals of the scriptural religions was that they loosened the grip of spirits on every aspect of daily life. The truly pious were strengthened against assaults by unsatisfied spirits. People continued to face illness and misfortune, however, and for these the actions of angry spirits of the dead appeared a more immediate and direct explanation than scriptural notions of sin (Hoskins 1987:150-151). Ordinary Javanese Muslims in Banten told Scott (1606:172-173) that God was good and would not hurt them, but the devil (by which they must have meant spirits, *setan* in Malay) was constantly doing them harm so they directed all their ritual activity to appeasing him.

Islam had already incorporated some helpful popular compromises by the time its greatest Southeast Asian gains were made. The period following the fall of Baghdad was one in which the Sufi orders (*tariqa*) became the major instruments for the extension of the faith. While the founders and saints of the Sufi orders had been learned visionaries seeking a direct path to union with God, at the popular level Sufism by the fifteenth century represented a means of linking the individual with the spiritual power (Ar. *baraqa*; Malay *berkat*) of holy men, apostles, rulers and other remarkable people. The power of these dead saints was invoked to help the living through the spiritual genealogy which linked each Sufi teacher to the venerated founder of his order, but also through visitations (*ziyara*) to the tombs of holy men, where offerings were frequently made.

Such practices were particularly popular in Southeast Asia, where the *berkat* of dead saints could be invoked for similar purposes to the spirits of the ancestors. The newly Muslim population made pilgrimages and offerings at holy tombs — those of the apostles thought to have introduced Islam to each area, such as the nine walis of Java or Dato ri Bandang in Makassar; of popularizers of the Sufi orders like Abdurrauf of Singkil, in Aceh, and Shaikh Yusuf of Makassar; and of certain powerful kings such as Iskandar Muda in Aceh. The strength of this saint-veneration as early as the sixteenth century is confirmed by the protest of a strictly orthodox Javanese handbook against it: "It is unbelief to say that the great imams are superior to the prophets, or to put the saints (*wali*) above the prophets, and even above our lord Muhammad" (Drewes 1978:38-39).

There is no doubt that despite rapid acceptance of the form of Muslim funerals, Southeast Asians continued to fear that the dead would trouble them unless ritually satisfied. In Banda in 1599, the dead were quickly buried in a white cloth, as prescribed, but when the Dutch asked Bandanese *why* they continued to pray for several days at the graveside they were told it was to prevent the dead from "standing up", which would otherwise surely happen causing great misfortune to all (*Tweede Schipvaart* 1601:90). Austronesians adopted with particular enthusiasm the widespread Muslim practice of returning at the third, seventh, fortieth and hundredth days after the burial, to feast at the grave (Martin 1604:49; Gervaise 1701:140-147; Raffles 1817 I:327; Ali Haji 1866:76).

> According to the official or learned conception this is done in order to bestow on the deceased the recompense earned by his good work; according to the popular notion it is to let them enjoy the actual savour of the good things of the feast (Snouck Hurgronje 1893 I:221).

Honouring the dead has continued to be a great preoccupation of Southeast Asian Muslims. Whereas in the Arab world the seventh month of the Muslim year is considered most appropriate for such commemoration, in Indonesia it is the beginning and end of the fasting month (the ninth) when ancestors are especially remembered. Feasts were (and in some places still are) held at grave sites just before the fast commences, and at its end, and the forgiveness of elders is asked — the dead as well as the living. Although the origins of these practices lie in obscurity, they may initially have represented another creative Muslim response to the need to make offerings to the spirits of the dead.

Arabic terms and prayers were adopted quickly even for purposes which had been closely associated with the spirits. *Do'a* became the standard term for an invocation or a blessing to ward off evil (Houtman 1603:107, 165). *Roh* (plural *arwah*) was accepted as a Muslim equivalent of the Austronesian concept of *semangat* (soul-substance or spirit — Endicott 1970:28-51), while potent graves were referred to by Arabic words which reinterpreted their power in Islamic terms — *kramat* (sacred [grave]), *berkat* (spiritual power), and *ziarah* (pilgrimage — Houtman 1603:250).

THE IDEA OF THE SACRED

When we move from the externals which could be observed by outsiders to the belief systems of individual Austronesians, it must be immediately acknowledged that the sources are inadequate to allow us to confirm or deny any of the great hypotheses about religious change. Yet to dodge it is in a sense to trivialize one of the most momentous intellectual passages for an individual or a society into a matter of outward social conformity. I have little doubt that there was a large-scale movement towards a more modern *mentalité* in the fifteenth and sixteenth centuries,[1] but it is almost impossible to explicate this without frequent reference to religious change at a much later period when there were ethnographers to record it.

The religions of the Austronesians were characterized by a baffling diversity of spirits and practices. When the Dutch attempted to investigate the religion of Seram (central Maluku) in 1684, their conclusion was that "the informants differed so widely that it was impossible to describe the system, and moreover they are so superstitious that it would almost take a book of paper to note the details of each negeri" (cited Knaap 1987:71). Modern ethnographers have faced similar difficulties. Conklin discerned 1500 distinct spirits among the Ifugao (Luzon), and Volkman (1985:34) "perhaps thousands" among Toraja. This has not prevented either contemporary missionaries and observers or modern scholars from identifying an underlying pattern of Austronesian or Southeast Asian belief.

As in other pre-modern traditions, there was no distinction between a religious and a secular dimension. The material world was suffused with spiritual forces, and to survive and flourish in it everybody had to know how to manipulate them. In a sense it is modern religions, notably Christianity, Judaism, and modernist Islam, by largely abandoning their "functions of explanation, prediction and control" of everyday events, and withdrawing to an other-worldly personal piety where they do not compete directly with scientific understandings of nature (Horton 1971:104), which created the category "primitive religion". The older religious systems of the Austronesians, on the other hand, can only be understood as intimately involved in every significant event of daily life (for modern explanations, see Hoskins 1987:139; Volkman 1985:33). Ritual and shamanistic activity was usually designed for immediate practical ends. Spiritual forces had to be manipulated to cure illness, ensure fertility, increase power, safeguard the living particularly at dangerous life crises, and ensure that the dead were assisted through the most traumatic of all transitions into a contented afterlife. Feasting and animal sacrifice was made to ensure the spirits were on side for every personal crisis, including

> the recovery of a sick person, the prosperous voyage of those embarking on the sea, a good harvest in the sowed lands, a propitious result in wars, a successful delivery in childbirth, and a happy outcome in married life (Plasencia 1589:191).

Even when Filipinos wanted to pick a fruit from a tree, plant or harvest rice, cross a stream or pass any major landmark, they would ask permission from the protective spirit and make some appropriate offering (Chirino 1604:298-299; Ortiz 1731, cited Rafael 1988:112). European observers were struck by the feasts and offerings to the spirits of the dead to aid the sick, and the attribution of illness and premature death to incorrect ritual or malign manipulation of the spirit world by some enemy.

In the African context, Horton (1971:101) has described a two-tier cosmology in which "lesser spirits" controlled the affairs of the local community, while a "supreme being" presided remotely over the entire cosmos. The supreme being was of greater interest to Africans who were drawn out of the local society for reasons such as trade, administration or enslavement, but for those immersed in the settled agricultural community had little role. Southeast Asia too had a concept of a somewhat remote creator, often named with reference to Sanskrit terminology — *Batara Guru* (*Betala* in Tagalog) or *dewata* — even though grounded in a specifically local mythology. Muslim and Christian missionaries naturally took special interest in these shadowy notions of a supreme creator god, but declined to use them to translate their own awesome concepts. Arabic *Allah* and Spanish *Dios* became the terms for God in Malay and Tagalog respectively. For older uses such as validating oaths, however, older terms seemed to carry more weight, especially in Javanese, Bugis and Makassarese (Noorduyn 1955:279; Andaya 1981:107-112).

Horton (1971) makes the point for Africa that even without new religions larger numbers of people would have directed their attention and ritual to the high god as the expansion of trade, communication and writing rendered local spirits unhelpful. The religion of spirits was not readily portable, and those who moved into the cosmopolitan trading cities had need of a personal faith which was universally valid. A similar point has been made for northern Thailand by O'Connor (1989), and for Sumba by Hoskins (1987:146).

The way in which the rulers of Wajo and Tallo', the two most commercialized states in South Sulawesi, moved towards monotheism before they accepted Islam (Noorduyn 1955:262-263; Reid 1981:14-15) suggests a similar kind of interpretation.

In a period of dynamic commercialization and urbanization, the consistency of scriptural monotheism was as much an advantage as its portability. Christian missionaries presented overwhelming evidence of the real terror in which many Austronesians lived because of the demands of malevolent spirits, and saw their task as the casting out of these demons in the name of Christ (Chirino 1604:300; Velarde 1749:71). Islam did not share this desire to make war on the spirits, since good *djinn* as well as bad were familiar themes. But Islam offered a refuge from the domination of these demanding spirits in a different vision of the cosmos. This was a predictable, moral world, in which the devout would be protected by God from all that the spirits could do, and would eventually be rewarded by an afterlife in paradise. Even the poor and the powerless, whose suffering at the hands of the spirits might not end with death, could hope to be rewarded in a Muslim heaven if they lived lives of personal virtue.

This new vision must have encouraged what Weber characterized as a rationalization of religion, or an "increase in distance ... between man and the sacred" (Geertz 1973:174). It depended on a simple but consistent concept of eternal reward and punishment, graphically illustrated in the Koran and much other Islamic literature. Preachers of both Islam and Christianity rendered into Austronesian vernaculars the torments which awaited in hell those foolish enough to prefer earthly pleasures to their eternal welfare, and those who rejected the true faith for its rivals (see examples in Rafael 1988:179-184; Hamzah Fansuri, *Poems* 1986:76, 92, 132).

Although the prominence of heaven and hell were new, the concepts may not have been. In their desire to find evocative terms to translate the Muslim and Christian heaven, proselytists made use of already localized words. Malay-speaking Muslims adopted the Sanskrit *swarga*, the abode of Siva, and *naraka* for heaven and hell respectively (Malay *surga* and *neraka*). The Spanish used Tagalog *langit* (sky) or other terms implying profound peace and contentment when discussing the joys of heaven.

In a moral universe, individuals provided heroic examples of moral and spiritual eminence. The ascetism of the Muslim sufis was particularly appealing because it shared elements already familiar from Indian traditions. The closeness of the Sufi saint to God was popularly thought to be evident in his supernatural powers and the bright glow (Malay *cahaya*, personalizing Arabic *nur*) which suffused him. The writers of Malay histories certainly believed that these self-evident powers were sufficient to convert many (*Sejarah Melayu* 1612:129; *Hikayat Banjar* 1968:420), and external sources confirm that at least such outstanding Sufi masters as Hamzah Fansuri, Syamsud-din as-Samatrani and Abdurrauf of Singkel in Aceh, and Shaikh Yusuf in Makassar and Banten, were popularly revered even during their lifetimes.

There must have been few if any Austronesians who doubted that spirits continued to interfere with the living. But Islam and Christianity provided predictable channels to tame them and scholarly traditions within which to pursue explanatory problems in a rational framework.

POST-SCRIPT

I have argued elsewhere (Reid 1993a) that Islam also wrought changes, more slowly, in the Southeast Asian attitude to political power, tending to encourage greater concentrations of power in certain radically reforming rulers. Change in this, as in other respects, was neither all of a piece nor gradual and imperceptible. Islamization provided the potential for radical change by introducing an external set of ideals to which radical reformers could appeal with spasmodic hope of success. Some of the most radical changes came in the sixteenth and early seventeenth centuries, because socio-economic conditions gave sustenance to such radical visionaries (Reid 1993). Later phases of traumatically rapid socio-economic change occurred around the turn of the twentieth century, and in the 1970s and 1980s, giving further fuel to what is today often called fundamentalism. The Austronesians of Southeast Asia are no more inclined than anybody else, however, to sustain such idealisms over lengthy periods.

NOTES

1   The case for this is strongly made by Denys Lombard (1990, II:131-175).

REFERENCES

Ali Haji ibn Ahmad, Raja
   1866   *The precious gift (Tuhfat al-Nafis)*. Trans. Virginia Matheson and Barbara Andaya. Kuala Lumpur: Oxford University Press, 1982.

Andaya, Leonard
   1981   *The heritage of Arung Palakka: a history of South Sulawesi (Celebes) in the seventeenth century*. The Hague: Nijhoff for Koninklijk Instituut voor Taal-, Land- en Volkenkunde.

Babad Lombok (ed.)
   1979   *Lalu Wacana*. Jakarta: Departemen Pendidikan dan Kebudayaan Republik Indonesia.

Babad Tanah Jawi
   1987   *Babad Tanah Djawi: Javaansche Rijkskroniek*. W.L. Olthof's vertaling van de prozaversie van J.J. Meinsma lopende tot het jaar 1721. Revised edition by J.J. Ras. Dordrecht: Foris for Koninklijk Instituut voor Taal-, Land- en Volkenkunde.

Blair, E.H. and J.A. Robertson (eds)
   1903-9   *The Philippine islands, 1493-1898*. Cleveland: Arthur H. Clark, 55 vols.

Chirino, Pedro
   1604   *Relación de las Islas Filipinas: the Philippines in 1600*. Trans. Ramón Echevarria. Manila: Historical Conservation Society, 1969.

Couto, Diego do
  1645   *Da Asia*. 9 Decades. Lisbon: Regia Officina Typografica, 1778-88.
          Reprinted Lisbon, 1974.

Dampier, William
  1697   *A new voyage round the world*. Sir Albert Gray (ed.). London: Argonaut,
          1927.

Dias, Bathasar
  1559   Letter from Melaka 3 December 1559. In H. Jacobs (ed.) *Documenta
          Malucensia*, Vol. I, pp.301-307. Rome: IHSI, 1974.

Diaz, Casimiro
  1718   *Conquests of the Fillipinas islands*. Translated in E.H. Blair and J.A.
          Robertson (eds) *The Philippine Islands, 1493-1898*, 41:317-324.
          Cleveland: Arthur H. Clark, 55 vols.

Drewes, G.W.J.
  1978   *An early Javanese code of Muslim ethics*. The Hague: Nijhoff for
          Koninklijk Instituut voor Taal-, Land- en Volkenkunde.

Endicott, K.M.
  1970   *An analysis of Malay magic*. Oxford: Clarendon Press.

Geertz, Clifford
  1973   *The interpretation of cultures*. New York: Basic Books.

Gervaise, Nicolas
  1701   *An historical description of the kingdom of Macassar in the East Indies*.
          London: Tho. Leigh. Reprinted Farnborough, 1971.

Hamzah Fansuri
  1986   *Poems. The poems of Hamzah Fansuri*. G.W.J. Drewes and L.F. Brakel
          (eds). Dordrecht: Foris for Koninklijk Instituut voor Taal-, Land- en
          Volkenkunde.

Hikajat Bandjar
  1968   *Hikajat Bandjar: a study in Malay historiography*. In J.J. Ras, pp.228-521.
          The Hague: Nijhoff for Koninklijk Instituut voor Taal-, Land- en
          Volkenkunde.

Hikayat Patani
  1970   *Hikayat Patani. The story of Patani*. A. Teeuw and D.K. Wyatt (eds), Vol.
          I. The Hague: Koninklijk Instituut voor Taal-, Land- en Volkenkunde.

Horton, Robin
  1971   African conversion. *Africa* 41(2):85-108.

Hoskins, Janet
  1987   Entering the bitter house: spirit worship and conversion in West Sumba. In
          Rita Smith Kipp and Susan Rodgers (eds) *Indonesian religions in
          transition*, pp.136-160. Tucson: University of Arizona Press.

Houtman, Frederick de
1601   Cort Verhael. In W.S. Unger (ed.) *De oudste reizen van de Zeeuwen naar Oost-Indie, 1598-1604*, pp.64-111. The Hague: Nijhoff for Linschoten-Vereniging, 1948.
1603   *Le 'Spraeck ende woord-boek' de Frederick de Houtman*. D. Lombard (ed.). Paris: Ecole française d'Extrême-Orient, 1970.

Ibn Majid, Ahmad
1462   al-Mal'aqiya. Trans. in G.R. Tibbets, *A study of the Arabic texts containing material of South-east Asia*, pp.99-206. Leiden: E.J. Brill for the Royal Asiatic Society, 1979.

Jones, Russel
1979   Ten conversion myths from Indonesia. In Nehemia Levtzion (ed.) *Conversion to Islam*, pp.29-58. New York: Holmes & Meier.

Knaap, Gerrit
1987   *Kruidnagelen en Christenen: De Verenigde Oost-Indische Compagnie en de bevolking van Ambon 1656-1696*. Dordrecht: Foris for Koninklijk Instituut voor Taal-, Land- en Volkenkunde.

Lavezaris, Guido de
1574   Reply to Rada's opinion. In E.H. Blair and J.A. Robertson (eds) *The Philippine islands, 1493-1898*, III: 260-271. Cleveland: Arthur H. Clark, 55 vols.

Legazpi, Miguel López de
1569   Relation of the Filipinas islands, and of the character and conditions of their inhabitants. July 1569. In E.H. Blair and J.A. Robertson (eds) *The Philippine islands, 1493-1898*, 3:54-61. Cleveland: Arthur H. Clark, 55 vols.

Levtzion, Nehemia (ed.)
1979   *Conversion to Islam*. New York: Holmes & Meier.

Lombard, Denys
1990   *Le carrefour javanais. Essai d'histoire globale*, 3 vols. Paris: Editions de l'École des hautes études en science sociales.

Manguin, Pierre-Yves
1979   L'introduction de l'Islam au Campa. *Bulletin l'École française d'Extrême-Orient* 66:255-269.

Martin, François
1604   *Description du premier voyage faict aux Indes Orientales par les Français de Saint-Malo*. Paris.

Matthes, B.F.
1943   *Dr Benjamin Frederick Matthes: Zijn leven en arbeid*. H. van den Brink (ed.). Amsterdam: Nederlandsch Bijbelgenootschap.

Matelief, Cornelis
1608   Historische verhael vande treffelijcke reyse, gedaen naer de Oost-Indien ende China. In I. Commelin (ed.) *Begin ende Voortgangh va de Vereenighde Neederlandtsche Geoctroyeerde Oost-Indische Compagnie.* Amsterdam 1646. Reprinted Amsterdam 1974.

Noorduyn, J.
1955   *Een achttiende-eeuwse kroniek van Wadjo': Buginese historiografie.* The Hague: Smits.

Pigafetta, Antonio
1524   *First voyage round the world*, pp.1-108. Trans. J.A. Robertson. Manila: Filipiniana Book Guild, 1969.

Pinto, Fernao Mendes
1578   *The travels of Mendes Pinto.* Trans. Rebecca Catz. Chicago: University of Chicago Press, 1989.

Pires, Tomé
1515   *The Suma oriental of Tomé Pires.* Trans. A. Cortesão. London: Hakluyt, 1944.

Plasencia, Juan de
1589   Relation of the worship of the Tagalogs, their Gods, and their burials and superstitions. In E.H. Blair and J.A. Robertson (eds) *The Philippine islands, 1493-1898*, 7:185-196. Cleveland: Arthur H. Clark, 55 vols.

Rafael, Vicente
1988   *Contracting colonialism. Translation and Christian conversion in Tagalog society under early Spanish rule.* Ithaca: Cornell University Press.

Raffles, T.S.
1817   *The history of Java*, 2 vols. London: John Murray. Reprinted Kuala Lumpur, Oxford University Press, 1965.

Reid, Anthony
1981   A great seventeenth century Indonesian family: Matoaya and Pattingalloang of Makassar. *Masyarakat Indonesia* 8(1):1-28.
1988   *Southeast Asia in the age of commerce*, Vol. I: *The lands below the winds.* New Haven: Yale University Press.
1993   Islamization and Christianization in Southeast Asia: The critical phase, 1550-1650. In Anthony Reid (ed.) *Southeast Asia in the early modern era.* Ithaca: Cornell University Press.
1993a   Kings, kadis and charisma in the 17th century archipelago. In Anthony Reid (ed.) *The making of an Islamic political discourse in Southeast Asia*, pp.83-108. Clayton: Monash University Centre of Southeast Asian Studies.

Rhodes, Alexandre de
1653   *Rhodes of Vietnam: The travels and missions of Father Alexander de Rhodes in China and other kingdoms of the Orient.* Trans. S. Hertz. Westminster, Md: Newman Press, 1966.

Ricklefs, M.C.
1979   Six centuries of Islamization in Java. In Nehemia Levtzion (ed.)
Conversion to Islam, pp.100-128. New York: Holmes & Meier.

Robson, Stuart
1981   Java at the crossroads. *Bijdragen tot de Taal-, Lande- en Volkenkunde* 137.

Schrieke, B.
1957   *Indonesian sociological studies*, Vol. II. The Hague and Bandung: Van
Hoeve.

Schumacher, John N.
1979   *Readings in Philippine church history*. Quezon City: Ateneo de Manila.

Scott, Edmund
1606   An exact discourse of the subtitles, fashions, policies, religion, and
ceremonies of the East Indians. In Sir William Foster (ed.) *The voyage of
Henry Middleton to the Moluccas*, pp.81-176. London: Hakluyt Society,
1943.

Sejarah Melayu
1612   Romanized Malay text. In R.O. Winstedt (ed.) *The Malay annals; or
Sejarah Melayu*. The earliest recension from MS No. 18 of the Raffles
Collection in the Library of the Royal Asiatic Society, London. *Journal of
the Malayan/Malaysian Branch of the Royal Asiatic Society* 16, iii (1938).

Sja'ir Perang Mengkasar
1963   *The Rhymed chronicle of the Macassar war*. C. Skinner (ed.). The Hague:
Nijhoff for Koninklijk Instituut voor Taal-, Land- en Volkenkunde.

Snouck Hurgronje, C.
1893   *The Achehnese*, 2 vols. Trans. A.W.S. O'Sullivan. Leiden: E.J. Brill, 1906.

Tweede Schipvaart
1601   *De Tweede schipvaart der Nederlanders naar Oost-Indie onder Jacob
Cornelisz van Neck en Wijbrant Warwijck, 1598-1600*, Vol. II. J. Keuning
(ed.). The Hague: Nijhoff for Linschoten-Vereeniging, 1942.

Undang-undang Melaka
1976   *Undang-undang Melaka: The laws of Melaka*. Liaw Yock Fang (ed.). The
Hague: Nijhoff for Koninklijk Instituut voor Taal-, Land- en Volkenkunde.

Velarde, Pedro Murillo
1749   Jesuit missions in the seventeenth century. In E.H. Blair and J.A.
Robertson (eds) *The Philippine islands, 1493-1898*, 7:27-119. Cleveland:
Arthur H. Clark, 55 vols.

Volkman, Toby
1985   *Feasts of honor. Ritual and change in the Toraja Highlands*. Urbana:
University of Illinois Press.

Winstedt, Richard
  1969   *A history of classical Malay literature*, 2nd ed. Kuala Lumpur: Oxford
          University Press.

Wolters, O.W.
  1970   *The fall of Srivijaya in Malay history*. London: Lund Humphries.

17

CHRISTIANITY AND AUSTRONESIAN TRANSFORMATIONS: CHURCH, POLITY AND CULTURE IN THE PHILIPPINES AND THE PACIFIC

Aram A. Yengoyan

The Christianization and colonization of the Philippines and the Pacific Islanders under Spanish and American rule took divergent paths. Under Spanish rule, the Philippines was Christianized to a high degree, yet the Spanish Crown did not regard the colony as a primary income source. Under American rule, the conversion to Protestantism was primarily secondary to America's global civilizing role throughout the world in which enlightened democratic liberalism was the keystone to the modern rational nation/state.

In the Pacific similar processes occurred but on a smaller scale. Furthermore, given the absence of hegemonic Catholicism, European and American Protestant churches and sects flourished throughout Pacific Island societies. The impact of Protestant churches in the Pacific is still critical and has far-reaching consequences wherever Micronesians and Polynesians relocate.

Christianity in its many forms and expressions came into insular Southeast Asia and the Pacific with the colonial expansion of European states. In more specific terms, the Austronesian portion of Southeast Asia went through various phases in which Christianity and colonialism worked in some contexts within a common and unified framework, while in others the Church and the State diverged in separate directions. For instance, early Dutch colonial rule in Indonesia was primarily a political and economic venture, and it was only in the nineteenth century that Dutch versions of Protestantism and Catholicism became active forces within the colonial regime. However, whereas the Dutch domination of Indonesia was primarily economic, the Philippines and other parts of the Austronesian world represent a different ensuing pattern in which the Church played a much stronger and more lasting role.

Within this comparative framework I plan to focus on the kinds of interactions which took place in the Philippines between Christianity and "native" Philippine culture(s) during the period of Spanish colonial rule (1520s to 1900), and on the kinds of changes expressed through Christianity during the American regime from 1900 to 1945. Some of the issues also have a bearing on conversion to Christianity in Micronesia and Polynesia, though the scale of the conversion process, its impact on native cultures and its time duration were markedly different in Oceania in comparison to the Philippines. Furthermore, the commercial and economic aims of Spanish policy in the Philippines were not comparable to what happened in the Pacific Islands under German rule, nor were they congruent with what American and English interests envisioned as economic ends.

SPAIN AND CATHOLICISM IN THE PHILIPPINES

Spanish rule in the Philippines, which lasted for almost 400 years, was in many ways a departure from Spanish policy and domination in Latin America. By definition, Spanish colonial rule always involved a close linkage between the aims of the Crown and the Church, not only in terms of their own particular ends but also in how they understood each other's roles. Moreover, the bloody conquest in Mesoamerica, the Caribbean and Peru were to be avoided at all costs in the Philippines. Thus, pressure on the Crown to curtail the disastrous policy of human carnage on native peoples came from within the Church as well as through the writings of colonial church historians. Consequently, the Philippines were colonized in a more harmonious manner than Latin America, primarily because the Church was allowed to take the initiative.[1]

Throughout the initial 300 years of Spanish rule in the Philippines it was apparent that the colony was not going to render the quick and vast wealth which was found in Mexico and Peru. Thus, by the 1680s if not sooner, the Crown realized that the Philippine colony had to be sustained from the Iberian and Mexican treasuries and that it would be a costly as well as a long-term negative economic venture. As early as the 1660s the Crown wanted to withdraw from the Philippines, but the linkage of Crown and Church meant that if one party desired to pursue its ends, the other also had to take part. It was only in the 1820s that the Spanish colony received an economic boost through the galleon trade which linked Mexico with China and later in the 1850s, after gold was discovered in the northern Luzon cordillera. Both ventures came too late and could not turn the colony around from its situation of economic stagnation and fiscal demise.

In a unique way, the spread of Christianity throughout the lowlands of Luzon and the Bisayas was initiated without the kind of violence which occurred in Latin America. Different parts of the archipelago were allocated to different Church orders; thus, the Augustinians, Franciscans, Recollectos, Dominicans, Jesuits, and others were allotted certain areas and spheres of social action in which the local peoples would not only be converted to the teachings of the Church, but would also become part of the civilizing process. However, the policies of the religious orders, apart from the general framework of religious conversion, differed from one another in many important directions. Just as one still finds remnants of a utopian social framework based on the writings of St. Thomas More among the Tarascans of Michoacán, Mexico, similar processes also occurred in the Philippines. These local social variants not only initiated the civilizing process, but also promulgated each order's vision of an ideal society as isomorphic with the teachings and dogma of the Church.

Furthermore, the use of local languages or dialects was basic to the priesthood and was widespread. Virtually all of the Church orders conducted masses, baptisms, weddings and other holy functions in the local Austronesian languages. Thus, Spanish did not become a *lingua franca* as it had throughout Latin America, and even after 370 years of Spanish rule (ending about 1900), only ten per cent of the population could speak Spanish fluently. Although this policy and practice did have the virtue of maintaining local societies and cultures, it also limited social mobility. For example, local administrative officials were Spaniards, and it was only in the nineteenth century that a segment of the Spanish bureaucracy was penetrated by the Spanish mestizo class or by *indios*.

The conversion process throughout the lowlands and the plains of the Philippines required the sedentarization of the population into barrios, villages and towns. Like Mexico and Latin America, the plaza complex became the centre of local government, Church administration and economic activity. Major forces which attracted people to move from hinterland to the population centres were the pageantry of the mass, the sacredness of local festivals named after patron saints, and the existence of daily and weekly markets. Yet, throughout the first 200 to 300 years, an *indio* could only attain inclusion in Spanish cultural, religious, and political institutions by becoming baptized, for it was through this pivotal act that one became not only a Christian, but also obtained the status to work within the framework of Spanish institutions. As late as the 1960s and 1970s, this pattern of religious conversion still existed among the upland Mandaya of southeast Mindanao. Baptism was interpreted by some of the Protestant denominations and their missionaries as the beginnings of spiritual rebirth; however, the Mandaya saw baptism as the beginnings of being a Cebuano who occupied the coastal areas of eastern Davao. Baptism along with the cutting of hair and wearing Western clothing were all markers of the shift to being a Cebuano (Yengoyan 1966:324-327).

Throughout the western Bisayas, missions spread from the major towns and the *poblacions* to small towns. In their concern to baptize the population as well as to keep count of individuals and groups, missionaries attempted to systematize the population in various ways. Thus, in Capiz, which is located on the northern part of the island of Panay, the Dominicans not only baptized in large numbers, but each individual and each family was provided with a surname which was commonly of Spanish origin. Small towns and villages were also named by the missionaries, and, in most cases, all individuals and families from one town would have surnames starting with the letter A, the next town with B, the next town with C and so forth. Even today this pattern is still evident, and one can always note the degree to which individuals migrated from the town of their origin or have married into neighbouring towns. In many of the Tagalog speaking areas of central Luzon, this pattern of naming did not exist, or, if it was implemented, it did not have a lasting impact. To this day, a great majority of Tagalog and Zambal surnames are native pre-contact names which were not changed to Spanish.

The missionization of the coastal plains not only created a stable population which was linked to the Church, but it also created economic inducements which gradually attracted inland populations. This pattern is quite evident when one reads Alcina's (1960) account of how Catholic missions operated in Cebu in the 1650s.

The form of civilization which was embedded in the conversion process also meant that certain "native" customs and institutions had to be changed in accordance with the missionaries' criteria for producing ideal Christians. For instance, almost all existing forms of communalism were rendered obsolete in the "new order". Thus, the rules of collective land tenure, including institutions such as the *barangay* and *bayanihan* which stressed collective work activities, were gradually replaced through the introduction of concepts embracing private property in land, commodities and labour. In this way, rational action became the foundation and an expression of the "new order".

Nevertheless, missionization could not prevent the emergence of syncretism in religious expression between Christian and native beliefs. The experience from Latin America indicated that many aspects of Church dogma and practice had been violated or rendered obsolete through contact with local and native beliefs. These not only persisted but also corrupted dogma and practice in ways which were difficult to control, much less eradicate.

One of the best examples of this kind of religious syncretism, which the Church attempted to control, was the widespread belief in witchcraft. Throughout the Bisayas, especially in Panay and Negros, and in Bicol, witchcraft beliefs are still widespread and integral to local religious belief and thought. The common belief, still current, is that witchcraft represents a pre-Christian system which still lingers as part of magical as well as religious thought. In reality, the opposite is more nearly the case.

Prior to Spanish contact, most local cultures had a belief system of benevolent and malevolent spirits which inhabited various parts of the environment, most often dark areas such as forests and caves, or remote areas such as the sea and sky. This spirit world, commonly labelled *anito*, *asuwang* or *diwata*, occurred in lowland societies as well as among upland groups such as the Kalinga, Ifugao, and Mandaya. In all cases where we have accounts of such spirits they often have a corporeal existence, although never in an anthropomorphic form. Even now, the spirit-world of the Mandaya is divorced of anthropomorphism. However, among the lowland groups malevolent spirits do have an anthropomorphic expression which can have the form of a whole human, or the lower half of the body with a head placed on the torso, or a severed body with each half travelling in different directions to different localities.

This conjunction of malevolent spirits with humanized bodies first appears in missionary accounts from the Bisayas in the early 1600s; as the basis of witchcraft, it was part of seventeenth century Spanish culture in Iberia. After the introduction of witchcraft to the Philippines, the emerging syncretism evolved into a complex set of relationships which are now dominant throughout the Bisayas. To this day, the Church has attempted to argue that witchcraft in this form is a pre-contact pagan custom which must be erased.

In the Philippines, native attitudes and actions towards Spanish political hegemony and Catholic policy and practice were not passive. Throughout various areas of the Bisayas, such as Bohol, and parts of Luzon, the historical record indicates a number of regional and local armed uprisings against Spanish policy and Church abuse. Most of these rebellions, which might have lasted from a few weeks to about a year in some cases, were suppressed and controlled by the Crown and the Church. However, in numerous cases one finds that a miracle or a divine event occurred shortly after the uprising was suppressed. The exact nature of these divine events is difficult to assess, for the descriptions are either vague or poorly recorded. What is of particular interest, however, is that, once these "miracles" occurred in the locality of the previous rebellion, one seldom or never finds another uprising occurring in that specific locality. By invoking the mystical, the creation of these "miracles" denoted that the specific vicinity had become sacred due to divine intervention and that future political action in that area might bring forth irreparable harm or even death.

Although Catholic conversion in the Philippines was not passively accepted, the Church had a fairly free reign in accomplishing its ends. The Crown, economically crippled throughout this period due to the fact that quick wealth never resulted from the discovery of precious metals nor vast profits realized from commercial export crops, expressed its presence as the arena which embraced religious restructuring with the hope of minimal involvement and cost. The indigenization of the clergy only occurred during the latter part of Spanish rule, since the Spaniards thought Filipinos could not master the Latin liturgy, let alone the various mysteries of the faith. Although the indigenization of the faith gradually occurred in the late nineteenth century and into the twentieth century as a native Church, in reality, as the Filipino Jesuit Horacio de la Costa

(1972:119) cogently argued, it was "not a native church, but a church staffed by natives".

By 1900, and on the eve of the coming of American Protestantism, the Catholic faith was the dominant religious structure in the northern and central Philippines and was well implanted throughout most of Luzon, the Bisayas and parts of Mindanao. The Church canons were also the canons of the social fabric and thus the civilizing influence which ideally would fashion and refashion Filipino culture.

AMERICA AND PROTESTANTISM IN THE PHILIPPINES

American Protestant beliefs at the turn of the century expressed the American worldly mission based on nationalism, a sense of patriotism and what was described as benevolent imperialism. The politics of Protestantism in the American Philippines were closely linked to the idea that the enemy was not only Spain but also the Catholic Church, which had corrupted local peoples through a misguided sense of dogma and superstition. Thus, the conviction was that Protestantism would bring forth the best of Christianity combined with another type of civilizing process, one linked to Euro-American liberalism and democracy.

In the early stages of American missionary activity in the Philippines, the feeling was that, although the Filipino was already a Christian, the form of Christianity as expressed in Catholicism was a corruption from a decadent context (i.e. Spain) so that, in theory, the whole conversion process to Christianity might have to be redone. Furthermore, American attitudes at the beginning of the twentieth century were probably more anti-Catholic as well as being anti-Spanish. Thus, many Protestant Churches argued that baptism, as expressed in terms of what the various American Protestant Churches had to offer, was the start of "true" Christianity. Yet, after forty years of work, the impact was quite limited. Conversion of Catholics to Protestantism occurred, but the scale and intensity were minuscule in comparison to what had happened under Spanish rule. In some cases local élites did convert with the inducement that they would be educated in Church-run colleges in the United States, since most higher education in the Philippines was under the auspices of the Catholic Church.

Furthermore, the American Board of Missions continuously pressured the American colonial government through the Governor General's office, as well as the home government in Washington, to place restrictive measures on Catholic Church landholdings, to alter taxation policy towards the Church, and to create other limitations which would curtail the role of the Catholic Church. Although some restrictions were implemented, in most cases they failed to pass due to Catholic pressure in the United States.

By the 1910s a fair segment of Protestant missionary activity shifted from the Catholic lowlands to the non-Christian, "pagan" groups who inhabited the mountainous areas of northern Luzon as well as the interiors of Mindanao and some of the islands in the Bisayas. Non-Christian minorities had the virtue of not being contaminated by Spanish culture and Catholic belief; thus, they could be incorporated into Protestantism with less trouble, and they could also be acculturated into the American mould of democracy and liberalism. The prestigious Brent school was established in Baguio, where the colonial summer capital was located, and missionary activity moved north towards the Kalinga, Igorot, and Ifugao. Uplanders were brought to the United States as show pieces in the great international exhibitions (St Louis, Seattle, San Francisco, etc.) between 1900 and the 1920s. It was the American experience which would provide the guiding and divine hand to these people as they moved from loincloth to democracy.

Where conversion among the uplanders did occur, however, a number of forces worked against missionary efforts. Partly due to limited resources from the United States as well as a dire need for Church personnel and ordained ministers, the various Protestant denominations devoted their efforts to medical benefits through the creation of hospitals and medical staff who could minister to the health needs of the uplanders. To this day, most of these small field hospitals and infirmaries still operate, though the personnel are now primarily Filipino. Thus, the legacy of American Protestantism in the Philippines is essentially not religious, but lies in the establishment of medical facilities and schools through which Protestantism and Americanism combined to offer the fruits and benefits of Western civilization.

Yet, the conversion of the Philippines was not really the ultimate goal of the American Mission Board. Although the Philippines had to be secured for Protestantism, this was only the initial phase in the process by which American Protestantism moved on to the Asian scene. Laubach's (1925) invocation that "... unless the Philippines are saved we shall lose Asia" meant not only to save it from the Catholic Church, but also to use it as a springboard for practices and methods to be perfected in order to move towards India and China. A vast number of missionaries in these countries received their first taste of the Orient in the Philippines, yet the real gems for Christian conversion were the high civilizations of the Asian mainland.

In a broader perspective, Protestantism's major impact was through its role in the transmission of American values and institutions to a society which had just fought for its independence from Spanish rule, only to lose it again through American intervention. If the American military conquest of the

Philippines was in part brutal and even uncalled for, it was Protestantism which restored the dignity of American humanitarian efforts through a benevolent form of imperialism which focused on mass education as the vehicle of cultural progress.[2]

CHRISTIANITY IN THE PACIFIC

The impact of Christianity in the Pacific must be understood in terms of the initial contact situation and the kinds of changes which ensued soon after contact. Population decimation in both the high and low islands had a drastic and dire influence on social structures and also on local populations. European introduced diseases moved faster than actual contacts with Europeans, thus in most cases by the time local cultures were encountered by the Europeans, the negative toll of population decline and decimation had already rendered a context of vulnerability.

The extent to which this massive population reduction influenced social and cultural institutions is difficult to determine. Yet, one is reminded of Kroeber's (1948:403-405) classic discussion on how cultural fatigue brought forth internal changes and cultural breakdown in religious structures in Hawaii even prior to the onslaught of European missionary activity. The causal relationships between population decimation and cultural fatigue are not well understood but one can surmise that the influences might have been critical.

For instance, a parallel case is seen on the Micronesian atoll of Nukuoro. According to Vern Carroll (pers.comm. 1980), once the Nukuoro religious leaders were told by German missionaries that their gods were false and had no power, the local religious leaders dumped their religious paraphernalia into the lagoons and thus virtually ended the traditional belief structure and religious system. Events of this type occurred throughout many Micronesian islands from the 1860s to the 1880s. In some cases, the destruction of the native religious structure was simply effected by defecating on the paraphernalia, thus breaking all forms of cultural taboo.

The breakdown of these local cultures throughout the nineteenth century made them vulnerable to quick and partial conversion to Christianity which in most cases was rampant and had a lasting impact. At the same time, Protestant denominations and the Catholic Church operated in a way which was quite different from the Philippine experience. Whereas Spain and the United States provided a hegemonic canopy for Catholic and Protestant activity in the Philippines, this situation was different in Polynesia and Micronesia. Orders and denominations operated throughout the last 150 years in a relatively open context though the imperial powers could be sought for assistance if needed.

As noted by Hezel (1978), Protestant Churches were established early to be self-financed, self-governed as well as self-propagating. This form of self-support followed the American model of local self-rule in which churches were to be established and soon afterwards they were turned over to the people. Ideally, religious symbols, ceremonies and prayer would fit into local custom and tradition which would sustain the impact of the Church. Local congregations would provide pastors, contribute food staples and labour, and would not be a financial drain on the American Board of Foreign Missions. Native clergy was encouraged though they were never full accepted.

Catholicism was fundamentally founded on saving as many souls as possible. The paganism of local belief was recognized as a debilitating force in the conversion process, thus the Church took an active role in destroying anything which they perceived as deleterious for conversion. Furthermore, a native clergy was created as an ideal aim, but in reality the common feeling was always that local people could never intellectually comprehend the mysteries of the Mass.

Both Catholicism and Protestantism were very critical of local custom, though Catholics were somewhat more tolerant. If Micronesian culture was subversive to evangelicalism, the use of the native language was even more so. Whereas in the Philippines, the various Catholic orders dealt with the mass and ceremonies in the native vernacular, in Micronesia this was not encouraged. Furthermore, communalism in regard to land ownership and private property was opposed by both Catholics and Protestants in a most vociferous way. Just as in the Philippines, a virtuous Christian morality could only be developed and propagated by and through individual worth and responsibility which was only expressed through private property and the commoditization of goods and services.

Christianity did not arrive in a vacuum. The conversion of "heathens and pagans" to a world religion was one issue, the other was the civilizing influence which was actively pursued by the agents of conversion. When the results of civilizing are viewed comparatively between the Philippines and the Pacific, it is apparent that its impact was far greater and deeper among the various cultures in the Pacific. In part due to the encountered situation, Micronesians and Polynesians were more vulnerable to these direct and indirect messages of change and cultural/political domination. The Philippines went through the same process but the consequences were less direct and much more problematic, thus in part explaining how and why local cultures in the Philippines have maintained their own reproduction.

On reading the missionary history of Micronesia and Polynesia, one quickly notes that the number of Protestant denominations were very diverse, especially in Polynesia. This form of diversity did exist among the various

Protestant Churches in the Philippines but the range and scope of the diversity is much more limited. Almost all of the major Polynesian islands are characterized by this diversity and probably Tonga is one of the best cases of the multiplicity of these denominations. Korn (1978:398) notes that at least seven denominations of Protestantism existed in a village of 494 individuals of which seventy were Roman Catholics. Individuals have shifting affiliations which appear to fit well with social mobility or more precisely an upward mobility (Korn 1978:417).

What is of interest in the Tongan case is that culturally Tonga has been heavily missionized and most of the cultural and symbolic institutions have rapidly declined or no longer exist. In fact, many anthropologists and historians who have worked in Tonga could conclude that Protestantism (Methodism and now Mormonism) have historically reworked Tongan culture into a missionary framework. However, the idea of rank and hierarchy which is pivotal to Tongan social structure and social interaction is probably even more buttressed and anchored now, especially since it has been reinforced by Protestantism. Korn (1978:419) notes that the "social system is conducive to the proliferation of denominations". One could also turn this around by arguing that the social system based on rank and hierarchy is pushed to new cultural complexities and involutional peaks as a result of Protestant religious diversity. Consequently, Tongan culture might have collapsed due to Protestantism, but Tongan social structure and its nuances have pushed rank and hierarchy to new pinnacles of diversity and dominance.

Christianity in the Pacific is still the dominant idiom and expression for cultural reproduction both within the homelands of Pacific Islanders as well as in their overseas communities. The creation of Samoan communities in Hawaii and California is premised on the political and religious conjunction between the Church and local Samoan élites. Throughout California, the Samoan community is nearly always established through the initial creation of a church with its own minister. Ministers are invited (some Samoans say imported) from Samoa. The role of the Church is not limited to matters of the spirit, but also the creation of a political force through the establishment of bingo parlours, which are an important source of revenue. By law, bingo parlours, as tax free institutions, can only occur under Church sponsorship except on federal lands such as Native American reservations. Thus, over the past twenty years there has been a proliferation of Samoan Churches and attached bingo parlours throughout California. Although the bingo complex is only one idiom of Samoan cultural reproduction and community unity, it is a critical focus through which Samoan politics and culture are sustained in a new context.

CONCLUSION

The transformation of local cultures in the Philippines and the Pacific presents a range of historical and theoretical issues. The lasting impact of Spanish rule in the Philippines was a religious transformation which had a vital impact on local cultures as well as on the growth of national culture over the past fifty years. It was only in Mindanao and in the presence of Islam that limitations occurred on the spatial spread of Catholic influence throughout the archipelago. To a certain extent local social institutions were modified, but in the transformation from Spain to the United States and to nationhood, Philippine culture was maintained both in terms of interpersonal relationships and cultural institutions. The American presence left its legacy in a widespread public education system, which had both positive and negative influences.

In the Pacific, the effects of religious changes have had a more lasting influence on Micronesian and Polynesian cultures. If education was the means of enhancing oneself in the Philippines, the religious domain was as important in Polynesia as witnessed by the way that overseas Polynesian community activity is created and perpetuated.

Social engineering was also a by-product of religious transformations in both cases. Whereas much of this type of social utopianism did not materialize in the Philippines due to the limited number of Church personnel and the lack of interest on the part of the Crown, in Micronesia and Polynesia the long-term political influences had a drastic impact on cultural institutions. Civilizing the Pacific under the guise of religious change meant that whole institutions were in jeopardy of disappearance. The contemporary interest and concern for cultural creation in Micronesia is another expression of the cultural quest to establish tradition by small-scale societies which were demographically and culturally altered through Western imperialism, be it political and/or religious.

Theoretically, Christianity in the Philippines and in Oceania is also a system of thought and action which works primarily at the level of the individual. Furthermore it does not render any particular form of a social totality. In the spread of Christianity, one finds the spread of Christian teachings as expressed through the Bible, the tenets based on Christ, the Pentecost, the conception of the Resurrection, and a dedication to certain teachings in the New Testament. Consequently, the negation of encountered social orders takes the form of comprehending sources of indigenous "evil" or "falseness" which are gradually replaced by new sources of "goodness" and "truth". Although the totality of a new social order need not emerge — as Burridge (1978:19) notes, Christian communities are expressed in and through a wide range of types of social organization — another form of totality must occur within a dynamic Christian context. In this new totality, the individual is expressed as a distinct and responsible unit who bears rights, obligations and responsibilities towards fellow humans as well as to an evolving social order.

However, the evolving social order may take different social forms. Some forms are more compatible with Christianity, others are less so; yet, in each case one finds individuality as one feature which is constant. As Burridge (1978:15) concludes, the concept of individuality, a hallmark of Christianity, is generalized throughout the society in some cases. This in turn may create new social forms in which the cultural logic is based on individualism, thus forming social structures which are, in theory, harmonious with the way in which individualism has re-emerged. New social orders and new moralities would in turn create what Burridge (1978:15) terms the "new man", a conception of the individual closely linked to Christian visions as expressed through the Resurrection.

All societies depend on the activity of individual agents, mediating social structural, religious and philosophical tenets in the course of dealing with daily contingencies. From this process there also emerge new cultural and moral imperatives. However, cultures differ in terms of the depth of the constraints which are imposed on individuals. The dilemma for Christian conversion is not simply the question of substituting one set of religious tenets for another, rather, it involves the development of new forms of individuality from the complex matrix of social structural rules through which all individuals are intricately related.

Burridge (1978) notes that once Christian conversion has created the individual and individuality is expressed through rights, duties, obligations and responsibility, this form of individuality can only be sustained in and through the emergence of money as the medium of exchange. As Simmel (1978 [1907]), followed by Burridge, stresses, it is money which establishes markers between individuals as well as between groups, statuses, interest groups and eventually classes. In some sense, the individuality which is so vital and essential to Christianity is based on money since "Christianity was founded in a moneyed environment" (Burridge 1978:18). Money is the initial opening to the gradual evolving of new political relationships, for once the value of money is recognized, participation in a foreign political economy inevitably follows, thus embedding the initial adherence of a monetary economy to individualism.

Spanish Catholicism in the Philippines was always premised on the conviction that the teachings of Christ through the Church were the sole basis of conversion to Christianity. Whatever emerged as a by-product in terms of economy and society was another issue, though it was recognized that this by-product might not be ideal. Direct cultural tampering with the encountered social fabric was only done if the missionaries saw it as a hindrance to the conversion policy. Thus, the civilizing process was present, but only tangential to religious dogma and practice.

American forms of Protestantism were always linked to a coterminous connection between God's mission and America's mission. The civilizing role of America at the turn of the nineteenth century was expressed as a necessity and as a virtue, a sense of truth and reason which was manifest in what the American Enlightenment could offer the world. Religion was subsumed under the civilizing process. As a totalizing social experience based on the emergence of the "new man", American Protestantism in the Philippines and the Pacific was the moral equivalent of imperialism, or to put it in another way, Protestantism was the "happy face" of the new social order. In an ironic and sardonic way this has not changed, for the whole of the Protestant movement since the 1850s is still intact, reconfirming Arnold Rose's recent comment to an American missionary "Don't apologize. All Americans are missionaries."

NOTES

[1] This was not the case, however, in California where the Church totally controlled the colonization and missionization process. Local indigenous populations died in enormous numbers due to the introduction of Old World diseases. There were also a number of rebellions against the missionaries and border wars grew in strength from the late 1820s through the 1840s.

[2] One should consult Achutegui and Bernad (1961) and Clymer (1986) for interesting overviews of how Protestantism operated throughout the Philippines and how Filipinos reworked certain aspects of both Catholicism and Protestantism in the formation of native Philippine Churches such as Aglipayanism.

REFERENCES

Achutegui, Pedro S. de and Miguel A. Bernad
    1961   *Religious revolution in the Philippines: the life and times of Gregorio Aglipay 1860-1960*. 2nd ed., 3 vols. Manila: Ateneo de Manila Press.

Alcina, Francisco Ignacio
    1960   *The Muñoz text of Alcina's history of the Bisayan Islands*
    [1668]   *(1668): Part I, Book 3*. Philippine Studies Program, Department of Anthropology, University of Chicago.

Burridge, Kenelm O. L.
    1978   Introduction: missionary occasions. In James A. Boutilier, Daniel T. Hughes and Sharon W. Tiffany (eds) *Mission, church and sect in Oceania*. ASAO Monograph No. 6, pp.1-30. Ann Arbor: The University of Michigan Press.

Clymer, Kenton, J.
    1986   *Protestant missionaries in the Philippines, 1898-1916: an inquiry into the American colonial mentality*. Urbana: University of Illinois Press.

De la Costa, Horacio
   1972   The missionary apostolate in East and southeast Asia. *Studies in the International Apostolate of Jesuits* 1:111-128.

Hezel, Francis X.
   1978   Indigenization as a missionary goal in the Caroline and Marshall Islands. In James A. Boutilier, Daniel T. Hughes and Sharon W. Tiffany (eds) *Mission, church, and sect in Oceania*. ASAO Monograph No. 6, pp.251-273. Lanham, Maryland: University Press of America.

Korn, Shulamit R. Decktor
   1978   After the missionaries came: denominational diversity in the Tonga Islands. In James A. Boutilier, Daniel T. Hughes and Sharon W. Tiffany (eds) *Mission, church, and sect in Oceania*. ASAO Monograph No. 6, pp.395-422. Ann Arbor: The University of Michigan Press.

Kroeber, A.L.
   1948   *Anthropology*. New York: Harcourt, Brace and World, Inc.

Laubach, Frank C.
   1925   *The people of the Philippines: their religious progress and preparation for spiritual leadership in the Far East*. New York: George H. Doran Company.

Simmel, Georg
   1978   *The philosophy of money*. London: Routledge and Kegan Paul.
   [1907]

Yengoyan, Aram A.
   1966   Baptism and 'Bisayanization' among the Mandaya of Eastern Mindanao, Philippines. *Asian Studies* 4(2):324-327.

CONTRIBUTORS

K. ALEXANDER ADELAAR

(PhD, Leiden, 1985) Senior Lecturer, Department of Applied Linguistics and Language Studies, University of Melbourne, Parkville, Victoria 3052, Australia.

PETER BELLWOOD

(PhD, Cambridge, 1980) Reader, Department of Archaeology & Anthropology, The Faculties, The Australian National University, Canberra, ACT 0200, Australia.

KULDEEP BHATIA

(PhD, ANU, 1982) Head, Aboriginal & Torres Strait Islander Health Unit, Australian Institute of Health and Welfare, Canberra, ACT 2601, and Visiting Fellow, John Curtin School of Medical Research, The Australian National University, Canberra, ACT 0200, Australia.

TOM DUTTON

(PhD, ANU, 1969) Senior Fellow, Department of Linguistics, Research School of Pacific and Asian Studies, The Australian National University, Canberra, ACT 0200, Australia.

SIMON EASTEAL

(PhD, Griffith, 1983) Fellow, John Curtin School of Medical Research, The Australian National University, Canberra, ACT 0200, Australia.

JAMES J. FOX

(D.Phil, Oxford, 1968) Professor and Head, Department of Anthropology, Research School of Pacific and Asian Studies, The Australian National University, Canberra, ACT 0200, Australia. (Convenor of the Comparative Austronesian Project.)

COLIN P. GROVES

(PhD, London, 1966) Reader, Department of Archaeology & Anthropology, The Faculties, The Australian National University, Canberra, ACT 0200, Australia.

X. GAO

(PhD, ANU, 1993) Research Fellow, John Curtin School of Medical Research, The Australian National University, Canberra, ACT 0200, Australia.

ADRIAN HORRIDGE

(PhD, Cambridge, 1953), Emeritus Professor, University Fellow, Research School of Biological Sciences, The Australian National University, Canberra, ACT 0200, Australia.

ROBERT L. KIRK

(DSc, Western Australia, 1959) Department of Archaeology and Anthropology, The Faculties, The Australian National University, and formerly Head, Department of Human Genetics, John Curtin School of Medical Research, The Australian National University, Canberra, ACT 0200, Australia.]

ANDREW PAWLEY

(PhD, Auckland, 1967) Professor and Head, Department of Linguistics, Research School of Pacific and Asian Studies, The Australian National University, Canberra, ACT 0200, Australia.

ANTHONY REID

(PhD, Cambridge, 1965) Professor, Department of Pacific and Asian History, Research School of Pacific and Asian Studies, The Australian National University, Canberra, ACT 0200, Australia.

MALCOLM ROSS

(PhD, ANU, 1987) Fellow, Department of Linguistics, Research School of Pacific and Asian Studies, The Australian National University, Canberra, ACT 0200, Australia.

CLIFFORD SATHER

(PhD, Harvard, 1971) Southeast Asian Studies Program, University of Oregon, Eugene, Oregon, USA. Fulbright Fellow 1993-4, Department of Anthropology and Sociology, University of Malaya, Kuala Lumpur, Malaysia.

S.W. SERJEANTSON

(PhD, Hawaii, 1970) Professor, Director, Institute of Advanced Studies, and Deputy Vice Chancellor, The Australian National University, Canberra, ACT 0200, Australia.

MATTHEW SPRIGGS

(PhD, ANU, 1981) Senior Fellow, Department of Archaeology and Natural History, Research School of Pacific and Asian Studies, The Australian National University, Canberra, ACT 0200, Australia.

S. SUPOMO

(PhD, ANU, 1972) Reader, Southeast Asia Centre, The Faculties, The Australian National University, Canberra, ACT 0200, Australia.

NICHOLAS THOMAS

(PhD, ANU, 1986) ARC Senior Research Fellow, Department of Archaeology & Anthropology, The Faculties, The Australian National University, Canberra, ACT 0200, Australia.

DARRELL TRYON

(PhD, ANU, 1968) Senior Fellow, Department of Linguistics, Research School of Pacific and Asian Studies, The Australian National University, Canberra, ACT 0200, Australia.

ARAM A. YENGOYAN

(PhD, Chicago, 1964) Professor, Department of Anthropology, University of California at Davis, Davis, California 95616, U.S.A.

INDEX